Constitutional and International Law Perspectives

Gabriël A. Moens is Garrick Professor of Law, T.C. Beirne School of Law at the University of Queensland and Director of the Australian Institute of Foreign and Comparative Law. He is a member of the Editorial Board of the *American Journal of Jurisprudence* and an Associate Member of the International Academy of Comparative Law. He has received a number of awards for excellence in teaching and won The Australian Teaching Award in Law in 1999. He has studied in Europe and the United States as well as in Australia, gaining his PhD in law and philosophy at the University of Sydney.

Professor Richard Darrell Lumb

Constitutional and International Law Perspectives

Gabriël A. Moens

University of Queensland Press

First published 2000 by University of Queensland Press
Box 42, St Lucia, Queensland 4067 Australia

Printed in Australia by McPherson's Printing Group

Distributed in the USA and Canada by
International Specialized Book Services, Inc.,
5804 N.E. Hassalo Street, Portland, Oregon 97213–3640

ISBN 0 7022 3160 6

Contents

Foreword: Anthony A. Tarr *vii*

1 The Contribution of Professor Richard Darrell Lumb to the T C Beirne School of Law *Gabriël A. Moens and John Trone* *1*

PART ONE: CONSTITUTIONAL LAW

2 Federal Representation and the Framers of the Australian Constitution *Nicholas Aroney* *13*
3 Parliamentary Privilege: Contemporary Issues *Gerard Carney* *54*
4 The States and the Constitution *Leslie Zines* *98*
5 Federalism-based "fragmentation of the decision-making process" in foreign relations *John Trone* *115*
6 Restitution of Unauthorised Government Exactions: A Matter of Public Law Principle or Judicial Expediency? *Peter Butler* *127*
7 Constitutional Convention 1998 and the Future of Constitutional Reform *George Winterton* *151*

PART TWO: INTERNATIONAL LAW AND JURISPRUDENCE

8 Adjudication Theories and Hard Cases at Common Law *Alan Fogg* *167*
9 International Trade Law Revisited *Kevin Ryan* *182*
10 GATT — An Impediment to Conservation? The Gasoline Case *Peter Gillies* *202*
11 The Duty of Obeying the Law: the Court of Session, the Kirk and the Disruption of 1843 *Reid Mortensen* *230*

Appendix: Works by Professor Richard Darrell Lumb *267*

Foreword

Professor Richard Darrell Lumb commenced his association with the TC Beirne School of Law at the University of Queensland as a Lecturer in 1958. He provided distinguished service to the School and to the University for nearly 40 years. For seventeen of those years he was a Professor in the School.

It is therefore not only appropriate but a pleasure for the TC Beirne School of Law to sponsor this publication of a collection of essays in honour of the late Professor Lumb. It is fitting also that the University of Queensland Press should publish the book.

Professor Lumb forged a national and international reputation as a scholar. While his greatest research interest was undoubtedly Australian Constitutional Law, he published extensively in the fields of international law and jurisprudence. He was the author of three major books dealing with Australian Constitutional law and produced also a book on the international law of the sea. His Doctoral thesis and many of his early articles focussed on jurisprudence.

This collection of essays affords his former colleagues and friends an opportunity to celebrate and commemorate Professor Lumb's academic achievements. The division of the contributions into two parts – Constitutional Law and International Law and Jurisprudence – reflects Professor Lumb's research interests.

The high regard and respect in which Darrell Lumb was held is the motivation behind the publication of this collection. It serves as a memorial to his scholarship and to the very substantial contribution that he made to the study of law in the fields canvassed. It is a fitting tribute to a distinguished scholar and longstanding faculty member of the T C Beirne School of Law.

Anthony A Tarr
Sir Gerard Brennan Professor of Law
T C Beirne School of Law
31 January 2000

1

The Contribution of Professor Richard Darrell Lumb to the T C Beirne School of Law

Gabriël A Moens[1] *and John Trone*[2]

A life of scholarship

Richard Darrell Lumb was born on 1 May1934 in Melbourne. After graduating with an undergraduate law degree (1955) and a Master of Laws degree (1956) from the University of Melbourne, he set off for Oxford, from which he received his PhD (1958). The title of his PhD thesis was *Natural Law and Positive Law: The Doctrines of Aquinas and Suarez Compared with Later Theories*.

He served as a Tutor and Research Assistant at the University of Melbourne in 1955–56. He was appointed as a Lecturer in the University of Queensland Law School in 1958. Professor Lumb taught at the Law School for a period which nearly extended over four decades, from the late 1950s to the mid-1990s. His association with the Law School was longstanding and close, and it is this association to which this volume pays tribute.

In 1961 he was appointed an Associate to High Court Justice Sir Edward McTiernan. This was clearly an exciting and formative experience for the young scholar, for decades later he still vividly recalled his time with the Court. He often spoke of Sir Edward's kindly manner, the stern countenance of Chief Justice Sir Owen Dixon in the courtroom, and the long hours of work at the Court. In 1964 he was admitted as a barrister and solicitor of the High Court.

His academic career was marked by success from its earliest stages. He progressed rapidly in the Law School, being appointed a Senior Lecturer in 1963 and a Reader in 1967. In 1977, he was a Visiting Fellow at the Australian National University. He was appointed Professor in 1980.[3] The subject of his inaugural Professorial lecture was the emerging developments in the law of the sea of that time.[4]

As well as his extensive scholarly pursuits, Professor Lumb assumed important administrative responsibilities within the Law School. At various times he was Sub-Dean of the Faculty of Law (1967–68) and Head of the Department of Law (1974–75, 1984–85). Besides his own scholarship, he also contributed to the research side of academic life as co-editor of the *University of Queensland Law Journal* for several years (1964–68).

He had many personal and professional contacts and associations outside the university. For instance, he participated in a number of community organisations. He was a Patron of the Australian Family Foundation, legal adviser to the Brisbane Consumers Group and a member of Australians for Constitutional Monarchy.[5] He strongly supported the activities of his local church, reflecting his life-long Catholicism. He often advised governments in relation to legal issues.[6] Finally, he frequently spoke to and wrote in the press about legal aspects of current political issues.[7]

Professor Lumb became seriously ill in early 1995. Indefatigable as always, he quickly returned to work, but illness overtook him once again. During this final illness he remained on leave from the University until his death on 3 February 1997, aged 62. He is survived by his wife Moira and their three children, Stephen, Joanne, and Brendan.

His Published Scholarship

As the bibliography of Professor Lumb's works makes clear, he contributed dozens of articles to scholarly journals and edited collections of essays. Even more importantly, he published four books, each of which was a significant contribution to its subject area. These were also successful works, three of them going through more than one edition.

His first book was an examination of Australian state constitutional law[8], even today something of a neglected topic. In its most recent edition, this book remains the standard work on the subject. (He also wrote several journal articles regarding issues of state constitutional law.[9])

His second book was an account of the law of the sea, placing a particular emphasis on its implications for Australia.[10] (He also wrote numerous articles about this subject). In 1974 he coauthored what was to become his most significant work, an encyclopaedic annotation of the Commonwealth Constitution.[11] In its fifth edition this book today remains an important reference work and student textbook. Finally, a decade later he wrote his fourth book, *Australian Constitutionalism.*[12]

The subject matter of these books reflect two of Professor Lumb's major scholarly interests: Australian constitutional law (three books) and the international law of the sea (one book). Professor Lumb's third major research interest was jurisprudence, the subject of his PhD thesis and many of his early articles. He sometimes lamented that he had not continued to write regarding jurisprudence. He reflected that this experience was like so much of scholarship: so many interesting subjects to pursue and never enough time to pursue them all!

To each of these three subjects Professor Lumb contributed a strong body of scholarship. His greatest research interest was undoubtedly Australian constitutional law. His conception of the subject was very much an Australian one, concentrating on Australian (and occasionally British) authority and eschewing a comparative approach such as the High Court has taken in recent years.

He was strongly devoted to what he called a 'federalist' conception of federalism. This devotion permeates all of his writings on constitutional law. For instance, it is particularly apparent in his writings about the external affairs power of the Commonwealth Constitution.[13] He considered the High Court's interpretation of this 'great and important' power[14] to be potentially inimical to the Australian federal system.[15]

In the period in which Professor Lumb wrote most of his books and articles, federalism rather than implied rights and freedoms was the main source of constitutional controversy. So far as federalism was concerned, his views regarding constitutional issues were generally in the same vein as those of Sir Harry Gibbs and Sir Daryl Dawson, rather than those of Sir William Deane or Sir Anthony Mason.

Professor Lumb also wrote widely on international law issues. His writings on the law of the sea strongly reflect an emphasis that Australia should not sleep on its international rights, but should assert them so that they may be recognised and respected by other nations. He also displayed a strong interest in the development of international criminal law.[16]

Professor Lumb's writings concerning jurisprudence concentrate particularly on natural law.[17] His Master of Laws dealt with *Philosophy of Law and the Nuremberg War Crimes Trials.* Specifically, he wrote articles for publication in *Archiv für Rechts- und Sozialphilosphie*, which is a leading European journal on legal philosophy and theory. He was a founding member of the Australian Society of Legal Philosophy and published regularly in the Society's *Bulletin*. One of his memorable contributions is a paper, entitled *The Duty of Obeying the Law*; in it Professor Lumb eloquently expressed his commitment to the Rule of Law. Lest it be thought that constitutional law, international law, and jurisprudence exhausted his research interests, it should be emphasised that he also published many articles on other subjects, such as native title to land.[18]

The substantial scholastic contribution of Professor Lumb is strongly reflected in the extensive use others have made of this work. For instance, his writings have frequently been cited by the High Court in cases concerning constitutional law and native title.[19] His writings have also been constantly cited by other scholars, particularly since many of his books and articles are standard works on their subject.

Some Personal Reflections

To inject a more personal element into our discussion of Professor Lumb's career, we will briefly discuss our own experiences of working with Professor Lumb.

A Colleague's Perspective

Gabriël Moens writes:

When I joined the University of Queensland Law School in 1988, Professor Lumb was one of the first academics to welcome me to the School. It was immediately obvious to me that Professor Lumb was a very kind and collaborative academic. His kindness was sometimes mistaken as naiveté, especially by people who did not know him well. However, his kindness and willingness to help other people were genuine characteristics of a true gentleman. He always encouraged younger colleagues to reach their potential. He did this by generously giving of his time and engaging his colleagues in scholarly discussions.

Collaborating with Professor Lumb on the Annotated Constitution of the Australian Commonwealth was undoubtedly one of the highlights of my academic career. Before his death I was fortunate enough to have worked with him on the preparation of the fifth edition of this treatise. This work had developed a formidable reputation by the time I started work on the Annotation. It was obvious that Professor Lumb's standards of scholarship were very high: he meticulously paid attention to details, for example, consistency in footnoting and references.

Professor Lumb was collegiate in the best scholarly tradition. He took a keen interest in fostering the professional development of general and academic staff, and was an exceptional and eager mentor. A shared scholarly interest in constitutional law and jurisprudence quickly brought us closer together as colleagues. Together we taught (and talked!) constitutional law for ten years.

One of the most striking qualities about Professor Lumb was his truly exceptional intellect, which was always apparent in my many conversations with him over these years. His amazing encyclopedic knowledge of Australian constitutional case law also merited respect.

I considered Darrell to be a valued friend. I am very pleased to pay tribute to his memory and legacy with this edited collection of essays.

A Student's Perspective

John Trone writes:

My undergraduate studies brought me into contact with Professor Lumb as a student in his classes and as his research assistant. He was part of the team teaching two undergraduate subjects: Constitutional Law and International Law. In Constitutional Law he taught us about the defence power, the external affairs power and the judicature chapter of the Commonwealth Constitution. In International Law he taught us about the law of the sea. As a student I remember his willingness to discuss constitutional issues, and his ready encouragement of research and writing regarding these matters.

My second major contact with Professor Lumb was through my work as his student research assistant. He was always a considerate and encouraging employer. His kindness and patience were unrelenting, and he showed respect for the opinions of those who worked for him. I particularly recall his meticulous attention to detail. When I went to see him regarding research work for the Annotated Constitution, I would always come away with a long list of tasks requiring further clarification or research!

Conclusion

We have tried to give a succinct account of Professor Lumb's life and scholarly career. Some of the papers in this collection of essays elaborate upon the themes and issues which we have raised. It is hoped that these papers constitute a fitting tribute to Professor Lumb.

As an appendix to this chapter we hereby reproduce the oration by **Father Gregory Jordan, S.J.** at Professors Lumb's funeral on 7 February 1997, at St Thomas Aquinas Church, St Lucia:

With the death of Richard Darrell Lumb, Professor of Constitutional Law at the University of Queensland, Australia has lost a luminary of the world of legal scholarship, expert in the Constitutions of the States as well as of the Commonwealth, in International Law and Law of the Sea.

Born in Melbourne in 1934, he was educated at Xavier College by an outstanding generation of Jesuit priests, especially the legendary Fr. "Gerry" Owens, S.J., teacher of classics and history. He was only 16 when he entered the University of Melbourne, where he won the exhibition in Greek the first year, shared it in Property the second, shared that in Evidence the third, and received his LLB with Honours at the age of 20, when he was already tutoring in two subjects. We Jesuit scholastics were compelled to take note as his career took off with the award of the Archbishop Mannix Travelling Scholarship, designed by that great and liberal prelate to encourage young Catholics of talent to aim for excellence in an academic career. Darrell has surely already thanked His Grace, for it made possible his Oriel years, with a D.Phil. Oxon, 1959. His first and only permanent appointment was to the University of Queensland.

His list of credits, or as he would have seen them, of responsibilities, from then on would be better known to this congregation: Associate to Mr Justice McTiernan, Senior Puisne Judge of the High Court of Australia, Senior Lecturer, Barrister and Solicitor of the High Court, Co-editor of the University of Queensland Law Journal, Visiting Fellow at ANU, and, finally, in 1980, Professor. His books had already begun to appear, and he was well on his way to establishing his national and international reputation as an expert — in some areas at least **the** expert. This and more was predicted by Darrell's Oxford supervisor, David Daube, Regius Professor of Civil law. He wrote:

> I have never lost contact with Dr Lumb and I think I have read most of his publications: all of them dealing with very basic problems, meticulously argued, resulting in important fresh insights. What distinguishes Dr Lumb's writings from most is the broad historical basis on which he rests his work. It may well be this feature which will make his thoughts worth reading when more facile discussions of the present are long forgotten.
>
> It is not as if he were a mere savant, remote from the world. He has an extraordinarily wide range of interests, and he has successfully taught a large variety of subjects. He is a man of true kindness of character, and his pupils are bound to admire him and profit from his vast knowledge sympathetically and lucidly presented.

As a reference this employs terms that are rarely used in references now. Elsewhere Professor Daube wrote:

> Mr Lumb is in my view a young scholar of great promise. He has a knowledge of legal philosophy and allied matters remarkable in a person of his age, and with it the true spirit of a researcher, he is accurate, and he is ready to change his views at any time if the evidence points in a new direction. What is no doubt equally important; he can distinguish between what is relevant and interesting and what is not, and he is capable of original thought.
>
> His character is of the highest. He is a man to be trusted, absolutely reliable and utterly decent. He is animated by the finest principles, yet unassuming, friendly and of an equable temperament. He is a good mixer, and would certainly make an excellent teacher and counsellor of younger men. I shall be very sorry if he leaves this country; I could not wish for a better colleague.

These encomia of the young Darrell Lumb are remarkably prescient, and his confrères of later years will recognize in them the true academic he was to become. Possessed of a brilliant and well-stocked mind, he avoided any temptation to intellectual arrogance, being notable for his humility beginning middle and end. He gave himself to a lifelong pursuit of objective truth which, as Pope John Paul II has often emphasised, is the true vocation of the scholar and the scholar's best service to mankind: but he always gave liberally of himself, and his expert advice to young students and academics. He was always warm with people, believing the pastoral role was integral to an academic calling. One colleague describes Darrell as a "real gentleman — as if he had stepped out of the 19th Century to be with us".

His influence on his students was deep, not simply because of a technical brilliance, but because of the spirit of the whole man.

The year 1980 saw Darrell's appointment as Professor. It also was a landmark in that he was diagnosed as having a form of leukaemia. The prospects for Darrell did not look good, but the illness was held at bay by use of a new drug, Interferon. It remained a closely guarded secret with Darrell continuing to work as if there were not a cloud in the sky, optimistic, bearing it with remarkable strength, and never letting it bother his colleagues.

Later, at the age of 55, he suffered two heart attacks, which greatly impaired his health, until, two years ago, he suffered the stroke which was a severe one and deprived him of the pleasures of conversation. He never complained; he was always positive, resilient in the face of these blows. Where did he draw that great strength?

Darrell's Catholic faith was not superficial compliance with a tradition, but in his bones. His humility was a fact and known, but it extended to his religious life, to the core of the man. It is remarkable that in this era when it is fashionable for many individuals to be their own Pope, his luminous intellect bowed in the obedience of faith. It is impossible to do justice to him without taking into account his faith and his fidelity.

Darrell was disturbed by the drift of our times, by the directions in which politicians were leading us, states rights eroded and federation threatened; the directions universities were heading, not to mention his own profession, which shaped his whole approach to life, convinced as he was of the need for a solid constitutional foundation, and a framework of laws that were in harmony with morality — not just with ethics — if we are to temper the passions and chaos in the affairs of men. He who was so scrupulous to preserve even minor achievements of the past deplored the carefree rejection of key components in the Western tradition. The only organisation outside his professional and academic life to which he lent his name was the Australian Family Association, to which he was Patron and consultant. Originally regarded as a maverick lobby group on the Australian scene, its philosophy appealed to Darrell, who would have liked the title of their conference in the International Year of the Family, viz., "The Family — there is no other way". The deterioration of the position of the family, and the unhappy consequences of it, increasingly recognized with alarm by both right and left, have only served to underline how far sighted Darrell was in his concerns.

He is now, finally, at rest. He has played the role that was assigned to him, by the gifts Providence showered on him, though within the limitations health imposed. He could not have done more. My poor words are over. The best sermon on Darrell was his own life though he would never have thought of it that way.

He who knew the dialogues of scholars so well has now entered that eternal conversation of the Blessed Trinity, light and truth itself, and the supreme law of love.

Notes

1. Garrick Professor of Law, The University of Queensland.
2. BA/LLB (Hons), PhD (Qld).
3. See "Law expert appointed Professor", *Cairns Post*, 25 June 1980, p 6.
4. See *New Bearings in the Law of the Sea* University of Queensland Inaugural Lectures, No 56, 29 April 1981 (St Lucia: University of Queensland Press, 1981).
5. See Lloyd Waddy, "The Republic: Will Blinky be the Only Bill? " (1994) 4 *Upholding the Australian Constitution* 251 at 271.
6. Eg "'Think tank' for State", *Courier Mail*, 12 September 1973, p 1; "Cowen refuses 'think money'", *Courier Mail*, 13 September 1973, p 2.
7. Eg R D Lumb, "School aid's legal basis", *Courier Mail*, 28 September 1962, p 2 (establishment of religion); R D Lumb, "Money aid to schools", *Courier Mail*, 26 November 1962 (establishment of religion); "Group supports Govt Viet policy", *Courier Mail*, 7 July 1966, p 7 (Vietnam War); "War objection seminar point", *Courier Mail*, 29 July 1968, p 8 (conscientious objection); "People's right on boundary", *Courier Mail*, 20 May 1972, p 3 (alteration of State boundaries); "Susan puts in her claim", *Courier Mail*, 4 July 1972, p 1 (voting rights under s 41 of the Constitution); "Academic hits at Bill publicity", *Courier Mail*, 27 March 1974, p 19 (1974 referendums); R D Lumb, "Sir John has the power", *Courier Mail*, 26 November 1975, p 5 (dismissal of Whitlam government); R D Lumb, "Constitution revision", *Courier Mail*, 10 May 1978, p 4 (revision of State Constitution); R D Lumb, "A point of law", *Australian*, 27 December 1982, p 6 (Tasmanian Dam dispute); Helen Trinca and Jane Cadzow, "Federal system completely disrupted", *Weekend Australian*, 2-3 July 1983, p 9 (*Tasmanian Dam Case*); Editorial, "Time of Trial", *Examiner*, 4 July 1983 (*Tasmanian Dam Case*); Ray Owen, "Referendum: The great danger to State aid", *Catholic Leader*, 24 July 1988, pp 1, 5 (1988 referendum on establishment of religion).
8. R D Lumb, *The Constitutions of the Australian States* (St Lucia: University of Queensland Press, 1963).

9. See eg R D Lumb, "The New South Wales Legislative Council Abolition Case" (1961) 4 *University of Queensland Law Journal* 23; R D Lumb, "Methods of Alteration of State Constitutions in the United States and Australia" (1982) 13 *Federal Law Review* 1; R D Lumb, "Manner and Form in the Australian Constitutional System Post Australia Acts" (1992) 12 *Queensland Lawyer* 177.
10. R D Lumb, *The Law of the Sea and Australian Off-shore Areas* (St Lucia: University of Queensland Press, 1966).
11. R D Lumb and K W Ryan, *The Constitution of the Commonwealth of Australia, Annotated* (Sydney: Butterworths, 1974).
12. R D Lumb, *Australian Constitutionalism* (Sydney: Butterworths, 1983).
13. s 51(xxix), *Commonwealth Constitution* (1900).
14. *R* v *Burgess; Ex parte Henry* (1936) 55 CLR 608 at 687 (Evatt and McTiernan JJ).
15. See eg R D Lumb, "The Franklin Dam Decision and the External Affairs Power: A Comment" (1984) 13 *University of Queensland Law Journal* 138; R D Lumb, "The External Affairs Power and Constitutional Reform" (1988) 62 *Australian Law Journal* 679.
16. See eg R D Lumb, "Legality and Legitimacy: The Limits of the Duty of Obedience to the State" in C H Alexandrowicz (ed), *Studies in the History of the Law of Nations* (The Hague: Martinus Nijhoff, 1970), 52.
17. See eg R D Lumb, "The Scholastic Doctrine of Natural Law" (1959) 2 *Melbourne University Law Review* 205; R D Lumb, "Natural Law and Legal Positivism" (1959) 11 *Journal of Legal Education* 503; R D Lumb, "Natural Law — An Unchanging Standard?" (1960) 6 *The Catholic Lawyer* 224; R D Lumb, "The Duty of Obeying the Law" in Ilmar Tammelo, Anthony Blackshield and Enid Campbell (eds), *Australian Studies in Legal Philosophy* (Berlin: Hermann Luchterhand, 1963), 195.
18. See eg R D Lumb, "Is Australia an 'Occupied' or 'Conquered' Country — How Legal Status of Australia in International Law Affects the Land Rights Question" (December 1984) 11 *Queensland Bar News* 16; R D Lumb, "Aboriginal Land Rights: Judicial Approaches in Perspective" (1988) 64 *Australian Law Journal* 273; R D Lumb, "Native Title to Land in Australia: Recent High Court Decisions" (1993) 42 *International and Comparative Law Quarterly* 84; R D Lumb, "The *Mabo* Case: Public Law Aspects" in M A Stephenson and S Ratnapala (eds), *Mabo: A Judicial Revolution* (St Lucia: University of Queensland Press, 1993), 1; R D Lumb, "*Mabo* and Aboriginal Title in Queensland" (1993) 14 *Queensland Lawyer* 15; R D Lumb, "Constitutional Issues and the Native Title Act, 1993 (Cth)" in M A Stephenson (ed), *Mabo: The Native Title Legislation* (St Lucia: University of Queensland Press, 1995), 26.
19. Eg *Wacando* v *Commonwealth* (1981) 148 CLR 1 at 8, 9 (Gibbs CJ); *Attorney-General (Vict); Ex rel Black v Commonwealth* (1981) 146 CLR 559 at 613 (Mason J); *Kirmani* v *Captain Cook Cruises Pty Ltd (No 1)* (1985) 159 CLR 351 at 362 (Gibbs CJ), 403, 411 (Brennan J); *Mabo* v *Queensland (No 1)* (1988) 166 CLR 186 at 238 (Dawson J); *Mabo* v *Queensland (No 2)* (1992) 175 CLR 1 at 114 n 28; *Wik Peoples* v *Queensland* (1996) 187 CLR 1 at 207 n 775 (Kirby J); *Kable* v *Director of Public Prosecutions (NSW)* (1996) 189 CLR 51 at 71 n 79 (Dawson J), 113 n 224 (McHugh J); *Commonwealth* v *Mewett* (1997) 191 CLR 471 at 498 n 106 (Dawson J); *Commonwealth* v *WMC Resources Ltd* (1998) 194 CLR 1 at 21 n 61 (Toohey J), 40 n 141 (McHugh J), 76 n 238 (Kirby J), [1998] HCA 8 (paras 28, 94, 209); *Egan* v *Willis* (1998) 195 CLR 424 at 502, [1998] HCA 71 (para 154) (Kirby J); *Re Governor, Goulburn Correctional Centre*; *Ex parte Eastman*

(1999) 73 ALJR 1324 at 1326 n 8, [1999] HCA 44 (para 7) (Gleeson CJ, McHugh and Callinan JJ). Other Australian courts and tribunals have also cited his writings. See eg *Fullmer* v *Cape York Cattle Company* [1987] 1 Qd R 6 at 15 (Master Lee, QC); *Coco* v *Newnham* (1990) 97 ALR 419 at 438, 450, 453-454, 456 (Lee J) (Qld SC); *Re Commissioner of Water Resources* [1991] 1 Qd R 549 at 555 (Byrne J); *Brown* v *Administration of Norfolk Island* (1991) 29 FCR 511 at 531 (Lockhart J); *Australian Health Insurance Association* v *Esso Australia Ltd* (1993) 41 FCR 450 at 486 (Sheppard J); *Arrowcrest Group Pty Ltd* v *Gill* (1993) 46 FCR 90 at 102 (French J); *Chau* v *Director of Public Prosecutions (NSW)* (1995) 37 NSWLR 639 at 650 (Kirby P); *Re Waanyi Peoples* (1995) 124 FLR 1 at 24 (French J) (NNTT); *Sande* v *Registrar, Supreme Court of Queensland* (1996) 64 FCR 123 at 130-131 (Lockhart J); *Strachan* v *Graves* (1997) 141 FLR 283 at 289 (Underwood J) (Tas SC); *Carnes* v *Essenberg*, Qld CA, [1999] QCA 339, 23 August 1999 (Chesterman J).

Part 1
Constitutional Law

2

Federal representation and the framers of the Australian Constitution

*Nicholas Aroney**

> I should like it to be distinctly understood that, as far as I am concerned, I do not intend that we shall take 40,000 people wherever we can find them and say, 'You shall have one member,' as in many of the colonies, and particularly in Victoria, if we did so we would do a grave injury to the country and confer a benefit on the towns. I understand we are to allow each colony to fix what may be considered fair constituencies and allot the colonies one member for every 40,000 of their population.
>
> — Sir George Turner, Premier of Victoria, National Australasian Convention, Adelaide, 1987.[1]
>
> [W]here you have different districts and separate local interests, those districts should be represented irrespective of the fact that they contain a minority of population ... It is not one vote, one value, and it ought not to be, and no one wishes that it should be in local politics. Why, then, do we ask for it in federal politics?
>
> — Bernhard Ringrose Wise, National Australasian Convention, Sydney 1987.[2]

Introduction

It is an honour to contribute to a book published in honour of Professor Darrell Lumb. In their classic work, *The Constitution of the Commonwealth of Australia Annotated*, Professors R D Lumb and G A Moens point out:

> The Federal nature of the Constitution is proclaimed in the first paragraph of the preamble which refers to the agreement on the part of the people of the colonies to unite in 'one indissoluble Federal Commonwealth ...'[3]

When Dr John Quick and Robert Randolph Garran came to discuss the federal principle as developed in the Australian Constitution in their magisterial *Annotated Constitution of the Australian Commonwealth*, they further observed that:

> The Federal idea ... pervades and largely dominates the structure of the newly-created community, its Parliamentary executive and judiciary departments.[4]

* The author wishes to thank Professors Greg Craven and Jeff Goldsworthy for their helpful comments on earlier versions of this paper.

However, in his equally important work, *The Constitution of the Commonwealth of Australia*, Professor W Harrison Moore concluded:

> The predominant feature of the Australian Constitution is the prevalence of the democratic principle, in its most modern guise. It is true that, in a federal government, the simple democratic plan of pure majority rule must make compromises with the principle of State right. But that is the only compromise which it makes in Australia.[5]

Different views, obviously, of what is most important in the Australian Constitution. Which one is correct? The current emphasis on fundamental doctrines and their implications in High Court constitutional adjudication leads to a number of questions. What is the basis on which constitutional implications are to be drawn? Do they turn on contemporary needs? Political philosophy? Logic? Intention? As between the various fundamental doctrines embodied in the Constitution, what are their respective places in the total constitutional framework? Which are the more important, the more fundamental, the more controlling? In the case of a conflict between principles, how are they ranked? Does one doctrine have greater explanatory power than the others? What, in Galligan's words, is the 'hierarchy of institutional design'?[6]

One undoubtedly important topic in constitutional adjudication concerns the impact of democracy and federalism on the system of political representation. On a number of recent occasions the High Court has been asked to rule on questions concerning these matters.[7] One of the recurrent issues concerns equality of voting power, or the question of whether or not the Australian Constitution requires that federal electoral divisions be, within the bounds of practicality, of equal size having regard to the number of voters or people.[8] Federalism and democracy bear on this question, something which the record of the debates held at the Australasian Federal Conventions of 1891 and 1897–98 clearly reveal. In the minds of its framers the Australian Constitution undoubtedly attempted to provide for a system of *federal representation*, to 'adapt representative government to federalism', as Justice Gummow recently put it in *McGinty v. Western Australia*.[9]

The intentions of the framers are relevant to the implications which flow from the Australian Constitution,[10] and in fact the Convention Debates reveal a great deal about the relative place of federalism and democratic theory in the Constitution.[11] Most of the framers thought that federalism required some form of federal representation in the national Parliament, reflecting the American model of the Senate as a States' House. However, an important minority of them held that federalism required but two independent spheres of government, a national one embracing the whole territory of the nation, and a regional government for each of the constituent territories — with no need for some mechanism of State representation in the national Parliament.[12] On either view, though to varying degrees, federalism involves a qualification of national majoritarianism, and therefore of majoritarian conceptions of democracy. Whether *federalism* and *democracy* are antithetical, compatible or essential to one another is also a matter of debate. When democracy is defined in terms of national majoritarianism and federalism in terms of independence of territorial minorities within a nation, there is an obvious antithesis. Hence, 'to one who believes in the majoritarian notion of freedom, it is impossible to interpret federalism as other than a device for minority tyranny'; but there are others who say that 'democracy is achievable only in federations'.[13]

Under the Constitution the national Parliament is comprised of a Senate in which the people of the Original States elect an equal number of Senators for each State. In this, majoritarian democracy is decidedly compromised — in Justice Gummow's terms, a striking 'adaptation of representative government to federalism'. Even more importantly for the present discussion, this adaptation extends to the House of Representatives, since among other things Original States are guaranteed a minimum of five representatives therein.

In this context, the debate over equality of voting power can be characterised as a debate over federalism versus majoritarian democracy. The first step in this is to appreciate that there is an imperfect, but real, analogy between the States regarded as electorates for the purposes of representation in the Senate and local communities regarded as electorates for the purposes of the House. Clearly, when States having vastly different populations are equally represented in the Senate, it cannot reflect the majoritarian conception of democracy. By the same token, *if* majoritarian democracy is to be embodied in the House, local electorates must have more or less equal populations or, through the more direct and exacting mechanism, the entire nation must be treated as a single electorate. Yet in *Burke v. Western Australia*, when asked to find a requirement of equality of voting power in the Western Australian Constitution, the Supreme Court of Western Australia held that the decisive factor was that the Constitution authorised 'an electoral system whereby members are chosen by electors organized on a geographical basis — in provinces or in districts'.[14] Even though the implications of this answer were not fully worked out in the judgment, this was indeed the crucial point.[15] As soon as local electorates are admitted, a strict system of national majoritarianism is, for practical purposes, compromised. Moreover, representation by local electorates bears an important affinity with federal ideas because federalism as a theory is by no means limited to a union of what we call states or provinces. Pierre-Joseph Proudhon, for example, stated:

> Federation from the Latin *foedus*, genitive *foedeus*, which means pact, contract, treaty, agreement, alliance, and so on, is an agreement by which one or more heads of family, one or more towns, one or more groups or towns or states, assume reciprocal and equal commitments to perform one or more specific tasks, the responsibility for which rests exclusively with the officers of the federation.[16]

The tendency to read federalism as solely concerned with unions of *states* is a by-product of the superficial treatment of the United States federation as archetypal.[17] This orientation certainly impacted heavily on the framers of the Australian Constitution, concerned as they were with 'States' rights'. But the use of local electorates in representative systems within both 'democracies' and 'federations' is a vestigial — and perhaps more than merely vestigial — reminder of a deeper 'federal' orientation which has been inherited from medieval systems of representation. As Bogdanor and Butler have pointed out:

> The plurality system, as it developed in Britain and in countries influenced by Britain, was profoundly linked to the notion of territorial representation. 'The ancient idea of representation,' according to Maitland, comprised 'the representation of communities, of organised bodies of men, bodies which, whether called boroughs or counties, constantly act as wholes, and have common rights and duties.' MPs represented not segments of opinion, nor of course political parties, but constituencies. They were attorneys seeking the redress of grievances before committing their constituencies to the payment of the expenses of government ... It was this notion of representation which came to be adopted by the American colonists ...[18]

Likewise Bernard Bailyn observed that the American colonial towns and counties

> like their medieval counterparts, were largely autonomous, and they stood to lose more than they were likely to gain from a loose acquiescence in the action of central government ... Having little reason to identify their interests with those of the central government, they sought to keep the voices of local interests clear and distinct.[19]

In accordance with this perspective, the first 'federations' among the British colonies in America were established by the Fundamental Orders of Connecticut in 1639 and the Organisation of the Government of Rhode Island of 1642, which provided for the combination of towns into a colony-wide form of government, while leaving the town governments responsible, as before, for most local matters. The Fundamental Orders of Connecticut, for example, provided for annual elections of town deputies, the four deputies of each town receiving the largest vote then representing the town in the General Court of Connecticut.[20] It became significant for the Philadelphia Convention in 1787 that the Connecticut towns enjoyed equality of representation in the State's lower house. In turn, the Connecticut compromise, as it came to be called, took on the character of a necessary principle of federation, and was adopted as such by a significant majority of the framers of the Australian Constitution. James Bryce had taught the Australian framers that the Connecticut Orders were in fact the 'oldest truly political Constitution in America'.[21]

The persistent use of local electorates, usually justified on other than 'federalist' grounds, therefore points to a federal perspective which counterbalances arguments for equality of voting power aired in the name of representative democracy. Daniel Elazar has pointed out:

> While the United States has made a point of specifying the *unitary* character of the states as polities, many, if not most, states are constitutionally *unions* of their counties or towns under their own constitutional theories and were held to be such by their jurists until the twentieth century ... This is another aspect of state constitutionalism that also deserves exploration, particularly in light of the United States Supreme Court reapportionment decisions of the 1960s, which directly, if unthinkingly, assaulted the very foundations of this aspect of state constitutionalism.[22]

Some of the framers of the Australian Constitution perceived this analogy between the States regarded as electorates for the purposes of representation in the Senate and local communities as electorates for the purposes of representation in the House. One of the more important of them, Andrew Inglis Clark, when responding to the charge that representation of the States in the Senate would compromise majoritarian principles, pointed to the fact that equal electorates did not exist either in England or Australia at the time, so that majoritarianism was likewise compromised at this level.[23]

The framers and federal representation

The quality and nature of representation was a question of vital importance to the delegates to the two National Australasian Conventions held in the 1890s. Sir Henry Parkes' famous resolutions debated by the first convention held in Sydney in 1891, and Edmund Barton's similar resolutions debated at the first session of the second convention when it sat in Adelaide in 1897, set out the basic features of the proposed federal constitution.[24] Even at this early stage, the broad outlines of the constitution were reasonably identifiable, at least so far as a majority of the delegates were concerned.[25] Parkes' description of the executive shows a clear commitment to responsible government, since the advisers to the Governor-General were to be 'persons sitting in Parliament and whose term of office shall depend upon their possessing the confidence of the House of Representatives, expressed by the support of the majority'. At the same time, the federal principle was equally clearly in mind, since the 'Parliament [was] to consist of a Senate and a House of Representatives, the former consisting of an equal number of members from each province'. And as regards the question of electoral districting for the lower house, the democratic model seems to have been accepted as a general principle, since the House of Representatives was 'to be elected by districts formed on a population basis, and to possess the sole power of originating and amending all bills appropriating revenue or imposing taxation'.[26]

The debate on the resolutions reveals the federal ideas held by many of the framers. The resolutions embraced two different conceptions of representation which were to be applied to the Senate and to the House of Representatives respectively. The Senate was to represent the States as equal partners in federation; the House was to represent districts formed on 'a thoroughly popular basis'.[27] Clearly, if the Senate was to represent the States as equal partners, the population of each State would have nothing to do with it.

The question of equality of voting power in lower house elections turns on the basis on which electoral districts are divided. If the principle in Parkes' resolution were applied to electoral districting, each electorate would be of a tolerably equal population. However, section 29 of the Constitution leaves the determination of electorates to the State and Commonwealth Parliaments in their unfettered discretion. Throughout the various drafts and in its final form the provision was and is noticeably silent on the basis of districting, and elicited only the most cursory consideration by the delegates.[28] By contrast, the debate on what were to become sections 7 and 24 was extensive, and heated. Since the case for equality of voting power in federal elections turns on the language of section 24 of the Australian Constitution as copied from Article I, section 2 of the US Constitution,[29] aspects of the Australian debate on section 24 are relevant to the question of equality of voting power. The debate over section 7 is also relevant, since it contains the districting provisions for the Senate which correspond to those for the House addressed in section 29. These debates reflected the delegates' views of federal representation and gave them an opportunity to consider the possibility of entrenching some requirement that electorates be of equal size.

Parkes' resolutions

The debate over Parkes' resolutions, especially concerning the composition of the two houses of the federal Parliament, centred on the power of the Senate to amend the detail of financial bills. It was premised on the near universal understanding that the States would be equally represented in the Senate in order to safeguard their interests. This objective lead 'States' righters' to demand that the Senate have powers co-ordinate with the House of Representatives. However, the objection to co-ordinate powers was that this would allow an overall minority of the population to veto the decisions of the majority represented in the House. Nevertheless, equal representation and substantial power for the Senate remained largely unchallenged, and the majoritarian position focussed on the maintenance of responsible government as a democratic principle, that is, a government responsible solely to the popular house, principally through control of government finance in the form of appropriation, tax and perhaps loan bills. The majoritarian or democratic strategy was to seek a qualification of the powers of the Senate over financial measures. The level of control concerned the questions of initiative, veto in whole (rejection) and veto in detail (amendment). Thus at the heart of the debate over Parkes' resolutions were contending views of representation, federalism and democracy. An examination of the arguments canvassed reflects the relative depth of their comprehension of federal and democratic theory and practice, especially as it related to the issue of representation.

A fairly consistent theme was the degree to which federal and State oriented points of view prevailed over the democratic and national. In the first place, equality of representation of the States in the Senate was almost universally accepted. Even Alfred Deakin, a key exponent of the democratic and nationalistic perspective, levelled his attack on the powers and not the composition of the Senate.[30] In accepting equal representation, the more nationalistic and democratically inclined delegates, mostly from the two larger States and especially Victoria, were forced to concede a significant qualification of the majoritarian and national principle.[31]

For Deakin, the very nature of the 'States' was a fundamental point of difference which ultimately bore on the question of representation. In response to an interjection from Sir Samuel Griffith, Deakin pointed out that the colonial boundaries were but artificial divisions, and stated:

> I cannot conceive of an entity called the state apart from the people whose interests it embodies; nor can I conceive anything within the state which can claim an equal authority with the final verdict, after solemn consideration, of the majority of its citizens. If the hon. Gentleman [Griffith] has any metaphysical entity in his mind which can be placed above this, I shall be glad to learn its nature ...[32]

But in 1891 at least, this challenge to 'States' rights did not prevail against Griffith's rejoinder that the States were to be understood as 'aggregations of their own people' and that 'the majorities of the separate States might be of a different opinion from the majority of the people of Australia, taken as one!'[33]

Barton developed these premises by pointing out that it would be 'possible for the representative principle to be preserved and instituted from its very foundation in two chambers just as well as in one', and that the Senate could be 'part of the organ by which the will of the people is expressed'. Accordingly, one chamber 'called *par excellence* the House of Representatives' would represent the people organised in localities, and the other would represent the people organised as States.[34] As Charles Kingston later put it, 'while the electors are the same, the electorates are different'.[35]

For some delegates the rationale for equal representation was that the Senate would thereby be the guardian of 'States' rights'. Deakin countered by challenging them to define States' rights, and having defined them, to show how in the exercise of limited federal legislative power those rights could be infringed. Behind this was the view that States' rights were the residual legislative powers of the States and that they were to be protected by the express division of powers in the Constitution and the enforcement of that division by the High Court.[36] However, this did not prevail against Barton's response that what were actually at stake were States' *interests*. This was perhaps better put by Richard Chaffey Baker, who pointed out that equal representation in the Senate would enable the people organised as States to have a say on federal policy *within* its areas of legislative competence. It would not just be a matter of the Senate protecting States' rights understood as the residue of powers retained by the States and lying *outside* federal power; it would be a matter of protecting States' interests by enabling them to 'have a voice as states concerning the powers which are delegated to the federal government'.[37]

While Deakin's democratic and nationalistic position was forceful and consistent in terms of its premises, it contained the important concession of equality of representation. Six years later Henry Bournes Higgins[38] was not prepared to concede this without argument and a division. The concession of equal representation was a prerequisite to the consent of the smaller colonies, but in the hands of the South Australians the need for compromise was elevated into a *principle* of federalism. Baker maintained that federation is a 'compact made between the constituent states'.[39] John Alexander Cockburn added that federation is 'a compromise and essentially a bargain' and for that reason a compromise between separation and union.[40] Kingston reminded the Convention:

> we are dealing with autonomous States, who have long enjoyed the blessing of self-government, and who should not be asked — and who, if asked, would not be likely to accede to the request — to sacrifice any of their existing powers other than those which it is absolutely necessary should be surrendered in the national interest.[41]

Almost mercenary in manner, John Hannah Gordon thought that the constitution would be 'a mere commercial treaty. We are not here to raise a national standard, but to enter into a bargain, colony with colony, on terms which we think advantageous to each.'[42] A number of delegates were conscious that equal representation in the Senate was the expression of this compromise between unification and confederation in the composition of the federal organs of government.[43] For some, this was a cardinal principle of federation; for others merely a compromise, but always an unavoidable one against which all of the arguments of Deakin and later Isaacs and Higgins could not prevail.

Moreover, John Murtagh Macrossan's perception that the party system would continue to provide the motive force in federal politics so that Senators would vote along party lines seemed to fall on deaf ears — even though Bryce (upon whom the framers relied more than any other) had emphasised the operation of the party system in the United States.[44] Bryce accordingly taught that the Senate had never protected the small States against the large States' dominance of the House of Representatives, and this was urged against the States' righters. However, he had also praised the Senate, and those in favour of co-ordinate powers were not reticent in citing Bryce to this effect, even if it meant acknowledging that the small State — large State question had become a non-issue in the United States.[45]

A final line of argument was to characterise the Senate as an upper house, with the implication that it lacked democratic credentials and its powers should be subordinate to the more popular lower house. The response was that the Senate was to be properly understood as the States' House. In 1891, the latter view tended to prevail, though it was to be modified in 1897 with the move towards direct election. Along these lines, Sir Thomas McIlwraith contested the implicit assumption that the Senate would represent the monied class.[46] Baker repulsed the insinuation by pointing out that the Senate would *not* be a nominated body or elected by a property-owning constituency.[47] Anticipating 1897, Baker and Cockburn supported the Senate as a 'council of states' provided that it was directly elected.[48] Some, however, embraced the suggestion that the Senate would function as an upper house. Nicholas Fitzgerald accepted that the Senate would be a 'conservative' institution which would check the passions and impetuosity of 'the people's will'.[49] Parkes thought that the Senate would be like the House of Lords, representative of a 'moral and just conservatism', though it would embody 'the only conservatism possible in a democracy — the conservatism of service, of length of experience, and weight of character'.[50]

All in all, the attack on equal representation did not succeed, even on the basis of indirect election. Deakin's 1891 concession that he would allow wide powers for the Senate if its composition was elective meant that in 1897 Higgins' attack on equal representation in a directly elected Senate was doomed to failure.[51]

If the impregnability of equality of representation was a victory of federal principles over democratic ones, the democratic response was to seek to limit the powers of the Senate in the name of responsible government. Nevertheless, there was again a definite limit in the degree to which the democrats could compromise the powers of the Senate; their opponents were alert to the dilution of the Senate's powers. The Senate's powers could be limited in two ways. The first, and most important, was to limit the Senate's powers over financial bills, a device which bore an intimate relation to the responsible government issue. The second, in the case of all kinds of bills, was to provide for a deadlock-breaking mechanism to reduce the long term capacity of the Senate to resist the will of the House of Representatives. The latter device seemed to enjoy a significant level of support, although the 1891 Bill did not contain a deadlock provision. James Munro argued that if the Senate could amend money bills then, contrary to Griffith's view of the matter, deadlocks would be very likely and the views of a section of the people would prevail; a minority would govern the majority. Andrew Joseph Thynne, with Deakin's support, proposed that after the example of Switzerland deadlocks between the two houses could be resolved 'on sound democratic lines', a popular referendum in which the views of the *people* as a whole and the people of the States would be decisive.[52] But in 1891 this did not prevail. It was met by the considerable authority of Griffith, who thought that a really serious deadlock would be tantamount to 'revolution', and that:

> Every constitutional government consists of two or more parts, each one of which can put the machine out of gear. That is the essence of constitutional government. The only means of avoiding collision is to have autocracy.[53]

Baker echoed this orientation when he warned that responsible government, though democratic, tends to centralisation of power, whereas federalism diversifies it.[54] With support from most of his fellow South Australians, he persistently promoted a Swiss executive appointed by both houses of the legislature and composed of ministers from each State.[55] Cockburn saw that federalism lead to the loss of Parliamentary sovereignty — in the constitutive and legislative sense — replacing the 'High Court of Parliament' with a judiciary as supreme arbiter of constitutional issues. It was, he thought, doubtful whether responsible government could survive the demise of Parliamentary sovereignty, and it might be necessary to follow the Swiss system.[56]

Against the federalist approach of the leading South Australians and

Queenslanders, the democrats consistently promoted responsible government and, as a corollary, lower house control of financial legislation. Henry John Wrixon pointed out that '[f]inance is government, and government is finance, and under the English system of government one or other house must appoint the executive'.[57] It followed that finance and government should be in the final control of the House of Representatives so that the majority of the Australian population would determine the executive government. If the Senate were to control money bills, 'the real effect of it is to give the determining power of government into the hands of, it may be, a small minority of the people'.[58]

In any case, John Winthrop Hackett's warning was well heeded in 1891:

> there will be one of two alternatives — either responsible government will kill federation, or federation in the form in which we shall, I hope, be prepared to accept it, will kill responsible government.[59]

While federalism did not kill responsible government in 1891, it did prolong its hesitating conception until 1897. For in 1891, Griffith's suggestion was convincing. While favouring both equal representation in the Senate *and* responsible government, he had asked at the outset whether a Senate having such a composition and powers could be compatible with responsible government. Since responsible government was a recent and evolving institution, he suggested the delegates leave the constitution 'elastic as to allow of any necessary development that may take place'.[60] As a result, the 1891 Bill provided in Chapter II, Clause 4 that ministers of State 'shall be capable of being chosen and of sitting as Members of either House of the Parliament'. Thus while responsible government was part of the 'democratic' platform, in 1891 at least, the matter was left open.[61]

The only point, then, at which the principle of federal representation was compromised lay in the limitation of the Senate's powers over financial bills. On this, there was a range of views. Munro thought that the House 'ought to be supreme in questions of finance'.[62] Deakin denied the Senate an absolute power of veto, although he conceded greater powers if it should act 'under the control, and only by the authority of the people'.[63] Barton maintained that the Senate should have equal powers with respect to financial and taxation bills provided it be directly elected.[64] Baker sought full power over financial bills,[65] while Kingston, a dissentient among the dominant South Australian opinion, only tentatively supported a power of amendment.[66] Griffith pointed out that the distinction between veto and amendment was insignificant, since the power of rejection was the really important power, the power which could bring down a government.[67] Fitzgerald supported the veto in detail exercised by a 'conservative' Senate acting as a 'check on the people's will'.[68] Andrew Inglis Clark thought that the strongest argument against amendment was that it would amount to control of the majority by the minority. However, the answer to this was that British responsible government was not, in any case, 'founded on the principle of an absolute rule of the majority' since despite agitation to the contrary

> single and equal electoral districts have never yet been adopted in England, and have not been adopted, so far as I know, in any of the Australian colonies. The electoral districts remain at the present time, both in the Australian colonies and in England, very unequal in numbers, and as to the amount of representation assigned to them; and the consequence is that many important measures are decided in the House of Commons, and are decided in every colonial legislature, by a majority in that legislature who were returned by, and who represent, an absolute minority of electors.[69]

For Clark, the remedy lay in the Hare system of proportional representation for which Clark himself became famous when it was implemented in Tasmania. It did not lie in limiting the powers of the Senate on what were for him speciously democratic grounds. Representative government, for Clark, did not require equality of voting power but a genuine attempt to 'get the intelligence and judgment of the community'. In all electoral systems, even with equal electoral districts, a minority could prevent a majority from getting its way. The important thing was that a minority have the opportunity to be represented, put their case, and ultimately become a majority. But those who oppose equal representation of the States and equal powers for the Senate, Clark pointed out, do not take their principle of majoritarianism to its logical conclusion and adopt the French system under which the majority was given an absolutely dominant voice.[70]

Parkes' resolution originally provided that the House would 'possess the sole power of originating and amending all bills appropriating revenue or imposing taxation'. Sir John Downer sought to amend the resolution by deleting the reference to amendment, and later moved that the Senate should have a power of veto in detail.[71] The first amendment was successful. Wrixon proposed a further amendment limiting the power to one of rejection, not amendment, countering Downer's second proposal.[72] Positions were stated and a crisis reached, with veiled threats of a 'packing up of portmanteaux' and a failure of federation.[73] Others sought compromise or reference to a committee.[74] However, Downer was convinced by Griffith that the power of veto in whole was the significant power and was prepared to let the matter go to committee.[75] Thus a compromise was reached, Downer and Wrixon withdrawing their amendments, so that the resolution as agreed was silent on the question of veto — in whole or in part.[76] In due course, following the consideration in committee and the debate on Griffith's draft bill, the Convention agreed to the terms of Chapter I, Clause 55, which limited the power of the Senate over taxation and appropriation bills to rejection.[77]

Beyond the confrontation between responsible government and Senatorial power, a significant number of delegates saw federalism, a strong Senate and independent State government as the more progressive and genuinely representative alternative. Ironically, Deakin used classically conservative arguments in favour of responsible government and the dominance of the lower house — as 'institutions which have the sanction of long experience'.[78] On the other hand, Cockburn emphatically saw the independence of the South Australian people to determine local policy as an important facilitator of progress. Progress and resolution of social problems could be best solved at the local level, rather than through uniform laws promulgated by a Parliament representing an overall majority of Australians.[79] Lieutenant-Colonel William Collard Smith was surprised that Cockburn, whose 'instincts were liberal ... almost democratic and socialistic', should support a powerful Senate since it would actually represent wealth. Cockburn responded that the opposite would be the case.[80]

Federalism was also promoted as progressive and democratic by Macrossan, who observed that Switzerland was the most democratic country in the world, yet one of the most federal also.[81] Clark noted that E A Freeman, the 'eminent historian' who had 'studied most closely, and written the most exhaustively on federal government' thought that federal government

> in its highest and most elaborate development is the most finished and the most artificial production of political ingenuity. It is hardly possible that federal government can attain its perfect form except in a highly refined age, and among a people whose political education has already stretched over many generations.[82]

It was also noted that American federalism and separation of powers had developed on the basis of English institutions as they existed prior to the Reform Acts and the development of responsible government.[83]

The final matter to note on Parkes' resolutions, and not the least significant, is that representation in the House was described in different ways: as representing the *people* as a whole, the *majority* of the people as a whole, the people grouped in *localities* and the people as *individuals*. There were occasional comments to the effect that the electorates would probably be equal, or more or less equal.[84] Baker stated that '[t]he House of Representatives is elected by the people grouped in electoral constituencies containing probably an equal number of voters ...'[85] But by the same token, important qualifications of the democratic nature of the House (let alone the Senate) were to be heard at this early stage. Nicholas John Brown proposed that the smaller States enjoy a minimum level of representation in the House (he suggested a minimum of 12).[86] Secondly, despite the language of Parkes' resolution (which focused on the local electorates), the principle of proportional representation was defined in terms of the States, rather than electorates.[87] This became the language of the Australian Constitution in its final form.

Barton's resolutions

The debate on Barton's resolutions identifies what was distinctive about the Second Convention of 1897–98. First of all, the discussion was more sophisticated. The issues of 1891 had been well aired over the ensuing six years, and in 1897 the representatives of the five colonies built on the earlier discussion and demonstrated deeper knowledge of the available models, history and theory of federal government. The Adelaide Convention began by debating fresh resolutions instead of building directly on the 1891 Bill, even though the resolutions were not particularly different from those of 1891. This time round the framers were directly elected by the people of the respective colonies, and as 'representatives' were influenced by the manner of their own election, demonstrating a marked preference for direct election. The Constitution Bill produced in 1898 was in a number of respects more 'democratic' and 'nationalistic' than the Bill of 1891.[88] It remains to be seen, however, whether and in what respects the democratic or federalist perspectives prevailed. As La Nauze pointed out, 'the formal requirements of democracy would at some point be confronted with those of federalism'.[89]

One aspect was strikingly democratic. The recital to the resolutions recounted that 'in order to enlarge the powers of self-government of the people of Australia, it is desirable to create a Federal Government which shall exercise authority throughout the Federated Colonies ...'[90] This language has lead a member of the High Court to hold that the Constitution is ultimately concerned with self-government, meaning representative and responsible government.[91] The comments of the representatives on this expression show that it was intended to focus attention away from the objection that federation would mean the 'surrender' of powers of colonial self-government, as the first resolution provided.[92] Henry Dobson (no democrat) did 'not care whether the Bill [was] on an ultra-democratic, a democratic, a liberal, or a conservative basis. It [would] enable the people of Australasia to acquire a larger measure of self-government ...'[93] Cockburn, emphatically a 'democrat' *and* a States' righter, thought that the enlargement of the powers of self-government had to do with *autonomy*, the ability of the colonies to 'manage [their] own affairs'.

In this sense, federation would secure autonomy by 'safeguarding us against all possible aggression'. It was therefore imperative that there also be safeguards against 'these powers [of local self-government] being unduly encroached upon by the federal or central authority' — against that 'vortex that continually tends to draw everything to the centre, and to increase the centralizing powers'. For as he said later, 'local government, self-government, and government by the people are analogous terms ... centralization is opposed to all three, and there can be no government by the people if the Government is far distant from the people'.[94]

By the same token, Bernhard Ringrose Wise exalted in the recital as a declaration that the Constitution 'emanates from the people, and that it is for the benefit of the people as a whole'.[95] The declaration indicated where the 'seat of sovereignty' lay, and would, like the words 'We, the people of the United States', assist the High Court in settling the question of ultimate sovereignty.[96] He hoped that the recital would be adopted as the preamble of the Constitution Bill. However, the preamble which was ultimately adopted was more of a compromise between the democratic and nationalistic orientations:

> Whereas the people of [the colonies] have agreed to unite in one indissoluble Federal Commonwealth ...

It compares with the federalist orientation of Parkes' recital of 1891 ('in order to establish and secure an enduring foundation for the structure of a federal government') and the confederal language of the preamble to the 1891 Bill ('Whereas the Australasian Colonies ... have ... agreed to unite in one Federal Commonwealth'). It seems that something of Cockburn's vision ultimately prevailed, since 'local government, self-government, and government by the people are analogous terms'.[97]

There were nevertheless decided democratic elements introduced in 1897, and the change in orientation was apparent from the beginning. Of greatest importance was the movement towards a directly elected Senate. Barton's resolution left the matter open but when, in his introductory speech, Barton noted that some representatives approved direct election, he was met by a resounding 'hear, hear' from the Convention — while the alternative view brought forth no response. When he turned to the House of Representatives, which was to be elected on a population basis, he was again met by a resounding 'hear, hear', for on this 'there can perhaps be no denial' — again, 'hear, hear'.[98]

For some members of the Convention, direct election was necessary because the upper houses in some of the colonial legislatures were nominated or elected on a limited franchise, and this would prejudice the choice which the State legislatures would make.[99] Others pointed to failures in the American system and demands for reform.[100] Following Deakin's lead in 1891, a significant number felt that the powers of the Senate would turn on its composition and were explicit about their change of mind since 1891.[101] Deakin, who had seconded Barton's resolutions, was delighted to observe the shift in viewpoint. With the 'general sense' and 'common influence' of the Convention in this direction, he could now be in the majority on certain points.[102]

Necessarily connected to a shift to direct election, was the question of how many electorates the States would be divided into, and who would decide such questions. Different views were expressed and the full arguments will have to wait until the debate over what was to become section 7 is examined. But at this early stage, Barton staked out his preference for the States to vote as single electorates in order to express the principle that each State as a whole would be especially represented in the Senate. He acknowledged that this view happened to coincide with the way 'in which we stand elected now to this Convention'.[103] Another reason was so that the composition of the House and the Senate would be sufficiently different.[104]

Another dominant and relatively new concern in 1897 concerned the question of the franchise, for the 1891 Bill had left the franchise to the States and did not prohibit plural voting, meaning a right to cast more than one vote.[105] On the whole, the viewpoints were liberal for the time. One recurring aphorism was 'one man, one vote', which in popular parlance bears a close relation to the idea of equality of voting power. However, the representatives at the Convention did not mean equality of voting power when they used this expression. 'One vote, one value' would have been more accurate if this had been the case. They were rather concerned to proscribe plural voting — a different (though related) matter.[106] That 'one man, one vote' did *not* mean 'one vote, one value' appears explicitly from almost every representative who spoke to the matter.[107] For instance, Sir George Turner supported 'one man, one vote' while treating it quite separately from the number of electors who would be represented by each member of the House.[108] William Arthur Trenwith, an opponent of equal representation in the Senate and a proponent of equality of voting power, also supported 'one man, one vote'; but he saw these as different issues.[109] Perhaps the clearest expression of this distinction came from Quick, the moving force behind the new scheme of an elected Convention. He supported a liberal franchise which should be fixed in the Constitution. The words which he used were very clear: 'no person ... shall vote more than once at any federal election'. But he distinguished this from the size and boundaries of House of Representative electorates, which he regarded as 'a mere matter of detail', to be left to the State Parliaments, subject to federal supervision as it 'should see fit'.[110]

Barton's resolutions referred to 'districts formed on a population basis' and there was a discussion of how the proportion of members to voters should be worked out. Turner emphatically denied any implication of equality of electorates and in this view was supported by Deakin.[111] According to Deakin, the key principle of the federation must be 'the rule of the majority', for 'our whole history is the history of a struggle to give more and more effect to that principle' and this must not be put at risk. Wise interjected that 'if that principle were in full force in Victoria, Melbourne and the suburbs would return nearly half the members'. Deakin, however, saw this as 'another branch of the subject', having to do with differences in the numerical strength of electoral divisions based on 'the sacrifices imposed upon the respective voters. It is scarcely a qualification, and practically the principle of the rule of the majority is not departed from.'[112]

Nevertheless, responsible government fared better at Adelaide. Cabinet government fitted in well with the more nationalistic tone of 1897.[113] This was a triumph of British over American and Swiss models of executive government, supported, ironically enough, by conservative arguments favouring Anglo-Saxon institutions over Continental ones, experience over theory and the familiar over 'unfound novelties', as Higgins put it. There was again the interesting confrontation between the two kinds of liberal-democrats which first appeared in 1891. On one hand, Higgins and Isaac Isaacs, liberals from Victoria, insisted on majority rule in a strong national government; on the other hand, Cockburn and the other liberals from South Australia argued for 'local government, self government, and government by the people'. Higgins warned the 'small state radicals' that 'the stiffest Tories are leaning all their hopes upon equal representation in the Senate', since the experience of America showed that the small states with equal representation were but 'pocket borough[s] for the silver kings'.[114] Isaacs delighted in pointing out that far from representing an essential *principle* of federation, equal representation in the Senate was actually a *compromise* achieved at the Philadelphia Convention between the two logically coherent positions of confederation and national union; and that the Senate was originally intended to be an upper house.[115] But the South Australian Gordon responded that the 'genius ... of South Australian politics, has been local government', to which he contrasted 'a huge system of centralisation'.[116] Likewise Cockburn cited one Canadian writer that 'State rights and provincial rights are the strongest bulwarks against despotism. In a Federation, diversity is freedom, uniformity is bondage.'[117]

Charting a middle course typical of those from New South Wales, Wise pointed out that the same *logical* and *theoretical* majoritarian arguments had been put in 1787 and had had to succumb before the *practical* need for a federal pact to which the delegates of all the States would agree. As with the celebrated Connecticut compromise in the United States, Australian federation would necessarily rest on a compromise over equal representation, despite the complications of responsible government, financial control and deadlocks.[118] In this spirit, Deakin was prepared to concede equal representation in the Senate and to acknowledge the need to make 'divisions ... of the colony in order to recognise the different interests'.[119]

Representatives continued to maintain that the lower chamber would be the 'people's house', representing 'every unit in each of the States equally'.[120] But an important concession of the democratic principle in the House lay in James Thomas Walker's proposal for the House that there be 'one member for every 60,000, with a minimum of four for the less populous states'.[121] In his address in reply, Barton traded scholarship with Isaacs in one of their typical confrontations, this time over the referendum,[122] citing E A Freeman to the effect that the English system of representative government grew out of a union of constituent political units, from *mark* to *hundred* to *shire*, a progression suggesting that the English Parliament is constituted more like federal Switzerland than majoritarian France.[123]

Section 7

The debate over Parkes' and Barton's resolutions leads into the debate over what became section 7 of the Constitution. The discussion of the various precursors of section 7 took up a substantial proportion of the debates as a whole. The attention given to the composition of the Senate in 1891 and 1897–98 reflects the significance which the delegates accorded to the issue of federal representation.

In 1891, following the precedent of the United States Constitution (as it then stood),[124] Clark's draft bill provided that senators would be chosen by the State Parliaments.[125] This reflected the mode of representation in the Federal Council of Australasia and under the American Articles of Confederation; it also reflected the position of the delegates at the First Convention.[126] The Griffith Bill followed the Clark scheme in this respect, despite suggestions to the contrary by Deakin and Kingston.[127] As noted, however, it is of abiding significance that from the first session held in Adelaide in 1897, the consensus view had shifted to a direct election of senators by the people of each State.[128]

Nonetheless, the Adelaide amendment retained a federalist focus in two important respects. First, it retained equality of representation for the States, and second, as Frederick William Holder was later to point out, the choice was to be made 'by the people of the State *as one electorate*'.[129] At Adelaide and Sydney, attempts were made by Higgins, supported by proposals of the New South Wales Parliament, to democratise the Senate even further by removing equality of representation for the States, and by William McMillan to qualify the principle that the people of each State should vote as one electorate. In the event, equality of representation for original States was preserved, but McMillan was partly successful, since the federal Parliament was given power to divide the States into electorates.[130] At Sydney and then at Melbourne, a further proposal to introduce an additional discretion in the State Parliaments to determine the number of intra-State electorates was rejected.[131] If successful, this would have placed the determination of Senatorial districting on the same basis as districting for the House of Representatives under section 29. Accordingly, the debate over districting for the Senate sheds light on the views of the delegates on the principles of districting as a whole, and the distinctions which they drew between upper and lower house representation, and between federal and democratic representation. Indeed, the dearth of debate on section 29 means that we must turn to the debate over section 7 for information about the delegates' views as relevant to section 29.[132]

First of all, the attempts to compromise equality of representation of the States in the Senate were unsuccessful. The New South Wales Parliament proposed that representation in the Senate be proportionate to the population of each State, subject to a guarantee of at least three senators for each State.[133] Notably, the Senate continued to be composed of senators from each State regarded as a unit, but the population principle would have worked a significant qualification in the proposition that the Senate would represent the States as *equal* partners in the federal pact.

Higgins' argument at Adelaide and then at Sydney against equal representation was premised on the view that the proper end of all government, let alone of federal government, is the benefit of the people, regarded as a whole and regarded as individuals, without any 'arbitrary' institutions, such as States or local governmental units, intervening.[134] Thus the purpose of federation was to enlarge the powers of self-government of the people *as a whole*, not a minority of the people. He thought it absurd that 'a man in New South Wales is to be treated as equal only to one-eighth of a man in Tasmania', reflecting his individualist orientation. The particular implications of this on 'voting power' were noted. He thought, citing Edmund Burke, that 'all governments ... are mere contrivances for the benefit of the people', reflecting his orientation to nationalism. Higgins opposed mere 'league' or 'federacy', and opposed a compromise between federacy and federation (the idea that the Senate should be a house of confederacy where the States would be represented as equals). His conception of true federation required a central legislature which was fully national, with 'unification on the subjects which are federal, and a severance of the subjects which are not federal'. Where subjects were of general concern only a majority of the whole people were competent to rule on it. This required both houses to be popularly elected, in order to reflect the *national* consensus, the 'mass of the people'. He considered that the way to represent the States would be to require senators to vote by States or to allow the State Parliaments or governments to appoint senators.[135] Thus the provision as it stood was associated with the 'cause' of Southern American slavery, amounting to an 'ingenious device' to thwart 'the will of the people, as a mass', and to prevent 'liberal and radical legislation'. A liberal franchise would be negatived by grouping the people on a territorial rather than population basis. The 'best' of the Philadelphia Convention voted against equal representation in 1787 and the same should occur in Australia in 1897.

Joseph Hector Carruthers, who voted with Higgins, similarly objected that equal representation in the Senate would be analogous to the South Australian Legislative Council being composed of one member for all of Adelaide and another from 'some paltry, petty municipality'. Thus 'there should be ultimate rule by the people, not by broad acres, or arbitrary boundaries, or other accidental occurrences in our Australian civilisation'.[136] However, Higgins fell far short of prevailing, even though he was prepared to allow some weighting to the smaller States instead of a purely population basis; the vote being 32 to 5 in Adelaide and 41 to 5 in Sydney.[137] Higgins did not have the vote of Deakin or Isaacs on this point. Exposing Higgins' a-historical rationalism, Deakin pointed out that the question was 'not merely a question as to which form can be most logically deduced from certain premises which may or may not be generally accepted; it is a question between equal contracting parties, as to the terms and conditions on which they will enter the Federation'. Pushing Higgins to the logical conclusion of his premises, Deakin pointed out that pure majority rule would require a single chamber, indeed, the referendum instead of a legislature. The problem lay therefore in the premises. Moreover, while it is well-known Deakin foresaw that the operation of the party system would counter the function of the Senate as a States' House, it is not often recognised that Deakin also expected that the parties would adapt themselves to the electors of small and large States in proportion to their voting power, thus recognising the 'dignity' of each of these 'communities'.[138] Isaacs likewise took the practical course of voting with the inevitable majority, but not without pronouncing a very full argument against equal representation in principle.[139]

By contrast, John Quick maintained that the Connecticut compromise *was* an important political principle, based on the fact that the States were 'sovereign entities' and 'equal contracting parties'.[140] Patrick McMahon Glynn relied on the explanation of the *Federalist No 62*, that in a compound government of national and confederal elements, the Senate reflects the federal principle through equal representation. *The Federalist* justified the resulting limitation on absolute majority rule since 'the facility and excess of law-making seem to be the diseases to which our Governments are most liable'.[141] Downer anticipated and possibly foiled the argument that the US Senate does not in fact act as a 'States' House' (and that the Australian Senate would not either) when he pointed out that if the Senate is founded 'fairly', with equal representation of the States

> state rights will come very little into these matters, and the results will be highly satisfactory, because we shall know that we really have become so much one people that these smaller considerations never occur to anybody at all.[142]

Downer seemed to suggest that a 'successful' Senate would in fact be marked by a sense of unity and national purpose. If this is what he meant, it would follow that Senators from a particular State need not always (or even usually) vote as a block, but would rather involve themselves individually in national policy debate, and even align themselves with various political parties. It may be that Downer was also suggesting that equality of representation would ensure that the people of each State would feel properly represented as 'a people', and this security would free them to engage in national policy debates in a non-sectarian manner, knowing that they were entitled to that equal share of representation which befits an independent political body, and could make use of this whenever their sectional interests were in jeopardy. In this sense, equal representation in the Senate would serve to unify rather than divide the nation.

Moreover, Wise explicitly turned to the theme of districting to represent local interests, stating:

> where you have different districts and separate local interests, those districts should be represented irrespective of the fact that they contain a minority of population.

Therefore:

> It is not one vote, one value, and it ought not to be, and no one wishes that it should be in local politics. Why, then, do we ask for it in federal politics?[143]

It is significant that Higgins in fact supported this view when he interjected that 'it can be all met in fixing the districts!'[144]

As noted, there was a compromise over districting for the Senate. The federal Parliament was given power to divide the States into multiple electorates, but in the absence of legislation to that effect, each State would vote as one electorate. The various alternatives for senatorial districting were brought together in divers combinations. The alternatives were the entrenchment of each State as single electorates, entrenched multiple electorates for each State, Commonwealth Parliamentary determination and State Parliamentary determination. Those who wished to see each State represented as 'one corporate body' which was 'sovereign ... in essence, if not in form' supported the 'one electorate' provision, with or without a Commonwealth over-ride.[145] According to Barton, the House should represent *locality* and the Senate each *State as a whole*, as an outworking of the federal principle.[146] If the Senate were to be chosen by intra-state electorates, the sense in which it would represent the State as a whole would be compromised. Other delegates, along with the Parliaments of South Australia, Tasmania and Western Australia, shared this concern, but thought that this was best achieved by allowing each State to determine its representation in the Senate.[147] Cockburn supported this approach since 'the greater diversity we allow the greater our freedom from bondage will be'.[148] However, it was opposed by other delegates on the ground that it could lead to inconsistency, fracturing unified State representation, and gerrymandering.[149] Federal control was urged, against Sir Edward Braddon's concern that this could enable the Commonwealth to 'interfere in local and State elections'.[150]

Across this welter of views, thought was given to whether intra-State electorates for the Senate should be equal in population. Lyne, though voting with Higgins against equal representation in the Senate, was concerned that if the States voted as single electorates, the cities would 'obliterate' the country towns. At the same time, Lyne seemed to favour dividing the States up into six electorates of 'as nearly as possible an equal division of people'.[151] At Melbourne, Isaacs proposed that the State Parliaments be given a voice, subject to the superintendence of the Commonwealth and the fall back position of 'one electorate'. McMillan asked:

> Will there be any provision about having an equal number of electors in each district? Would the State Parliament have the right to divide the State as it likes?[152]

Isaacs responded that the State Parliaments would have power to determine electoral divisions as they pleased, and could thereby 'protect' the country against the dominance of the towns. Barton maintained that the Senate should represent each State voting as a whole and the House should represent localities, unless a system of proportional representation were to be adopted.[153] Deakin saw the House as representing individual electors rather than localities, but promoted the Hare system as means of representing every significant section of the population, and proper representation of city, country, town, agricultural and pastoral interests.[154] Sir John Forrest, who voted with Isaacs, expressed concern at the 'preponderating influence' of the 'larger centres of population' which would occur if the States were organised as single electorates.[155] McMillan's point was not taken up by the other speakers who addressed Isaacs' proposal, which was defeated 27 to 16. The suggestion of equal electorates was abandoned.

Thus during the discussion on what was to become section 7, the delegates expressly considered the possibility of entrenching a requirement that electoral divisions be of a size proportionate to population, but the suggestion was disregarded, even by Isaacs. The debate over section 24 gave further opportunity to consider the possibility of entrenching equality of electorate sizes. What was clear about section 7 however, was the significant 'infringements of simple majority rule' which it embodied, to the consternation of the Labor Party in New South Wales.[156]

Section 24

As adopted in 1891, chapter I, clause 24 of the draft bill provided:

> The House of Representatives shall be composed of Members chosen every three years by the people of the several States, according to their respective numbers; and until the Parliament of the Commonwealth otherwise provides, each State shall have one Representative for every thirty thousand of its people.
>
> Provided that in the case of any of the existing Colonies ... until the number of the people is such as to entitle the state to four Representatives it shall have four Representatives.

This precursor of section 24 reflected both democratic and federal principles. In contrast to the provisions for the Senate then envisaged, the members of the House were elected by the people, rather than by the Parliaments of the States. Moreover, representation was according to population, reflecting Parkes' and Barton's resolutions that the House of Representatives was 'to be elected by districts formed on a population basis': one representative for every 30,000 people.[157] These were the democratic elements. They contrasted markedly with the overwhelmingly State-oriented clause which governed the composition of the Senate. Yet they were not wholly democratic. The provision treated the *States* as the basic units entitled to a number of representatives proportionate to their respective populations, rather than providing for one representative for every unit of 30,000 people *as an electoral district*. Thus strictly speaking, the way was left open for electorates within a State to contain any number of people, so long as there was a correspondence of 30,000:1 between the total population of that State and its number of representatives.

Moreover, clause 24 contained three *decidedly* State-oriented or 'federal' elements. The first was that the House was to be composed of representatives chosen by 'the people of the several states', rather than by 'the people of the Commonwealth' as a whole. In this respect, clause 24 followed the precedent of Article 1, section 2 of the United States Constitution, with its focus on the States as constitutive elements of the federal body-politic. Next, the principle of proportionality to population was primarily directed to the States, rather than to the electoral divisions within the States: members of the House were to be chosen by the people of the several States according to their respective numbers. This was (and continues to be) a very important element for a number of reasons. First, the principle of proportionality to the populations of the States was carried through into the final version of section 24, whereas the 30,000 quota was dropped. Second, this was a constitutionally entrenched requirement, unlike the 30,000 quota, which was subject to the Parliament of the Commonwealth providing otherwise, so long as the representation continued to be proportional to the populations of each State.[158] Finally, even the proportionality principle as it applied to the States was substantially qualified by a guaranteed minimum of four representatives in the House for each State. This was an important federalising change to Clark's draft, which did not guarantee a minimum representation and in fact allocated only two representatives for Western Australia.

A clear nationalising modification lay in the substitution of 'people of the commonwealth' for 'people of the several states'. However, this was matched by a number of important State-oriented innovations.[159] First, the minimum level of representation for each State was lifted from four to five.[160] Second, the House was more often seen as representing *locality*, rather than the aggregate of *individuals* across the entire *national population*. Ironically, this led some to think that the Senate would be 'more "national" than the national chamber itself'.[161] Third, despite prolonged argument, the 30,000 quota was replaced by a 2:1 nexus between the size of the House and the size of the Senate. The principle of proportionality to the population of each State remained, but for this purpose the quota of population was tied to the size of the Senate, the total population of the nation and the population of each State.

The argument between those supporting a fixed quota of say 30,000 or 50,000 (subject to Parliamentary revision) and those supporting the 2:1 nexus sheds light on the delegates' respective visions of federal and national democracy and the degree to which the Australian Constitution embodies these principles.[162] It seems to have been Baker's successful motion in the Constitutional Committee that lead to the 2:1 nexus, but as Acting President and Chair of Committees, he did not speak to the issue in the Convention.[163]

As Chair of the Constitutional Committee, Barton briefly explained to the Convention that members of the House 'as before ... are to be chosen by the people of each State, according to the number of its population', but that the Committee had adopted the 2:1 nexus. The numbers of the 'States Assembly'[164] had been calculated against an Australian population of 3.6 million to produce a quota of 50,000. However, with the minimum of five members for each State, the calculation could produce slightly over a 2:1 ratio, so the bill would require a 2:1 nexus 'as nearly as practicably'.[165]

When the Convention came to debate clause 23 as it was then numbered, Barton called upon Richard Edward O'Connor to add to this explanation.[166] O'Connor explained that the new clause 23 had abandoned a 30,000 or 50,000 quota in favour of a 2:1 nexus in order to avoid the problem that a fixed quota, in the absence of Parliamentary amendment, would produce an alarmingly oversized lower house as the population of Australia grew (consistent with available forecasts).[167] However, Turner objected to the change on a number of grounds, one being that it is precisely the case that the House should increase with population, since it is to be the popular house by definition. This should translate into a fixed quota of 50,000, since in the House 'the people are represented as *individuals*'.[168] Turner and O'Connor debated the meaning and effect of the clause, with Turner concluding that the 2:1 nexus was introduced with the joint sitting as a means of resolving deadlocks in mind. The same concern was voiced by Higgins, arguing that representation in the House should be population-based, not State-based. In accordance with the democratic formula that 'the people ought to rule', the clause should revert to the fixed quota, whether that be 30,000, 40,000 or 50,000; and let Parliament adjust the quota as necessary in the light of overall population increases.[169] Isaacs also objected to the 2:1 nexus, but for the reason that it would weaken the representation of States with lower growth rates, such as was expected to be the case with Victoria and South Australia. For that reason the nexus was undemocratic and illiberal — even though the voting power of individuals in each State, as a State, would remain proportional or equal. While the proportionality to population between States was democratic, with respect to the size of constituencies, the nexus was 'conservative'. Thus Isaacs warned that Victorians would reject the nexus provision: while their population would be expected to increase, it would increase at a lower rate than the other States, and accordingly Victoria's proportion of the fixed number of seats in the House would in fact decrease.[170] On the contrary, in the United States, a gradual increase in the quota maintained proportionality to population, yet the growth in the size of the House was kept under control: there was a gradual increase in representation for all growing States, despite disparities in the rate of growth.[171]

Searching for a middle way, it seems, Deakin argued that the 2:1 nexus was appropriate for the time being, but that it should not be entrenched beyond ten or twenty years. He said:

> But as it is, this provision may last in the Constitution for fifty, 100 or 150 years. And which of us can foresee, or dare attempt to decree an iron condition which is to bind these colonies under circumstances to exist a hundred years hence.[172]

A similar argument was put by Trenwith when he later argued that 'it is unwise ... to tie the hands of people that are not yet born by our views as to what is right as to their proportion of representation in the two Houses'.[173]

Barton, a successful architect of compromise on other crucial issues, in this case actively promoted the 2:1 nexus. Replying to these arguments, he maintained that those from the larger States (he being from NSW) 'ought to be prepared to concede what are the principles of Federation' by ensuring a relative numerical strength between the two houses. While the United States did not maintain a fixed nexus between the houses, the relative strength of the Senate was supported through its executive powers. Where the Senate was not supported by the concession of extraordinary powers, a 2:1 nexus is an 'essential of Federation'.[174]

Turner proposed an amendment so as to alleviate the rigidity of the 2:1 nexus, by giving Parliament power to legislate to the contrary. However, his amendment (in its final form) was defeated by a vote of 26 to 9 and the convention approved the 2:1 nexus provision.[175]

In the debate on the second and third paragraphs of clause 23, two amendments were proposed. Whilst unsuccessful, they also shed light on the general views of the Convention. During debate on the second paragraph Vaiben Louis Solomon protested that the two large States would now dominate Parliament. The Senate no longer had any substantial power over money bills, and New South Wales and Victoria with a total of 50 members would control the House of Representatives — against only 26 members from the remaining four States. Objecting that 'representation purely on a population basis is not fair or equitable in any way', he proposed a sliding scale for the determination of numbers of representatives from each State. However, with numerous caustic interjections, his proposal was negatived.[176] In turn, during the debate on the third paragraph George Houston Reid proposed (but under pressure later withdrew) an amendment that the minimum representation for a State be reduced to from five to four, as in the 1891 Bill.[177]

Thus when sitting at Adelaide, the Convention debated and rejected, on one hand, two proposals — Reid's and Turner's — which would have democratised the House significantly, and on the other hand, rejected Solomon's proposal which would have significantly qualified its 'popular' character. The same ground was again covered in Sydney when proposals of the New South Wales and Victorian Legislative Assemblies to re-introduce the 30,000 quota were considered. Turner again supported the proposals, restating the view that the House was to 'represent the people in the various states *as individuals*'.[178] Barton repeated the response that the States as original parties to the federal pact would require equal representation in a Senate having a substantial level of power and standing, and this required a 2:1 nexus to keep the two houses in the proper balance.[179] Holder agreed, noting that the 2:1 nexus effectively amounted to a quota of 1/72 of the national population, rather than a fixed quota of 30,000 or 50,000. In making this point, it should be noted that like many of the delegates he spoke almost as if intra-State electoral divisions should reflect the quota, so that 'there should be one member to every seventy-second part of the population'.[180]

By the same token, when Isaacs came to debate the matter in Sydney, he noted that the small States were claiming the principle of equal representation in the Senate so that

> when we come to deal with the House of Representatives, it is our turn to claim and insist, as I take it, that *we shall have representation in that house on the basis of population*, uninterfered with by the number of people in the states, and absolutely independent of the constitution of the Senate.[181]

But Isaacs and Higgins were not altogether successful in this matter even when it came to the 'popular house'. O'Connor, responding in favour of the 2:1 nexus, went so far as to say that the clause only entrenched the nexus, *leaving the balance to Parliament.*[182] He also thought that in the lower house of the Commonwealth there would be less need for the representation of 'localities' than in the State legislatures, since federal legislative powers did not concern matters which were essentially of localised concern.[183]

The democratic theme was very clearly expressed by McMillan. He objected to the entrenchment of the 2:1 nexus by distinguishing sharply between the 'characteristics of representation' of the two houses. The Senate would represent each State 'in its corporate capacity'. In the House the method of representation should be calculated to 'ascertain the actual opinion of the people of the country' through the various 'constituencies' of 50,000, 60,000, 70,000 or 100,000 people, so as to represent 'all interests combined' in 'that great popular house'. Accordingly, there could be 'no analogy between the representation of the senate and the representation of the house of assembly'.[184] This view was directly contradicted by Clarke, speaking soon after, when he expressly noted that each colony should be able to apportion its own districts.[185]

The function of 'locality' or 'districts' in the system of representation for the Commonwealth Parliament came out again in Reid's attack on the entrenchment of the 2:1 nexus. Unlike McMillan's focus on the individual, Reid thought that the House would essentially represent locality, reflected in the use of the fixed quotas (say of 30,000 population per representative).[186] But even with Reid the concern seems to have been with the position of the *States*, rather than the *localities* within each of the States. For instance, Reid objected to a unique proposal put forward by Glynn which happened to give South Australia a larger proportion of representatives. Glynn responded:

> You do not, even under the constitution, carry out the ratio of population with the strictest accuracy. You find ... for instance in South Australia — that in some electorates 2,000 people return two members, while in others 15,000 people return only the same number of members. Under federation or pure consolidation you cannot carry out any absolute strictness of principle in regard to representation.[187]

Glynn and Reid revealed here a common focus on the States as wholes, rather than electoral divisions within each State.

The delegates who stressed the population basis for representation in the House generally rejected the 2:1 nexus and supported the fixed quota (eg Isaacs, Higgins, Kingston, Quick, Reid, Turner, McMillan, Peacock). Given that these delegates were ultimately unsuccessful, it is rather difficult to see how section 24 can be taken to imply a requirement of equality of voting power. On balance, it seems that a majority at the convention saw section 24 as embodying federalism as much as democracy. Certainly, on the 2:1 nexus issue, the O'Connor/Barton position was upheld by a vote of 26 to 17.

Some outstanding points remain to be addressed, however. First of all, it was not until the Melbourne sitting of the second convention that section 24 was amended to read 'chosen by the people of the Commonwealth'.[188] There is some significance in the difference of expression, and it could be argued that the change introduced in Melbourne nullified any 'federalist' implication to be derived from the debates in Adelaide and Sydney. But by the same token, Barton's 'there shall be one member for each quota of the people of the State' (which of itself could imply an equality of population for each electoral district)[189] reverted at Melbourne into language more like its final form, viz 'the number of members to which each state is entitled', 'the number of members chosen in the several states', 'the number of members to be chosen in each state', then finally, 'the number of members chosen in the several

States'.[190] These expressions focus on the States rather than electoral districts, and do little to support an implication of equal electorates.

Moreover, since the division in Sydney had not been with a full convention, in Melbourne Turner decided to test 'the feeling the convention' once again, and proposed the 50,000 quota subject to Parliamentary adjustment. In the debate, Isaacs reiterated that the compromise on the Senate as a State's House called for a corresponding compromise on the House of Representatives to make it a truly popular house. He criticised the 2:1 nexus as 'conservative' and 'anti-popular'. Seemingly threatening to campaign against the bill should the 2:1 nexus be carried at the convention, Isaacs argued that it turned the constitution from 'a free and democratic constitution', a 'liberal constitution' with male and hopefully female franchise, into a constitution more conservative than any colonial one, and even more conservative than the British.[191]

However, Barton carried the day with a vote of 25 to 15,[192] arguing that the 50,000 quota is 'aimed, whether directly or not, at the subversion of every principle of federal government'. In response to an interjection by Isaacs, Barton alleged that Isaacs was seeking indirectly but intentionally to undermine the Senate as representing the States in their corporate capacities. For, 'we are dealing with a Federal Constitution, and we do presume to preserve some equilibrium of power as respects the two Houses'.[193]

Thus the debate on sections 7 and 24 demonstrates that the delegates chose not to entrench a requirement of equal-sized electorates. The tone and pattern of the debate makes it difficult to conclude that equality of voting power or electorates of equal size was an intended implication of the language of section 24, particularly since the 30,000/50,000 quota was rejected in favour of the 2:1 nexus, itself premised on federal considerations.

Section 29

What remains then are the terms of section 29 itself, which leaves it completely to the Federal and State Parliaments to determine the existence and size of electoral divisions. The provision went through three important stages, but resulting in a provision having an effect very much like its American counterpart.[194] However, unlike the US provision, from Clark's draft onwards the relevant provision was consistently *explicit* about the power of the parliaments to determine electoral districting. Clause 31 of the 1891 Bill provided:

> The electoral divisions of the several States for the purpose of returning members of the House of Representatives shall be determined from time to time by the Parliaments of the several States.[195]

Consistent with the general tendency of the Second Convention, at Sydney in 1897 the clause was approved in the following form:

> Until the Parliament otherwise provides, the electoral divisions of the several States for the purpose of returning members of the House of Representatives, and the number of members to be chosen for each electoral division, shall be determined from time to time by the Parliaments of the several States. Until division each state shall be one electorate.[196]

Then, upon a motion by Barton, the words 'No electoral district shall be formed out of parts of different States' were added, in order to forestall any contrary implication due to the change to section 24 previously noted, now providing for a choice by 'the people of the Commonwealth'.[197]

The State orientation in the 1891 Bill was commuted in favour of Commonwealth supervision at the Second Convention. Barton explained the change as responsive to the danger of 'gerrymander'. While the making of electoral divisions 'is properly left in the hands of the Parliaments of the several states', the amendment was to ensure

> a reserve power proposed to be given to the Parliament of the federation, not to be exercised in any ordinary case but in case there should happen to be some such state of things as once occurred in the United States. It is a reserve power left to the Parliament of the federation to see that the House, which is the most important of the federal legislature should not have its efficiency impaired or its representation made, I would not say, corrupt but ineffective or improper by any course that might be taken by a state.[198]

In 1901 Quick and Garran referred to both the gerrymander and malapportionment as explanations. They noted in respect of malapportionment that US courts intervened where State laws were clearly in contravention of State constitution equality requirements. However, they reflected a more centralist orientation than Barton, stating that in section 29

> State Parliaments are, for the time being, exercising a delegated authority; they are acting merely as legislative agents of the Federal Parliament, which may, at any time, interpose and undertake the work. This ultimate control over electoral divisions is another illustration of the national principles on which the House of Representatives is founded.[199]

While this reflects the legal meaning of the words 'until the Parliament of the Commonwealth otherwise provides', especially when read with subsection 51(xxxvi), it is also an important and proto-typical example of the way in which a literal reading of the Constitution has often led to an expansion of Commonwealth legislative power, against the apparent intention of at least some of the framers of the Constitution. In the first place, Barton clearly saw parliamentary override in section 29 as a 'reserve power', 'not to be exercised in any ordinary case'. Secondly, the amendment to section 29 requiring that no division shall be 'formed out of parts of different States' is capable of a more State-oriented nuance: that it preserves the integrity of the House as representative of the States on a State-wide proportionate basis.[200] Thirdly, it was clear that Barton saw the expression 'until the Parliament of the Commonwealth otherwise provides' in terms of the referendum issue. While certain parts of the Constitution were entrenched, and the basic law could not be changed except by referendum, at significant points Barton's bill left the 'amendment' of the Constitution to Parliament, meaning that the Constitution made provision in a particular matter, but left it open to Parliament to change the constitution of the houses of Parliament if it thought fit. 'Parliament should have power from time to time to legislate without the form of referendum being gone through.'[201] This reflected Barton's basic antipathy for the referendum. Following Freeman, he saw Parliament as embodying the constituent elements of the body politic, and had resisted recourse to the more 'primitive' referendum of our Teutonic 'forefathers'.[202] Moreover, Barton believed that the 'irresistible implication' to be drawn from such provisions was that Parliament should have this *power* of amendment — so far from his intention was it that provisions of this nature would allow far-ranging implied limitations on legislative power 'necessary' for a system of representative democracy! Parliament, not the High Court, was to guard against the gerrymander.[203] And this Parliament, it must be remembered, would itself reflect federal and democratic principles in the structure of the two houses.

By the same token, Quick and Garran noted that the amendment of section 24 to read 'chosen by the people of the Commonwealth' was 'an index of the national character of the Constitution, and of the existence of a national citizenship'. This directs one back to the debate over section 24. While that provision clearly took on a relatively more nationalistic flavour in certain respects, the principle of representation adopted for the House was one of proportionality to State-wide population. This contrasted markedly from the decidedly democratic focus on the electoral divisions themselves as being 'formed on a population basis' along the lines of the Parkes resolution, the terms of the precursor to section 24 and the 50,000 quota proposal by Turner. As noted, the 2:1 nexus was adopted specifically with the deadlock procedure in mind, but for this very reason the result in sections 24 and 29 is one of balance between the federal and democratic principles. This balance was carried against the objection of Isaacs and others that this was to compromise the democratic character of the Constitution too far, especially after they had compromised so much on the Senate to start with.

Conclusion

In the early stages of the debate, when the conventions considered Parkes' and Barton's resolutions, one might have expected that the Constitution would expressly require that House of Representatives districts be formed 'on a population basis' with a fairly high degree of equality of voting power. However, the debate over the powers and composition of the Senate at this early stage revealed a compelling concern with federalism and the special role of the States as local units of government in the system of national representation.

In the upshot, the Constitution did not entrench a requirement of equal districts for the House of Representatives. Section 29 expressly gives final power over districting to the national Parliament as a safeguard against gerrymanders, but it does not entrench an equality of electoral districts. Section 29 was adopted in the conventions without much discussion. However, the debate over sections 7 and 24 demonstrates the degree to which 'federal', as opposed to 'individual-democratic', considerations dominated the thinking of a decisive majority of the framers.

To this degree, a 'federal theory' can be discerned in three important respects. The first is summed up in Cockburn's aphorism that 'local government, self-government and government by the people are analogous terms'. As such, the Constitution was certainly about 'government by the people,' and perhaps even 'popular sovereignty'. But this idea of popular government did not mean national majoritarian government, for it was understood primarily in terms of local government, but in such a way that a wider, 'federal' level of government was not excluded. As such, the idea likewise implies that there were understood to be numerous configurations of 'the people': of the locality, of the State and of the Federation. Thus if a theory of 'popular sovereignty' is presupposed by the federal constitutional system, it is a theory which contemplates varying configurations of 'people[s]' constituting their governments in their varying capacities, as sections 51(xxxviii) and 128 seem to envisage.

The second aspect of a theory of federalism to be discerned in these debates is seen in Deakin's point of departure from Higgins' rationalism: that 'it is a question between equal contracting parties, as to the terms and conditions on which they will enter the Federation'. Presupposing that federalism is indeed akin to covenant or treaty, it is expected that the parties will make historically conditioned choices. Accordingly, the abstract philosopher will no doubt find plenty to quibble about in the result, but in doing so, the rationalist may well be proposing something other than federalism. Even the federalist may express concern about the consistency or the expediency of those choices and ask whether too much might have been conceded by one or other of the parties. But federalism must always involve freedom of contract, and with that goes a fundamental respect for the historically conditioned choices which the parties have negotiated and recorded in the Constitution.

The final element of federal theory is to be seen in Barton's recognition that parliamentary representation was founded in something like Freeman's federative principle, 'from mark, to hundred, to shire',[204] and that therefore, as Clark saw, there was an analogy between the Senate as representative of the States and the House as representative of localities. This, as has been discussed, militates against the majoritarian demand for electorates of equal size in both the Senate and the House. It strongly suggests that equality of voting power is not an implication of the Australian Constitution, but gives distinctively *federal* reasons for this conclusion.

Moreover, the Australian Constitution was very much modelled on the United States Constitution. The various versions of the Constitution Bill can ultimately be traced to Clark's draft produced in 1891. Clark, of course, was enamoured with the American Constitution and modelled his draft on the US precedent, except that he was explicit about the power of the Commonwealth and State parliaments to determine electoral districts. Clark's draft deeply influenced Griffith's draft and the Constitution Bill which was adopted by the 1891 convention. In turn, the 1891 bill was clearly recognisable in the Barton draft of 1897, which, after amendments in committee of the whole and alterations agreed to by the colonial premiers in 1899, and subject to the changes to the judicial system required by the Crown Law Officers in England, became the Australian Constitution.[205] It is not without significance that these three key players, Clark, Griffith and Barton, shared reasonably similar views about the nature of federation and democracy, implemented these ideas in their draft constitutions, and carried much of the debate in the conventions on the issues discussed in this chapter. It can fairly be said that it was their vision of federal representation which generally, and in certain respects decidedly, shaped the form and substance of sections 7, 24 and 29. If equality of voting power is not entrenched in the Australian Constitution, it is largely due to the adaptation of representative government to federalism worked out and carried by these three important figures.

Notes

1. *Official Record of the Debates of the Australasian Federal Convention.* Legal Books, Sydney, 1986 (Adelaide 1897) at 41. The *Debates* will henceforth be cited by speaker, city, date and page as appropriate.
2. Sydney 1897 at 317.
3. 5th edn, Butterworths, Sydney, 1995 at 14; 3rd edn, 1981 at 36.
4. Angus & Robertson, Sydney, 1901 at 332.
5. 1st edn, John Murray, London, 1902 at 327; see at 102.
6. Galligan B, *A Federal Republic: Australia's Constitutional System of Government*, Cambridge University Press, 1995 at 7, also see at 8, 38, 188.
7. *Australian Capital Television Pty Ltd v. Commonwealth of Australia (No. 2)* (1992) 177 CLR 106; *Nationwide News Pty Ltd v. Wills* (1992) 177 CLR 1; *Theophanous v. The Herald and Weekly Times Limited* (1994) 124 ALR 1; *Stephens v. West Australian Newspapers Limited* (1994) 124 ALR 80; *Langer v. Commonwealth of Australia* (1996) 134 ALR 400; *Muldowney v. South Australia* (1996) 136 ALR 18.
8. *Attorney-General of the Commonwealth (ex rel McKinlay) v. Commonwealth of Australia* (1975) 135 CLR 1; *Burke v. Western Australia* [1982] WAR 248; *McGinty v. Western Australia* (1996) 134 ALR 289.
9. (1996) 134 ALR 289 at 374. Of course, 'federation' from the point of view of independent states is a *unifying* notion, in contrast to a loose 'confederation'. But from the viewpoint of a consolidated unitary government, federation is a *decentralising* idea.
10. Goldsworthy J, 'Implications in Language, Law and the Constitution' in Lindell G (ed.), *Future Directions in Australian Constitutional Law*, Federation Press, Annandale, NSW, 1994; 'Originalism in Constitutional Interpretation' (1997) 25 *FLR* 1.
11. See Galligan B and Warden J, 'The Design of the Senate' in Craven G (ed.), *The Convention Debates 1891–1898: Commentaries, Indices and Guide*, Vol. VI, Legal Books, Sydney, 1986.
12. See Sampford CJG, 'Responsible Government and the Logic of Federalism: An Australian Paradox?' (1990) *Public Law* 90 at 93. The definition is adopted from Davis SR, *The Federal Principle: A Journey Through Time in Quest of a Meaning*, University of California Press, 1978 at 121–2.
13. Frenkel M, *Federal Theory*, Centre for Research on Federal Financial Relations, Canberra, 1986 at 10, 26. See McWilliams WC, 'Democracy and the Citizen: Community, Dignity, and the Crisis of Contemporary Politics in America' in Goldwin RA & Schambra WA (eds), *How Democratic Is the Constitution?* American Enterprise Institute for Public Policy, Washington, 1980 at 93; Pound R, 'Law and Federal Government' in Pound, McIlwain & Nichols, *Federalism as a Democratic Process*, Rutgers University Press, New Brunswick, 1942.
14. [1982] WAR 248 at 252, 256 per Chief Justice Burt.
15. See Diamond M, 'The Electoral College and thc Idea of Federal Democracy' (1978) 8 (1) *Publius: The Journal of Federalism* 63.
16. Proudhon PJ, *The Principle of Federation*, University of Toronto Press, Toronto, 1979 at 38.
17. Davis, n 12 ch. 4; see Lutz DS, *Popular Consent and Popular Control: Whig Political Theory in the Early State Constitutions*, Louisiana State University Press, 1980, ch. 7.
18. Bogdanor V and Butler D, *Democracy and Elections: Electoral systems and their political consequences*, Cambridge University Press, 1983 at 2–3. The quotation from Maitland

FW appears in *The Constitutional History of England*, Cambridge University Press, 1955 at 363. Cf McIlwain CH, 'The Historical Background of Federal Government: Some Sources of Our American Federalism' in Pound, McIlwain & Nichols, n 13.

19. Bailyn B, *The Ideological Origins of the American Revolution*, Belknap Press, Cambridge, MA, 1967 at 164. While it was beyond the scope of Bailyn's thesis explicitly to connect the principle of territorial representation to American federalism, see the suggestive comments at 228–9. Bailyn is cited by Bogdanor and Butler, n 18 at 3. But contrast Moore, n 5 at 330.
20. Lutz DS, *The Origins of American Constitutionalism*, Louisiana State University Press, 1988, ch. 4.
21. Bryce J, *The American Commonwealth*, Vol I, 2nd edn, Macmillan, 1889 at 415.
22. Elazar DJ, *The American Constitutional Tradition*, University of Nebraska Press, 1988 at 113. See Galligan B, n 6 at 69, 71; Wechsler H, 'The Political Safeguards of Federalism' (1954) 54 *Columbia Law Review* 543 at 551; Dixon RG, *Democratic Representation: Reapportionment in Law and Politics*, Oxford University Press, New York, 1968, ch IV; *Baker v. Carr* 369 US 186 (1961) per Frankfurter and Harlan JJ.
23. Sydney 1891 at 247. Also see Wise, Sydney 1897 at 317.
24. Sydney 1891 at 23, 499–500; Adelaide 1987 at 17, 395.
25. La Nauze JA, *The Making of the Australian Constitution*, Melbourne University Press, Carlton, 1972 at 40.
26. Sydney 1891 at 23. It seems that Parkes changed the first draft of his resolution as a result of discussions with a smaller group including Clark and Griffith: n 25 at 35–8. Subsequently, important changes were introduced in the Convention as it was finally approved: Sydney 1891 at 499–500. Compare Barton's resolution as adopted at Adelaide in 1987 at 17, 395.
27. Sydney 1891 at 26. Parkes' first draft referred to 'districts possessing severally an equality of representation': n 25 at 35–8. Notably, the resolution as presented to the Convention was not substantially changed on these points before it was approved: Sydney 1891 at 500.
28. Adelaide 1897 at 715; Sydney 1897 at 454–5; Melbourne 1897 at 1840, 2528.
29. See *Wesberry v. Sanders* 376 US 1 (1963).
30. Sydney 1891 at 68–88. In committee, he proposed a directly elected Senate: La Nauze, n 25 at 47.
31. Eg Wrixon, Sydney 1891 at 215.
32. Sydney 1891 at 74–5.
33. Sydney 1891 at 78. In Griffith's 1891 Draft Commonwealth of Australia Bill senators were chosen by the State legislatures. They were not directly elected by the people of the various States.
34. Sydney 1891 at 91. Also see McIlwraith at 63.
35. Sydney 1891 at 159. Also see Baker at 111.
36. Sydney 1891 at 79, 82.
37. Sydney 1891 at 111, 113. See Moore, n 5 at 123.
38. La Nauze described Higgins as 'an obstinate individualist radical,' though 'learned and courteous, [and therefore] heard with attention while he argued a hopeless case': n 25 at 102, 120.
39. Sydney 1891 at 111.
40. Sydney 1891 at 197, 199.
41. Sydney 1891 at 153.

42. Sydney 1891 at 451.
43. Eg Hackett, Sydney 1891 at 278; Parkes at 445.
44. Sydney 1891 at 434. Also see Deakin, Adelaide at 287–8. Bryce committed much of the second volume of his American Commonwealth to an analysis of the role of parties as the motive force in American politics. On Bryce's impact on the framers, see La Nauze, n 25 at 18–9.
45. Rutledge, Sydney 1891 at 147–8. See Bryce, n 21, vol 1 at 93–120.
46. Sydney 1891 at 63.
47. Sydney 1891 at 111.
48. Sydney 1891 at 111, 200.
49. Sydney 1891 at 171.
50. Sydney 1891 at 319.
51. See Deakin, Sydney 1891 at 74 and Adelaide 1897 at 650–1; Higgins, Adelaide 1897 at 641–9. Deakin's comments in 1897 explain why in 1891 he did not contest equal representation: he clearly saw the necessity for compromise on equal representation. Nevertheless, in 1891 his speeches stressed logic; in 1897 they stressed conciliation against Higgins' insistent maintenance of principle. Even Isaacs 'deserted' Higgins on equal representation for reasons of political necessity: Adelaide, 1897 at 660.
52. Sydney 1891 at 441.
53. Sydney 1891 at 429–31. Compare Thynne at 106.
54. Sydney 1891 at 439–40.
55. Sydney 1891 at 440, 465–6. See Baker RC, *The Executive in a Federation*, Bristow CE, Government Printer, Adelaide, 1897; also Downer at 102, Bird at 122, Smith at 135, Kingston at 162.
56. Sydney 1891 at 198.
57. Sydney 1891 at 214.
58. Sydney 1891 at 215.
59. Sydney 1891 at 280.
60. Sydney 1891 at 35–8, 40–1.
61. To complete the story, at Adelaide in 1897, the relevant clause was amended to prohibit a Minister of State from holding office for more than three months unless becoming a member of Parliament (section 64): Adelaide 1897 at 1233, Melbourne 1898 at 2534.
62. Sydney 1891 at 53.
63. Sydney 1891 at 78.
64. Sydney 1891 at 91–3.
65. Sydney 1891 at 113.
66. Sydney 1891 at 163.
67. Sydney 1891 at 35–8, 40–1, 427–9.
68. Sydney 1891 at 171–2.
69. Sydney 1891 at 247.
70. Sydney 1891 at 247–51.
71. Sydney 1891 at 375–6, 380.
72. Sydney 1891 at 381.
73. See Barton, Sydney 1891 at 417, Munro at 389, McIlwraith at 396, Smith at 397–8, Kingston at 403.
74. Barton, Sydney 1891 at 414, 418, Bray at 459.
75. Sydney 1891 at 442–4.

76. Sydney 1891 at 463.
77. Sydney 1891 at 706, 762, 953–4. In due course Barton's draft of 1897 limited the Senate's powers over annual appropriation bills only, but taxation bills were later included at Reid's initiative. This was essentially carried through the Sydney and Melbourne sessions, although drafting changes ultimately created the problematic form of the present section 53, which specifically denies a power of amendment but is silent on rejection: Adelaide 1897 at 480, 484, 575, 1232, Sydney 1897 at 467, 481, 537, Melbourne 1898 at 2532–3.
78. Sydney 1891 at 84. See also Rutledge at 144.
79. Sydney 1891 at 201. See also Gordon at 451, who thought likewise.
80. Sydney 1891 at 399.
81. Sydney 1891 at 433.
82. Sydney 1891 at 243.
83. Sydney 1891 at 279.
84. Sydney 1891 at 26.
85. Sydney 1891 at 111.
86. This was supported by Wrixon, but opposed by Macrossan on democratic grounds: Sydney 1891 at 208, 215, 436.
87. Cuthbert, Sydney 1891 at 290.
88. See Quick J and Garran R, n 4 at 135; La Nauze, n 25 at 72, 79–80, 94–5, 124, 128, 137, 152. One important area of 'democratisation' which will not be discussed here was the shift towards popular referendum for the adoption and amendment of the constitution. But even here, the democrats did not win on every point. Compare Sydney 1891 at 884, 894, 897, 963–4, Adelaide 1897 at 1020–4, 1028–30, 1242–3, Melbourne 1898 at 715–6, 765–6, 769–72, 2543; Quick J and Garran R at 988. Another area of relative democratisation lay in the deadlock provision of section 57 and the substantial debate which this engendered at Sydney in 1897. But again this was significantly tempered by the adoption of a joint sitting in conjunction with the 2:1 nexus instead of a referendum.
89. Note 25 at 95, and compare at 125.
90. Adelaide 1897 at 17. The reference was ultimately changed to 'Australasia:' at 395.
91. *Australian Capital Television Pty Ltd v. Commonwealth* (1992) 177 CLR 106, 228 per McHugh J.
92. La Nauze, n 25 at 112–13.
93. Adelaide 1897 at 191.
94. Adelaide 1897 at 338–9. He also said: 'Of course majorities must rule, for there would be no possible good government without majorities ruling, but I do not think the majority in South Australia should be governed by the majority in Victoria, or in New South Wales:' at 340.
95. Adelaide 1897 at 115. Praising his own words it appears. Barton at 366 attributed the expression to Wise. See also Carruthers at 87, Symon, at 127: federation will not 'curtail the liberties of the people'; Isaacs at 170, Higgins at 643.
96. However, Wise himself declaimed against districts of equal size: at 290.
97. Adelaide 1897 at 338–9; see La Nauze, n 25 at 128.
98. Adelaide 1897 at 22.
99. Turner, Adelaide 1897 at 39.
100. Isaacs, Adelaide 1897 at 176.
101. Quick, Adelaide 1897 at 189; Downer at 209–10.

102. Deakin, Adelaide 1897 at 285. Despite the 'great change of opinion' some maintained their preference for the State legislatures choosing their senators, e.g. Forrest at 248.
103. Adelaide 1897 at 26.
104. Reid, Adelaide 1897 at 270.
105. Barton and Cockburn respectively argued for federal control and a more liberal franchise in 1891 without success: Sydney 1891 at 91, 200, 628, 636. In 1897, Holder favoured an adult franchise: Adelaide at 149; Downer a liberal one: at 212; Lyne a franchise at age 25 or 30 for the Senate: at 161; Dobson sought a vote per person plus a vote for thrift: at 192; he was criticised by Fysh: at 242; Forrest wanted to leave the matter to the States: at 246–50.
106. Contrast *McKinlay's Case* (1975) 135 CLR 1, 72 per Murphy J.
107. For example Fraser, Adelaide 1897 at 79 and Isaacs at 437. Except see Carruthers, Sydney 1897 at 271.
108. Adelaide 1897 at 41. Also see Forrest at 250.
109. Adelaide 1897 at 330–2.
110. Adelaide 1897 at 187.
111. Adelaide 1897 at 41. See the extract at the beginning of this chapter.
112. Adelaide 1897 at 289–90.
113. For example, see Glynn, Adelaide 1897 at 72, and Wise's change of mind at 106–7.
114. Higgins, Adelaide 1897 at 101–2.
115. Adelaide 1897 at 171–3.
116. Adelaide 1897 at 318.
117. Adelaide 1897 at 339. The author was an unidentified 'Mr Watson': see Craven, n 11, vol. VI at 254.
118. Adelaide 1897 at 105–10.
119. Adelaide 1897 at 290.
120. Trenwith, Adelaide 1897 at 331.
121. Adelaide 1897 at 309. This had been the position in 1891; Walker was maintaining this position in case the discussion over the 30, 40, 50 or 60 thousand ratios had clouded the principle of minimum representation.
122. See La Nauze, n 25 at 121; Isaacs, Adelaide 1897 at 180, 392, 394.
123. Adelaide 1897 at 388. The citation was from Freeman EA, *The Growth of the English Constitution from the Earliest Times*, Macmillan and Co, London, 1898 at 9–10, see at 37, 60, 66; and see *The History of the Norman Conquest of England*, Clarendon Press, Oxford, 1870, vol I at 79–99; vol V at 461.
124. The 17th Amendment (1913) introduced the direct election of US senators by the people of each State.
125. It would appear that Kingston's draft was in the same terms: La Nauze, n 25 at 24–6, 295–6.
126. La Nauze, 25 at 2.
127. Sydney 1891 at 158.
128. Adelaide 1897 at 641, 1190, 1210, 1223.
129. Sydney 1897 at 388. The significance of this is discussed below.
130. Adelaide 1897 at 641, 670; Sydney 1897 at 259–62, 355, 368–71, 390–1.
131. Sydney 1897 at 381–2; Melbourne 1897 at 1992–3, 1928.
132. For the same reason, section 29 as the Australian framers understood it must be read in the light of the United States experience under the corresponding Article I, section 4, sub-section 1.
133. Quick and Garran, n 4 at 183; Sydney 1897 at 358.

134. Adelaide 1897 at 379, 641ff; Sydney 1897 at 259–65, 345–1.
135. In the early federal Parliaments, Senate election results reflected the predominant perspectives of the various States on the protection–free trade issue. Moreover, opposition supporters in the Senate declined to acknowledge a formal leader as improper in a States' House: Sawer G, *Australian Federal Politics and Law 1901–1929*, Melbourne University Press, 1972 at 18–19. In due course this attitude declined as party organisation and discipline was consolidated. But see Odgers JR, *Australian Senate Practice*, Royal Australian Institute of Public Administration, Canberra, 6th edn, 1991 at 7–18.
136. Adelaide 1897 at 540–1.
137. Adelaide 1897 at 668; Sydney 1897 at 355.
138. Deakin, Adelaide 1897 at 650–1; Sydney 1897 at 331–6. See Downer at 267, Glynn at 276.
139. Isaacs, Adelaide 1897 at 660; Sydney 1897 at 303–13; compare Isaacs' *Australian Democracy and Our Constitutional System*, Horticultural Press, Melbourne, 1939 at 33–4.
140. Adelaide 1897 at 656. See Elazar, n 22 at 23–5.
141. Adelaide 1897 at 664–5; Sydney 1897 at 276–82; see Symon's reliance on Freeman on this point, Sydney 1897 at 291–6. Glynn incorrectly referred to No 72 and attributed it to Hamilton rather than Madison: *The Federalist Papers*, The New American Library of World Literature, New York at 377. It seems he corrected the error when addressing the South Australian Legislative Assembly: Hunt EM, *American Precedents in Australian Federation*, AMS Press, New York, 1963 at 108.
142. Sydney 1897 at 269.
143. Sydney 1897 at 317.
144. Note 143.
145. For example, Barton, Holder, O'Connor, Glynn, Reid, Downer, Kingston, Quick. See Sydney 1897 at 360, 366, 371–3, 374, 377, 388, 380, 382, 387; Melbourne 1898 at 1923–4.
146. Adelaide 1897 at 669; Sydney 1897 at 360–1, 377; Melbourne 1898 at 1923–4.
147. That is, Symon, Brown and Clarke: Sydney 1897 at 294, 364, 367, 384.
148. Sydney 1897 at 379.
149. For example McMillan, Higgins, Downer respectively: Sydney 1897 at 369–72.
150. Sydney 1897 at 383.
151. Lyne, Sydney 1897, 364–6, 369, 385–6; Adelaide 1897 at 668–9; similarly, Howe at 381.
152. Melbourne 1898 at 1923.
153. Melbourne 1898 at 1925.
154. Melbourne 1898 at 1925–7.
155. Melbourne 1898 at 1927.
156. La Nauze, n 25 at 166.
157. See La Nauze, n 25 at 53.
158. Incidentally, a 1933 House of Representatives redistribution proposal which reduced South Australia's representation from seven to six was thought by the then Premier of South Australia to be a matter of sufficient interest to the State for him to make a personal representation to the Commonwealth Government on behalf of the South Australian MPs: Patterson PA, 'Federal Electorates and Proportionate Distribution' (1968) 42 *Australian Law Journal* 127 at 130.
159. These innovations were unfortunately not emphasised by Quick and Garran: n 4 at 450, 466. Compare Quick and Garran, para 113 at 455 with para 103 and para 104 at 447–50.

160. The US Constitution required that each State should have at least one representative: Art I, sec 2, sub-sec 3.
161. Moore, n 5 at 98.
162. Its significance was recently noted in *McGinty* (1996) 134 ALR 289 at 383 per Gummow J.
163. La Nauze, n 25 at 138. It is perhaps not insignificant that the nexus was Baker's idea. His wider theory of federalism was deeply influenced by the Swiss example, with its reliance on mechanisms of federal representation rather than a division of powers enforced by the judiciary. See Baker, n 55.
164. As the Senate had come to be called in the Barton bill. Higgins also sought a new name for the other house: 'National Assembly': Adelaide 1897 at 481. Both were unsuccessful.
165. Adelaide 1897 at 435–7.
166. Adelaide 1897 at 683. Barton's fatigue was noticeable (at 682) and O'Connor had drafted the provision (at 436).
167. Adelaide 1897 at 683–6.
168. Adelaide 1897 at 686, 701, emphasis added. See the debate between Turner and O'Connor at 687–8.
169. Adelaide 1897 at 692. See also Reid at 269 suggesting a 60,000 quota.
170. This in fact occurred for Victoria in the 1906, 1911 and 1921 redistributions: Patterson, n 158 at 129.
171. Adelaide 1897 at 694–8.
172. Adelaide 1897 at 702–3.
173. Adelaide 1897 at 708.
174. Adelaide 1897 at 703–7.
175. Adelaide 1897 at 709–10.
176. Adelaide 1897 at 710–13. Quick and Garran indicate that his proposal 'was not taken seriously and was negatived without division': n 4 at 447.
177. Adelaide 1897 at 714–15.
178. Sydney 1897 at 420–1.
179. Sydney 1897 at 423.
180. Sydney 1897 at 424. The 1/72 proportion was calculated by reference to the total number of Members of the House, itself calculated as twice the number of senators, given six senators for each of the six States.
181. Sydney 1897 at 425, emphasis added.
182. Sydney 1897 at 429. This substantiates the *McKinlay* focus on the conscious entrenchment of the nexus requirement in section 24 and the rejection of the implication of equality of voting power both in *McKinlay* and *McGinty*.
183. Sydney 189 at 434.
184. Sydney 1897 at 436–7.
185. Sydney 1897 at 442.
186. Sydney 1897 at 445.
187. Sydney 1987 at 446–7.
188. Melbourne 1898 at 1827–8.
189. These words were introduced at Adelaide by Barton: Adelaide 1897 at 683, 1191, 1225.
190. Melbourne 1898 at 1827–8, 1838, 2435.
191. Melbourne 1898 at 1831–4.
192. Quick and Garran, n 4 at 447, say 25 to 10, but see Melbourne 1898 at 1837.

193. Melbourne 1898 at 1835.
194. Art I, sec 4, sub-sec 1: 'The Times, Places and Manner of holding Elections for Senators and Representatives shall be prescribed in each State by the Legislature thereof; but the Congress may at any time by Law make or alter such Regulations, except as to the Place of Choosing Senators.'
195. Sydney 1891 at 948.
196. Sydney 1897 at 454.
197. Melbourne 1898 at 1840; Quick and Garran, n 4 at 465–6. Thence, with subsequent verbal amendments, the provision took its present form.
198. Sydney 1897 at 454. This followed the approach of the US Constitution: *Wesberry v. Sanders* 376 US 1 at 30–40 per Harlan J (dissenting).
199. Quick and Garran, n 4 at 466.
200. Melbourne 1898 at 1840.
201. Adelaide 1897 at 455.
202. Adelaide 1897 at 388.
203. Quick and Garran, n 4 at 466. Compare Berger R, *Government by Judiciary: the Transformation of the Fourteenth Amendment*, Harvard University Press, Cambridge, MS, 1977.
204. Freeman's influence on Clark is noted by Reynolds J, 'A I Clark's American Sympathies and his Influence on Australian Federation' (1958) 32. *Australian Law Journal* 62 at 64. See Melbourne 1890 at 110; Sydney 1891 at 243.
205. La Nauze, n 25 at 239–69.

3
Parliamentary privilege: contemporary issues

Gerard Carney

Introduction

It is an honour to be invited to contribute a chapter to this book of essays which celebrates the academic achievements of the late Professor Darrell Lumb. Professor Lumb was a colleague of mine during 1989 when I lectured in constitutional law at the University of Queensland and we shared a common interest in State constitutional law. I have selected this topic on parliamentary privilege in view of his deep and abiding concern with the appropriate role of constitutional law in maintaining the stability of our governmental system as a parliamentary democracy. Parliamentary privilege is an integral component in determining the appropriate relationship between Parliament and the Executive and between Parliament and the Judiciary. In recent times a range of issues has arisen involving the determination of the scope of these privileges and the respective jurisdiction of the courts and of Parliament. This chapter endeavours to chronicle some of those issues. It begins with an outline of the historical development of parliamentary privilege in England and subsequently in Australia in order to place the discussion of the contemporary issues in their appropriate context.

Historical origins of parliamentary privilege

The powers, rights and immunities known as parliamentary privileges took centuries to evolve and were won incrementally by the English Parliament or by either of its Houses after numerous power struggles with the Crown and with the courts. Their purpose was then and still is the protection of Parliament from outside interference by the Crown and the courts. And given the intense struggles from which these privileges emerged, they have been jealously guarded ever since.

It was interference by the Crown at the end of the fourteenth century which first aroused the concern of Parliament to protect itself.[1] The House of Commons struggled against the Crown to assert its right to debate any matter, to initiate legislation even if contrary to the interests of the Crown and to control its own elections. It also asserted the right to determine exclusively the exercise of its privileges which were derived from the common law and custom of Parliament, in particular, the freedom of speech in Parliament. According to Erskine May,[2] the Members of the House of Commons enjoyed by the end of the fifteenth century a traditional right of freedom of speech within the House.[3] That freedom was, however, a matter of contention throughout the reigns of Elizabeth I and James I, culminating in the Protestation of 1621 when the House of Commons declared inter alia the freedom of speech of its members.[4] But it was not until the House of Lords decision in *Eliot's Case*[5] in 1629 that freedom of speech was recognised as a legal right. In that case, Sir John Eliot and two other Members of the House of Commons were arrested at the instigation of the Crown for uttering allegedly seditious language during debate in the House and for assaulting the Speaker. The House of Lords declared their arrest for the seditious statements to be invalid as against the law and privilege of Parliament. It has been said that the actions of the Crown in this helped ignite the Civil War.[6] Further problems arose after the Restoration in *Jay v. Topham*[7] in 1682 and *Williams' Case* in 1684 in both of which the proceedings of Parliament were questioned. These decisions provided the immediate reason[8] for the inclusion of the privilege of freedom of speech as Article 9 of the *Bill of Rights* 1689 in relation to the speeches, debates and proceedings of Parliament.[9]

In the end, the power struggle between the Parliament and the Crown was resolved by the subjection of the royal prerogative to parliamentary control. The *Bill of Rights* 1689 confirmed the paramountcy of Parliament over the Crown, yet measures were still required to curtail Crown attempts to influence the House of Commons through its members. Accordingly, at around this time, the first limitations were introduced on the holding of public office while a member of Parliament.[10] This measure along with s. III of the *Act of Settlement* 1701 which provided for the appointment of judges during good behaviour were designed to curtail the influence of the Crown and promote the independence of the Parliament and the Judiciary.

On the other hand, the power struggle between Parliament, especially the House of Commons, and the Common Law Courts prolonged into the nineteenth century. Essential to an understanding of this conflict is the notion of Parliament as a judicial body often described as the 'High Court of Parliament'. This character derives from its earliest origins as a court of justice in the thirteenth century hearing private petitions for the redress of grievances in special judicial decisions of the Curia Regis.[11] Only at the end of the fourteenth century did those who attended Parliament, originally at the invitation of the sovereign, attain the right to do so. The greater barons and churchmen became the Lords in Parliament while the representatives of the counties and boroughs formed the Commons. The former continued to exercise judicial power but the Commons became increasingly concerned with political matters.[12]

In order to assert its dominance over the Crown and the other Courts, Parliament asserted and relied upon its judicial character as the High Court of Parliament although it appears not to have acted as a court as such since the sixteenth century.[13] Nevertheless, Parliament developed certain powers, rights and immunities similar to those acquired by other Courts.

First, there evolved the law of Parliament, *lex et consuetudo parliamenti*, comprising the privileges of Parliament. Secondly, the need to ensure the independence of Parliament free from outside interference resulted in the adoption of privileges enjoyed by the other Courts: immunity from prosecution for what is said in Parliament and power to punish for contempt. Thirdly, during that period of history when different Courts possessed different jurisdictions so that the administration of the law was marked by different bodies and different bodies of law, Parliament claimed immunity from the other Courts relying upon its status as the highest Court of the land. Hence, it refused to subject itself to the common law. Finally, this immunity from the common law eventually was claimed by the House of Commons alone in order to ensure its independence from the House of Lords, all of whose Members were eligible to participate when it convened as the highest Common Law Court.

Professor Campbell suggests that the Commons might have been prepared to allow the Lords during the Tudor and Stuart periods to review the exercise of parliamentary privilege had they been independent of the Crown.[14] This independence was only achieved later through s. III of the *Act of Settlement* 1701. Meanwhile, *Eliot's* Case in 1629 convinced the Commons to continue to assert its exclusive role in reviewing the exercise of parliamentary privilege. Judges who transgressed into the area of privilege were liable to be brought before the House for contempt.[15] Nevertheless, the securing of judicial independence by the *Act of Settlement* 1701 brought no change in the Commons' view. The courts did not challenge this, aware no doubt that their fate lay now with Parliament's power to address the Crown for their removal. Indeed if parliamentary privilege were raised in court proceedings by way of defence, the court's ability to determine whether such a claim could be made was not recognised until the nineteenth century in *Stockdale v. Hansard*.[16]

The struggle which ensued between the House of Commons and the Courts gradually resolved itself in a similar manner to the resolution of the struggle between the Crown and the Courts over the royal prerogative. The Courts assumed the jurisdiction to decide only whether a particular parliamentary privilege existed at common law; judicial review of the manner of its exercise was denied: *Stockdale v. Hansard*. Moreover, no new privileges could be asserted by one House — only Parliament could alter its privileges by legislation.[17]

The factors which contributed to this negotiated settlement were summed up by Carl Wittke:

> ... this settlement of the relation between privilege and the law, could be brought about only after the idea of separate codes of law had disappeared, and the notion that *les parliamenti*, like the rest, was part of the common law, had been evolved; after the nature of the English Supreme Court had been radically altered; and after the democratization of the lower house had made substantial progress.[18]

Hence, the establishment by the House of Lords of the separate body of Law Lords substantially removed the cause of rivalry between the two Houses of Parliament, while the electoral reforms of the 1830s made the House of Commons more representative of the people and so more secure from outside interference by the Crown and the Courts.

It is evident from this short history that parliamentary privileges were Parliament's response to threats posed by the Crown and by the Courts often at the instigation of the Crown to the capacity of Parliament to function as the sovereign legislature. Parliament has used its privileges to secure this independence and the dignity due its sovereignty. Although Maitland was of the view at the beginning of the twentieth century that '[t]heir importance in the past has been great; their importance in the present we are apt, I think, to overrate',[19] their justification today rests on the same basis on which they originally evolved, namely, the capacity of the Parliament to perform its legislative functions free from unnecessary interference. The dominance of the Executive today demands the maintenance of parliamentary privilege to preserve in some measure the capacity of Parliament to protect its members from Executive assault and to ensure that responsible government is not petrified. The role of Parliament as a check on the performance of the Executive is as equally important if not more so in this age than in the past.

Although the history of parliamentary privilege may portray at times a petulant obsession on the part of Parliament with its dignity, this was the lesson of bitter experience at the hands of the Crown. Those lessons ought not to be forgotten now or regarded as irrelevant. Fajgenbaum and Hanks rightly point out that the justification of parliamentary privilege must be found now in Parliament's political supremacy rather than in its judicial origins.[20] This fact necessitates a closer examination of the role of parliamentary privilege today and whether it can claim any justification for its present nature and scope in a different political environment from that from which it emerged. What were not directly considered in the power struggles between Parliament, the Crown and the Courts were the interests of the people. Since this is the overriding concern of modern systems of government, it should be an important factor in assessing the justification of parliamentary privilege today.

Parliamentary privilege in Australia

Colonial and State position

Reliance on parliamentary privilege in the American colonies during the eighteenth century resulted in the development of principles which came to affect the position in colonial Australia. Indeed, there were constant battles between the legislators who claimed privileges as of right and the Governors who recognised only those privileges conferred by grace and favour. This latter view was also the view held in England until an opinion was given in 1815 by British law officers on the privileges of the House of Assembly in Lower Canada.[21] Their view was that the grant of legislative power conferred 'such privileges as are incidental to, and necessary to enable them to perform their functions in deliberating and advising upon, and consenting to laws for the peace, welfare and good government of the Province'.

Accordingly, by virtue of this principle of necessity, colonial legislatures were not immediately possessed of all the privileges of the House of Commons. The Judicial Committee of the Privy Council in *Kielly v. Carson*[22] endorsed this view by according a colonial legislature 'such [privileges] as are necessary to the existence of such a body, and the proper exercise of the functions which it is intended to execute'.[23] In that case it was held that it was not necessary for the exercise of the functions of the House of Assembly of Newfoundland as a local legislature to punish persons for contempt committed outside the Assembly. The power of the House of Commons to so commit was distinguished as one derived 'by virtue of ancient usage and prescription'.[24] Professor Campbell suggests that this decision, two years after the House of Commons had found the Sheriff of Middlesex[25] guilty of contempt, may have been decided on the basis that the power of contempt 'was unnecessary and too dangerous to be entrusted to inexperienced colonial politicians'.[26]

The Privy Council in *Doyle v. Falconer*[27] took *Kielly v. Carson* one further step in holding that the Legislative Assembly of Dominica did not possess the power to punish for contempt committed *within* the House. *Kielley v. Carson*, while it refused to acknowledge the power to *punish* for contempt, accepted that a colonial legislature had the power to suspend or expel a member for unworthy conduct without inflicting further punishment for contempt.[28]

Other privileges applying by the principle of necessity include the immunity of freedom of speech[29] and the power to order the production of documents.

This last mentioned privilege was recently upheld by the High Court in *Egan v. Willis.*[30] A majority[31] of the Court affirmed the decision of the NSW Court of Appeal that the NSW Legislative Council possessed the inherent common law power to order one of its members who was also the State Treasurer to produce certain 'state papers' relating to the government's consideration of a report of a Royal Commission into a gold mine. This power was necessary to enable the House to review the conduct of the Executive Government. The joint judgment of Gaudron, Gummow and Hayne JJ referred to 'the immediate interrelation between that superintendence and the law-making function in which the Legislative Council participates, together with the Legislative Assembly and the Crown'.[32]

The NSW Court of Appeal had also upheld the power of the Council to order the suspension and removal of the member from the House although not from the precincts of Parliament. The Court distinguished between measures which were merely enforcement in nature and those which were punitive. The suspension of a member to enforce its order to produce documents was necessary for the functioning of the House and so was within the inherent power of the House. On the other hand, suspension of a member solely as punishment for non-compliance was beyond the inherent power of the House.[33] This distinction was not embraced by a majority of the High Court. While upholding the power to suspend the minister for non-compliance with its order, the joint judgment of Gaudron, Gummow and Hayne JJ acknowledged that there may be limits to the power of the House to enforce its orders, but considered 'to distinguish between punishing and merely inducing compliance may very well be difficult'.[34] In any event, the House had acted within its powers by suspending the member 'for a limited time'.[35]

McHugh J dissented on the ground that while the House has the power to suspend a member who obstructs the business of the House, it is for the House and not for the Courts to decide whether a member has so obstructed the House.[36] His Honour regarded the principle of *Stockdale v. Hansard*[37] as applicable here, namely, that 'matters affecting the internal administration of the House of Commons are outside the jurisdiction of the common law courts'.[38] In addition, his Honour applied a stricter test as to the inherent powers of the House, namely, whether 'it would be impossible, in the absence of the power asserted, to carry out the relevant function'.[39] Accordingly, in his Honour's view, the House possessed no power to order the production of documents from a citizen but members who were ministers were in a different position in view of the principle of responsible government.[40]

Whether a House possesses the inherent power to call for the production of documents by a minister in respect of which the Executive claims public interest immunity or legal professional privilege was left open in *Egan v. Willis*. But the issue was subsequently decided by the NSW Court of Appeal in *Egan v. Chadwick*.[41] The Court unanimously held that it was reasonably necessary for the performance of the function of the Legislative Council to hold the Executive to account that it possess the capacity to call for the production of *all* Executive documents. However, the Court split on whether exceptions might arise to such claims. The majority of Spigelman CJ and Meagher JA held that the production of Executive documents would be precluded if this were inconsistent with the principle of responsible government. The only instance of such inconsistency they declared was in the case of documents recording the deliberations of cabinet under public interest immunity.[42] Priestley JA dissented on this point holding that 'no *legal right* to *absolute* secrecy is given to any group of men and women in government'.[43]

Given the evident uncertainty experienced by colonial legislatures as to the scope of their powers, it became accepted during the nineteenth century that legislation enacted pursuant to the power to make laws for the peace, order and good government of the colony could confer the privileges of the House of Commons on each House.[44] Hence the prescription of the power to punish for contempt was made by legislation and generally within fairly confined limits.[45]

Accordingly, there were two sources of parliamentary privileges for the Australian colonies: those privileges which at common law were necessary for the exercise of their functions and for their self-protection and those conferred by local legislation. A third source has been cited, at least in relation to Art 9 of the *Bill of Rights* 1689, that of inherited statutory law.[46] The difficulty in relying on inherited statutory law is the test of inheritance: the statute must have been able to be applied to the conditions in New South Wales on 25 July 1828.[47] Freedom of speech is unlikely to have been applicable at that time given the absence of a representative legislature in New South Wales until 1842.[48] However, this freedom is accepted as applying under the common law principle of necessity.[49]

The only certain basis for the incorporation of all the privileges of the House of Commons in colonial legislatures is by their wholesale adoption by statute. Apart from New South Wales[50] and to a limited extent in Tasmania,[51] this has been provided for in the other States of Queensland,[52] Victoria,[53] South Australia[54] and Western Australia.[55]

The Commonwealth position

The only source of parliamentary privileges for the Commonwealth Parliament is s. 49 of the Constitution:

> The powers, privileges, and immunities of the Senate and of the House of Representatives, and of the members and the committees of each House, shall be such as are declared by the Parliament, and until declared shall be those of the Commons House of Parliament of the United Kingdom, and of its members and committees, at the establishment of the Commonwealth.

Privileges of the House of Commons as at 1901 continue to apply at the Commonwealth level since Parliament has not yet declared comprehensively its privileges pursuant to s. 49. However, to the extent it has declared certain privileges, any corresponding privileges of the House of Commons no longer apply. Such declarations have been made in the *Parliamentary Papers Act 1908* (Cwlth) and the *Parliamentary Proceedings Broadcasting Act 1946* (Cwlth) which extend immunity to the publication and broadcasting of parliamentary proceedings. The *Parliamentary Privileges Act 1987* (Cwlth) (the '1987 Act') is not a comprehensive declaration, being enacted only in respect of certain privileges, namely, to regulate the power to commit for contempt, to abrogate the power to expel a member and to remove doubts as to the scope of the freedom of speech in Art 9 of the *Bill of Rights*.

By s. 49 of the Constitution, parliamentary privileges are part of the ordinary law and therefore may only be altered by legislation enacted pursuant to s. 49.[56] Neither House alone may alter its privileges, although by s. 50 each may regulate by standing orders the mode of their exercise.

Definition of parliamentary privilege

Professor Enid Campbell has defined parliamentary privilege in terms of individual and collective privileges:

> The privileges of parliament refer to those rights, powers and immunities which in law belong to the individual members and officers of a parliament and to the Houses of Parliament acting in a collective capacity.[57]

Odgers'[58] draws a clear distinction between immunities and powers, classifying them as follows:

1. Immunities

Immunity of proceedings from impeachment and question: Art 9 *Bill of Rights* freedom of speech (only substantive immunity). Three minor immunities of members, witnesses and parliamentary officers:

- immunity from arrest in civil causes
- exemption from service as a juror
- exemption from compulsory attendance in a court or tribunal.

2. Powers

Power of each House to:

- determine their own constitution
- conduct inquiries
- punish contempts.[59]

Abrogation of parliamentary privilege

Despite the sanctity which surrounds parliamentary privileges, especially the freedom of speech in Art 9 of the *Bill of Rights* 1689, they are all vulnerable to abrogation or amendment by statute. It has been said at times that any statutory abrogation or amendment of parliamentary privilege must be done expressly, that is, by an express declaration.[60] This view appears inconsistent with the general principle that rights may be amended by statute expressly or by 'necessary implication'. It has also been said that such an express declaration is required at the Commonwealth level by virtue of s. 49 of the Constitution.

The principal authority relied on at general law for Parliament to use express words when abrogating parliamentary privilege is the decision of the House of Lords in *The Duke of Newcastle v. Morris*.[61] An argument was put in that case that new bankruptcy legislation which applied to all debtors whether traders or non-traders did not apply to non-traders who were members of Parliament because unlike earlier legislation no reservation had been inserted in respect of their privileges, in particular, the immunity from arrest. The House of Lords rejected this interpretation, holding that all members were subject to the legislation as debtors, but, in the course of doing so, accepted that their privileges were not abrogated, in particular, the immunity from arrest. While requiring express words in the statute to abrogate their privileges in this case, the Lord Chancellor, Lord Hatherley, relied on the fact that all previous bankruptcy legislation had expressly reserved them:

> It seems to me that a more sound and reasonable interpretation of such an Act of Parliament would be, that the privilege which had been established by Common Law and *recognised on many occasions by Act of Parliament*, should be held to be a continous privilege not abrogated or struck at unless by express words in the statute ... (emphasis added).

This decision must be considered in the light of the previous legislation which expressly reserved parliamentary privilege. In the absence of such a legislative history of express reservation, abrogation might not require express language. The preferable approach is to adopt the presumption recognised by the rules of statutory interpretation that the legislature does not intend to override fundamental common law principles, especially those concerned with individual rights, unless it has indicated a clear intention to do so. Rights which have enjoyed the benefit of this presumption under the general law include the right against self-incrimination and the right to compensation upon acquisition of property rights.[62] The position is clearly stated by Isaacs J in *Ex parte Walsh and Johnson: Re Yates*:[63]

> ... even where Parliament confessedly possesses plenary power within its own territory, the full literal intention will not ordinarily be ascribed to general words where that would conflict with recognised principles that Parliament would prima facie be expected to respect.

But as Mason ACJ, Wilson and Dawson JJ observed in *Pyneboard Pty Ltd v. Trade Practices Commission*, this presumption is rebuttable by virtue of 'the general principle that a statute will not be construed to take away a common law right unless the legislative intent to do so clearly emerges whether by express words or by necessary implication'.[64]

The test is solely one of ascertaining the intention of Parliament having regard to the language of the statute interpreted in its historical context.[65] The importance of the historical context is well illustrated by the rejection by the House of Lords in *In re Parliamentary Privilege Act*,[66] of the argument that the *Parliamentary Privilege Act* 1700 (Imp) had impliedly repealed Art 9 of the *Bill of Rights*. That Act and its predecessors beginning with the Act 12 & 13 Will 3, c 3 in 1700 permitted the commencement of suits against members of Parliament from the dissolution or prorogation of Parliament until the meeting of a new Parliament 'any privilege of Parliament to the contrary notwithstanding'. The argument that this abrogation of privilege extended to the freedom of speech in Parliament was rejected since Parliament's intention was only to abrogate the privilege against civil proceedings being brought against members for the period of forty days after Parliament's dissolution and forty days prior to its meeting again.[67]

The preferable view to adopt would appear to be that the presumption against the abrogation of fundamental rights is particularly strong in relation to parliamentary privileges given their importance to the effective functioning of Parliament. Parliament is unlikely to intend to alter its privileges without making its intention clear. Accordingly, a court will require very clear evidence of Parliament's intention before parliamentary privilege is abrogated by statute.[68] In some cases an express intention may be necessary; in others it may not.[69]

Commonwealth position

In 1983 a Joint Opinion of the Commonwealth Attorney-General, Senator Gareth Evans, and the Commonwealth Solicitor-General, Sir Maurice Byers, was given that Commonwealth secrecy provisions did not abrogate the freedom of speech enjoyed by members of State Parliaments.[70] The Joint Opinion arose out of revelations made in the South Australian House of Assembly by Mr Peter Duncan which appeared to be based on evidence given in camera to the Hope Royal Commission on Australia's security and intelligence agencies. On the issue of statutory abrogation of parliamentary privilege, the Joint Opinion expressed this view:

> [I]t is clear that parliamentary privilege is considered to be so valuable and essential to the workings of responsible government that express words in a statute are necessary before it may be taken away: see *Duke of Newcastle v. Morris* (1870) LR 4 HL 661 at 671, 677 and 680. In the case of the Parliament of the Commonwealth, s. 49 of the Constitution requires an express declaration.[71]

The first point has already been dealt with. The second requires closer examination as it suggests that s. 49 prevents the Commonwealth impliedly amending its privileges. Section 49 which has been cited earlier contains two limbs. One limb adopts the powers, privileges and immunities of the House of Commons as at 1901 until they are declared by the Commonwealth Parliament. The other limb empowers the Commonwealth Parliament to so declare. Although the High Court in *R v. Richards; Ex parte Fitzpatrick and Browne*[72] referred to this limb as contemplating a comprehensive enactment of privileges, it did so in the context of an argument that the privilege of the House of Commons to commit for contempt was not available as the Commonwealth had declared its privileges for the purposes of s. 49 by enacting the *Parliamentary Papers Act 1908* (Cwlth) and the *Parliamentary Proceedings Broadcasting Act 1946* (Cwlth). The Court made it clear that the privileges of the House of Commons continue to apply until such time as the Parliament pursuant to s. 49 has comprehensively declared its privileges. This still has not occurred.

It must follow, however, that its privileges, including those derived from the House of Commons, are amenable to ad hoc amendment and abrogation by Commonwealth legislation just as the privileges of the House of Commons in 1901 were subject to legislative change. But what is the legislative source of authority for these ad hoc amendments? In *R v. Richards; Ex parte Fitzpatrick and Browne*[73] the view was expressed that both the *Parliamentary Papers Act 1908* (Cwlth) and the *Parliamentary Proceedings Broadcasting Act 1946* (Cwlth) were enacted pursuant to s. 51(xxxix) as laws incidental to the execution of an exercise of power by Parliament rather than pursuant to s.

51(xxxvi) and s. 49. Of course, s. 51(xxxix) alone is not a legislative power; it must be incidental to another power and, although the judgment omits to refer to that power, it presumably must be s. 49. If ad hoc amendments do not constitute an exercise of the first limb of s. 49 as such, s. 49 cannot be relied on to support the need for an express declaration. Parliament must simply indicate its intention clearly in accordance with the principles of interpretation outlined earlier.

The issue of statutory abrogation of parliamentary privilege arises in relation to witnesses appearing before Parliament or its committees when they are asked to provide evidence which they are under either a statutory or a general law duty not to disclose. It is clear that by virtue of Art 9 of the *Bill of Rights* no witness can be impugned for disclosing information contrary to a duty of confidentiality under the general law. The difficulty lies in respect of statutory duties of confidentiality which have the potential to override the privilege of freedom of speech. Parliament needs to express in very clear words its intention to abrogate the freedom of speech when imposing these statutory duties.

Odgers'[74] asserts that witnesses appearing before a House or a parliamentary committee of the Commonwealth Parliament are immune from prosecution for disclosing information which they are prohibited by statute from disclosing. Two grounds are relied on: (i) the immunity accorded evidence given to a House or a committee by s. 16 of the 1987 Act; and (ii) that the relevant statutes do not expressly abrogate the immunity afforded by parliamentary privilege. As noted earlier, express abrogation may be unnecessary in some cases where Parliament's intention is clear. This view was expressed by the Commonwealth Solicitor-General in 1991 when the issue arose as to whether witnesses appearing before the Parliamentary Joint Committee on the National Crime Authority were protected by parliamentary privilege if they disclosed information contrary to secrecy provisions in the *National Crime Authority Act 1984* (Cwlth). A detailed account of the various opinions given by the Solicitor-General and the Attorney-General's Department is given in *Odgers'*.[75] The final opinion of the Solicitor-General concluded that the secrecy provisions abrogated parliamentary privilege by 'necessary intendment'. In other words, express words were not required to amend parliamentary privilege. Nevertheless, *Odgers'* regards this issue as unresolved.[76]

Commonwealth abrogation of State parliamentary privilege

The Joint Opinion referred to earlier in relation to the revelations made by Mr Peter Duncan in 1983 in the South Australian House of Assembly also raised the issue whether Commonwealth legislation could abrogate State parliamentary privileges. That Opinion concluded that Mr Duncan was not in breach of the relevant Commonwealth secrecy provisions since they did not purport to abrogate the parliamentary privilege of freedom of speech under s. 38 of the *Constitution Act 1934* (SA). But it was the view expressed in the Joint Opinion that federal legislation was capable in certain cases, such as in time of war, of abrogating State parliamentary privilege which prompted the Senate to refer that issue to its Standing Committee on Constitutional and Legal Affairs. The Senate Committee in its 1985 Report cited earlier, *Commonwealth Law Making Power and the Privilege of Freedom of Speech in State Parliaments*,[77] by a majority reached the contrary conclusion on two grounds:[78] (i) that since State parliamentary privilege formed part of the 'Constitution' of each State, s. 106 prevented the Commonwealth's legislative powers being used to abrogate that privilege even in time of war; and (ii) abrogation of the privilege would infringe that limb of the *Melbourne Corporation* principle which protects the capacity of the State to function as such. The latter of these grounds is the more persuasive since s. 106 is made subject to the Constitution.[79] Contrary to the view expressed in the Joint Opinion that the *Melbourne Corporation* principle is confined to interference with State executive power, the High Court in *Western Australia v. Commonwealth, Native Title Act Case*[80] has since held that it also protects State legislative power. Moreover, a Commonwealth law which purported to abrogate State parliamentary privilege would impair the very 'machinery of government', the Parliament, which according to the *Native Title Act Case*, the *Melbourne Corporation* principle protects.[81]

Freedom of speech

Probably the most significant parliamentary privilege is that of freedom of speech enshrined in Article 9 of the *Bill of Rights 1689*:

> ... that the freedom of speech and debates or proceedings in Parliament ought not to be impeached or questioned in any court or place out of Parliament.

As noted earlier, Art 9 declared what had probably been established at law by the House of Lords decision in *Eliot's Case.*[82] The freedom of speech conferred refers to three activities within Parliament: a speech, a debate and a proceeding.[83] The essence of this privilege of freedom of speech is that no liability attaches to what a Member says or does in a speech, a debate or in parliamentary proceedings. The clear implication from that position, although it is not always appreciated, is that Members remain accountable to their House for what they say and do in the House.[84]

Without this freedom, it has been said that Parliament would have developed into 'polite but ineffectual debating societies'.[85] It has also been regarded as the key to parliamentary supremacy over the Crown and its ministers.[86] As the essential privilege for securing the independence of Parliament, it ensures the capacity of those in whom is vested the sovereign authority of the state to be informed of all points of view in resolving the policy and legislative issues put before them in Parliament. An environment is created in which the members of Parliament are entirely free to canvass their views without fear of being unfairly challenged outside Parliament by the Executive or by the people through the courts. Despite Executive dominance of the Parliament arising through the party system, the Parliament has thereby retained its capacity to criticise the Executive. Moreover, the investigatory role of parliamentary committees would otherwise be severely hampered without freedom of speech for its witnesses.

Yet problems do arise from this freedom. Reputations are sometimes ruined. With every freedom there is a cost and this is the cost of securing the independence of Parliament. Rules of conduct must, however, regulate members in their exercise of the freedom. But these need to be administered by the House. It is in this context that there is a call for provision to be made for a citizen's right of reply. Given the cost which the community must bear by according the Parliament the privilege of freedom of speech, the community is entitled to a precise clarification of the scope of Art 9. Yet, the meaning of 'proceedings in Parliament' and the extent of the restriction of not being 'impeached or questioned', remain unresolved at the State level. And even at the Commonwealth level, the definition provided by the 1987 Act requires clarification. It is proposed to consider here the difficulties which have arisen in relation to the scope of the freedom in terms of the activities covered and the effect of the freedom on the admissibility of evidence in legal proceedings.

Scope of freedom of speech: nature of activities

The freedom of speech in Art 9 of the *Bill of Rights* is confined, as previously noted, to three activities: speeches, debates and the proceedings of Parliament. While the nature and scope of the former two activities are fairly clear, that is not the case with parliamentary proceedings. The core of parliamentary proceedings includes of course the proceedings of parliamentary sittings which include speeches and debates, as well as the passage of legislation. Also included are the tabling of motions and amendments to motions or bills and the tabling, asking and answering of questions to ministers and other members. A register of members' pecuniary interests might also attract the privilege.[87] The proceedings of parliamentary committees including the evidence given by any person to those committees are also covered[88] as are those who present petitions to Parliament.[89] The principal difficulty arising from the generality of the expression 'proceedings in Parliament' is to define its outer limits and, in particular, the activities associated with speeches, debates and proceedings which are entitled to freedom of speech. The determination of the scope of the privilege in this respect lies squarely with the courts or Parliament and not with either House alone to determine.

It is clear that members are not protected by the privilege in respect of all their parliamentary duties when performed outside parliamentary proceedings. However, the closer the relevant activity is connected to the proceedings of Parliament, the easier it is to argue that it should be protected by privilege.[90] If the activity relates to the member's constituency duties only, then it is unlikely to fall within the scope of the privilege. What is important is the degree of connection to parliamentary business. In this context, two categories of communication may be considered: (i) communications between members or between a member and a minister; and (ii) communications between members and constituents or other persons.[91]

Communications between members or between a member and a minister

Communications between members or between a member and a minister which appear entitled to protection because of their close relationship to parliamentary business include any discussion of drafts of oral questions, questions on notice, or motions and any discussion of draft speeches to be made in the House.[92]

Communications between a member and a minister in relation to constituency matters have an uncertain status. In the *Strauss Case*,[93] the House of Commons refused by a narrow vote of 218 to 213 to accept the report of its Privileges Committee that a letter written by Mr Strauss MP to a minister which was critical of the London Electricity Board was protected by parliamentary privilege.[94] It is submitted, however, that privilege attaching to a communication between a member and a minister on a constitutency matter is justified given the efficiency, discreteness and utility of such a communication when Parliament is not sitting.[95]

A further area of uncertain status relates to parliamentary committees: whether informal meetings between members of parliamentary committees and even whether formal meetings of parliamentary committees convened outside the precincts of Parliament are covered by parliamentary privilege.[96]

All of these forms of communication described so far, except that in the *Strauss Case*, were recognised as entitled to protection by the Commonwealth Joint Select Committee on Parliamentary Privilege in its 1984 Report.[97] In recommending the adoption of a statutory provision to extend the scope of 'proceedings in Parliament' to cover these communications, the Committee confined its recommendations to defamation proceedings.[98] The following provisions were proposed:[99]

(1) That the Parliament adopt an expanded definition of proceedings in Parliament in the following terms — 'That without in any way limiting the generality of the 9th Article of the Bill of Rights or the interpretation that would otherwise be given to it, for the purposes of a defence of absolute privilege in actions or prosecutions for defamation the expression 'proceedings in Parliament' shall include:

(a) all things said, done or written by a Member or by an officer of either House of Parliament or by any person ordered or authorised to attend before such House, in or in the presence of such House and in the course of the sitting of such House and for the purposes of the business being or about to be transacted, wherever such sitting may be held and whether or not it be held in the presence of strangers to such House: provided that for the purpose aforesaid the expression 'House' shall be deemed to include any Committee, sub-committee or other group or body of Members or Members and officers of either or both of the Houses of Parliament appointed by or with the authority of such House or Houses for the purposes of carrying out any of the functions of or representing such House or Houses;

(b) questions and notices of motion appearing, or intended to appear, on the Notice Paper, and drafts of questions and motions which, in the case of draft questions, are to be put either orally or as questions on notice, and in the case of draft motions, are intended to be moved, and draft speeches intended to be made in either House, provided in each case they are published no more widely than is reasonably necessary;

(c) written replies or supplementary written replies to questions asked by a Member of a Minister of the Crown with or without notice as provided for in the procedures of the House;

(d) communications between Members and the Clerk or other officers of the House related to the proceedings of the House falling within (a), (b) and (c).

These recommendations have been given substantial effect by the *Parliamentary Privileges Act 1987* (Cwlth) which is examined below. Although an exposure draft of the 1984 Report had included a provision to accord privilege to the *Strauss* situation, this was deleted from the Final Report. The Committee preferred to make no recommendation on this situation given the need for compelling reasons before further eroding the protection of reputation by an extension of absolute privilege.[100]

Finally, it should be noted that merely because a member communicates within the precincts of the House, this does not attract the privilege of freedom of speech. This has been firmly established by the 'Zircon affair' in the House of Commons.[101] In 1987 an attempt was made by a number of members of that House to screen a film in one of the meeting rooms of the House, despite the fact that the BBC had agreed not to screen it because of the danger it posed to national security by revealing details of a secret defence project, code named, 'Zircon'. Moreover, the High Court had granted an injunction against one of the producers of the film, Mr Duncan Campbell, from revealing directly or indirectly any details of the Zircon project. After unsuccessfully applying for an injunction to prevent the members from screening the film, the Attorney-General requested the Speaker to issue an order prohibiting the film's screening. This, the Speaker was reluctant to do, until advised on Privy Counsellor terms of the threat to national security.

The subsequent report of the Committee of Privileges condoned the action taken by the Speaker. The Committee found no breach of privilege arose as a result of the ban on the film. The privilege of freedom of speech, according to the Committee, was limited to the debates and proceedings in Parliament. It did not extend to activities occurring simply within the precincts of Parliament, such as the screening of a film in one of the rooms of the House of Commons.[102]

Communications between members and constituents or other persons

It has been held that correspondence between a member and a constituent, even on a matter of parliamentary business, is not protected by freedom of speech as a 'proceeding in Parliament'.[103] While it may not seem unreasonable to regard the provision of information for the purpose of a parliamentary speech or debate to be incidental to the parliamentary functions of a member, the wide ranging circumstances in which such information may be provided preclude absolute immunity attaching to such communications as a general rule. Distinctions might otherwise have to be drawn between information supplied to a member voluntarily or at the member's request, information which is relevant or irrelevant and information which is actually used by the member or not used. Appreciation of such difficulties may explain the lack of support for the extension of the privilege to this situation.

Another explanation is that communications between a constituent and a member are nevertheless likely to attract the protection of qualified privilege.[104] This defence which may be defeated by proof of malice requires that the person making the defamatory statement has an interest or duty in making it and that the persons to whom it is made have a corresponding interest or duty in receiving it. This defence of qualified privilege has recently been expanded by *Lange v. Australian Broadcasting Corporation*[105] to conform to the implied freedom of political discussion in relation to government and political matters. This unanimous decision of the High Court overturned the special constitutional defence recognised by a majority of the Court in *Theophanous v. Herald and Weekly Times Ltd.*[106] Instead the Court expanded the common law defence to cover 'a person who mistakenly but honestly publishes a government or political matter to a large audience'.[107]

Parliamentary Privileges Act 1987 (Cwlth): 'proceedings in Parliament'

In the case of the Commonwealth Parliament, a statutory definition of 'proceedings in Parliament' is provided in s. 16(2) of the *Parliamentary Privileges Act 1987* (Cwlth). This definition is intended, 'in addition to any other operation', to declare the position under Art 9 of the *Bill of Rights 1689.*

Section 16(2) provides:

> "proceedings of Parliament" means all words spoken and acts done in the course of, or for purposes of or incidental to, the transacting of the business of a House or of a committee, and, without limiting the generality of the foregoing, includes —
>
> (a) the giving of evidence before a House or a committee, and evidence so given;
> (b) the presentation or submission of a document to a House or a committee;
> (c) the preparation of a document for purposes of or incidental to the transacting of any such business; and
> (d) the formulation, making or publication of a document, including a report, by or pursuant to an order of a House or a committee and the document so formulated, made or published.

The actual scope of this statutory definition is not readily apparent. By limiting it to 'the transacting of the business of a House or of a committee', the recommendations of the 1984 Joint Select Committee Report on Parliamentary Privilege are adopted. Thus, communications between members or between a member and a minister, such as in the *Strauss* case, on a constituency matter unconnected with parliamentary business, are not covered by this statutory definition.[108] This accords with the view ultimately taken by the House of Commons in the *Strauss* case. However, s. 16(2) appears to extend beyond the Report's recommendations to cover communications between members and constituents or other persons if these communications satisfy the restriction that they occur 'for purposes of or incidental to the transacting of the business of a House or of a committee'.[109]

The scope of s. 16(2) was considered by the Queensland Court of Appeal in *O'Chee v. Rowley*[110] where Senator O'Chee was sued for defamation in respect of a radio interview he gave on commercial fishing of marlin in protected fields in North Queensland. The Senator had asked a question on that issue in the Senate prior to the interview and thereafter had made a speech in the House on the same issue. He claimed that 43 documents relevant to the proceedings were privileged under s. 16(2) on the basis that they 'were created, prepared, brought into existence or came into [his] possession for the purposes of or incidental to the transacting of the business of the Senate'. The trial judge, Williams J, classified these documents generally as comprising: letters addressed to the Senator; reports prepared for other persons on long line tuna fishing in marlin waters; a diary note by the Senator of an 'attendance on constituent'; letters exchanged between the Senator and another member of Parliament; and notes of telephone conversations made by the Senator.

Williams J applied[111] to s. 16(2) the traditional view of the general law espoused in *Erskine May*[112] and adopted by Allen J in *AJ Grassby*[113] that no parliamentary privilege attaches to communications between informants and members in circumstances where the member is asked to raise a matter in Parliament. No privilege arose whether the member actively sought the document to raise in Parliament or whether it was simply provided to the member in the hope that it would be raised there. However, this narrow approach to the operation of s. 16(2) was rejected on appeal to the Queensland Court of Appeal.

Moynihan J agreed with the reasoning of McPherson JA for allowing the appeal but along with Fitzgerald P required further particulars by supplementary affidavit before concluding that the documents were privileged under s. 16. Only McPherson JA was prepared to accept their privileged status on the basis of the particulars already provided. Subject to these evidentiary requirements, Moynihan J accepted the interpretation of s. 16 by McPherson JA.[114] As to the meaning of 'proceedings in Parliament', his Honour considered that all those documents written by the Senator, comprising diary notes, file notes of attendances and conversations and letters, were documents within s. 16(2)(c) having been prepared for the purpose of or incidental to the transaction of Senate business (i.e. the question he asked in the Senate and the subsequent debate).

As for those documents sent to the Senator, these only fell within s. 16 once 'the member or his or her agent does some act with respect to it for the purposes of transacting business in the House'.[115] Such an *act* might be 'procuring, obtaining or retaining possession' of documents for the purpose of being sufficiently informed on a topic before raising it in Parliament. Hence, unsolicited mail may become privileged if the member 'elects to keep it for purposes of transacting business of a House'.[116] As well, other documents dated subsequent to the matter being discussed in the Senate, are not necessarily incapable of being privileged given that they may have been generated in anticipation of further parliamentary debate — even if two to three months after the last Senate discussion.[117] On the interpretation of 'proceedings in Parliament' in s. 16(2), McPherson JA concluded:

> By s. 16(2) of the 1987 Act proceedings in Parliament include the preparation of a document for purposes of or incidental to the transacting of any business of a House. More generally, such proceedings include all acts done for such purposes, together with any acts that are incidental to them. Bringing documents into existence for such purposes; or, for those purposes, collecting or assembling them; or coming into possession of them, are therefore capable of amounting to 'proceedings in Parliament'.[118]

The next issue was whether by requiring the production of these documents within s. 16(2)(c) this was to question or impeach 'the preparation' of these documents for the purpose of transacting the business of the Senate — this being the effect of engrafting the definition in s. 16(2)(c) onto Art 9. His Honour concluded that this was so in that disclosure would impair their preparation retrospectively.[119] Finally, s. 16(4) which specifically prevents a court or tribunal from admitting a document or oral evidence taken in camera by a House, was held not to define exhaustively the position on the production of documents in legal proceedings.

Queensland has also attempted to define 'proceedings in Parliament' in s. 3 of the *Parliamentary Proceedings Act 1990* (Qld) in terms substantially identical to those of the Commonwealth definition. The only differences are that the Queensland definition expressly refers to proceedings before an inquiry held under the authority of the House (ss. 2 and 3(3)) and includes documents 'laid before' as well as presented or submitted to the House, a committee or inquiry (s. 3(3)(d)).

Effect of freedom of speech: admissibility of evidence concerning parliamentary proceedings

A further difficult aspect of the freedom of speech provided by Art 9 is to determine the extent to which reference to speeches, debates or proceedings is permitted in legal proceedings and for what purpose. It is proposed here to consider this issue both under the general law and under the *Parliamentary Privileges Act 1987* (Cwlth) with particular reference to criminal and defamation proceedings.

The fundamental protection derived from Art 9 is that no action may be brought against a member or a witness for what they have said or done in the course of parliamentary proceedings. This principle applies to criminal[120] and civil[121] proceedings. The rationale for this privilege, as explained earlier, is to enable that absolutely free exchange of views in the performance of the legislative function and in the increasingly important investigatory role of the Houses of Parliament.

A significant difficulty which has arisen is whether the privilege also denies reliance on what is said in Parliament, not as the basis of legal proceedings against that person, but in *support* of an action based on events occurring outside Parliament.[122] It is clearly accepted by all authorities that the proceedings of Parliament may be referred to for the purpose of proving as a fact that certain events occurred in the course of those proceedings.[123] For example, Hansard may be cited to establish that a member made a particular statement in Parliament on a certain day. Even so, parliamentary practice has required the approval of the House before reference could be made to its proceedings for that limited purpose in court.[124]

But the issue on which the authorities are divided is whether inferences and submissions can be made on the basis of the evidence of those proceedings, not for the purpose of imposing legal consequences on the member or witness, but simply in 'support' of those proceedings whether brought by or against the member or witness. In *Church of Scientology of California v. Johnson-Smith*[125] Browne J held that Art 9 precluded reference to parliamentary statements by a member to support the plaintiff's claim that the member in making defamatory statements outside Parliament had been motivated by malice, thereby negating the member's claim of qualified privilege. His Honour[126] accepted the Attorney-General's submission:

> that what is said or done in the House in the course of proceedings there cannot be examined outside Parliament for the purpose of supporting a cause of action even though the cause of action itself arises out of something done outside the House. In my view this conclusion is supported both by principle and authority.

Two principles underlying Art 9 were relied on: first, '[t]he House must have complete control over its own proceedings and its own members'; and secondly, 'a member must have a complete right of free speech in the House without any fear that his motives or intentions or reasoning will be questioned or held against him thereafter'.[127]

The authorities relied on were not on point factually but contain statements supportive of a wide view of Art 9 precluding the questioning of statements made in the course of parliamentary proceedings. In *Stockdale v. Hansard*,[128] Lord Denman said 'that whatever is done within the walls of either assembly must pass without question in any other place',[129] while Patteson J observed 'that whatever is said or done in either House should not be liable to examination elsewhere'.[130] Reliance was also placed on statements in *Ex parte Wason*[131] especially that by Lush J: 'I am clearly of opinion that we ought not to allow it to be doubted for a moment that the motives or intentions of members of either House cannot be inquired into by criminal proceedings with respect to anything they may do or say in the House.'[132] Little weight, however, ought to be attached to this quote for it contemplates proceedings against a member for what the member has said or done in Parliament. *Dingle v. Associated Newspapers Ltd*[133] was regarded as analogous[134] in that Pearson J denied reference to a select committee report, an extract of which was published as part of an alleged libel, for the purpose of impugning it.[135]

A wide view of the scope of the privilege has also been expressed in a series of decisions in Australia. In *R v. Turnbull*[136] a former State Treasurer was charged with official corruption and his parliamentary statements were excluded. For what purpose the Crown wished to rely on them is unclear but Gibson J regarded the privilege as protecting members from *use* being made of such statements.[137] In *Holding v. Jennings*[138] Anderson J recognised:

> [I]t is clear law that no proceedings, either civil or criminal, may be taken against a member of Parliament for anything said or done by him in Parliament, and a member is not examinable outside Parliament concerning anything said by him in Parliament: see *Ex parte Wason* (1869) LR 4 QB at p 573; *Bradlaugh v. Gossett* (1884) 12 QBD 271 at p 275; *Stockdale v. Hansard* (1837) 9 AD & E 1; *Dillon v. Balfour* (1887) 20 LR Ir 600; Blackstone, 1 Com 163; *R v. Creevey* (1813) 1 M & s. 273; *Chubb v. Salomons* (1852) 3 Car & Kir 75.

In *Comalco Ltd v. Australian Broadcasting Corporation*[139] Blackburn CJ considered the privilege as preventing 'the substance of what was said in Parliament to be the subject of any submission or inference'.

However, the wide view of the effect of the privilege espoused in *Church of Scientology* was rejected by Hunt J in *R v. Murphy.*[140] His Honour permitted in that case, for the purpose of testing their credibility, the cross-examination of witnesses on their prior statements made to a parliamentary committee. The case was the second of two criminal prosecutions brought against Justice Lionel Murphy for attempting to pervert the course of justice. The same ruling had been made by Cantor J in the first trial[141] while also upholding the right of the Crown to cross-examine Justice Murphy on a written statement he had given to a Senate committee. Senate committees had been investigating allegations against the Justice to ascertain whether an address for removal was warranted under s. 72 of the Constitution. Before both trial judges, counsel representing the Senate argued that such evidence was inadmissible by virtue of parliamentary privilege.

Hunt J confined the privilege under Art 9 to prevent reliance on what is said in Parliament or to its committees for the purpose of bringing an action against that person, not when the action was based on conduct occurring outside Parliament and the evidence is used to establish a motive or intention. His Honour thereby confined the privilege to ensuring that no legal consequences are visited upon the witness for what was said in Parliament or to its committees:

> I remain of the view that what is meant by the declaration that "freedom of speech ... in parliament ought not to be impeached or questioned in any court or place out of parliament" is that no court proceedings (or proceedings of a similar nature) having legal consequences against a member of parliament (or a witness before a parliamentary committee) are permitted which by those legal consequences have the effect of preventing that member (or committee witness) exercising his freedom of speech in parliament (or before a committee) or of punishing him for having done so.
>
> Cross-examination going to the credit of a witness in curial proceedings — based upon the inconsistency between his evidence before a parliamentary committee and his evidence in court, or even upon the untruthfulness of the former — does not of itself visit legal consequences upon the witness, and neither (where the witness is a party) do the proceedings themselves visit such consequences upon him as a result of what he had said or done before the parliamentary committee. If, as a result of such cross-examination, the party to the proceedings is not believed by the tribunal of fact — and for that reason loses his case (or he is convicted) — that result is a consequence of what is seen by that tribunal to be the true facts given in evidence before them; it cannot logically be said to be a consequence of what the party had said to the parliamentary committee. To resort once more to the language of causation, what the party said to the parliamentary committee may possibly be thought to be the causa sine qua non, but it was not the causa causans of the loss of his case. The causa causans or the real cause of that loss is that the jury accepted the case against him and not his own case, perhaps by reason of his lack of credit — which may have been revealed by what he said to the committee, but which existed in any event.[142]

In support of the approach taken by Hunt J are earlier statements in *Gipps v. McElhone*[143] where a defamation action was brought against a member of the New South Wales Parliament in relation to comments he made about the plaintiff to another member outside Parliament. Martin CJ[144] and Manning J[145] indicated they were prepared to allow reference to subsequent parliamentary statements made by the defendant for the purpose of establishing malice to defeat the defence of qualified privilege. However, the judgments made no reference to parliamentary privilege. Subsequent support for Hunt J is found in the Full Court of South Australia in *Wright and Advertiser v. Lewis*[146] which is discussed below in the context of defamation proceedings.

Since *R v. Murphy*, a number of decisions in Australia have approved the principle of the *Church of Scientology* and rejected the ruling of Hunt J.[147] In *R v. Jackson*[148] Carruthers J held evidence of what the accused had said in Parliament was inadmissible for the purpose of establishing that he had lied to Parliament as corrobative evidence of official corruption. His Honour followed *Church of Scientology* and expressly declined to follow *R v. Murphy*. Also, Beaumont J in *Amann Aviation Pty Ltd v. The Commonwealth*[149] disallowed reference to what had been said in Parliament for the purpose of proving that the Commonwealth was not ready and willing to proceed with a contract and hence was not entitled to terminate it. His Honour adopted a wide view of the privilege under the general law:

> On behalf of the applicant it is submitted that the tender of the extract from *Hansard* does not offend s. 16(3) because it is for the limited purpose of proving that the Senator made a statement in Parliament in which he admitted having the conversation alleged. It is true that, before the enactment of s. 16, it was permissible to use *Hansard* for the limited, but non-contentious, purpose of proving that a member of Parliament was present in the House on a particular day. According to the memorandum explaining the operation of s. 16(3)(c), this is still a legitimate approach. This would accord with the language of s. 16 and with its apparent purpose, that is to say, that a member of Parliament should be able to speak in Parliament "with impunity and without any fear of the consequences": per Gibbs ACJ in *Sankey v. Whitlam* (1978) 142 CLR 1 at 35. Where, as here, the subject-matter of the passage from *Hansard* is contentious in that it is sought to be used to impugn the conduct of the Senator, in the context of a denial by the respondent of any impropriety, it is almost inevitable that the tender of *Hansard* would lead to an examination of the circumstances in which the Senator came to make the statement and that this would further lead to an attempt to assess the credibility of this evidence and to compare it with other evidence already given. Such an examination, in a contentious area, cannot be reconciled with the complete freedom of speech envisaged by the Bill of Rights and the Act.[150]

Most recently, both the House of Lords in *Pepper v. Hart*[151] and the Privy Council in *Prebble v. Television New Zealand Ltd*[152] on appeal from the New Zealand Court of Appeal have accepted the decision in *Church of Scientology*. Only the Privy Council considered *R v. Murphy* and regarded the reasoning of Hunt J as incorrect.[153] The *Prebble* case is discussed below in the context of defamation proceedings.

Lord Browne-Wilkinson who delivered the principal judgment in *Pepper v. Hart* rejected any suggestion in *Church of Scientology* that Art 9 denied any reference to parliamentary speeches except for the purpose of what was said on a particular day.[154] But his Lordship's rejection of the wide terms of the effect of Art 9 in that case was only to allow reference to ministerial statements in Parliament to assist in the interpretation of ambiguous legislation. No support for the reasoning of Hunt J can be found in his Lordship's judgment. Indeed the following warning indicates acceptance of the wide effect of Art 9 not to permit the questioning of the intentions and motives of members: 'No doubt all judges will be astute to ensure that counsel does not in any way impugn or criticise the Minister's statements or his reasoning.'[155]

It seems to be suggested by Sir Clarrie Harders[156] that the ruling of Hunt J in *R v. Murphy* and the principle from *Church of Scientology* are reconcilable. In other words, there is the general principle that what is said in Parliament cannot be used to support an action which is based on events occurring outside Parliament, but as an exception to that principle what is said in Parliament by a person may be used to test his or her credibility in legal proceedings to which they are not a party.

Any reconciliation of *R v. Murphy* and *Church of Scientology* appears dubious.[157] The mere testing in a court of the credibility of someone who has given evidence to a parliamentary committee may have repercussions, even legal consequences, at a later time. There is the potential for conflict arising between a House taking action against a witness for contempt for misleading the House and the court taking action for perjury. And what of a witness in commercial proceedings who is a director of the company the subject of the proceedings? Principle and the weight of authority support *Church of Scientology* and its wide view of the privilege. That view accords with Blackstone's description of the privilege:

> whatever matter arises concerning either House of Parliament ought to be examined, discussed and adjudged in that House to which it relates and not elsewhere.[158]

This passage highlights one factor seemingly overlooked in the judicial debate on this issue, namely, that Art 9 precludes the speeches, debates and proceedings of Parliament from being impeached or questioned in any court *or in any other place out of Parliament*. To confine the protection afforded by Art 9 against the imposition of legal consequences on those who are engaged in parliamentary proceedings fails to give effect to the intention that other bodies apart from courts were to be precluded from questioning those proceedings. Such bodies would include those undertaking enquiries[159] (e.g. a royal commission) which lack the capacity to impose legal consequences on parliamentary statements.[160] Their role, however, is in part to question and probe the intentions of those it investigates. In so far as members of Parliament or parliamentary witnesses are called before these enquiries, unless they are protected by Art 9 in respect of their parliamentary statements, they are vulnerable to being questioned on their reasons, motives and even their sources of information in respect of those statements.

Official inquiries are not precluded from investigating issues or even allegations raised in Parliament provided no reference is made to parliamentary statements or a line of inquiry taken in connection with such statements.[161] Art 9 simply prevents the particular statements made in Parliament being examined as such, including ascertaining the undisclosed sources of information used. This was obviously understood by Townley J as Commissioner in *Royal Commission into Certain Crown Leaseholds*[162] who decided that a Senator could not be compelled to answer questions before the royal commission charged with the investigation of an allegation of corruption he made in the Senate:

> Whatever a member's constituents may do or say to him for what he has said in Parliament it seems to me that he may not be compulsorily examined as to it by the Executive Government or by the courts.

Investigation of the motives and intentions of members might also arise if they were to be interrogated by police or security personnel in respect of what they have said in Parliament. A comparable case arose in the *Sandys Case* in 1938 when Mr Sandys, a member of the House of Commons, wrote a letter to the Secretary of State for War advising that he had received information relating to British defence preparations. He was questioned by the Attorney-General and threatened with prosecution unless he revealed his sources of information and was also summoned to appear before a military court of inquiry. The Select Committee on the Official Secrets Act found these actions against the member constituted a clear breach of privilege.[163] A similar case arose in Australia in 1948 when Mr Fadden, then the Leader of the Country Party, was interrogated by security officers in his Parliament House office as to his informants for a statement he had made in Parliament.[164]

Given that such pressure is most likely to come from the Executive which establishes these enquiries or may authorise such interrogations, the independence of Parliament and of its members will otherwise be threatened if Art 9 is not given a wide operation. Most significantly, it would undermine the ability to speak freely as Gibbs ACJ in *Sankey v. Whitlam* observed:

> [O]ne important reason for the privilege stated in Art 9 is that a member of Parliament should be able to speak in Parliament with impunity and without fear of the consequences.[165]

Similarly, Lord Browne-Wilkinson in *Pepper v. Hart*[166] observed:

> Article 9 is a provision of the highest constitutional importance and should not be narrowly construed. It ensures the ability of democratically elected Members of

Parliament to discuss what they will (freedom of debate) and to say what they will (freedom of speech).

On this basis, the privilege must preclude *any* questioning of what is said or done by members and by the officers of Parliament within parliamentary proceedings. These considerations require the same protection for others who appear before Parliament or its committees.[167]

Accordingly, the wide view in *Church of Scientology* can be justified on the following grounds: (i) members and those appearing as witnesses must be entirely free and uninhibited in what they wish to say for the effective functioning of Parliament; (ii) to allow their statements to be examined for any purpose in court or other tribunals inhibits the freedom in (i); and (iii) any conflict between Parliament and the courts in relation to what has been said in Parliament must be avoided to preserve the dignity and effective functioning of Parliament.

A general privilege in such simple terms as Art 9 is prone to have certain undesirable consequences. Its undimished standing for over 300 years is a testimony to both the respect which it has earned and the indulgence it has enjoyed from those whom it protects. Nonetheless, a balanced assessment of the merits of a wide privilege as the price for the diminished rights of the individual is still required.

Parliamentary Privileges Act 1987 (Cwlth)

In response to the rulings of Cantor J and Hunt J, the President of the Senate introduced the bill for the *Parliamentary Privileges Act 1987* (Cwlth) which *Odgers'* cites as 'enacted primarily to settle a disagreement between the Senate and the Supreme Court of New South Wales'.[168] While the 1987 Act endeavours to resolve the position at the Commonwealth level, it of course does not do so at the State level. The relevant provisions of the Act are in s. 16 which provides as follows:

Parliamentary privilege in court proceedings

16 (1) For the avoidance of doubt, it is hereby declared and enacted that the provisions of article 9 of the Bill of Rights, 1688 apply in relation to the Parliament of the Commonwealth and, as so applying, are to be taken to have, in addition of any other operation, the effect of the subsequent provisions of this section.

(2) For the purposes of the provisions of article 9 of the Bill of Rights, 1688 as applying in relation to the Parliament, and for the purposes of this section, 'proceedings in Parliament' means all words spoken and acts done in the course of, or for purposes of or incidental to, the transacting of the business

of a House or of a committee, and, without limiting the generality of the foregoing, includes:
(a) the giving of evidence before a House or a committee, and evidence so given;
(b) the presentation or submission of a document to a House or a committee;
(c) the preparation of a document for purposes of or incidental to the transacting of any such business; and
(d) the formulation, making or publication of a document, including a report, by or pursuant to an order of a House or a committee and the document so formulated, made or published.

(3) In proceedings in any court or tribunal, it is not lawful for evidence to be tendered or received, questions asked or statements, submissions or comments made, concerning proceedings in Parliament, by way of, or for the purpose of:
(a) questioning or relying on the truth, motive, intention or good faith of anything forming part of those proceedings in Parliament;
(b) otherwise questioning or establishing the credibility, motive, intention or good faith of any person; or
(c) drawing, or inviting the drawing of, inferences or conclusions wholly or partly from anything forming part of those proceedings in Parliament.

(4) A court or tribunal shall not:
(a) require to be produced, or admit into evidence, a document that has been prepared for the purpose of submission, and submitted, to a House or a committee and has been directed by a House or a committee to be treated as evidence taken in camera, or admit evidence relating to such a document; or
(b) admit evidence concerning any oral evidence taken by a House or a committee in camera or require to be produced or admit into evidence a document recording or reporting any such oral evidence, unless a House or a committee has published, or authorised the publication of, that document or a report of that oral evidence.

(5) In relation to proceedings in a court or tribunal so far as they relate to:
(a) a question arising under section 57 of the Constitution; or
(b) the interpretation of an Act;

neither this section nor the Bill of Rights, 1688 shall be taken to prevent or restrict the admission in evidence of a record of proceedings in Parliament published by or with the authority of a House or a committee or the making of statements, submissions or comments based on that record.'

The terms of s. 16(2) and (3) are extraordinarily wide in their practical effect. This has been shown below[169] in relation to the protection afforded communications with members of parliament: see *O'Chee v. Rowley.*[170] Another recent example of the difficulties which may arise from s. 16 is the *Colston* affair. In April 1997 allegations were made that Senator Mal Colston had made false claims for travel allowances. He was then the Deputy President of the Senate and an independent senator having resigned from the ALP in 1996 after being re-elected a senator for Queensland. Statements in reply to these allegations were tabled in the Senate by the senator and by one of his staff in which she claimed responsibility for the mistaken claims. The senator duly refunded approximately $6,000 in allowances. When the staff member later retracted her statement, the Government referred the matter to the Federal Police for further investigation. At the same time there were attempts in the Senate to establish an inquiry by the Privileges Committee to decide whether the senator had misled the House. The Government objected to such an inquiry in view of the obstacles likely to arise from s. 16 in the police investigation and in any possible future prosecution.

Opinions from the Chief General Counsel of the Commonwealth, Mr Henry Burmester, and from the Clerk of the Senate, Mr Harry Evans, were raised to support the opposing views taken on the appropriateness of a Senate inquiry operating concurrently with a police investigation. Two principal difficulties were identified by the Commonwealth's Chief General Counsel:[171] first, the inability in subsequent legal proceedings to cross-examine any witnesses on evidence given to a Senate inquiry (which was the very reason for the enactment of s. 16); and secondly, the effect s. 16(3) may have on any documentation submitted to such an inquiry. The latter difficulty arises from the definition of 'proceedings in Parliament' in s. 16(2) which includes '(b) the presentation or submission of a document to a House or a committee'. If read literally, par (b) when read with subs (3) has an operation which is absurdly wide. In the context of the *Colston* affair, original travel documents if submitted as evidence to a Privileges Committee inquiry might be incapable of being used in any legal proceedings by virtue of s. 16(3)(b) for those documents would be tendered and used for the purpose of questioning the intention of any person, namely, Senator Colston. A similar difficulty arises under the *Parliamentary Papers Act 1990* (Qld) s. 3(3)(c) and (d). Within the accepted rules of statutory interpretation,[172] s. 16(2)(b) needs to be read down to avoid an absurd operation. Accordingly, it ought to be confined to documents prepared for presentation or submission to the Parliament or to a committee.

In view of the apparent width of s. 16, it is not surprising that challenges to its constitutional validity have been raised both judicially and extra-judicially. Beaumont J in *Amann Aviation Pty Ltd v. The Commonwealth*[173] upheld s. 16(3) as merely declaratory of the general law and hence not an impermissible interference in the judicial function in violation of Ch III of the Constitution.

On the other hand, Sir Clarrie Harders argued that in so far as s. 16 purported to deny the right to cross-examine witnesses on prior inconsistent statements, it was invalid for impermissibly interferring with the judicial function.[174] He also argued that it infringed Art 14.3(e) of the International Covenant on Civil and Political Rights.[175]

However, the most recent challenge to the validity of s. 16(3) is that in so far as it restricts the conduct of defamation proceedings, it needs to be read down so as not to infringe the implied freedom of political discussion under the Commonwealth Constitution. This is the view expressed by Pincus and Davies JJA in the Queensland Court of Appeal in *Laurance v. Katter.*[176] Before considering this issue further, the effect of freedom of speech both at general law and under s. 16 of the 1987 Act on defamation proceedings needs to be considered in the light of the above discussion.

Effect of freedom of speech in defamation proceedings

Where defamatory statements are made in a parliamentary speech, or as part of a debate or the proceedings of Parliament or of its committees, Art 9 precludes any action against those responsible for such statements whether or not a member of Parliament. Where defamatory statements are made by a member outside the 'proceedings of Parliament', no privilege attaches to those statements.

It can be appreciated in view of the above discussion that difficulties may arise, however, when defamation proceedings are brought in respect of statements made outside Parliament but reference to what has been said in Parliament is sought such as in *Church of Scientology*. In particular, recent cases demonstrate the difficulties which arise when a member of Parliament sues for defamation and reference to statements made in Parliament is required by either the member to establish the cause of action or by the defendant to establish a defence.

In *Prebble v. Television New Zealand Ltd*,[177] on appeal from the New Zealand Court of Appeal to the Privy Council, the plaintiff a former minister and member of the New Zealand House of Representatives sued the defendant for defamation in respect of a television program which the plaintiff claimed accused him of being party to a conspiracy to sell off state-owned assets on unduly favourable terms in return for political donations. The program referred to statements made in Parliament and the defendant wished to refer to those statements to establish the truth of its accusations. In doing so the defendant wished to allege that the plaintiff had misled the Parliament by suggesting that the government did not intend selling off state-owned assets.

The Privy Council upheld the view of the Court of Appeal of New Zealand that freedom of speech prevented reference to what was said in Parliament even in defamation proceedings brought by a member where the defendant wished to refer to the member's parliamentary statements only for the purpose of establishing a defence. The Board acknowledged the conflict which arises in such a case but gave paramountcy over the interests of the administration of justice to 'the need to ensure that the legislature can exercise its powers freely on behalf of its electors, with access to all relevant information'.[178] In the Board's view, the public interest in ensuring that members and witnesses appearing before parliamentary committees are not inhibited required a wide view of the privilege.

The Board rejected both of the defendant's arguments which would have confined the effect of the privilege. The first was based on the ruling in *R v. Murphy* that the privilege only precluded reference to statements made in Parliament where legal consequences were sought to be imposed against their maker. The Board regarded this view of Hunt J as erroneous[179] noting that s. 16(3) of the 1987 Act contained 'the true principle to be applied':

> This view [of Hunt J] discounts the basic concept underlying article 9, viz. the need to ensure so far as possible that a member of the legislature and witnesses before committees of the House can speak freely without fear that what they say will later be held against them in the courts. The important public interest protected by such privilege is to ensure that the member or witness *at the time he speaks* is not inhibited from stating fully and freely what he has to say. If there were any exceptions which permitted his statements to be questioned subsequently, at the time when he speaks in Parliament he would not know whether or not there would subsequently be a challenge to what he is saying. Therefore he would not have the confidence the privilege is designed to protect.
>
> Moreover to allow it to be suggested in cross-examination or submission that a member or witness was lying to the House could lead to exactly that conflict between the courts and Parliament which the wider principle of non-intervention is designed to avoid. Misleading the House is a contempt of the House punishable by the House: if a court were also to be permitted to decide whether or not a member or witness had misled the House there would be a serious risk of conflicting decisions on the issue.[180]

The second argument that privilege only arose when the member was sued for defamation was unsustainable since the privilege could not depend on who brought the proceedings.[181]

The Privy Council disagreed with the decision of the South Australian Court of Appeal in *Wright and Advertiser v. Lewis*[182] on which this second argument was based. In that case, the Court refused to strike out particulars of a defence and interrogatories in a defamation action brought by a member of the South Australian Parliament in respect of a letter published in a newspaper which accused the member of making unfounded and defamatory statements in Parliament. The particulars of the defence and interrogatories in referring to the statements made in Parliament were challenged by the member as infringing parliamentary privilege. The Court rejected this challenge, holding that privilege could not be raised in a case brought by a member.

King CJ allowed reference to the parliamentary statements for the purpose of defending defamation proceedings brought by the member, for to hold otherwise, would involve 'a gross distortion of the law of defamation'.[183] Nor would such reference inhibit the member's exercise of free speech in Parliament:

> There can be no doubt that some of the more general expressions of the ambit of Parliamentary privilege found in the cases and in learned writings, if understood literally, would have the effect of precluding a defendant from justifying imputations on a Member of Parliament in relation to his statements and conduct in the Parliament. But the authors of those general expressions were not confronted with that particular issue and there does not appear to be any interest of Parliament or the public which warrants such a rule. Freedom of speech and deliberation in the Parliament is the primary value sought to be protected by parliamentary privilege. To accord to a defendant the right to defend himself against an action for defamation by proving truth, would not impinge upon such freedom. A member would not be inhibited in the exercise of free speech or of his Parliamentary duties by fear of legal consequences, because he would be aware that his actions and motives could not be examined in court unless he instituted the proceedings which rendered such examination necessary. Only the member's action in launching proceedings alleging a false imputation could lead to an examination in court of the issue of the falsity of the imputation, and therefore of the member's statements and conduct. I cannot think of any other public or Parliamentary interest which could be impaired by such an examination in such circumstances.
>
> I do not think that a defendant, so defending himself, can be regarded in any real sense as impeaching or questioning the freedom of speech, debates or proceedings in Parliament as forbidden by Art 9; nor can the courts be fairly regarded as doing so if they permit a defendant to so defend himself. It would not be sought to visit any legal consequences on the member, nor to examine his actions or motives except so far as that examination might be rendered necessary by the member's own action. The object would be merely to repel the accusation made by the member that a false imputation had been made against him. If Parliamentary privilege operated to prevent a person, exposed to an action by a member for defamation, from defending himself by proving the truth of his criticism of the statements or conduct of the member, it would indeed be "turned into an abominable instrument of oppression": *Adam v. Ward*.[184]

White J expressly agreed with the judgment of King CJ but relied on two specific factors: (i) like in *Adam v. Ward,* the member's action came 'out of the blue', without any preceding altercation between the parties; and (ii) if reference were denied the defendant would be unable to disprove malice in order to maintain the defence of qualified privilege.[185] Olsson J adopted the view of North P in *News Media Ownership v. Finlay*[186] that the privilege is no more than 'a shield of defence'.[187] As noted earlier, his Honour regarded[188] *R v. Murphy* as not inconsistent with the principle from *Church of Scientology*.

Both of the cases relied on in *Wright and Advertiser v. Lewis,* the decision of the House of Lords in *Adam v. Ward*[189] and *News Media Ownership v. Finlay,*[190] were defamation actions brought by a member of Parliament in respect of criticism of his performance. Statements made by them in Parliament, while noted to be protected by absolute privilege, were still used for the purpose of establishing the cause of action or for arguing the defence of qualified privilege. Yet the issue whether such reliance infringed parliamentary privilege was not raised in either case.[191]

The harshness of the wide view of the privilege taken by the Privy Council in *Prebble* in relation to defamation actions is alleviated by the court's ability in an appropriately extreme case to avoid injustice by staying the action. However, in *Prebble* the order of the New Zealand Court of Appeal that the proceedings be stayed unless privilege was waived by the House of Representatives, was reversed by the Privy Council as the defendant was able 'to put forward the overwhelming majority of the matters upon which it relies in justification of the alleged libel'.[192] Extreme injustice is avoided but in other cases where a stay is not ordered, the parties may be clearly disadvantaged.

Where a member of Parliament is prevented from relying on his or her own statements in Parliament, another approach may have been to allow the member to waive the benefit of the privilege. However, the authorities deny that waiver is possible even by the House concerned, for the privilege is for the benefit of the Parliament and not simply for the benefit of the individual member.[193]

The difficulties which may arise when a member sues rather than when being sued, identified in *Prebble* and *Wright*, have recently been identified as arising under s. 16 of the 1987 Act by the Queensland Court of Appeal in *Laurance v. Katter.*[194] In that case, a member of the Commonwealth Parliament was sued for defamation for saying outside Parliament on national radio and television that his statements made in Parliament were 'backed up with the hardest of hard evidence'. The plaintiff wished to incorporate the member's parliamentary statements with this statement made outside Parliament in order to establish defamation. The plaintiff demurred to the member's defence which claimed that s. 16 of the 1987 Act precluded reference to what he had said in Parliament.

On the authorities considered above, under the general law there would appear to be little chance of success in being able to incorporate the parliamentary statements as part of the allegedly defamatory statement. This is not an action brought by a member nor is it simply using the parliamentary statements for the purpose of 'supporting' the action. Had the defendant actually repeated his parliamentary statements outside Parliament rather than merely referred to them, it is unlikely that privilege would attach to them.[195] Nevertheless, two arguments have been put to support the privilege extending that far. First, the repetition of parliamentary statements outside Parliament remain part of the proceedings of Parliament and secondly, to deny privilege is in effect to question the identical statements made inside Parliament under privilege. The first of these arguments was mentioned by Zelling ACJ in *Australian Broadcasting Corporation v. Chatterton*[196] where in obiter his Honour regarded it as arguable that privilege attached to the same statements made outside Parliament.[197] Prior J disagreed, rejecting both of the arguments above.[198] The same view was adopted by Lieff J in *Stopforth v. Goyer*.[199] The member may, however, rely on qualified privilege where publication is to a limited audience.

All members of the Court in *Laurance v. Katter*[200] acknowledged that s. 16 of the 1987 Act was drafted in extraordinarily wide terms. In their view, its terms if taken literally, were capable of preventing a member from relying on his or her own parliamentary statements in order to prove the elements of a defamation action and of preventing a defendant in the same way from establishing a defence. Pincus JA posed the example of how untenable s. 16 was in a case where a member is critical of someone under privilege and that person's response is the subject of a defamation action brought by the member. The defendant is then unable to refer to what the member originally said of the defendant under privilege to justify the response. Of course, this is the position under the general law according to the Privy Council in *Prebble,* subject to the overriding qualification that in an appropriate case the action should be stayed.

While a majority of the Court (Pincus and Davies JJA) concluded that s. 16(3) could not validly operate in that manner and so allowed in part the demurrer, Fitzgerald P in dissent upheld the validity of the provision despite the wide net it cast. In noting that s. 16(3) may prevent a member from suing in defamation for even a malicious publication of known falsehoods concerning his proceedings in Parliament, his Honour opined:

> I do not find that particularly surprising or objectionable. Parliamentary "powers,

> privileges and immunities" belong to Parliament ... not the individual members, and it is not unjust or unreasonable that the public interest which they are intended to serve has adverse consequences for parliamentarians as well as ordinary citizens who are without recourse for defamation published of them by a member of parliament in Parliament. Indeed, the defamed member of parliament at least has a public and absolutely privileged forum in which to respond to maliciously false defamation by an ordinary citizen, as well as the opportunity to achieve vindication by having the citizen punished by the material House for contempt.[201]

However, the majority, noting also the difficulties for a defendant in such a case, confined the operation of s. 16(3) to avoid that result. Davies JA derived from the context of s. 16 an overriding requirement in s. 16(3) that evidence concerning the proceedings of Parliament would only be inadmissible 'if that would impeach or question the freedom of proceedings in Parliament', observing this would also 'achieve a satisfactory balance between the public interest in protecting the freedom of political discussion and the competing public interest in protecting the freedom of speech in Parliament which s. 49 of the Constitution authorises'.[202] His Honour concluded that condition was not satisfied in this case. Pincus JA took a different approach reading down s. 16(3) so as not to apply to defamation proceedings in order to avoid infringing the implied freedom of political discussion under the Constitution.[203]

On the other hand, Fitzgerald P in dissent provides[204] a persuasive argument against there being any infringement of the implied freedom of political discussion: how can s. 49 be subject to such an implied freedom when the unqualified adoption of the privileges of the House of Commons as at 1901 could not have been intended to be subject to that freedom? This argument appears unassailable if s. 16 is merely declaratory of the privileges of the House of Commons as at 1901.[205] For the intention is quite clear in s. 49 that it was those privileges which were to be enjoyed by the Parliament. That evident intention in s. 49 precludes any implication of a restriction such as the implied freedom of political discussion.

If s. 16 is not merely declaratory of the general law,[206] the issue is whether the implied freedom operates as a restriction on the legislative power pursuant to which the 1987 Act is enacted. That power appears to be either s. 49 or a combination of s. 49 and s. 51(xxxix).[207] There can be little doubt that the implied freedom restricts the legislative power in s. 49 (as distinct from the adoption of the House of Commons privileges) which declares the privileges of the very body whose deliberations are the subject of the protection afforded by the implied freedom. Moreover, both s. 49 and the implied freedom share the same underlying purpose: the protection of the processes of deliberation of policy, albeit at different levels, the former at the representative level and the latter at the community level.

If it is accepted that s. 16 burdens the freedom of political discussion in that it precludes reference to the proceedings of Parliament in support of any proceedings of a court or tribunal, the critical issue becomes whether the terms of s. 16 are reasonably appropriate and adapted for giving effect to a legitimate public interest, namely, the effective functioning and integrity of Parliament, and whether the burden imposed is only incidental and not disproportionate.[208] A relevant factor in assessing the proportionality of s. 16 is the extent to which it impairs the capacity of a defendant in defamation proceedings to establish the defence of qualified privilege as expanded in *Lange v. Australian Broadcasting Corporation*.[209]

The assessment to be made in the application of the implied freedom is whether the restrictions on the use outside Parliament of parliamentary proceedings are no more than is reasonably necessary to protect the functions and integrity of Parliament. The evidentiary difficulties faced by parties in legal proceedings must be weighed against the dual public interests of ensuring that members and witnesses are uninhibited in what they say or do in the course of parliamentary proceedings and of avoiding conflict between Parliament and the courts. If the narrow view of the freedom of speech under Art 9 adopted by Hunt J in *R v. Murphy* were seen to adequately protect these public interests, s. 16 would need to be read down accordingly. But for the reasons given earlier, it is submitted that these public interests are only adequately protected by the wide view given in *Church of Scientology* and *Prebble*. In so far as s. 16 gives effect to that view, it would be valid. However, any operation beyond that would be open to challenge, unless, for example, s. 16(2)(b) is read down in the manner suggested earlier, that is, confined to documents prepared for presentation or submission to the Parliament or to a committee.

Conclusion

It is surprising that despite several centuries of evolution the precise scope and effect of parliamentary privilege remains obscure. This chapter only touches on a few of the issues awaiting resolution. Central to them all is an appreciation of how far these privileges must extend to ensure the efficacy of Parliament without at the same time unreasonably impairing individual rights, especially those of freedom of speech and reputation. While an assessment of parliamentary privilege is desirable, the implied freedom of political discussion may vest that task in the High Court rather than in the Parliament, at least in relation to the privileges of the Commonwealth Parliament.

Notes

1. Maurice L Gwyer (ed.), *Anson's Law and Custom of the Constitution*, Vol 1 *Parliament*, 5th edn 1922 at 166–7 cites *Haxey's Case* in 1397 where Haxey had been condemned as a traitor for introducing certain bills in Parliament. This judgment was later reversed by Henry IV and the House of Lords. According to FW Maitland, *The Constitutional History of England*, Cambridge 1909 at 241, Haxey may not have been a member of the House of Commons but a clerical proctor. In 1512 in *Strode's Case*, the Court of Stannay fined Richard Strode for introducing legislation to control the tin mines in Cornwall. An Act (4 Hen VIII, c 8) was later passed declaring void the proceedings taken against Strode and having a general operation.
2. *Erskine May's Treatise on The Law, Privileges, Proceedings and Usage of Parliament*, 21st edn at 291.
3. This accords with the view in GR Elton, *The Tudor Constitution*, 1962 at 254 that freedom of speech within Parliament appears not to have been raised as a privilege before the reign of Henry VIII. FW Maitland, *The Constitutional History of England*, 1909 at 242 states that the first time the freedom was claimed of the King by the Speaker at the beginning of a session was in 1541.
4. FW Maitland, *The Constitutional History of England*, 1909 at 242–243.
5. CJ (1667–87) 19, 25; LJ (1666–75) 166, 223.
6. FW Maitland, *The Constitutional History of England*, 1909 at 322.
7. (1682) 12 St Tr 822.
8. See the opinion of Lord Denning on the *Strauss Case* in GF Lock, 'Parliamentary Privilege and the Courts: The Avoidance of Conflict' [1985] Public Law 64 at 88.
9. FW Maitland, *The Constitutional History of England*, 1909 at 321 asserts that no member of the House of Commons since the Restoration has been punished for words spoken in the House.
10. The first such measure was prescribed by the *Act of Settlement* 1701 but this was repealed before it took effect and was replaced in 1707 by s. 24 of the Statute 6 Anne, c 7.
11. Enid Campbell, *Parliamentary Privilege in Australia*, 1966 at 3.
12. Ibid.
13. GR Elton, *The Tudor Constitution*, 1962 at 229.
14. Campbell, supra 11 at 4–5.
15. See Campbell, ibid at 5 where in fn 6 there is cited the case when Sir Francis Pemberton and Sir Thomas Jones as judges of the Court of King's Bench were held in contempt of the House of Commons in 1689 for their judgment in *Jay v. Topham* (1684) 12 St Tr 822.
16. (1839) 9 A & E 1; 3 St Tr NS 736.
17. Declared in 1704: 'neither House of Parliament hath any power, by any vote or declaration, to create to themselves any new privilege that is not warranted by the known laws and customs of Parliament', CJ (1702–1704) 555, 560.
18. Carl Wittke, *The History of English Parliamentary Privilege*, 1921 Columbus (Ohio), republished 1970 Da Capo Press, New York at 205.
19. FW Maitland, *The Constitutional History of England*, 1909 at 374.
20. *Australian Constitutional Law: Cases, Materials and Text*, 1972 Butterworths at 170.
21. Letter by W Garrow and S Shepherd to Lord Bathurst, 30 December 1815, reprinted in WPM Kennedy, *Documents on the Canadian Constitution 1759–1915*, Toronto 1908 at 297–9 — cited in fn 16 in Campbell, supra 11.
22. (1842) 4 Moo P C 63. Cf *Beaumont v. Barrett* (1836) 1 Moo P C 59 where the Judicial

Committee of the Privy Council previously upheld the privilege of the Legislative Assembly of Jamaica to commit for contempt of the Assembly.

23. (1842) 4 Moo P C 63 at 88.
24. Fagjenbaum and Hanks, supra 20, dispute this view at 169ff.
25. (1840) 11 Ad & E 273.
26. Supra 11 at 20.
27. (1866) LR 1 PC 328.
28. See *Doyle v. Falconer* (1866) LR 1 PC 328 at 340; followed in *Barton v. Taylor* (1886) 11 App Cas 197 at 204 which confined the power to suspend for the period of the current sitting; *Harnett v. Crick* [1908] AC 470; *Willis v. Perry* (1912) 13 CLR 593 at 597; *Armstrong v. Budd* (1969) 89 WN (Pt 2) (NSW) 241 where Wallace P at 402 applied the doctrine of necessity to the conditions in 1969. Necessity is determined at the date of the exercise of the power: *Egan v. Willis & Cahill* (1996) 40 NSWLR 650 at 7 per Mahoney P and at 5 per Priestley JA.
29. See *Gipps v. McElhone* (1881) 2 LR (NSWR) 18; *R v. Turnbull* [1958] Tas SR 80; *Chenard and Co v. Joachim Arissol* [1949] AC 127.
30. (1998) 195 CLR 424 dismissing the appeal from the NSW Court of Appeal (1996) 40 NSWLR 650.
31. Gaudron, Gummow, Kirby, Hayne and Callinan JJ; McHugh J dissented.
32. (1998) 195 CLR 424 at 453 [47].
33. (1996) 40 NSWLR 650 at 664–7 per Gleeson CJ; at 677–8 and 683 per Mahoney P; at 692–3 per Priestley JA.
34. (1998) 195 CLR 424 at 455 [55].
35. Ibid. at 455 [54]. See also Kirby J at 505 [159] and Callinan J at 514 [194] who both accepted the suspension as not punitive.
36. Ibid at 478–9 [108–109].
37. (1839) 9 Ad & E 1 at 203.
38. This paper does not consider the scope of judicial review in relation to parliamentary privilege.
39. (1998) 195 CLR 424 at 467 [81].
40. Ibid. at 472 [93] and 475–6 [102].
41. [1999] NSWCA 176.
42. Ibid. at [69–71] per Spigelman CJ; [154] per Meagher JA.
43. [1999] NSWCA 176 at [143].
44. *Doyle v. Falconer* (1866) LR 1 PC 328 at 341.
45. For example, ss. 41–46 *Constitution Act 1867* (Qld).
46. For example, the Report of the Senate Standing Committee on Constitutional and Legal Affairs in 1985 on *Commonwealth Law Making Power and the Privilege of Freedom of Speech in State Parliaments* (PP235/1985) at pars 2.8 to 2.39 considered three bases for the incorporation of the freedom of speech in Art 9 of the *Bill of Rights* in the privileges of the colonial State Parliaments: (i) as inherited law; (ii) implied by the doctrine of necessity; and (iii) colonial statute.
47. s. 24 *Australian Courts Act 1828* (Imp), Act 9 Geo IV, c 83; see *Quan Yick v. Hinds* (1905) 2 CLR 345.
48. The first representative legislature was established by Act 5 and 6 Vic, c 76 (1842). Cf. the view of Campbell, supra 11 at 29 that the relevant statutes were not inherited as they were

of purely local operation in England. This precludes application by paramountcy but not by inheritance.

49. See *Gipps v. McElhone* (1881) 2 LR (NSWR) 18; *R v. Turnbull* [1958] Tas SR 80; *Chenard and Co v. Joachim Arissol* [1949] AC 127.
50. See *Egan v. Willis & Cahill* (1996) 40 NSWLR 650 at 19 per Gleeson CJ.
51. *Parliamentary Privilege Act 1858* (Tas), see s. 17. Kirby J in *Egan v. Willis* at fn 200 noted adoption 'to a lesser extent in Tasmania'.
52. *Constitution Act 1867* (Q) s. 40A.
53. *Constitution Act 1975* (Vic) s. 19(1): as at 21 July 1855. See *Dill v. Murphy* (1864) 1 Moo PCC(NS) 487.
54. *Constitution Act 1934* (SA) ss. 9 and 38: as at 24 October 1856.
55. *Parliamentary Privileges Act 1891* (WA) s. 1: 'for the time being'.
56. Harry Evans (ed.), *Odgers' Australian Senate Practice*, 7th edn at 29 (electronic copy of 30/9/96).
57. Campbell, supra 11 at 1. See also *Odgers'* ibid. at 28: 'refers to an immunity from the ordinary law which is recognised by the law as a right of the Houses and their members'.
58. Supra 44 at 30–61.
59. *Odgers'* (ibid.) notes at 28–9 that the power to punish for contempt is a power to punish for offences against the House and it is not an offshoot of the immunities nor is it intended to protect those immunities — that role is for the courts. At times it was erroneously considered necessary to find a corresponding immunity to establish a contempt of the House. This led to the fabrication of immunities.
60. See Laurie Marquet, 'Commonwealth and State — A Privileged Compact?' (1986) 1 Legislative Studies 20 at 21; Report of the Select Committee on the Official Secrets Act (UK), HC 101 (1938–1939). A recent example is the *Special Commissions of Inquiry Amendment Act 1997* (NSW) which was upheld in *Arena v. Nader* (NSW Court of Appeal — 10 October 1997).
61. (1870) LR 4 HL 661.
62. See *Clissold v. Perry* (1904) 1 CLR 363 at 373; *Commonwealth v. Hazeldell Ltd* (1918) 25 CLR 552 at 563.
63. (1925) 37 CLR 36 at 93.
64. (1983) 152 CLR 328 at 341. See, for example, *Hawkins v. Gathercole* (1855) 24 LJ Ch 332 where the ecclesiastical privilege against distress was held not to be abrogated by statute.
65. See *McGinty v. Western Australia* (1996) 186 CLR 140 at 177; 134 ALR 289 at 302.
66. [1958] AC 331.
67. See the dissent of Lord Denning which as a dissenting opinion of the Judicial Committee was unable to be published although it has been published since as an Annexure in GF Lock, 'Parliamentary Privilege and the Courts: The Avoidance of Conflict' [1985] Public Law 64 at 88. Lord Denning at 85 regarded the 1770 Act as directed to the Houses and Art 9 directed to the Courts so that no conflict was possible.
68. In *Aboriginal Legal Service of Western Australian (Inc) v. Western Australia* (1993) 9 WAR 297, Rowland J at 304 accepted the submission that 'clear words in a statute' were required to limit parliamentary privileges.
69. See *Criminal Justice Commission v. Nationwide News Pty Ltd* [1996] 2 Qd R 444 at 453–4 per Fitzgerald P.
70. In Appendix II to the 1985 Report of the Senate Standing Committee on Constitutional

and Legal Affairs, *Commonwealth Law Making Power and the Privilege of Freedom of Speech in State Parliaments*, PP235/1985 at 85.

71. Ibid. at 86 (para. 8).
72. (1955) 92 CLR 157 at 168.
73. Ibid.
74. Supra 44 at 44.
75. Ibid. at 44–7.
76. Ibid. at 47. See Campbell supra 11 who at 168 requires express words to abrogate privilege but when discussing the effect of statutory secrecy provisions at 171–2 omits reference to this issue.
77. PP 235/1985.
78. Ibid. see conclusions (1) and (2) on p. xix and chapter 3.
79. Cf. the Joint Opinion regarded s. 106 not as a restriction on Commonwealth legislative power (pars 5 and 6 at p. 86 of the report).
80. (1995) 183 CLR 373 at 477.
81. Ibid. at 481.
82. CJ (1667–87) 19; LJ (1666–75) 166.
83. *In re Parliamentary Privilege Act 1770* [1958] AC 331 at 350.
84. See Joint Select Committee on Parliamentary Privilege, Final Report, PP 219/1984 at para. 5.4.
85. Campbell, supra 11 at 28.
86. Ibid.
87. Cf. *Rost v. Edwards* [1990] 2 WLR 1280 at 1293 per Popplewell J holding House of Commons register not privileged.
88. *Goffin v. Donnelly* (1881) 6 QBD 307.
89. *Lake v. King* (1667) 1 Wms s. 131.
90. The typing of a statement to be made by a member in Parliament is covered: *Holding v. Jennings* [1979] VR 289.
91. See generally SA de Smith, *Constitutional Law and Administrative Law*, 5th edn by Harry Street and Rodney Brazier, Penguin Books, 1985 at 328–31.
92. See the 1967 Report of the House of Commons Select Committee on Parliamentary Privilege, HC 34, 1966–1967 at para. 91. Cf Joint Select Committee on Parliamentary Privilege, Final Report, PP 219/1984 at para. 5.8.
93. Report from the House of Commons Committee of Privileges HC (1956–57); H.C. Deb. 591 (8.7.58).
94. Lord Denning considered the letter privileged in his dissent in *In re Parliamentary Privilege Act, 1770* [1958] AC 331 published later as an Annexure in GF Lock, 'Parliamentary Privilege and the Courts: The Avoidance of Conflict' [1985] Public Law 64 at 83.
95. See the Joint Select Committee on Parliamentary Privilege, Final Report, PP 219/1984 at paras 5.14–5.15.
96. Ibid. at paras 5.24 and 5.25. Cf *Re Quellet (No 1)* (1967) 67 DLR (3d) 73 at 85.
97. PP219/1984.
98. Ibid at para 5.27.
99. Ibid. at para. 5.29. In formulating the recommended provisions, the Committee acknowledged the assistance from the recommendations of the 1967 House of Commons Report on Parliamentary Privilege and the 1976–1977 recommendations of the Privileges Committee which reviewed those 1967 recommendations (*Third Report from the Committee of*

Privileges. Recommendations of the Select Committee on Parliamentary Privilege HC 417 (1976–77)).

100. At para. 5.22.
101. See *Report of the House of Commons Committee of Privileges on National Security* (Zircon Report) HC 365 (1987).
102. Ibid. at paras 16 and 35.
103. *R v. Rule* [1937] 2 KB 375; *Rivlin v. Bilainkin* [1935] 1QB 485; *R v. Grassby* (1992) 55 A Crim R 419 at 428–9. Activities preceding the presentation of a petition were not regarded as privileged by the Marks Royal Commission in Western Australia: see *Report of the Royal Commission into Use of Executive Power*, November 1995 at p. 22. This issue was left open in *Halden v. Marks* (1996) 17 WAR 447.
104. See *Meekins v. Henson* [1964] 1 QB 472; *Egger v. Chelmsford* [1965] 1 QB 248.
105. (1997) 145 ALR 96.
106. (1994) 182 CLR 104.
107. (1997) 145 ALR 96 at 114.
108. As noted earlier, an exposure draft of the 1984 Report had included a provision to accord privilege to the *Strauss* situation but it was deleted from the Final Report (para. 5.22).
109. *Odgers'* at 38–9 agrees with this position. Another notable feature of this statutory definition is that it incorporates 'acts done', as well as 'words spoken'. So it would seem that the act of revealing a confidential document is capable of attracting privilege.
110. (1997) 150 ALR 199.
111. Unreported judgment of 18 April 1997 at p. 8.
112. Supra 2 at 132–3.
113. (1991) 55 A Crim R 419 at 430–1.
114. (1997) 150 ALR 199 at 215.
115. Ibid. at 10 per McPherson JA.
116. Ibid. at 11.
117. Ibid.
118. Ibid. at 20.
119. Ibid. at 13–14.
120. See *Ex parte Wason* (1869) LR 4 QB 573.
121. See *Dillon v. Balfour* (1887) 20 Irish LR 600.
122. See *Church of Scientology of California v. Johnson-Smith* [1972] 1 QB 522; *R v. Turnbull* [1958] Tas SR 80; cf. *R v. Murphy* (1986) 5 NSWLR 18.0
123. See *Church of Scientology of California v. Johnson-Smith* [1972] 1 QB 522 at 527; *Mundey v. Askin* [1982] 2 NSWLR 369 at 373 (CA); *Rost v. Edwards* [1990] 2 WLR 1280.
124. This requirement was abolished by the Senate in respect of its proceedings by Privileges Resolution No 10 (25 February 1988). On the practice of the House of Commons: see C J Boulton (ed.), *Erskine May's Treatise on The Law, Privileges, Proceedings and Usage of Parliament*, 21st edn at 91.
125. [1971] 3 WLR 434.
126. Ibid. at 437.
127. Ibid. at 437.
128. (1839) 9 Ad & E 1; 112 ER 1112.
129. Ibid. at 114.
130. Ibid. at 209.
131. (1869) LR 4 QB 573.

132. Ibid. at 577.
133. [1960] 2 QB 405.
134. Supra 113 at 438.
135. This view was approved of by the Court of Queen's Bench in *R v. Secretary of State for Trade; Ex parte Anderson Strathclyde plc* [1983] 2 All ER 233 which refused to refer to ministerial statements made in Parliament which were relied on for an application for judicial review of a decision made by the minister outside Parliament. This case has been overruled by the House of Lords in *Pepper v. Hart* [1993] AC 593 at 639.
136. [1958] Tas SR 80.
137. Ibid. at 83.
138. [1979] VR 289 at 291.
139. (1983) 78 FLR 449 at 453.
140. (1986) 5 NSWLR 18 at 33–8.
141. Judgment of 5 June 1985 unreported.
142. (1986) 5 NSWLR 18 at 38–9.
143. (1881) 2 NSWR 18.
144. Ibid. at 23.
145. Ibid. at 25.
146. (1990) 53 SASR 416.
147. See *Australian Broadcasting Commission v. Chatterton* (1986) 46 SASR 1 at 18 per Zelling ACJ; cf. Prior J at 35–6; *AJ Grassby* (1991) 55 A Crim R 419 at 430–2 per Allen J.
148. (1987) 8 NSWLR 116.
149. (1988) 19 FCR 223.
150. Ibid. at 230–1.
151. [1993] AC 593.
152. [1995] 1 AC 321.
153. Ibid. at 333.
154. [1993] AC 593 at 639.
155. Ibid.
156. 'Parliamentary Privilege — Parliament versus the Courts: Cross-examination of Committee Witnesses' (1993) 67 ALJ 109 at 122. See reply by Harry Evans in (1993) 67 ALJ at 457.
157. Cf. Olson J in *Wright and Advertiser v. Lewis* (1990) 53 SASR 416 at 447.
158. *Commentaries on the Laws of England* Vol 1 at 163.
159. See 'Privilege of Parliament' (1944) 18 ALJ 70 at 74–6 per Lowe J's ruling as the Royal Commissioner to investigate certain questions concerning the 'Brisbane Line' in 1943 and parliamentary statements by Mr Ward MHR that a royal commission came within Art 9 as 'a place out of Parliament' and that it could not require Mr Ward to give evidence relating to statements made by him in the House of Representatives; followed by Townley J as Commissioner in *Royal Commission into Certain Crown Leaseholds* (1956) St R Qd 225 at 229. See also RD Lumb & GA Moens, *The Constitution of the Commonwealth of Australia*, 5th edn 1995 at 108–9. Cf. Campbell supra 11 at 39–40.
160. Section 16 of the *Parliamentary Privileges Act 1987* (Cwlth) declares the use of parliamentary proceedings in a court or tribunal, the latter being defined in s. 3(1) to mean any person or body having the power to examine witnesses on oath.
161. Campbell, supra 11 at 41. See also DR Mummery, 'Freedom of Speech in Parliament'

(1978) 94 LQR 276 at 284–5 and T Carmody, 'Royal Commissions, Parliamentary Privilege and Cabinet Secrecy' (1995) 11 QUTLJ 49.
162. (1956) St R Qd 225 at 230.
163. HC 101 (1938–39).
164. See Campbell, supra 11 at 43.
165. (1978) 142 CLR 1 at 35. At 35, his Honour specifically observed that no reference to the proceedings of Parliament was sought to found the charges or 'to support' them.
166. [1993] AC 593 at 638.
167. The freedom of speech accorded witnesses appearing before parliamentary committees is a more recent extension of the privilege: CJ (1818) 389.
168. Ibid. Sir Clarrie Harders was very critical of s. 16, especially in denying the right to cross-examine witnesses for the purpose of testing their credibility.
169. See fn 98.
170. (1997) 150 ALR 199.
171. Memorandum from Chief General Counsel re '*Parliamentary Privileges Act 1987*, s. 16: Impact of Criminal Investigation', dated 18 April 1997.
172. See *Grey v. Pearson* [1857] 6 HLC at 106.
173. (1988) 19 FCR 223 at 231.
174. Sir Clarrie Harders 'Parliamentary Privilege — Parliament versus the Courts: Cross-examination of Committee Witnesses' (1993) 67 ALJ 109 at 140.
175. Ibid. at 142 which provides 'In the determination of any criminal charge against him, everyone shall be entitled to the following minimum guarantees, in full equality: ... (e) To examine, or have examined, the witnesses against him and to obtain the attendance and examination of witnesses on his behalf under the same conditions as witnesses against him.'
176. (1996) 141 ALR 447 (Qld Court of Appeal). Special leave to appeal to the High Court was granted but the matter was settled in May 1998.
177. [1995] 1 AC 321.
178. Ibid. at 336.
179. Relied on at 333 'the long line of dicta that courts will not allow any challenge to what is said or done in Parliament' and that it was inconsistent with the *Church of Scientology Case* which had been approved by the House of Lords in *Pepper v. Hart* [1993] AC 593 and by *Comalco Ltd v. Australian Broadcasting Corporation* (1983) 78 FLR 449 both of which held 'that it would be a breach of privilege to allow what is said in Parliament to be the subject matter of investigation or submission'.
180. [1995] 1 AC 321 at 334.
181. It might also have been rejected since '[t]he important public interest protected by such privilege is to ensure that the member or witness *at the time he speaks* is not inhibited from stating fully and freely what he has to say' (said in respect of the first argument at 334).
182. (1990) 53 SASR 416.
183. Ibid. at 421–2.
184. Ibid. at 426–7.
185. Ibid. at 431 and 432–3.
186. [1970] NZLR 1089.
187. Supra 170 at 447.
188. (1990) 53 SASR 416 at 447.
189. [1917] AC 309.

190. [1970] NZLR 1089.
191. The reason for this was surmised by White J to be that it is up to the parties to raise the issue and not for the court to raise it: (1990) 53 SASR 416 at 430.
192. [1995] 1 AC 321 at 339.
193. See ruling of Speaker in 1952 PD Cth vol 219 pp. 1991–3, 2104–5; *Australian Broadcasting Commission v. Chatterton* (1986) 46 SASR 1 at 20 per Zelling ACJ.
194. (1996) 141 ALR 447 (Qld Court of Appeal).
195. See *R v. Abingdon* (1793) 1 Esp 226 at 228, 170 ER 337 at 338; *R v. Creevy* (1813) 1 M & s. 273, 105 ER 102; see also JA Pettifer (ed.), *House of Representative Practice,* 1981 at 646.
196. Supra 135.
197. Ibid. at 18–19.
198. Ibid. at 35–6. See also *R v. Lord Abingdon* (1793) 1 Esp 226, 170 ER 337; *R v. Creevy* (1813) 1 M & s. 273, 105 ER 102.
199. (1978) 87 DLR (3d) 373; cf. *Roman Corp Ltd v. Hudsons Bay Oil & Gas Co Ltd* (1972) 23 DLR (3d) 292, affirmed (1973) 36 DLR (3d) 413; *Re Clark and Attorney-General of Canada* (1977) 81 DLR (3d) 33.
200. (1996) 141 ALR 447 per Fitzgerald P at 480, per Pincus JA at 482 and per Davies JA at 488.
201. Ibid. at 480.
202. Ibid. at 490.
203. Ibid. at 486.
204. Ibid. at 453.
205. Is so according to *Prebble* [1995] 1 AC 321 at 333.
206. Not according to Pincus JA at 5 and Sir Clarrie Harders 144 at 119.
207. See *R v. Richards; Ex parte Fitzpatrick and Browne* (1955) 92 CLR 157 at 168.
208. See *Australian Capital Television Pty Ltd v. The Commonwealth* (1992) 177 CLR 106 at 142–4, 157–62, 169.
209. (1997) 145 ALR 96.

4
The States and the Constitution

Leslie Zines

In his constitutional work the States of Australia were of prime interest to the late Professor Darrell Lumb. His writings concern both the State constitutions and the place of the States in the federal union. It is appropriate therefore that there be a chapter on the latter topic in a book published in his honour. What makes it even more appropriate is that the High Court has in the last few years delivered a number of decisions that have as their focus the position of the States in the Constitution.

For present purposes I propose to deal with the following areas:

(a) The legislative powers of the States;

(b) State immunity from federal law;

(c) The States and representative government; and

(d) The Constitution and State courts.

All these topics have involved the High Court making fairly broad constitutional implications.

Legislative powers

For nearly eighty years we have witnessed the steady and seemingly inevitable increase in federal power in Australia and, therefore, the reduction and decline of the exclusive legislative and executive power of the States. While this trend has a similarity in result to what occurred in the United States, the method of achieving it has been different. In America, the commerce clause was the vehicle, while in Australia it has been the result of a broad interpretation of various federal powers, but particularly the corporations power (s. 51(xx)) and, to a lesser extent, the external affairs power (s. 51(xxix)). So satisfied has the Commonwealth been with judicial decisions based on those powers that there has been little in the way of novel or adventurous use of s. 5l(i). In each of the prefaces to the second, third and fourth editions of *The High Court and the Constitution* I said that the commerce power remained the least explored in modern times.

The only political and social outcry in Australia to expansion of federal power that had any resemblance to the strong emotional reaction to United States Supreme Court decisions in the 1930s was in respect of the interpretation given to the external affairs power in *Commonwealth v. Tasmania* (the

Tasmanian Dam case).[1] Both the majority and minority judges expressed themselves in somewhat combative language. The judgments in turn reflected the political debate outside the courtroom. Attempts were made by the States and others in the Australian Constitutional Convention and in submissions to the Constitutional Commission to have the external affairs power formally amended.

There was no such strong reaction to the expansion of the scope of the corporations power in *Tasmanian Dam* to include the control of all corporation activities done for the purposes of trade. (Three majority judges — Mason, Murphy and Deane JJ — went further and upheld Commonwealth regulation of all acts done by s. 51 (xx) corporations.)

When the decision in *Tasmanian Dam* relating to treaties was followed in 1996 in *Victoria v. Commonwealth*[2] there did not seem to be a murmur from the States or the media. The court unanimously upheld many of the provisions of the amendments made in 1993 to the Industrial Relations Act on the basis of the external affairs power. The provisions gave effect to ILO conventions relating to minimum wages, equal remuneration, discrimination in employment, wrongful dismissal and the right to strike.

The political 'respectability' of federal use of s. 51 (xxix) to achieve domestic social goals occurred when Mr John Howard said that, not being an ideologue, he would be prepared to use the external affairs power as a last resort to implement his industrial relations policy. So far as I am aware there was no protest from any State or political groups. Other provisions of the Industrial Relations Act depended on the corporations power. Western Australia conceded that the Commonwealth had power to control all the industrial relations of the corporations even though that went beyond the ratio of *Tasmanian Dam*, which was limited to the control of acts done for the purposes of trade.

It is, I think, clear that the States and the public came to accept as normal Commonwealth legislation which would have caused dispute and even some passion a decade or so earlier. There will, no doubt, be many more cases where the validity of Commonwealth legislation will be challenged for lack of power. There may also be further attempts to formally alter the external affairs power. I believe, however, that the issue of the powers of the Commonwealth and the States inter se will not in the future be the great constitutional battle ground that it has been for most of this century.

State immunity from federal law

Although experience has affirmed that the early doctrine of the reserved powers of the States has clearly been 'exploded', the same cannot be said unreservedly of the other pre-*Engineers* principle, namely, the doctrine of intergovernmental immunity, sometimes called the doctrine of the immunity of instrumentalities.

The *Engineers* case[3] had, of course, held that Commonwealth laws can 'bind ... the people of every State considered as individuals or as political organisms called States ... in other words, bind both the Crown and subjects'.[4] The national nature of the Commonwealth government and parliament was emphasised. In that parliament were represented all the people of all the States. They could deal with any abuse of power in respect of their States through the political and democratic process. Express provisions of the Constitution were brought to the fore and implications of a broad nature, such as federalism, were to be avoided.

The concept of federalism, however, continued to haunt and fascinate. It was relied on twenty-five years after *Engineers* in *Melbourne Corporation v. Commonwealth*,[5] where the *Engineers* principle was qualified to a degree by relying on the federal framework of the Constitution. The framework prevented the Commonwealth from acting with the purpose of controlling a State in the exercise of its functions, and discrimination would usually be evidence of that purpose. The principle was applied in only one other case, namely, *Queensland Electricity Commission v. Commonwealth*[6] which held invalid special provisions of the Conciliation and Arbitration Act relating to an industrial dispute between a Queensland State authority and a trade union in the electricity industry, on the ground that it placed a special burden or disability on the State.

It was made clear, however, that a law which did not discriminate against the States could also be invalid on implied federal grounds. Dixon J had declared that:

> The foundation of the Constitution is the conception of a central government and a number of State governments separately organized. The Constitution predicates their continued existence as independent entities.[7]

In later cases the formulation that was most favoured relating to this implication was that the Commonwealth could not impair the existence of the States or their capacity to function as governments.[8]

The court has always insisted that these implied principles do not mean a return to the doctrine of reserved powers. There has, therefore, been an attempt to extract from the federal concept an essential element of separate independent State organisations of government divorced from their general powers and functions. The principle is that the States should remain independent entities with a capacity to exercise whatever powers and functions they have.

There is, however, some difficulty in determining whether a federal law operates merely to reduce or impair the areas or subjects over which the State may effectively legislate or exercise executive authority or whether it impairs its capacity to act as a government. The limited nature of the restriction was clear from various cases upholding laws that had a considerable effect on the States and their functions. These included (a) provisions imposing on the States federal payroll tax[9] and fringe benefits tax in respect of benefits provided to Crown servants, members of parliament, ministers and judges,[10] (b) provisions prohibiting the States, on grounds of heritage protection, from developing their own land without the consent of a federal minister,[11] and (c) provisions requiring a State to abide by federal law forbidding racial discrimination in exercising a statutory power to approve or refuse approval for transfers of Crown leases.[12]

In *Western Australia v. Commonwealth (Native Title Act* case)[13] the court gave some clues as to what was involved in the implied restriction regarding non-discriminatory laws. Western Australia argued that the native title legislation interferred with its power to control land and resources for various purposes. In rejecting this submission a joint judgment said:[14]

> The Act does not purport to affect the machinery of government of the State. The constitution of the three branches of government is unimpaired; the capacity of the States to engage the servants it needs is unaffected; the acquisition of goods and services is not impeded; nor is any impediment placed in the way of acquiring land needed for the discharge of the essential functions of the State save in one respect, namely, the payment of compensation.

This paragraph treated as relevant to a State's capacity as a government its ability to acquire servants and resources with which to carry out its functions. This was tested in *Re Australian Education Union; ex parte Victoria*,[15] where Victoria challenged the power of the Commonwealth to authorise the Industrial Relations Commission to bind a State in respect of a number of awards and proposed awards covering all, or nearly all, the public service of Victoria of its authorities. A joint judgment of six judges upheld most of the action of the Commission with the exception of two cases. Those cases involved provisions of interim awards which the court said restricted the offer of voluntary severance deals made to Crown employees.

The High Court declared that critical to a State's capacity to function as a government was its right to determine the number and identity of the persons it wishes to employ, the term of employment and the number and identity of the persons it desires to dismiss, with or without notice, on redundancy grounds. Subject to an exception, the court upheld the making of federal awards prescribing minimum wages and working conditions, at least if it takes account of the special functions and responsibilities of the employees. The issues of promotions and transfers and termination of appointment on other grounds were left open.

As an exception to the general principle laid down by the court, it was held that federal awards could not prescribe any minimum salaries or conditions for persons employed 'at the higher levels of government'. This category includes 'Ministers, ministerial assistants and advisors, heads of department and high level statutory office holders, parliamentary officers and judges and possibly others as well'.[16]

Leaving aside this excluded class, the decision is consistent with the views expressed in the *Payroll Tax case*[17] and the *Second Fringe Benefits Tax case*[18] that merely because a Commonwealth law has economic consequences for the operations of government does not mean that it breaches the implied restriction. It has, however, been criticised on the ground that a State might just as easily be prevented from employing the number or type of persons that it wants by a federal award fixing minimum employment conditions as by more direct command. The argument is that if freedom to employ and dismiss is essential to the capacity of a State it is unrealistic to ignore the economic consequences of federal laws. That was a major ground of Dawson J's dissent on that issue. It is a view with which I disagree.

The effect of prescribed wages and salaries on governmental policy regarding employment and redundancy will depend on political and economic circumstances, which will vary from time to time. Whether the State will raise taxes, reduce expenditure in other directions or take other steps to have a service of the size and kind that it wants will depend on many varied circumstances, including the outlook and political complexion of the Government, the situation in an upper House (and sometimes in a lower House), when an election is due, the size of any budget surplus or deficit and the weighing and balancing of conflicting social interests and policies. All this is left to a State Government and Parliament to determine in the light of the prescribed terms. There is no room for such determination in the case of a legislative command. Similarly the cost of running the governmental services, including the public service, will be affected by Commonwealth sales taxes and customs and excise duties. The best security for the independence and existence of a State in these circumstances is the restriction against discriminatory laws. If, for example, the power to tax is the power to destroy, then while that limitation operates the Commonwealth could not destroy a State unless it destroyed everyone else in the process.

The exception of persons in high office seems to me to be only of token value, a result of brooding over abstract concepts, rather than dealing with practical affairs. As a practical matter (as Dawson J pointed out) it is difficult to believe that to prescribe minimum salaries for these office holders under a non-discriminatory law would affect the capacity of a State to function as a government when federal law will have determined the conditions of all, or nearly all, others, perhaps tens of thousands.

This aspect of the decision is difficult to reconcile with the *Second Fringe Benefits Tax* case. The majority in that case followed *Payroll* in looking at whether the particular tax in fact interferred with or was likely to interfere with the State's capacity. Brennan J dissented insofar as the tax was applied to benefits given to officers of 'the essential organs of State', namely ministers, Supreme Court judges and State members of parliament.[19] The majority took a more practical view. In *Re Australian Education Union* the exception from federal regulation of persons in high office is not the same as the class Brennan J made reference to in the earlier case, but the reasoning is similar, namely that there is a class of persons so central to the government of a State that their employment conditions should not be affected by federal law, regardless of the practical effect on the capacity of the State to exercise its functions.

One result of the case seems to be that the Racial Discrimination Act and the Sex Discrimination Act of the Commonwealth do not apply to State appointments and terminations of appointment on grounds of redundancy.

One source of unnecessary complexity has crept into this area in the past few years. It concerns the operation of s. 106 of the Constitution, which provides, in part, that 'the Constitution of each State shall, subject to this Constitution, continue ... as at the establishment of the Commonwealth.' Until recently, no Commonwealth law had been held invalid on the ground that it was inconsistent with s. 106. Indeed there is a technical difficulty in concluding that either s. 51 is limited by s. 106, or vice versa, because both sections are expressly declared to be subject to the Constitution. In 1930 in the *Australian Railways Union v. Victoria Railways Commissioners*[20] Dixon J said that possibly s. 106 might provide the ground for concluding that a federal law could not provide for the imposition of monetary obligations on the States which are not subject to the condition that funds shall be appropriated by the Parliaments of the State.[21]

For nearly sixty years, however, the protection of the existence and capacity of the States was said to depend upon a restriction implied from the federal nature of the Constitution, although s. 106 was of course an important element of the Constitution's federal framework.

In *Re Tracey, ex parte Ryan*,[22] however, s. 106 was referred to among the reasons for declaring invalid a Commonwealth provision providing that where a person had been acquitted or convicted of an offence by court martial that person was, in effect, not liable to be tried for substantially the same offence by a State court applying State law. Five judges held that this provision was not authorised by the defence power. Brennan and Toohey JJ also held that because the State courts were an essential branch of government, s. 106 prevented the Commonwealth from prohibiting them from exercising their jurisdiction. Mason CJ, Wilson and Dawson JJ expressed doubts whether such provisions could be sustained 'having regard to s. 106'.

It seems to me that the implied restrictions based on federalism would have lead to the same result. They would also prevent attempts to enforce federally imposed monetary obligations on a State in the absence of parliamentary appropriation. The object of the implied restriction in ensuring the independent operation and framework of State organisations of government clearly preserves the integrity of the operation of responsible government, the relationship between the organs of government, parliamentary debate, the freedom of the judiciary and so on.

All these matters could also be regarded as part of the State Constitutions. I am of the view, however, that it is better to recognise clearly that what is in issue is the federal nature of the Constitution and that to that end, it is necessary to safeguard the existence and independence of the States. To concentrate on the notion of 'State Constitution' is to direct argument to semantic and technical issues. What is a State Constitution? It cannot be the Constitution Act, because anything may be included in such an Act. Also principles fundamental to State government may be in other legislation. Some federal laws may be regarded as affecting a State Constitution, which would, nevertheless, not be inconsistent with State independence and capacity to govern. This occurred in *Port MacDonnell Professional Fishermen's Association Inc v. South Australia*[23] which upheld a Commonwealth Act, passed under s. 51(xxxviii) with the consent of State Parliaments, extending the territorial limits of State legislative power. The court said it did not have to consider the general dilemma posed by the relationship of s. 51 and s. 106 because in the case of s. 51(xxxviii) its purpose was such that it must be given full force and effect.

In *Re Australian Education Union*, the High Court was far from clear as to the relationship of the implied restrictions and s. 106. At one point the judgment seems to treat s. 106 as simply part of the constitutional foundation for the implied restrictions, that is, as part of the federal framework. But the judgment then goes on to talk of the impairment of 'the existence of the States and *their Constitutions* and their capacity to function as Governments' (emphasis added).[24] This adds an express new element to the usual description of the restrictions on Commonwealth power to bind the States. For the most part, however, the scope of the restriction is described in the judgment in the usual manner.

The States and representative government

In *Australian Capital Television Pty Ltd v. Commonwealth*[25] the High Court held invalid a federal Act which, subject to exceptions, prohibited political broadcasting on radio and television during election periods. The Act imposed its prohibitions in relation to all, including State, elections. Five judges (Mason CJ, Deane, Toohey, Gaudron and McHugh JJ) held the Act invalid in respect of both Commonwealth and State elections. Brennan J regarded it as invalid only in respect of State elections; while Dawson J held it fully valid.

A majority of the court held that a system of representative government in the Commonwealth sphere was implied in the Constitution and that freedom of communication on political and governmental matters was essential to that system. The most important provisions that gave rise to the implication are sections 7 and 24, which provide, in part, that senators and members of the House of Representatives, respectively, shall be 'directly chosen by the people'.

How did these provisions and the implication derived from them protect communication about *State* public affairs from Commonwealth control? Brennan and McHugh JJ held the provisions relating to State elections invalid on the ground that they impaired the capacity of the State to function as an independent government — the principle discussed above.

For the majority, however, there was no practical way of unravelling those forms of political communication that concerned federal matters from those that related to State governmental affairs. The inter-relationship of State and federal politics and policies was evidenced by national political parties, the range of matters debated in the Commonwealth Parliament and federal control and influence in respect of many matters over which the Commonwealth does not have direct legislative power, sometimes by use of the appropriation or grants powers.[26]

In 1994 in *Theophanous v. Herald and Weekly Times Ltd*[27] and *Stephens v. West Australian Newspapers Ltd*[28] a majority held that the States were also prevented by the Constitution from impairing communication on governmental affairs, whether Commonwealth or State. These cases concerned suits for defamation brought, respectively, by members of the Commonwealth and Western Australian Parliaments. Again, the majority emphasised the intermingling of State and federal political issues. In the earlier cases, however, remarks were made by Deane, Toohey and Gaudron JJ which might have suggested that the Commonwealth Constitution prescribed representative government for the States. It was mentioned that the Constitution refers to State parliaments, voters and electoral systems,[29] although, in the case of the latter, in provisions that are transitional.

In *McGinty v. Western Australia*[30] it was made clear that the basis of the constitutional restriction on State power (and which resulted in constitutional alteration to the common law of defamation) related to the upholding of representative government at the federal level. In that case it was accepted by nearly all the judges that any implications that might be drawn from the Constitution as to the principle of 'one vote, one value' did not apply to the system of elections in respect of State legislatures. While the Constitution assumed a form of State representative government it did not prescribe such a system, expressly or impliedly.[31] The only dissent from that view was from Gaudron J who said that the Constitution impliedly required the States to be and remain 'essentially democratic', but that requirement stopped 'considerably short' of requiring equality of voting power.

The position therefore, seemed to be that insofar as the States were restricted in controlling political communication in State affairs, under the Constitution, it was because representative government at the Commonwealth level required freedom of communication of *all* public affairs, whether primarily of concern to Commonwealth, State or local government.

Theophanous and *Stephens* gave rise to judicial disagreements on two fronts, namely, first, whether the implication of federal representative government (or the interpretation of the words 'chosen by the people') requires the restriction of the States in respect of State political matters and, secondly, whether common law rights and duties of persons inter se are subject to the implication. In *Theophanous* and *Stephens* three judges — Brennan, Dawson and McHugh JJ — were opposed to these propositions for varying reasons. In *McGinty* Gummow J expressed some concern about the reasoning in those cases and whether the limitation on power extended to controlling what he called 'the general law'. In March 1997 these propositions were challenged in the High Court in *Levy v. Victoria* and *Lange v. Australian Broadcasting Corporation*. In this chapter I am not concerned with the issue of the effect of the implied freedom on the common law or other private rights of action.

In *Lange v. Australian Broadcasting Corporation*[32] a unanimous High Court upheld the implication of freedom of communication on political and governmental matters. That freedom, the court said, was drawn from ss. 7, 24, 64 and 128 and related sections of the Constitution and 'can extend only so far as is necessary to give effect to those sections'. The focus of attention is, therefore, the freedoms necessary to ensure the constitutionally prescribed system in the federal sphere.

The court did not go to the length of following the earlier case by holding that representative government under, for example, ss. 7 and 24 requires freedom of communication of *all* public affairs, whether primarily of concern to Commonwealth, State or local government. The judges did, however, recognise that *many* such affairs would be relevant. In *Lange* the court extended the common law defence of qualified privilege in defamation cases to encompass communication to the public on governmental or political matters. The judgment mentioned that this went beyond the freedom dictated by the Constitution. It added, however:

> Of course, the discussion of matters at State, Territory or local level might bear on the choice that the people have to make in federal elections or voting to amend the Constitution, and on their evaluation of the performance of federal ministers and their departments. The existence of national political parties operating at federal, State, Territory and local government levels, the financial dependence of State, Territory and local government on federal funding and policies, and the increasing integration of social, economic and political matters in Australia make this conclusion inevitable.[33]

It is, I think, unfortunate that the court has not gone to the length of holding that all political and governmental matters in Australia are indivisible for present purposes. In *Levy v. Victoria*,[34] for example, it was held that the Victorian duck hunting regulations were not inconsistent with the implied freedom of the plaintiff to protest against laws permitting and regulating duck hunting. In the result it was, therefore, unnecessary for the court to determine whether communication relating to those laws came within the constitutionally protected category. However two judges suggested it did not. Brennan J said it seemed like 'a discrete State issue'.[35] McHugh J said that the issue seemed 'remote from choosing members of the Senate or House of Representatives'.[36]

In my opinion this attempt to preserve separate fields of communication on public affairs could give rise to a great deal of litigation and fine, but arid, distinctions.

Even if, in theory, some matters seem clearly of exclusive or primary concern to the States, such as the behaviour of State ministers or members of parliament, practical politics may indicate otherwise. That distinction, for example, would not, in recent times, seem so clear to Western Australians. One only has to consider the disputes regarding Dr Carmen Lawrence and Senator Crichton-Browne that went on in both State and federal parliaments and in political parties at a national and State branch level. Clearly the issue is not resolved by looking at Commonwealth legislative powers. The great federal involvement in the passage of the new gun ownership laws and in education are illustrative of that.[37]

Insofar as the Constitution does restrict State power in the name of federal representative government it seems that those restrictions will operate in relation to freedom of assembly and association for political or public purposes. The same may be true of the right to demonstrate and parade, and perhaps to engage in symbolic acts to make a political point. The law challenged in *Levy* is a case in point. McHugh J said in that case, that the freedom extended to 'signs, symbols, gestures and images' and that 'any mode of expressive conduct is capable of communicating a political or governmental message to those who witness it'.[38]

While these freedoms would be subject to countervailing social interests the High Court would examine whether the law went beyond what was reasonably necessary to achieve the legitimate goal.[39] This involves a balancing of the countervailing social interest and the implied freedom, and raises the issue of proportionality.[40]

It was on these grounds that the High Court laid down new principles of defamation law where the protected area of communication was involved. It was on the same grounds that the court was divided in *Australian Capital Television*, and also in *Cunliffe v. Commonwealth*[41] in relation to legislation prohibiting unregistered persons from advising aliens on immigration matters. It is likely that legislation regulating demonstrations, in the interest of motorists or of other pedestrians, for example, would be invalid if it gave a wide discretion to police or an official in granting or refusing a permit or if the criteria for exercising the discretion did not have regard to the implied freedoms of assembly and communication.

I should mention that State Constitution Acts may have entrenched provisions designed to secure some aspects of representative government. In *Stephens v. West Australia Newspapers*, for example, the implied freedom was held to operate also by virtue of entrenched provisions of the Constitution Act of Western Australia. Also, in *McGinty* Toohey and Gaudron JJ, while agreeing that the Commonwealth Constitution did not affect the validity of State electoral divisions, held, in dissent, that the State entrenched provisions did. I am concerned, however, only with the Commonwealth Constitution.

State courts

The Constitution, of course, had a great impact on the courts of the earlier colonies. It created a national court of appeal, made provision for federal jurisdiction to be conferred on State courts and authorised the creation of federal courts.

The express guarantees which governed federal courts, however, were not made applicable to those of the States, such as the provisions of s. 72 relating to the appointment, tenure and remuneration of federal judges, and the separation of the judicial power of the Commonwealth implied in Chapter III. However, it was held that, in investing State courts with federal jurisdiction, the Commonwealth had to 'take a [State] court as it finds it'.[42] It has been repeatedly said that the Commonwealth Parliament may not, under s. 77 or s. 51(xxxix), affect or alter the constitution of a State court or the organisation through which its jurisdiction and powers are organised.[43] Further, the Commonwealth cannot, under s. 77, authorise or require State courts to exercise non-judicial functions.[44] But, until September 1996, it had always been assumed that the State parliaments could do so, subject to the State's own constitution.

Kable v. Director of Public Prosecutions[45] changed all that to a considerable degree. A New South Wales Act applied to, and only to, a named person, Gregory Wayne Kable, who had been convicted of the manslaughter of his wife. The Act was passed a short while before he was due to be released from prison. It appears he had sent letters to several persons threatening to kill them when he came out of gaol. The Act declared that its object was to protect the community by providing for Kable's preventive detention. The Supreme Court was empowered to make an order that he be detained if satisfied on reasonable grounds that he was more likely than not to commit a serious act of violence and that it was appropriate for the protection of persons or the community that he be held in custody. In construing the Act, the need to protect the community was to be given paramount consideration. The standard of proof was on the balance of probabilities, and the court could have regard to specified material which would not otherwise have been admissible.

The High Court, by a majority of four to two, held the Act invalid as inconsistent with Chapter III of the Constitution (Toohey, Gaudron, McHugh and Gummow JJ; Brennan CJ and Dawson J, dissenting). It was generally accepted that neither the Commonwealth nor State Constitutions prescribed a separation of powers so far as State courts were concerned. Nothing in Chapter III, the judges said, prevented the State parliament, generally speaking, from conferring non-judicial power on the courts. The principle in the *Boilermakers* case, therefore, did not apply.

What the State could not do, however, was to give to a court which exercised the judicial power of the Commonwealth powers or functions that were 'incompatible with' or 'repugnant to' the exercise of such judicial power. The functions given to the Supreme Court in respect to Mr Kable were held to be of that nature.

In this regard the majority applied the same principle that they had in earlier cases to determine whether functions conferred on a federal judge as persona designata were invalid because of the separation of judicial power.[46] The incompatibility in both cases arises where the judges are prevented from acting in accordance with the judicial process or the provision diminishes public confidence in the integrity of the court in exercising federal jurisdiction.[47]

The broadest restrictions on State power were stated in the judgments of Gaudron, McHugh and Gummow JJ. Each referred to all the courts exercising the judicial power of the Commonwealth as an 'integrated' system[48] and said that the Constitution did not provide for two different grades of federal justice or judicial power.[49]

McHugh and Gummow JJ took the issue of an integrated justice system further than the others. Much of their argument has at its foundation section 73 of the Constitution. That section sets out exhaustively the appellate jurisdiction of the High Court in respect of federal and State matters (subject to a limited power of Parliament to make exceptions). The only judgments of State courts exercising State jurisdiction from which an appeal lies to the High Court are those of the Supreme Courts. McHugh and Gummow JJ found from this provision relating to appeals from the Supreme Courts that it was an object of the Constitution to ensure the unity of the common law as a national system. It followed, they thought, that it would not be open to a State to abolish its Supreme Court or vest judicial power in bodies from which there could be no ultimate appeal to the High Court.[50] McHugh J suggested that to prevent appeals to, or review by, the Supreme Court in relation to decisions of the lower courts might be inconsistent with the integrated system required by Chapter III. That is because if there was no Supreme Court appeal or review the matter could not get to the High Court (unless of course, the lower court had been exercising federal jurisdiction). These questions did not, of course, arise directly from the issues before the court, but they were stated in reply to a submission that the State court system stood outside, and had no constitutional relationship with, the federal judicature.

A second strand of the integration theory was relied on by all the majority judges. It is that the Constitution both implies and requires that the States have courts in which the Commonwealth may vest jurisdiction under s. 77. As Gaudron J put it:[51]

> Were [the States] free to abolish their courts, the autochthonous expedient, more precisely the provisions of Ch. III which postulate an integrated judicial system,

would be frustrated in their entirety. To this extent, at least, the States are not free to legislate as they please.

It followed that the States could not authorise or require their courts to exercise functions or processes which were incompatible with the exercise of the judicial power of the Commonwealth.

Toohey J's judgment seems to differ from the other three majority judgments in that he confines himself to incompatible aspects operating while the State court is actually exercising federal jurisdiction. At first sight it might seem odd that an action brought by the State Director of Public Prosecutions under the State Act should be regarded as federal jurisdiction. That came about, however, because Kable pleaded that the Act was unconstitutional. It thus became a matter 'arising under the Constitution or involving its interpretation' under s. 76(i) of the Constitution. It therefore attracted s. 39 of the Judiciary Act, which vests State courts with federal jurisdiction.

It would appear, therefore, that for Toohey J the issue of incompatibility arose when the court was exercising the judicial power of the Commonwealth. For the other three majority judges the issue arises at all times because the exercise of any function or jurisdiction may affect public confidence in the integrity of a court in which is vested federal judicial power. Toohey J did not oppose this broader interpretation, but did not feel the need to consider it for purposes of the case.

Even on Toohey J's more limited view, however, a matter can be converted to federal jurisdiction by the defendant pleading the principle in *Kable*. This, in my opinion, makes his approach undesirable because too much depends on particular circumstances relating to the behaviour of defendants. It also seems undoubtedly the case that public perception of the court when exercising federal jurisdiction can clearly be affected by its exercise of other powers, functions and jurisdiction. As McHugh J said,[52] it remains the same court consisting of the same judges.

This case has given rise to a number of uncertainties. As the *Boilermakers* doctrine remains inapplicable to State courts it is clear that the functions of an administrative appeals tribunal may be given to the Supreme Courts even though they cannot be conferred on federal courts. Yet, it is also clear that the decision in *Kable* produces a situation where, in certain circumstances, the result is the same as if a separation of powers did apply.[53] This is the case where non-judicial powers are repugnant to the exercise of judicial functions and where judicial powers are to be exercised in a manner not consistent with due process. The recent decisions relating to what functions may or may not be conferred on a federal judge as persona designata are now applicable to the powers that may be conferred on a State court or presumably (despite an apparent contrary view of Gaudron J)[54] on a State judge as persona designata.

Nevertheless, the absence of a principle of separation of powers in the State systems remains significant. It is not correct to say, in my view, that a concern for individual liberty or even the rule of law is at the basis of the *Kable* decision. The judgments do not say that the New South Wales Parliament cannot enact that Mr Kable shall be imprisoned for life or until the Attorney-General directs. Indeed McHugh J affirms that it can.[55]

What the Parliament cannot do is dress up a legislative or executive decision with the objective and impartial clothing of the judiciary. Gummow J quoted a United States Supreme Court judgment which said that the reputation of the judiciary 'may not be borrowed by the political Branches to cloak their work in the neutral colours of judicial action'.[56] If one were concerned simply with the individual in the case, rather than that principle, it might be argued that it was better for Mr Kable to have a judge determine the issue rather than an official. Indeed Gove J refused to issue a further detention order against him and he was released.

As I mentioned, Kable no doubt restricts State power to control the judicial process. In the federal sphere there are several pronouncements in recent years to the effect that provisions contrary to natural justice or due process are inconsistent with the exercise of judicial power.[57] Similar statements about 'the judicial process' were made in *Kable.*[58]

Even if the requirement of due process was limited to the exercise of federal jurisdiction,[59] it is clear that no State legislature could safely legislate to impair natural justice in respect of State jurisdiction because, as explained earlier, of the manner in which it can be converted to federal jurisdiction by pleading Chapter III or a federal statutory defence.

It may be that the implication of an 'integrated' judicial system and a uniform common law, put forward by McHugh and Gummow JJ, and based on the position of the High Court as an ultimate court of appeal in all matters, will give rise to more far-reaching arguments than are foreseen in the judgments.

If the Supreme Courts did not exist the High Court would have no appellate jurisdiction in relation to judgments of State courts exercising State jurisdiction. Therefore, both these judges reason that the Constitution requires their preservation. The same result would, however, follow if jurisdiction were vested in lower courts from which there was no appeal to the Supreme Court or which the Supreme Court could not review. Without expressing a concluded view, McHugh J said that such a situation would seem inconsistent with the integrated system that Chapter III and covering Cl.5 envisaged.[60] Gummow J also said that the State could not vest the judicial power of the State in bodies from which there could be no ultimate appeal to the High Court.[61]

If these premises are accepted, is it not a reasonable argument that none of the judicial power of the State can be exercised by the legislature or vested in administrative or executive bodies, from which there is no appeal to a court, because it would impair the constitutional positions of the Supreme Court as at the apex of the State judicial system, the High Court as at the apex of the national system and the guaranteed unity of the common law.

If that argument should ever succeed the States would have acquired that degree of separation of judicial power that existed in the federal sphere until *Boilermakers*. The principle was that only courts could exercise the judicial power, but those courts could have non-judicial power conferred on them if not inconsistent with their judicial functions.

This, however, is in the realm of conjecture and it is important to remember that Toohey and Gaudron JJ relied only on the need of State courts to exercise federal jurisdiction.

Notes

1. (1983) 158 CLR 1.
2. (1996) 187 CLR 416.
3. (1920) 28 CLR 129.
4. Note 3 at 153.
5. (1947) 74 CLR 31.
6. (1985) 159 CLR 192.
7. (1947) 74 CLR 31 at 82.
8. Zines L, *The High Court and the Constitution*, 4th edn, Butterworths, Sydney, 1997 at 328–32.
9. *Victoria v. Commonwealth* (1971) 122 CLR 353.
10. *State Chamber of Commerce and Industry v. Commonwealth* (1987) 163 CLR 329.
11. *Commonwealth v. Tasmania* (1983) 158 CLR 1.
12. *Koowarta v. Bjelke-Petersen* (1982) 153 CLR 168.
13. (1995) 183 CLR 373.
14. Note 13 at 481.
15. (1995) 184 CLR 188.
16. Note 15 at 233.
17. *Victoria v. Commonwealth* (1971) 122 CLR 353.
18. *State Chamber of Commerce and Industry v. Commonwealth* (1987) 163 CLR 329.
19. Note 18 at 362–4.
20. (1930) 44 CLR 319 at 391–2.
21. See also *Garnishee (No.1)* case (1932) 46 CLR 155 at 176.
22. (1989) 166 CLR 518.
23. (1989) 168 CLR 340.
24. 184 CLR at 229–30.
25. (1992) 177 CLR 106.

26. Note 25 at 142, 168–99 216–7.
27. (1994) 182 CLR 1.
28. (1994) 182 CLR 211.
29. *Nationwide News Pty Ltd v. Wills* (1992) 177 CLR 1 at 75; *Australian Capital Television Pty Ltd v. Commonwealth* (1992) 177 CLR 106 at 216.
30. (1996) 186 CLR 140.
31. Note 30 at 175, 189, 208–10, 291–4.
32. (1997) 189 CLR 520.
33. Note 32 at 571–2.
34. (1997) 189 CLR 579.
35. Note 34 at 596.
36. Note 34 at 626.
37. For a different view see Carney G, 'The Implied Freedom of Political Discussion — Its Impact on State Constitutions' (1995) 23 *FL Rev* 180.
38. *Levy* 189 CLR 579 at 622–3.
39. Note 8 at 381–3.
40. *Leask v. Commonwealth* (1996) 187 CLR 579.
41. (1994) 182 CLR 272.
42. *Federated Saw Mill Etc Association v. Alexander* (1912) 15 CLR 308 at 313.
43. *Le Mesurier v. Connor* (1929) 42 CLR 481; Cowen Z and Zines L, *Federal Jurisdiction in Australia*, 2nd edn, Oxford University Press, Melbourne, 1978 at 185.
44. *Queen Victoria Memorial Hospital v. Thomton* (1953) 87 CLR 144.
45. (1996) 189 CLR 51.
46. *Grollo v. Palmer* (1995) 184 CLR 348; *Wilson v. Minister for Aboriginal and Torres Strait Island Affairs* (1996) 138 ALR 220.
47. *Kable* 189 CLR at 98, 107, 116, 132–3.
48. Note 47 at 102, 112, 114–5, 137–9.
49. Note 47 at 103, 115, 127.
50. Note 47 at 109–10, 137–9.
51. Note 47 at 103.
52. Note 47 at 114.
53. Note 47 at 118–9.
54. Note 47 at 104. Cf. McHugh J at 117–8.
55. Note 47 at 121.
56. Note 47 at 133.
57. For example *Leeth v. Commonwealth* (1992) 174 CLR 455 at 470; *Chu Kheng Kim v. Minister for Immigration* (1992) 176 CLR 1 at 27. Note 8 at 202–4.
58. 138 ALR at 107, 122, 132.
59. Note 58 at 116, McHugh J said that 'neither the Commonwealth nor State parliaments can legislate in a way that permits the Supreme Court *while exercising federal judicial power* to disregard the rules of natural justice …' (emphasis added). The rest of his judgment, however, seems to take the broader view described earlier in the text.
60. Note 58 at 114.
61. Note 58 at 139. He said the State could not do this in combination with abolishing its Supreme Court. However, it is suggested that the reasoning would also apply where the Supreme Court continued to exist, but substantial jurisdiction was conferred on other courts and there was no appeal or review by the Supreme Court.

5

Federalism-based 'fragmentation of the decision-making process' in foreign relations

John Trone

Introduction

Throughout his scholarly career Professor Lumb was keenly interested in both international law and the external affairs power of the Australian Constitution,[1] which are closely related topics. For instance, in a well-known 1988 article[2] he argued that the external affairs power required limitation by constitutional amendment if it supported legislation on any subject of 'international concern', even in the absence of a treaty concerning that subject, or beyond the scope of such a treaty.[3]

However, it is less well known that, before he was lured away by the technicalities of the law of the sea, Professor Lumb wrote extensively on the then-emerging international law of human rights. I shall touch on these writings because they bring out the importance Professor Lumb then attached to the development of and observance of international law.

Professor Lumb's writings show an early recognition of the extraordinary effect that international legal rules would come to exert upon national legal systems. In 1963, when explaining a now notable source of human rights,[4] the Treaty of Rome,[5] to an Australian audience, he wrote with considerable prescience that:

> [i]t may well be that English commercial law will undergo a profound transformation in the next two decades. Political federation however is not an immediate end of the Treaty, although political unity is envisaged in the preamble to the Treaty and the achievement of economic union will make political federation more feasible.[6]

We have since seen such epochal legal developments as the United Kingdom's entry to the then Common Market,[7] the *Factortame* judgment,[8] and the Maastricht (Union) Treaty.[9]

In 1970 Professor Lumb welcomed the formulation of international standards of human rights, which had gained momentum since the Nuremberg Trials. He wrote:

> The developments which the [Nuremberg] Trials set in train, or at least contributed to, are still continuing. The Genocide Convention,[10] the Declaration of Human

> Rights[11] and now the draft Covenant on Civil and Political Rights[12] have been the result of the demand for enshrinement of basic human rights in fundamental documents which will be binding on those who wield sovereign power. In this respect the Human Rights Year may be characterised as a further positive achievement within the international legal order.[13]

He lauded the development of international criminal law at the Nuremberg trials, stating that the trials 'stand out as a milestone in the history of the struggle for the international recognition of human rights'.[14]

Not only did he support the development of international *rules* regarding human rights: he also commended the introduction of procedures for ensuring their *observance*. Professor Lumb supported the imposition of international criminal liability on those committing war crimes and crimes against humanity, whether they be the 'triggermen', the propagandists or the lawyers who collaborated in such iniquities.[15] He insisted that 'a secure international order can be built upon the basis of individual responsibility for offences against that order'.[16] Professor Lumb also wrote favourably[17] of the enforcement machinery developed under the European Convention on Human Rights.[18]

All such international obligations depend for their efficacy upon the rule that gives legal expression to the moral imperative that a nation must observe its international commitments. That rule is expressed by the Latin phrase '*Pacta sunt servanda*' ('treaties are to be obeyed').[19] Under this rule, every treaty in force must be performed in good faith by the parties to it.[20] The *Restatement on Foreign Relations* calls this 'perhaps the most important principle of international law'.[21]

The core of this rule is that treaty obligations must be performed. Aside from observance of such binding obligations being a matter of national honour (since great nations keep their word),[22] the keeping of such promises must be an indispensable foundation for a more 'secure international order'.[23]

This paper discusses how the American and Australian Constitutions have both denied federalism-based 'fragmentation of the decision-making process' in foreign affairs. Why this denial is important is emphasised throughout. This denial is essential because it better ensures the observance of Australia's and America's international commitments than would any federally fragmented decision-making process. This denial thus promotes *pacta sunt servanda*. Finally, a distinction in the manner in which each constitution regulates federal supremacy over foreign affairs is discussed.

Fragmented decision-making and foreign relations

It is well known that the external affairs power of the Australian Constitution has been held to permit the federal Parliament to implement any treaty obligation undertaken by Australia. The *Tasmanian Dam* case[24] definitively established this in 1983, but arguably the position has been clear since 1936.[25]

Hence the Australian Constitution does not impose upon the federal government a federalism-based 'fragmentation of the decision-making process' in foreign relations. This phrase was originally used by Sir Anthony Mason. He argued that 'fragmentation of the decision-making process as it affects the assumption and implementation by Australia of its international obligations' was 'altogether too disturbing to contemplate'.[26]

In response, in the most recent external affairs decision of the High Court, *Victoria v. Commonwealth*,[27] Justice Dawson argued that 'a "fragmentation" of the decision-making process [in treaty implementation] is part and parcel of a federal system'.[28] In support of his views, Justice Dawson cited United States Supreme Court authority concerning the Congressional power over interstate commerce.[29]

Justice Dawson failed to mention the views of the United States Supreme Court on the area most relevant to external affairs — treaty-making and treaty-implementation — where there is no federalism-based fragmentation of the decision-making process whatever. Indeed, the American constitutional example stands as a powerful refutation of the notion that the federal division of powers, in the absence of a treaty obligation, should stand in the path of federal implementation of the nation's international obligations. In the following section the manner in which the American Constitution denies any federalism-based fragmentation of the nation's foreign relations is outlined.

The American constitutional position

The President's power to make treaties with the advice and consent of the Senate[30] enables the United States to undertake both self-executing and non-self-executing treaty obligations. Without going into the minutiae of the distinction,[31] self-executing treaty obligations have direct effect in American law without need for further legislative action, whereas non-self-executing treaties require legislative implementation by Congress.[32]

Under the Constitution's 'necessary and proper' clause, Congress has the power to enact such implementing legislation.[33] Under this clause Congress may make laws which are 'necessary and proper' for carrying into execution powers vested by the Constitution 'in the Government of the United States, or in any Department or Officer thereof'.[34] The treaty-making power is such a power.

Provided that they do not infringe constitutional prohibitions such as those in the Bill of Rights,[35] treaty-implementing statutes and self-executing treaties are supreme over State laws by virtue of the supremacy clause, the American equivalent of section 109 of the Australian Constitution.[36] The supremacy clause provides that treaty-implementing statutes and treaties made in pursuance of the Constitution are the supreme law of the land, anything in the Constitution or laws of any State to the contrary notwithstanding.[37]

The power to make self-executing treaties or to enact legislation implementing non-self-executing treaties is in no way limited by considerations of federalism. There is no federalism-based fragmentation of the decision-making process so far as the treaty obligations of the United States are concerned.

Under its power to implement treaties Congress may make laws which would otherwise be beyond its delegated powers. This reflects the determination of the founders of the American federal system that the national government be able to fulfil the international commitments of the United States. The intention of the framers of the American Constitution regarding the observance of treaty obligations is recounted in the following section.

From the first

As Justice Black observed decades ago, 'international relations, [is] the one aspect of [American] government that from the first has been most generally conceded imperatively to demand broad national authority'.[38]

Indeed the inability of the central government to enforce treaties in the face of contrary State laws was one of the principal reasons for the swift demise of the Articles of Confederation (1781–1789),[39] which were soon replaced by the present United States Constitution.

While the treaty-making power under the Articles of Confederation was not limited by the federal distribution of powers in the absence of treaty, the Articles contained no provision for the supremacy of federal treaties over state laws. Many States frustrated the observance of federal treaties by enacting inconsistent laws. The nation was left in breach of its obligations but the nation was powerless to remedy the default of its component parts.

Hence Alexander Hamilton saw the 'fragmentation of the decision-making process' that Justice Dawson supported as one of the worst defects of the Confederation:

> The treaties of the United States, under the present Constitution, are liable to the infractions of thirteen different Legislatures, and as many different courts of final jurisdiction, acting under the authority of those Legislatures. The faith, the reputation, the peace of the whole union, are thus continually at the mercy of the prejudices, the passions, and the interests of every member of which it is composed.

Is it possible that foreign nations can either respect or confide in such a government? Is it possible that the people of America will longer consent to trust their honor, their happiness, their safety on so precarious a foundation?[40]

Having suffered a fragmentation of the decision-making process concerning the observance of treaties, one of the principal purposes of the framers of the present Constitution was that the nation would henceforth be able to enforce the commitments it made to foreign nations. The framers retained the plenary[41] treaty-making power of the Articles, uninhibited as it was by the federal distribution of powers in the absence of treaty. But they remedied the fatal defect of the Articles by expressly providing in the supremacy clause of the new Constitution that State constitutions and laws were subordinate to federal treaties.[42]

Given this background, it should come as no surprise that within the first decade of the Constitution's existence the United States Supreme Court held in *Ware v. Hylton*[43] that under the supremacy clause a Virginia law impeding the collection of a debt was subordinate to the Treaty of Peace with Great Britain.[44]

So as long ago as 1796 the treaty-making power and the supremacy clause were construed by the United States Supreme Court to permit the making of self-executing[45] treaties dealing with subject matters otherwise beyond federal legislative power.[46] In *Ware* Justice Chase gave no credence to federalism-based fragmentation of the decision-making process concerning treaty obligations. He stated: 'A treaty cannot be the *supreme law* of the land, that is of all the *United States*, if any act of a *State Legislature* can stand in its way.'[47]

Such centralised decision-making regarding the undertaking and observance of treaty obligations has remained the law of the United States to the present day. This uninterrupted line of authority is traced in the following section.

The 1790s to the 1990s

In the following centuries, the United States Supreme Court has consistently adhered to the view that State and local laws concerning inheritance,[48] real property[49] and aliens[50] must give way to federal treaties with which they are inconsistent.[51] No area of State jurisdiction has ever been found by judicial decision to offer the opportunity for a State to frustrate the performance of the international obligations of the United States.

The Congressional power to implement non-self-executing treaties concerning matters otherwise beyond federal legislative was not challenged until 1920. As a result of that challenge the United States Supreme Court rendered its famous Migratory Birds decision, *Missouri v. Holland*.[52] In this case, some seventy-five years ago, counsel for the State of Missouri made arguments strikingly similar to those that would be put to and definitively rejected by the High Court in the *Tasmanian Dam case*[53] sixty years later. Both the Supreme Court and the High Court reached essentially the same answer, but the American court did so to little controversy many decades earlier.

Just as the Australian High Court would decide in the *Tasmanian Dam* case, the United States Supreme Court held that the Congressional power of treaty-implementation was co-extensive with the power of making treaties. In so doing the Court simply applied its manifold earlier authorities concerning self-executing treaties to the Congressional power to implement non-self-executing treaties.[54]

As regards Justice Dawson reference to fragmentation of decision-making under the interstate commerce clause, *Missouri v. Holland* pointedly illustrates that authority concerning the limits of the interstate commerce clause is utterly inapposite when considering the scope of the treaty-implementing power of Congress. This is because in *Holland* itself, while a law enacted under the interstate commerce clause had been held to be beyond power, a substantially similar law enacted under the power to implement treaties was held to be valid.

Congressional legislation protecting migratory birds[55] had been invalidated as beyond the power to regulate interstate commerce.[56] Subsequently a treaty dealing with the protection of migratory birds was made with Great Britain.[57] Legislation implementing the treaty was enacted under the necessary and proper clause.[58] When the State of Missouri challenged this legislation, the Supreme Court upheld the statute as 'necessary and proper' to carry out the obligations assumed under the treaty with Great Britain.

Writing for the Court,[59] Justice Oliver Wendell Holmes noted that while in the absence of treaty a great body of matters might be solely the subject of legislation enacted by the states, that was not so where a treaty obligation concerning such a subject was involved. 'No doubt the great body of private relations usually falls within the control of the State, but a treaty may override its power.'[60] Similarly, where implementing legislation is necessary, while in the absence of treaty 'an act of Congress could not deal with [a matter] ... a treaty followed by such an act could'.[61]

Finally, Missouri claimed that the treaty and the statute were void as infringing the Tenth Amendment, which provides that '[t]he powers not delegated to the United States by the Constitution, nor prohibited by it to the states, are reserved to the states respectively, or to the people'.[62] The Tenth Amendment thus limits the federal government to the exercise of powers delegated to it. However, as Holmes observed, the treaty-making power is expressly delegated to the Federal Government.[63] No 'invisible radiation'[64] from that Amendment cripples[65] the treaty-making power.

Holland demonstrates that the Constitution contains no limitation upon the subject matter of international agreements which may be implemented by Congressional legislation. The law stated in *Holland* remains the law today.

It might be mentioned for sake of completeness that nothing has come of the 'international concern' limitation once put forward 'as a suggestion'[66] in an extra-judicial speech by Charles Evans Hughes. Hughes speculated that the treaty power might extend only to 'matters of international concern', and not to the making of 'laws for the people of the United States in their internal concerns'.[67] However, no Justice of the Supreme Court, including Hughes himself, has ever invoked such a limitation in an Opinion.

In the United States then, central power in foreign relations has not been the subject of serious judicial challenge. As will be discussed in the following section, it has only once been subject to serious political challenge. The failure of that political challenge emphasises how secure central power in foreign relations is and must be.

The Bricker Amendment: back to the past

Only once in American history has there been a serious attempt to subordinate the treaty-making and implementing powers of the federal government to the federal division of powers in the absence of a treaty. In the early 1950s the proponents of the 'Bricker Amendment' sought to abolish the self-executing treaty and to confine the legislative power to implement treaties to the delegated powers of Congress in the absence of treaty.[68] Not surprisingly, the criticism was frequently made that the Bricker Amendment would return America to the foreign policy chaos of the Articles of Confederation.

However, the impetus for the Bricker Amendment lay not in abstract concern for federalism but in American racial politics. Its origins lay in fears that human rights treaties might provide a basis for federal legislation prevailing over racially discriminatory laws then in force in numerous States.[69] It is notable that in other areas most of the Bricker proponents supported treaties cutting across 'States' rights'.[70]

Consider then these motivations for the Bricker Amendment. Consider also the extraordinarily strong opposition to it from those intimately concerned with foreign relations, including then President Eisenhower[71] and Secretary of State Dulles.[72] It is clear that the Bricker Amendment does not provide a sound foundation for arguments that centralised treaty-making and implementation have been contrary to the interests of the United States. Few indeed would invoke it as such today.

Rather, it is an indication of how uncontroversial and accepted the law on this topic is that federalism based challenges to treaties and treaty-implementing legislation are virtually unheard of in the United States today. The United States Supreme Court has not even mentioned the issue for decades.

Finally, an oft-cited distinction between how the American and Australian Constitutions regulate federal supremacy over foreign affairs is discussed in the following section. That distinction is the role of the United States Senate, but it is not as significant a distinction as is commonly supposed by foreign observers.

A distinction

It is well known that the American Constitution requires that treaties be approved by two-thirds of senators present at the time of voting.[73] Obviously no similar equivalent requirement exists under the Australian Constitution.

The role of the United States Senate is often put forward by those who wish to downplay the centralisation of decision-making regarding foreign relations in the United States. However, such reliance is misconceived. The participation of the United States Senate in the making of treaties represents a rather minimalist representation of State governments. Three points about the role of the Senate should be noted.

Firstly, the United States Senate is a Federal body, a part of the Federal legislature. Having experienced State control over the observance of treaty commitments, the Framers of the United States Constitution left representation of State interests in foreign relations to a part of the federal government, rather than to the State governments themselves. Hence the role of the United States Senate gives no support to the notion that Australian State legislatures or State executives should have any power of decision-making as to the undertaking or observance of treaty commitments.

Secondly, the influence of the States upon the Senate has become very indirect indeed. While senators were originally appointed by the State legislatures,[74] today senators are elected by the people.[75] The Senate is not a house of the States.

Thirdly, the two-thirds requirement for approval of treaty ratification is much less significant today than it was at the time of the rejection of the Treaty of Versailles.[76] In recent years it has been avoided in a number of important instances through the use of congressional-executive agreements.[77] Such agreements are signed and ratified by the executive and approved by statute or joint resolution passed by *simple majorities* of both Houses, also signed by the executive.[78] Many constitutional scholars take the view that the congressional-executive agreement is a completely 'interchangeable' substitute for treaty approval by the Senate.[79] If this is correct, no distinction of substance exists between the manner in which the American and Australian constitutions regulate foreign relations.

Conclusion

The constitutional experience of the United States gives no support whatsoever to claims that the federal government in Australia should be unable to enforce the international engagements of the nation. It seems at best misconceived for Justice Dawson to have invoked United States law as in any way supporting a 'fragmentation of the decision-making process' in foreign relations.

The highest courts of Australia and the United States have thus converged in resolving this issue. Given the American experience, the controversy in Australia over the scope of the external affairs power seems an unduly insular perpetuation of ideas rejected long ago in the United States. A federalism-based 'fragmentation of the decision-making process' in foreign relations would not promote the observance of either nation's international obligations.

Notes

1. *Australian Constitution*, s. 51(xxix) ('The Parliament shall, subject to this Constitution, have power to make laws for the peace, order and good government of the Commonwealth with respect to ... External affairs').
2. Lumb RD, 'The external affairs power and constitutional reform' (1988) 62 *Australian Law Journal* 679.
3. Note 2 at 682, 687.
4. For example *Stauder v. City of Ulm, Sozialamt (Case 29/69)* [1969] ECR 419; *Nold v. Commission (Case 4/73)* [1974] ECR 491.
5. *Treaty establishing the European Economic Community*, Rome, 25 March 1957, 298 UNTS 11.
6. Lumb RD, 'The Treaty of Rome and the European Economic Community' (1963) 4 *University of Queensland Law Journal* 297 at 303.
7. *Treaty concerning the accession of Denmark, Ireland, Norway and the United Kingdom to the European Economic Community and Euratom*, Brussels, 22 January 1972, 1375 UNTS 2.
8. *R v. Secretary of State for Transport; ex parte Factortame (Case C 213/89)* [1990] ECR 2433; *R v. Secretary of State for Transport; ex parte Factortame Ltd (No. 2)* [1991] 1 AC 603.
9. *Treaty on European Union*, Maastricht, 7 February 1992, 31 ILM 247, OJ 1992 C 224/1.
10. *Convention on the Prevention and Punishment of the Crime of Genocide*, Paris, 9 December 1948, 78 UNTS 277.
11. *Universal Declaration of Human Rights*, Paris, 10 December 1948, GA Res 217A (III), UN GAOR, 3rd sess, Part I, Resolutions (A/810) at 71.

12. *International Covenant on Civil and Political Rights*, New York, 19 December 1966, 999 UNTS 171.
13. Lumb RD, 'Legality and legitimacy: the limits of the duty of obedience to the State' in Alexandrowicz CH, ed., *Studies in the History of the Law of Nations* (The Hague: Martinus Nijhoff, 1970), 52 at 82.
14. Note 13 at 52–3.
15. Note 13 at 74.
16. Lumb RD, 'Individual responsibility for aggressive war: the crime against peace' (1959) 3 *University of Queensland Law Journal* 333 at 334.
17. Note 16 at 333.
18. *Convention for the Protection of human rights and fundamental freedoms*, Rome, 4 November 1950, 213 UNTS 221.
19. Setear JK, 'An iterative perspective on treaties: a synthesis of international relations theory and international law' (1996) 37 *Harvard International Law Journal* 139 at 159; citing Chayes A and Chayes A, 'On compliance' (1993) 47 *International Organization* 175 at 185.
20. Art 26, *Vienna Convention on the law of treaties*, Vienna, 23 May 1969, 1155 UNTS 331 at 339.
21. American Law Institute, *Restatement of the Law (Third): Foreign Relations Law of the United States* (St Paul, Minn: American Law Institute, 1987), I: 190 (s. 321, Comment a).
22. Compare *FPC v. Tuscarora Indian Nation* 362 US 99, 142 (1960) per Black J, dissenting.
23. Note 16 at 334.
24. (1983) 158 CLR 1.
25. *R v. Burgess; ex parte Henry* (1936) 55 CLR 608.
26. *Koowarta v. Bjelke-Petersen* (1982) 153 CLR 168 at 225 per Mason J.
27. (1996) 187 CLR 416.
28. Note 27 at 568 per Dawson J.
29. *United States v. Lopez* 514 US 549 (1995). See *US Constitution*, Art I, s. 8, cl 3.
30. *US Constitution*, Art 2, s. 2, cl 2.
31. The literature on the subject is extensive. See, for example, Vàzquez CM, 'The four doctrines of self-executing treaties' (1995) 89 *American Journal of International Law* 695; Damrosch LF, 'The role of the United States Senate concerning "self-executing" and "non-self-executing" treaties' (1991) 67 *Chicago Kent Law Review* 515; Paust JJ, 'Self-executing treaties' (1988) 82 *American Journal of International Law* 760; Iwasawa Y, 'The doctrine of self-executing treaties in the United States: a critical analysis' (1986) 26 *Virginia Journal of International Law* 627. Note also *Sei Fujii v. State* 38 Cal 2d 718, 721–2; 242 P 2d 617, 620–1 (1952).
32. See *Foster v. Neilson* 27 US (2 Pet) 253, 314 (1829) per Marshall CJ, for the Court. See note 21 at I: 42–43 (s. 111).
33. *Neely v. Henkel* 180 US 109, 121 (1901) per Harlan J, for the Court.
34. *US Constitution*, Art I, s. 8, cl 18.
35. *Reid v. Covert* 354 US 1 (1957).
36. Section 109 of the *Australian Constitution* reads: 'When a law of a State is inconsistent with a law of the Commonwealth, the latter shall prevail, and the former shall, to the extent of the inconsistency, be invalid.'
37. *US Constitution*, Art 6, cl 2.
38. *Hines v. Davidowitz* 312 US 52, 68 (1941) per Black J, for the Court.

39. The Articles of Confederation came into force in 1781. The present United States Constitution came into force in 1789.
40. Hamilton A, 'Federalist No 22', in Hamilton A, Madison J, and Jay J, *The Federalist Papers* (Cooke J, ed.) Cleveland: World Publishing Company, 1961 at 144.
41. Save, of course, for constitutional prohibitions such as the Bill of Rights: see *Reid v. Covert* 354 US 1 (1957).
42. *US Constitution*, Art 6, cl 2.
43. 3 US (3 Dall) 199 (1796).
44. *Definitive Treaty of Peace and Friendship between the United States and Great Britain*, Paris, 3 September 1783, 48 CTS 487, 8 Stat 80. This treaty was made before the entry into force of the present Constitution. The supremacy clause of the present Constitution applies to treaties made both before and after its entry into force: note 43 at 237 per Chase J.
45. Use of the term 'self-executing' treaty began only in 1829, see *Foster v. Neilson* 27 US (2 Pet) 253 (1829) at 314, but the concept described by that phrase dates back at least as far as *Ware v. Hylton* 3 US (3 Dall) 199 (1796).
46. *Ware v. Hylton* 3 US (3 Dall) 199, 236 (1796) per Chase J.
47. Note 46 at 236 per Chase J (emphasis in original).
48. *Hauenstein v. Lynham* 100 US 483 (1880); *Orr v. Hodgson* 17 US (4 Wheat) 453 (1819).
49. *Chirac v. Chirac* 15 US (2 Wheat) 260 (1817); *Carneal v. Banks* 23 US (10 Wheat) 181 (1825); *Hughes v. Edwards* 22 US (9 Wheat) 489 (1824); *Fairfax's Devisee v. Hunter's Lessee* 11 US (7 Cranch) 603 (1813); *Santovincenzo v. Egan* 284 US 30 (1931).
50. *In re Ah Chong* 2 F 733 (CCD Cal 1880); *Baker v. Portland* 2 Fed Cas 472 (Case No 777) (CCD Ore 1879); *In re Tiburcio Parrott* 1 F 481 (CCD Cal 1880).
51. These authorities are multiplied many times over. Those given here are but examples.
52. 252 US 416 (1920).
53. (1983) 158 CLR 1.
54. Corwin ES, *The Constitution and What It Means Today*, Princeton, NJ: Princeton University Press, 1958 at 110.
55. *Migratory Bird Act of 1913*, 4 March 1913, ch 145, 37 Stat 847.
56. *United States v. Shauver* 214 F 154 (ED Ark 1914); *United States v. McCullagh* 221 F 288 (ED Kan 1915); *State v. Sawyer* 113 Me 458, 94 A 886 (1915); *State v. McCullagh* 96 Kan 786, 153 P 557 (1915).
57. *Convention between Great Britain and the United States for the Protection of Migratory Birds*, Washington, 16 August 1916, 221 CTS 408, 39 Stat 1702.
58. *Migratory Bird Treaty Act*, 3 July 1918, ch 128, s. 2, 40 Stat 755; 16 USC 703 to 708, 709a, 710, 711 (1994).
59. Two Justices dissented without opinion: *Missouri v. Holland* 252 US 416, 435 (1920) per Van Devanter and Pitney JJ, dissenting.
60. Note 59 at 434 per Holmes J, for the Court.
61. Note 59 at 433 per Holmes J, for the Court.
62. *US Constitution*, Tenth Amendment.
63. *Missouri v. Holland* 252 US 416, 432 (1920) per Holmes J, for the Court.
64. Note 63 at 433–4 per Holmes J, for the Court.
65. Compare Chafee Z Jr, 'Amending the Constitution to cripple treaties' (1952) 12 *Louisiana Law Review* 345.

66. Henkin L, ' "International concern" and the treaty power of the United States' (1969) 63 *American Journal of International Law* 272 at 274.
67. [1929] *Proceedings of the American Society of International Law* 194 at 196. Compare *Koowarta v. Bjelke-Petersen* (1982) 153 CLR 168 at 216–17 per Stephen J.
68. The relevant clause of the proposed Amendment stated: 'A treaty shall become effective as internal law in the United States only through legislation which would be valid in the absence of treaty.' Section 1, SJ Res 43, 16 February 1953. See also Section 2, S J Res 1, 15 June 1953.
69. As Covey Oliver stated: 'The hindsight of history shows that the basic issue was not really one of federalism ... The real fight was as to what treaties should be used for. The neoisolationists did not object to the classic powers of princes to make treaties about alliances, war, and peace and other remote things ... [T]hey did not want the supremacy clause used to authorise legislation that would override the outrageous evasions of the post-Civil War amendments to the Constitution (and their implementing legislation) that had come to be the internal law of the United States.' Oliver CT, 'The enforcement of treaties by a federal state' (1974) 141 *Academie de droit international Recueil des Cours* 331 at 387.
70. See Dulles JF, 'The challenge of our time: peace with justice' (1953) 39 *American Bar Association Journal* 1063 at 1064.
71. See *Public Papers of the Presidents of the United States: Dwight D Eisenhower, 1953*, Washington: US Government Printing Office, 1960 at 510; Eisenhower DD, *The White House years: mandate for change, 1953–1956*, Heinemann, London, 1963 at 277–85; Ferrell RH, ed., *The diary of James C Hagerty: Eisenhower in Mid-course*, Indiana University Press, Bloomington, 1983 at 5–14; *Department of State, Foreign Relations of the United States 1952–1954*, Vol I, US Government Printing Office, Washington, 1983 at 1782–856; Reichard GW, 'Eisenhower and the Bricker Amendment' (1974) 6 *Prologue* 88; Tananbaum DA, 'The Bricker Amendment controversy: its origins and Eisenhower's role' (1985) 9 *Diplomatic History* 73.
72. See Dulles JF, 'The making of treaties and executive agreements' (1953) 28 *US Department of State Bulletin* 591; US Congress Senate Committee on the Judiciary, *Hearings on S J Res 1 & 43 before a subcommittee of the Senate Committee on the Judiciary*, 83d Cong, 1st Sess, US Government Printing Office, Washington, 1953 at 825–9; Gerson LL, *John Foster Dulles*, Cooper Square Publishers, New York, 1967 at 118–22.
73. *US Constitution*, Art 2, s. 2, cl 2.
74. *US Constitution*, Art I, s. 3, cl 1.
75. *US Constitution*, Amendment XVII.
76. *Treaty of Peace between the Allied and Associated Powers and Germany, Versailles*, 28 June 1919, 225 CTS 188, 5 Wiktor 1.
77. For example 139 *Congressional Record* S16712 (daily edn, 20 November 1993) [*North American Free Trade Agreement*, Washington, Ottawa, Mexico, 8, 11, 14, 17 December 1992, 32 ILM 296, 605; Can TS 1994 No 2].
78. See Ackerman B and Golove D, 'Is NAFTA constitutional ?' (1995) 108 *Harvard Law Review* 799.
79. The term originates in McDougal MS and Lans A, 'Treaties and congressional-executive or presidential agreements: interchangeable instruments of national policy' (1945) 54 *Yale Law Journal* 181 and 534.

6

Restitution of unauthorised government exactions: a matter of public law principle or judicial expediency?

Peter Butler

Introduction

The relationship between ruler and ruled, state and subject, was a question that occupied much of Darrell Lumb's writings. Likewise, the clear imperative to uphold the precepts of the rule of law[1] was a theme that, I recall from undergraduate days, permeated his lectures in Introduction to Law, Constitutional Law and Jurisprudence, and animated his unswerving commitment, as a true jurist, towards providing the foundation for the legal respect for human dignity. Both these subjects are relevant to the question that I consider in this paper, in wishing to pay my own tribute to him. That question is — should a subject under the general law in Australia be able to recover back from the government or other public authority taxes or other imposts on the simple ground that they have been levied without legislative authority?

The absence of legislative authority may have been caused by the public authority purporting to effect an exaction under state or federal legislation which is constitutionally ultra vires, having been made without or contrary to or in excess of the powers conferred by statute. The exactions may have been required under regulations which may be determined to be beyond the regulation-making power conferred by statute. Local government authorities may require the payment of rates and charges unlawfully in excess of their powers to make by-laws. At any level of government public officials may insist on the payment of monies on the basis of an erroneous interpretation of the legislative authority. All such situations may be regarded as constituting an unlawful demand or exaction.[2] Yet, by an unfortunate development private law principles governing relations between subject and subject have been imported into what is clearly the public law area. As a result, the focus for establishing restitutionary liability has not been on the unlawfulness of the public authority's exaction, but on the payer's intention,[3] and whether it has been affected by any vitiating or qualifying circumstance. The case law suggests that the payments are normally made in circumstances where the payer and public authority share the same legal error.[4] In many instances there will be the added aggravating circumstance that the payer was misled by the presumption that the statute, regulation or by-law was validly enacted.[5] In some instances the public authority has engaged in some form of compulsion.[6] The traditional general rule that developed under English common law denied recovery for money paid under a mistake of law, whether the payer made the payment spontaneously or was misled as to the legal position into paying. However, money paid under a mistake of fact or under certain forms of compulsion has generally been recoverable. In addition, recovery was available where there has been an agreement or understanding to repay in the event that there is no obligation, or where a right of recovery has been explicitly created by statute.[7]

In Canada,[8] Australia,[9] South Africa,[10] Scotland,[11] and, most recently, England,[12] the highest appellate courts, one by one, have eliminated the distinction between mistakes of law and of fact for the purpose of founding restitutionary liability, and have endorsed restitution by a private payer against a public authority for mistaken payment. It is thus open to a taxpayer to invoke mistake of whatever kind (fact or law) as an unjust factor affording restitutionary relief. In a few instances, a taxpayer may know, or have strong grounds for believing, that the tax demand is invalid; yet it complies with the demand for fear that its commercial reputation will be damaged. That taxpayer cannot claim relief on the basis that its intention was vitiated by mistake.[13] In *Woolwich Equitable Building Society v. Inland Revenue Commissioners*[14] the House of Lords, by a narrow decision, held that, in such circumstances, relief was available on the basis of the public authority's ultra vires or unlawful demand. However, in principle, that ground should govern, even if the public authority has unlawfully exacted in error for other reasons. In *Woolwich* a majority were inclined to the view that there was no valid distinction to be made between taxes or charges exacted because the public authority misconstrued or misapplied a relevant statute or regulation which was valid, and taxes or charges exacted under an ultra vires statute or regulation.[15] In contrast, the majority of the Supreme Court of Canada in *Air Canada v. British Columbia*[16] rejected a right to restitution of tax paid in error of law where the exaction is under an invalid statute rather than on the basis of a misconstruction or misapplication of a statute. In Australia, the High Court has yet to decide whether or not an ultra vires or unlawful demand provides a ground for restitutionary relief, and, if so, the scope of operation of such ground. In the recent decision of *Commissioner of State Revenue (Vic) v. Royal Insurance Australia Ltd*,[17] the court was not required to consider such issue: the overpayments in question had not been made under statutory provisions that were held to be invalid.

This paper argues for recognition of the *Woolwich* principle in Australian public law against the background of existing authority. At the same time it is submitted that a wider view should be taken of the public law principle of recovery which informs *Woolwich*. The principle should cover not just a payment pursuant to an *invalid statute*; it should also embrace any exaction made without the authority of a statute, so as to include payments made pursuant to a misinterpretation of a statute. In so doing, it examines an important distinction, in this context, between private law and public law regimes, and the ascendant policy reasons that, on balance, inform and support the ultra vires ground, or, more precisely, the ground *without legislative authority*. It then considers whether appropriate countervailing defences or bars should be available in the light of potential fiscal disruption.

Existing judicial authorities

England — The Woolwich principle

The plaintiff, a building society, paid tax on interest and dividends as required by the Revenue under regulations. It questioned the validity of the regulations in judicial review proceedings. However, to avoid adverse publicity which might arise for failing to pay and to avoid the danger of incurring penalties, it paid three instalments of tax, but without prejudice to its right to recover those sums if it transpired that the regulations were void. Its challenge was ultimately successful. The Revenue repaid the instalments but refused to repay interest in respect of the period from the respective dates of payment up to the date of judgment. In order to recover interest under s. 35A of the *Supreme Court Act 1981* (UK), Woolwich had to show that the principal was repayable from the dates of the original payments. Woolwich obviously had not been mistaken, nor had it paid with the intention of closing the transaction. It could not prove compulsion, including that by way of a demand colore officii, because the tax had not been paid for performance of a duty. Nor could it show entitlement to interest based on contract. However, it succeeded on appeal by majority, both the English Court of Appeal and the House of Lords recognising a new restitutionary right based solely on payment of money pursuant to an ultra vires demand by a public authority.

The *Woolwich* decision in the House of Lords has been criticised for its lack of clarity as to the unjust factor on which recovery is based.[18] In the House of Lords Lord Goff delivered the principal opinion, with which Lord Browne-Wilkinson expressly and Lord Slynn impliedly agreed.[19] Lord Browne-Wilkinson and Lord Slynn also delivered separate reasons. Lord Browne-Wilkinson shared with Lord Goff a separate majority strand of principle based on failure of consideration.[20] A person pays a tax on the assumption that a liability has accrued due by reason of a demand made pursuant to an Act of Parliament, and that the payment will discharge that liability. If the demand is a nullity there can be no accrued liability, so that the payment is made on a basis which fails. But the true rationale for relief, as Professor Birks has explained,[21] is the unauthorised or unlawful nature of the demand itself which generates the nullity. The injustice lies in the exaction without authority.[22] Lord Browne-Wilkinson and Lord Slynn also found a different third ground of recovery in the notion of compulsion or duress.[23]

Lord Goff advanced five reasons applicable to the Crown and public authorities as supportive of a new restitutionary right. First, the *Bill of Rights 1688*, article 4, establishes the principle that taxes should not be levied without the authority of Parliament. 'Full effect can only be given to that principle if the return of taxes exacted under an unlawful demand can be enforced as a matter of right.'[24] Secondly, the coercive power of the State implicitly backs any demand for taxation. Thirdly, the law as it stood penalised the good citizen who assumed that any demand for tax was lawful, and paid what was asked for.[25] Fourthly, the comparison between the position of the Crown that can recover ipso facto money paid out of the consolidated fund without lawful authority and that of the citizen who could not obtain repayment is 'most unattractive'.[26] Finally, he pointed to a right under European law to repayment of sums levied by a public body contrary to the rules of European Community law.[27]

North American authorities

In North America the prevailing view is to deny a general right of recovery of an unconstitutional tax. This view governs even in jurisdictions which allow recovery based on mistake of law.[28] The position is well illustrated by the approach taken by the Supreme Court of Canada in *Air Canada v. British Columbia.*[29] There Air Canada and a number of other airlines had paid large sums of money to the government of British Columbia under the *Gasoline Tax Act 1968* (BC). That Act as then framed was outside the powers of the state legislature on the ground that it was not a direct tax within the meaning of s. 92 of the *Constitution Act 1867* (Can). The province enacted a new statute that imposed a similar tax that was a valid direct tax, and, by an amendment, sought to make it retrospective and to 'confiscate' the taxes collected previously as 'indirect taxes'. By a majority the Supreme Court held that the amendment was effective to bar the recovery of the unconstitutional taxes. As an additional reason La Forest J (Lamer and L'Heureux-Dube JJ concurring), after recognising the general recoverability of money paid under a mistake of law, rejected a right of recovery in relation to an unconstitutional or ultra vires statute. One exception was conceded: recovery might be permitted where the relationship between the particular taxpayer and the state was 'unjust or oppressive', or involved 'discrimination, oppression, or abuse of authority'. His reasons for a general rule denying recovery, in line with the United States authorities, were pragmatic: because of the potential disruption of government finances that recovery would cause, and to save government from the inefficient course of reimposing the tax on the same or other taxpayers.[30] However, La Forest J added, the rule against recovery of an unconstitutional and ultra vires levy should not apply where a tax is exacted from a taxpayer through a misapplication of the law.[31]

Wilson J, in a strong dissenting judgment, was of the view that mistake should not provide a basis for recovery in relation to moneys paid under unconstitutional legislation.[32] Rather, the principle for recovery lay in the fact that the statute was unconstitutional or ultra vires. She rejected the view that the prospect of fiscal disruption was sufficient to cast the burden of governmental error on the innocent taxpayer, as opposed to taxpayers as a whole, in the following persuasive passage:

> What is the policy that requires such a dramatic reversal of principle? Why should the individual taxpayer, as opposed to taxpayers as a whole, bear the burden of government's mistake? I would respectfully suggest that it is grossly unfair that X, who may not be (as in this case) a large corporate enterprise, should absorb the cost of government's unconstitutional act. If it is appropriate for the courts to adopt some kind of policy in order to protect government against itself (and I cannot say that the idea particularly appeals to me) it should be one which distributes the loss fairly across the public. The loss should not fall on the totally innocent taxpayer whose only fault is that it paid what the legislature improperly said was due. I find it quite ironic to describe such a person as 'asserting a right to disrupt the government by demanding a refund' or 'creating fiscal chaos' or 'requesting a new generation to pay for the expenditures of the old'. By refusing to adopt such a policy the courts are not 'visiting the sins of the fathers on the children'. The 'sin' in this case (if it can be so described) is that of the government, and government has means available to it to protect against the consequences of it. It should not, in my opinion, be done by the courts and certainly not at the expense of the individual taxpayers.[33]

Lord Goff expressed preference for this position in *Woolwich*[34] as did Mason CJ in *Commission of State Revenue v. Royal Insurance Australia Ltd.*[35] Furthermore, as Professor Hogg has argued,[36] the rule against recovery is inconsistent with an earlier Supreme Court of Canada decision, *Amax Potash v. Government of Saskatchewan.*[37] There it was held that the Saskatchewan legislature could not enact a statute purporting to bar the recovery of taxes that had been paid to the Saskatchewan government under an unconstitutional statute. A principle of federalism demanded that a restriction on the province's legislative power to tax could not be evaded by the indirect means of barring recovery of taxes levied in violation of the restriction. It is true that *Amax Potash* did not expressly decide that the taxes paid in that case were recoverable. But, as Professor Hogg observed, it is pointless to deny validity to the province's attempt to make the taxes irrecoverable if the taxes were already irrecoverable anyway.[38]

The Australian position

The leading case in Australia is still *Mason v. New South Wales*,[39] decided almost 40 years ago. The plaintiffs were transport operators who carried goods by road between Victoria and New South Wales. Under the *State Transport (Co-ordination) Act 1931* (NSW) they were required as part of a licensing scheme to pay for permits for their journeys. The plaintiffs made the payments, under protest, at a time when the legal advice in the industry was that the scheme, although it had been upheld as valid by the High Court, would be struck down by the Privy Council as being in violation of s. 92 of the Australian Constitution. Just as in *Woolwich*, then, as indicated by their protestations, there was no question that the plaintiffs proceeded under a mistake of law. Following declaration by the Privy Council that the scheme was indeed invalid as being in violation of s. 92,[40] the plaintiffs sought recovery of the amount of their payments. The majority of the High Court upheld their claim. While the actual ratio is by no means clear, it would seem to be based on private law duress, consisting in the plaintiffs' apprehension that, if they did not obtain licences, their vehicle would be seized under powers purportedly bestowed by the unconstitutional Act.[41]

At the outset Kitto J identified the question as one to be resolved according to private law principles — 'the same body of law as would govern the case if the parties were subject and subject'.[42] He recognised that a person who pays in response to the requirements of an invalid statute will not be regarded as having made the payment under duress just because he was obeying the de facto command of a legislature. However, duress may be found inhering in an Act which contains provisions which attach to non-payment consequences other than a bare liability to be sued.[43] Menzies J quoted a statement of O'Connor J in *Sargood Bros v. The Commonwealth*[44] that regarded 'payments thus demanded colore officii as being made under duress', noting that it was made in a case where there was a well-recognised power of seizure to enforce the demand which was made. He identified the situation in *Mason*, not as one where the money was demanded under colour of an office, but rather 'as demanded under colour of an Act of Parliament'. But he regarded the same principle as applicable in each case. 'The ultimate question is whether payment was made voluntarily or under compulsion'. *Hooper v. Exeter Corporation* (demand under colour of private Act) could properly be cited for this general proposition.[45] Later, however, unlike Kitto J, he watered down the duress principle that compulsion inheres in an Act of Parliament that contains a power of seizure; he conceded the possibility that, if nothing had been proved beyond the mere existence of such a power, that would not have been enough to prove that the payments were involuntary. He thus ultimately fell back on his acceptance of the finding that the plaintiffs believed that their vehicles would be seized.[46]

Dixon CJ alone expressed doubt whether the law to be applied in the present case was private law, the law relating to the recovery by one subject from another. He first emphasised that the demand was made with the full authority of the State under the terms of a public general statute which was later held to be constitutionally invalid.[47] He then reiterated his reservations that he had not been able completely to reconcile himself with the view that if the weight of a de facto governmental authority manifested in a money demand was not resisted, the money belonged to the Crown, unless the payment was the outcome of some recognised form of duress.[48] He most likely had in mind the general constitutional principle enshrined in the *Bill of Rights* that no moneys can be exacted by government without legislative authority.[49]

Reluctantly, he deferred to modern English authority:[50] 'But English authority seems now to say that moneys paid to the Crown as and for taxes cannot be recovered from the Crown upon its turning out that the moneys were not exigible notwithstanding that they were demanded by the Crown, unless the circumstances were such that they would be recoverable between subject and subject, e.g., as involuntary payments or payments made under a mistake of fact'. Shorn of those cases that turned on the application of private law principles (which would now include recovery for mistake of law), the logical inference to be drawn from Dixon CJ's judgment is that the right to recovery comes back to the question whether the moneys are recoverable from the Crown or public authority because the law did not authorise the Crown or public authority to collect the moneys.[51] This is borne out by his approach a short time later in *Cam & Sons Pty Ltd v. Ramsay*.[52]

Cam is a case that has been for the most part, overlooked and, in my opinion, underrated. It concerned a claim by a fish vendor for recovery of moneys charged as commission by a statutory marketing authority under the *Fisheries and Oyster Farms Act 1935* on all fish that was required to be brought to and sold in the fish market. In making payments to the marketing authority, the company deviated from what the law prescribed for its own advantage in making an arrangement to sell its fish with officers at the authority. In denying recovery Dixon CJ emphasised that the moneys in question would have been receivable by the authority had the law been observed.[53] In the course of his judgment, in which Kitto J and Windeyer J concurred, Dixon CJ first identified cases not covered by the question at hand, namely colore officii cases, and the case of an exaction under a threat of some consequence not sanctioned by law such as *Mason*. He then expounded public law principles in which an injustice occurs where the government acts outside its authority in exacting from the subject:

> There cannot, of course, be any taxation of the subject without Act of Parliament and that constitutional principle has been treated as settled by the fourth declaration contained in the *Bill of Rights* … No one denies the general constitutional principle that no moneys can be exacted by government without legislative authority and without such authority no moneys can be demanded or raised by government as a condition of exercising a power or discretion to the exercise of which the subject is entitled or giving effect to a right with which he is invested by law.[54]

In that exposition, given in the context of a restitutionary claim, he has skilfully absorbed and refined the principles of the earlier identified cases, based on notions of duress, into a broader public law principle that is based on the absence of legislative authority. However, in a third decision of the High Court, *Bell Bros Pty Ltd v. Shire of Serpentine-Jarrahdale,* Kitto J, who provided the majority reasoning for the court, Barwick J and Menzies J agreeing, declined to accept counsel's (J L Toohey QC's) submission that earlier cases, including *Cam,* put the right of recovery on a much broader (public law) basis,[55] and placed renewed emphasis on private law principles.[56] There the court allowed restitution in respect of fees paid for licences to quarry on private land. Barwick J, in concurring with Kitto J's reasons, agreed that the payments were obtained by 'that kind of extortion commonly covered by the description of payments exacted colore officii'.[57]

Since the decisions of *Air Canada* and *Woolwich* the High Court has not been required to consider in direct focus whether the *Woolwich* principle forms part of the corpus of Australian law. In cases where the recovery of taxes has been in issue, the Court has been careful to acknowledge the existence of the principle, but has distinguished it from the case under consideration. Such a case is *Royal Insurance*,[58] which provides an instructive insight into the scope of operation of the *Woolwich* principle. *Royal Insurance* was concerned with the recoverability by an insurance company, Royal, of overpaid taxes, that is, any taxes paid for which there is no legal liability as well as excessive payments of those which the payer is liable to pay. The overpayments occurred as a result of two amendments to the *Stamps Act 1958* (Vic), that abolished stamp duty on workers' compensation insurance. The Act contained a general provision,

s. 111(1), stating that where the chief revenue officer 'finds in any case that duty has been overpaid he may refund to the [payer] the amount of duty to be overpaid'. The majority of the Court, Brennan J, with Toohey and McHugh JJ concurring, held that s. 111(1) contained a power which had to be exercised in the subject payer's favour, once an over-payment was found to have been made and the Commissioner came under 'a legal liability to refund the amount'.[59] That liability was founded on private law restitutionary principles. Mason CJ held that the s. 111(1) power should not be regarded as authority to refuse a refund which a taxpayer is entitled to according to the principles of the general law.[60] One claim concerned duty that Royal continued to pay upon certain premiums in ignorance that liability had been abolished by the statutory amendments in relation to those premiums. Such payments were made under a mistake of law, not by reason of an unlawful exaction. Absent an honest claim of right to retain the tax because the Commissioner was 'taken to have known at all material times that the statutory liability had been repealed and that she had no entitlement to retain these amounts',[61] the majority found she was liable to refund the overpayment. However, due to an oversight the initial abolishing amendment Act only applied to 'wages policies'. Stamp duty on an overlooked second kind of policy known as a 'cost plus policy' was not abolished until some two years later by a second amending Act, which was given retrospective effect. Royal paid a large amount of duty in respect of cost plus premiums during the period in which it was lawfully payable. That second amending Act made no express provision for the refunding of duty paid in respect of the receipt of cost plus premiums during the period that the amendment operated with retrospective effect. The majority held that, in relation to that large amount paid for cost plus policies during that period, there was no mistake affecting the payment. However, in order to give retrospective effect to the second amendment, it was necessary to impose an implied statutory duty on the revenue to refund the amount of the payments made during the retrospective period of operation.[62] The majority regarded the payments in question as being 'quite different in principle' from those in *Air Canada* and *Woolwich*, which had been made under statutory provisions that were held to be invalid.[63] Moreover, by reason of the retrospective operation of the second amendment, it could not be said that any of the duty overpaid could be described as paid 'under the authority or purported authority of any Act', so as to fall within the more restrictive twelve month period of limitation prescribed for the bringing of recovery action against the Crown.[64] It also follows that, even if, as I advocate, a wider version of the *Woolwich* principle be declared, it could not be said that such wider version was applicable — it could not be said that at the relevant time of payment any *exaction* had been made without the authority of a statute.

Mason CJ, having reasoned strainedly,[65] in the context of legislation changed by subsequent retrospective legislation, that Royal had made all the payments as a result of a causative mistake of law, was not concerned to examine *Woolwich*. In his view *Woolwich* recognised a prima facie right of recovery based solely on payment of money pursuant to an ultra vires demand by a public authority. He considered that, prima facie, causative mistake was all that was required where the recipient has no legal entitlement to receive or retain the moneys. He went on to consider as possible that 'the absence of any legitimate basis for retention of the money (by a revenue officer) might itself ground a claim for unjust enrichment without the need to show causative mistake on the part of (the payer)'.[66] That proposition would seem questionable in the light of his later view, shared by the other members of the Court, that the imposts sought to be recovered were *not* 'paid under the authority or purported authority of any Act'.[67] In the absence of a factor vitiating the payer's intention where there has not been an exaction or purported exaction without the authority or under pretence of an Act of Parliament, it is difficult to discern an injustice in the receipt by the Revenue of the overpayments made by Royal.[68]

The upshot from *Royal Insurance* is that, in relation to the recovery of overpayments of taxes or other imposts, private law restitutionary rules operate, at least where there is not an unlawful exaction. As regards the situation where there is an unlawful exaction, the majority in *Royal Insurance* adopted a neutral stance in their attitude to the *Woolwich* principle, leaving to the appropriate occasion to choose between the views of the majority and minority of the Supreme Court of Canada in *Air Canada*. However, Mason CJ in the context of rejecting a defence of disruption to public finances found 'compelling' the dissenting views of Wilson J against denying a right of recovery on the ground of adverse fiscal consequences.[69] Other Australian judges have also shown a receptivity to the adoption of the *Woolwich* principle.[70]

A matter of public law principle or judicial expediency?

As a matter of practical necessity society requires that the state, operating through its representative government by the consent of its citizens, appropriates a citizen's property (money) by way of taxation to a consolidated revenue fund, and *in return* provides the citizen with a bundle of public services which cannot be provided on a user pay basis because of the enormous coordination problems involved and the impossibility of achieving unanimous consent about funding ; for example, national security, domestic law enforcement, a passable road system. (A levy by way of tax is to be distinguished from a payment for services rendered.) In addition to the provision of such public services, the revenue raised by taxation enables government to make the transfer payments necessary to guarantee a certain minimum level of well-being and to honour the claims of need, to which a competitive price system gives no consideration.[71] Where there has been an overpayment of taxes it is possible that a large number of taxpayers may be affected. In such circumstances there is an element of public interest telling against repayment.

So, in *Air Canada,* as already noted, La Forest J rejected a right of recovery of unconstitutional and ultra vires levies. The central policy concerns that influenced him to reject recovery as a general rule and that have influenced other North American judges are the potential disruption to government finances and the inefficiency of reimposing a new set of taxes on the same or other taxpayers.[72] Judges in the United Kingdom[73] and in Australia[74] have expressed similar concerns. For example, in the course of upholding the validity of an ad hoc statutory bar to safeguard revenue that had been unlawfully exacted, Starke J observed in *Werrin v. The Commonwealth,* 'The prompt collection of revenues is of the utmost public importance both for the performance of functions of government and the meeting of public liabilities. It would upset public finance unless some safeguards were provided against mistakes in assessment or the illegal exaction and collection of taxes'.[75] More recently the Court hesitated in reconsidering the franchise decisions relating to liquor and tobacco, because it recognised that the States (and Territories) had put in place financial arrangements of great importance in order to finance the operations of government.[76] Nonetheless, principle finally prevailed over expediency in *Ha v. New South Wales,*[77] where the court decreed, as beyond power and invalid, provisions of a state statute which were held to have imposed duties of excise. Once so characterised, the duties, in accordance with s. 90 of the Commonwealth Constitution, fell within the exclusive power of the Commonwealth Parliament. The judgement, the majority acknowledged, had the most serious implications for the revenue of the States and Territories. It elicited a creative legislative rescue package on the part of the Commonwealth for the benefit of the States.[78]

It is my contention that, on balance, the overall public interest can best be served by recognition of a public law rule whereby the subject has a prima facie right of recovery, from the government or other public authorities, of taxes and other imposts that have been levied without authority. I discuss in the next section whether that rule should be subject to appropriate countervailing defences or bars that may be able to be invoked by the public authority in the public interest.[79] As already noted, the principle of paramount constitutional importance that governs the exaction of taxes is declared by the *Bill of Rights*, article 4, that no moneys can be exacted by a government or a public authority without legislative authority.[80] It is from that fundamental constitutional principle that the restitutionary rule stems as a corollary from the necessary requirement of impartial and regular adherence to the principle of legality in the enforcement of taxation laws for the collection of taxes.[81] The rules embodied within the *Bill of Rights*, article 4, and its restitutionary corollary are clearly emanations of a different legal order (public law — the law of legislation) than those rules which govern 'private transactions' between subject and subject (private law — the law of liberty).[82] Recently in *Kleinwort Benson Ltd v. Lincoln City Council* Lord Goff has described the true position as consisting of 'two separate and distinct regimes'.[83] Indeed, that the rules are of a distinctly different order is made manifest by the correlative right of recovery of the state against the citizen where a transfer is made from consolidated revenue without legislative authority.[84] Such a right is automatic, uninformed by private law rules which govern vitiated or qualified transfers of money or other property between subjects. To deny recognition of an automatic right of recovery by the subject against the state in the converse situation is to undermine and distort in this context the integrity of this distinct legal order.

Two additional practical reasons make adherence to the principle of legality necessary: first, to render the government or other public authority properly accountable for its exercise of the grant of exclusive statutory exaction power in regard to the collection of taxes; and, secondly, to encourage ongoing cooperation on the part of citizens in the prompt payment of taxes.

Accountability on the part of government for the exercise of exclusive, extraordinary statutory exactions[85]

Public authorities as created and designed by the state through legislation generally have the *exclusive* legal right to at least the more extreme forms of coercion. The kinds of duress that private bodies and associations can employ is more strictly limited and is regulated both by the private law as supplemented by legislation and also by market forces.[86] It is this crucial distinction that provides the policy rationale for the distinct public law right encapsulated in *Woolwich*, directed to protecting the citizen from the unlawful behaviour of the revenue authorities.[87] There are allied considerations that support a public law duty of accountability. The public law duty to restore unauthorised exactions will foster a disciplined approach to such exactions and accord proper recognition to values of equity and fairness and ethical responsibility on the part of the public authority.[88] These are important considerations, bearing in mind that the only leverage that the citizen can wield is the casting of a single vote at the ballot box every three years or so.

Encouragement of cooperative payment of taxes by the subject[89]

The conditions for a stable and ordered society necessary to achieve liberty depend on maintaining the rule of law. Even in a well-ordered society the coercive powers of the state are to some extent necessary for the attainment of social cooperation. Citizens may lack full confidence in one another to comply with the recognised private rules of just conduct and the legislative commands of the state. A general awareness or suspicion that others may be tempted not to honour their legal duties may eventually cause the system to break down. That is certainly true of a taxation system. The theory is that while the public services provided from taxation revenue are extremely difficult to value in the individual case and will be likely to differ in value between citizens, where the bundle of public services is extensive and randomised, the odd imbalances that appear in individual cases will tend to balance out in the long run. While that is the theory, a senior English judge has described the position differently: 'All rates and taxes are supposed to be expended for the benefit of those who pay them, and some really are so'.[90] It requires little reflection to realise that a tax system that operated on a voluntary basis would be especially unstable. For that reason compulsion is an essential feature of taxation.[91] By a public coercive system of penalties the government removes the grounds for thinking that others are not complying with the rules. Wilson J in *Air Canada* expressed the resultant position in the following words:

> The taxpayer, assuming the validity of the statute as I believe it is entitled to do, considers itself obligated to pay. Citizens are expected to be law-abiding. They are expected to pay their taxes. Pay first and object later is the general rule. The payments are made pursuant to a perceived obligation to pay which results from the combined presumption of constitutional validity of duly enacted legislation and the holding out of such validity by the legislature. In such circumstances I consider it quite unrealistic to expect the taxpayer to make its payments 'under protest'. Any taxpayer paying taxes exigible under a statute which it has no reason to believe or suspect is other than valid should be viewed as having paid pursuant to the statutory obligation to do so.[92]

When taxes have been unlawfully exacted from the subject under such a coercive system, but without authority, a necessary corollary is that the subject has prima facie an automatic right of recovery. To reverse such a principle for policy reasons would sap a taxpayer's confidence in the justice of the rule of law. In the words of Vaisey J in *Sebel Products Ltd v. Commissioners of Customs and Excise*, it would tempt a taxpayer 'to find too ready an excuse (to evade his liability) in the plea that the Revenue Authorities will, if they can, keep in their coffers, if they can get it there, money which the taxpayer was under no obligation to pay to them'.[93] As Vaisey J recognised, a rule that is conducive to such an outcome should be avoided 'in the public interest'. In much the same vein, Wilson J insisted that the burden of an unlawful exaction should be distributed fairly across the public.[94] In reality this may mean in some instances that substantially the same group of taxpayers will be levied subsequently pursuant to a lawful Act. Nonetheless, the insistence on legality communicates an important message of encouragement to the taxpaying subjects in addition to those administering the public Act in question.

The issue which divided the judges in *Woolwich* was whether or not it was appropriate that the old law should be changed judicially or by statutory reform. For Australia, it is submitted that, apart from the persuasive reasoning in the majority decision in *Woolwich* itself, clear authority for a public law right of recovery is to be found in Sir Owen Dixon's judgment in *Cam*, with which Kitto and Windeyer JJ agreed. There is also additional support in Dixon CJ's judgment in *Mason* and also that of Kitto J. While they both ultimately required proof of compulsion, each rightly emphasised the factor that underpins and justifies the distinct public law right. The demand had been made 'with the full authority of the State under the terms of a public general statute' (Dixon CJ);[95] 'under the *de facto* command of a legislature with superadded provisions which attach to non-payment consequences other than a bare liability to be sued' (Kitto J).[96]

Scope of restitutionary rule

As Beatson has persuasively argued, the *Woolwich* principle should apply wherever the sole power of a statutory authority or body to charge is given and is thereby limited by statute or subordinate legislation. The crucial issue is whether the only authority to exact the payment, whether for the provision of services or not, is the statute under which the payee is acting.[97] There must be a levying or exaction of the charge.[98] But just how the levy or exaction is effected should not be determinative. The principle should apply whether the payment is made pursuant to an express or implied demand, a process of self-assessment, or an otherwise manifested expectation of payment on the part of the payee authority.[99] The principle should apply wherever there is an unlawful exaction, that is, an exaction without legislative authority. Thus exactions pursuant to legislation that is constitutionally invalid and those pursuant to a misapplication of a valid statute are equally caught by the principle.[100] On the other hand, payments made for consideration in accordance with a commercial transaction, even where an element of the consideration is arrived at by wrongly assuming the legality of the charge, do not attract the principle.[101]

Countervailing bars or restrictions

The importance to individual citizens of being able to rely on the finality of their private transactions and the security of their receipts has long been recognised by the courts.[102] The task of maintaining a fair balance between a payer who confers an unintended benefit on the payee and the payee who purports to rely on the security of such payment is an ongoing, challenging task. As already noted, similar policy concerns have been recognised as applicable to public authorities. Recognition of the *Woolwich* principle in Australia will have a potential impact on the adequacy of public revenues for the proper provision of public services.

Should, then, there be unrestricted recovery of unlawful exactions as Wilson J supported in her dissenting judgement in *Air Canada*?[103] What possible bars or restrictions are appropriate and feasible in the context of a claim founded on the *Woolwich* principle? The critical moot point that is relevant to these questions is whether a claim for unlawful exactions displaces any other grounds of recovery available.[104] Once it is accepted that the right of recovery encapsulated in *Woolwich* is a public law right of a different legal order — the law of legislation — quite 'separate and distinct' from private law rights between subject and subject, it follows as a matter of logic and principle that the same separate regime — the law of legislation — should govern any countervailing bars or restrictions. Cornish's point sheets home that statutory public authorities that are subject to the *Woolwich* principle do not operate in the commercial marketplace (a position which, for the most part, will hold today).[105] If they make unauthorised exactions and have to repay, it is open to them, unlike the ordinary citizen or business enterprise, to exercise the power, or to seek the support of others to exercise, the power to raise revenue by other authorised legislative means. They may also invoke the power to introduce statutory restrictions and bars, with retrospective effect if necessary,[106] provided they are constitutional.[107] Wilson J recognised this in *Air Canada* when she said, 'The "sin" in this case (if it can be so described) is that of government and only government, and *government has the means available to it to protect against the consequences of it. It should not be by the courts and certainly not at the expense of individual taxpayers*'.[108]

Rather than the North American judicial response of a blanket rule of no recovery of ultra vires taxes because of the possible disruption to public revenue, some commentators who favour recovery of ultra vires taxes have suggested that a special defence of 'extreme disruption of public finances' should be recognised.[109] Cornish finds the notion of such special defence 'unattractive'. 'It would confer a discretion inherently difficult to exercise: and it seems to contain the imperative that, if governments are to exceed their taxing powers, this should be done on the grandest scale'.[110] The inherent flaw in the notion of the defence of 'fiscal disruption' is the difficulty of determining judicially just how much possible fiscal disruption is 'too much'. It was this very difficulty which led La Forest J and the majority in *Air Canada* to favour a general rule denying recovery,[111] but where the ostensible rationale for such denial might, in fact, be unfounded. The reality is that the judicial process and function is simply not fitted or equipped to make an informed judgement about the adequacy of public finances for effecting authorised public services. That is a matter of public policy for parliament ultimately to decide. Mason CJ rightly rejected the recognition of such 'a vague and amorphous defence': 'The remedy for any disruption of public finances occasioned by the recovery of money in conformity with the law of restitution lies in the hands of the legislature. It can determine who is to bare the burden of making up any shortfall in public funds.'[112]

Apart from the defence of fiscal disruption, other possible qualifications to the *Woolwich* principle that have been adopted in some other jurisdictions are also flawed. One such judicial expedient, prospective overruling, has been rejected by the High Court of Australia in *Ha*:

> This court has no power to overrule cases prospectively ... Prospective overruling is ... inconsistent with judicial power on the simple ground that the new regime that would be ushered in when the overruling took effect would alter existing rights and obligations. If an earlier case is erroneous and it is necessary to overrule it, it would be a perversion of judicial power to maintain in force that which is acknowledged not to be the law.[113]

The same reasoning renders inappropriate that judicial technique which was employed by the Irish Supreme Court in *Murphy v. Attorney-General.*[114] Such technique limits (a) the class of plaintiff eligible to recover taxes paid under the unlawful tax to those who had protested by instituting proceedings at the date of the declaration of invalidity, and (b) the amount of taxes recoverable to those paid after the date the government was 'put on notice' of the possible invalidity of the tax by the institution of proceedings challenging the legislation.

What about the defence of change of position?[115] Consistent with the view that the *Woolwich* principle is a 'separate and distinct' public law right, is it appropriate and feasible that this defence, an emanation of the private law restitutionary regime, be able to counter that right? I would argue that this defence is inapplicable. In any event, it is difficult to see how a public authority that has unlawfully exacted money from a citizen, backed by the exclusive coercive power of the state, can assert that it expended those moneys by *reason and only by reason* of their receipt rather than, at least to some extent, in reliance on the power to exact. To ignore the presence of the (unlawful) exaction for the purposes of the defence seems to contradict the policy that calls for recovery. Mason CJ's reference to the availability of the defence in *Royal Insurance* is not inconsistent with that view. It was made with reference to a situation where there was no unauthorised exaction, and which attracted the 'separate and distinct' private law regime.[116] In any event, there is the extreme difficulty of invoking the defence to show that the moneys received into consolidated revenue have, by reason of the receipt, been spent on other than ordinary public services. The English Law Commission has recommended that the defence should not apply to claims for the recovery of ultra vires taxes.[117]

On the other hand, it is considered that restitution will be denied where the honest claim for payment of an unauthorised tax or claim has been contractually compromised.[118] In that situation the countervailing policy of upholding the sanctity of binding agreements and the finality of litigation should prevail. However, the unsatisfactory notion of voluntary payment or submission[119] is inapplicable in actions to recover unauthorised (ultra vires) exactions by public authorities, because the voluntariness of the payer in making the payment is irrelevant where the prima facie basis of recovery is the illegality of the exaction.[120] In *Woolwich* Ralph Gibson LJ in the English Court of Appeal questioned whether it could be demonstrated that a taxpayer knew of the point of the illegality of the exaction and nevertheless made the payment with the apparent intention of not seeking to recover it.[121] Cornish has suggested that such might be the case where the taxpayer can be shown to have made the payment with the intent to bribe or to secure some commercial advantage, such as an exclusive licence, and is willing to pay for it, whether lawful or not.[122] He concurs with those decisions in various jurisdictions which deny recovery in such cases.[123] Is such a result in which the public authority is allowed to retain the payment received colore officii ultimately conducive to the attainment of an environment of integrity for the doing of business with government? Or would such an environment be more readily attained if public authorities were required, on detection of such payments, likewise to pay them back automatically on the basis of an unlawful exaction, or at least, not be permitted to retain them?[124]

Another possible defence that was adopted by La Forest J for the majority in *Air Canada,* but not by Wilson J,[125] is the defence of 'passing on' or 'windfall gain'. The argument is that, if the claimant taxpayer has transferred the burden of the tax to a third party purchaser, recovery should be denied because there is the possibility that the taxpayer will gain a windfall. If there is to be a windfall it should be enjoyed by the revenue. In *Royal Insurance*[126] the High Court rejected the availability of the defence under the general law. However, in *Mutual Pools*[127] it upheld as valid specific legislation which incorporated such a defence in a receptive context, under which the taxpayer was unable to recover where it could not show refundment to the third party purchaser of any of the tax that had been passed on.

Specific legislative schemes for recovery

Australian jurisdictions have many specific legislative schemes that define the terms for recovery of particular overpayments of taxes or other charges.[128] Beatson has noted from *Woolwich* 'that the assumption is that where there is a statutory framework, it replaces the common law within its sphere of application'.[129] This is the Australian experience. For example, in *Chippendale*[130] various sales tax provisions for recovery of overpaid tax were regarded as excluding any general restitutionary rights of recovery. In *SCI Operations*[131] the High Court held that as the right to the repayment of duty paid was based wholly in statute, restitutionary principles could not convert a statutory right to obtain a refund of money into a right to obtain a refund with interest. This approach is entirely appropriate, bearing in mind that the obligation to pay a tax or other charge arises, not from agreement or the common law, but from legislation.[132]

Conclusion

The adoption in Australia of the wide version of the *Woolwich* principle, which I here advocate, will bring the common law into line with the reasonable expectations of ordinary Australian taxpayers, and provide a right to citizens that is commensurate with a public authority's right to recover payments which it had no legislative authority to make. At the same time it will eliminate the citizen's present necessity to surmount unsatisfactory and unsettled concepts that have evolved for 'private transactions', if that citizen wishes to recover an unlawfully exacted tax or charge. Certainly, fiscal disruption to the public authority is a valid concern. But its extent should not be exaggerated, let alone presumed as the rationale for applying a blanket rule denying recovery for ultra vires transactions. Judicial expediency is not called for in this area. The enactment of constitutionally valid legislative regimes is the way forward, supplemented, if necessary, by such legislative restrictions or bars to the recovery of exactions found to be without legislative authority, as is judged necessary by parliament. Such enactments will rightly attract public scrutiny and accountability, and may cause political embarrassment. But a political resolution is the correct and principled outcome of upholding the principle of legality in a constitutional democracy.

Notes

1. See Lumb, 'Legality and Legitimacy: The Limits of the Duty of Obedience to the State' in Alexandrowicz (ed.) Grotian Society Papers 1968, Studies in the History of the Law of Nations, M Nijhoff — The Hague, 1970, p. 52. See also Mason, K, 'The Rule of Law' in Finn (ed.), *Essays on Law and Government, vol 1, Principles and Values* (1995), p. 114; Allen, *Law, Liberty and Justice* (1993), Ch. 2 (The Rule of Law), p. 20; Walker, *The Rule of Law, Foundation of Constitutional Democracy* (1988).
2. *Woolwich Equitable Building Society v. IRC* [1992] 3 WLR 366, 394 per Lord Goff, 413 per Lord Jauncey; see also 381 per Lord Keith.
3. Compare *Mason v. New South Wales* (1958–59) 102 CLR 108, 117 per Dixon CJ.
4. See, for example, *National Pari-Mutuel Association Ltd v. The King* (1930) 47 TLR 110; *Werrin v. The Commonwealth* (1938) 59 CLR 150.
5. *Air Canada v. British Columbia* (1989) 59 DLR (4th) 161, 168–9 per Wilson J; *Woolwich Equitable Building Society v. IRC* [1992] 3 WLR 366, 392–3 per Lord Goff.
6. *Sargood Brothers v. The Commonwealth* (1910) 11 CLR 258; *Mason v. New South Wales* (1959) 102 CLR 108; *Bell Bros Pty Ltd v. Shire of Serpentine–Jarrahdale* (1969) 121 CLR 137.
7. See generally *Woolwich Equitable Building Society v. IRC* [1992] 3 WLR 366, 384–5 per Lord Goff; Law Commission, *Restitution: Mistake of Law and Ultra Vires Public Authority Receipts and Payments*, Law Com No 227, 1994.
8. *Air Canada v. British Columbia* (1989) 59 DLR (4th) 161 (SCC).
9. *David Securities Pty Ltd v. Commonwealth Bank of Australia Ltd* (1992) 175 CLR 353 (HCA); *Commissioner of State Revenue (Vic) v. Royal Insurance Australia Ltd* (1994) 182 CLR 51 (HCA).
10. *Willis Faber Enthoven Pty Ltd v. Receiver of Revenue 1992* (4) SA 202 (A).
11. *Morgan Guarantee Trust Company of NY v. Lothian Regional Council* (1995) SLT 299.
12. *Kleinwort Benson Ltd v. Lincoln County Council* [1998] 3 WLR 1095 (HL).
13. See *Woolwich Equitable Building Society v. IRC* [1992] 3 WLR 366.
14. [1992] 3 WLR 366.
15. [1992] 3 WLR 366, 381 per Lord Keith, 394 per Lord Goff, 413 per Lord Jauncey, 421 per Lord Slynn; see also A Burrows, *The Law of Restitution* (London Butterworths, 1993), 353.
16. (1989) 59 DLR (4th) 161.
17. (1994) 182 CLR 51 at 67 per Mason CJ, 90 n 96 per Brennan J with whom Toohey and McHugh JJ agreed, 101 per Dawson J.
18. See McKendrick, 'Restitution of Unlawfully Demanded Tax' [1993] LMCLQ 88; Fitzgerald, 'Ultra Vires as an Unjust Factor in the Law of Unjust Enrichment' (1993) 2 Griffith LR 1.
19. [1992] 3 WLR 366, 390, 396 (Lord Goff), 414, 416 (Lord Browne-Wilkinson), 418, 421 (Lord Slynn).

20. Ibid., at 385–6 (Lord Goff), 414–15 (Lord Browne-Wilkinson).
21. Birks, 'When Money is Paid in Pursuance of a Void Authority — A Duty to Repay?' [1992] PL 580, 588.
22. Suarez, *De Legibus,* 1,8 quoted by Lumb, op cit., n 1, 64–5.
23. [1992] 3 WLR 366, 415 (Lord Browne-Wilkinson), 421 (Lord Slynn).
24. Ibid., 389.
25. Ibid., 389.
26. See *Auckland Harbour Board v. R* [1924] AC 318 followed in Australia in *Commonwealth v. Burns* [1971] VR 825; *Attorney-General v. Gray* [1977] 1 NSWLR 406.
27. Case 199/82 *Amministrazione delle Finanze dello Stato v. Spa San Georgio* [1983] ECR 3695.
28. See Field, *The Effect of an Unconstitutional Statute* (1971) Ch 10; Pannam, 'The Recovery of Unconstitutional Taxes in Australia and the United States' (1964) 42 Texas L Rev 177; *Mercury Machine Importing Corp v. City of New York* 154 NE 2d 400 (1957)(NYCA); Palmer, *Law of Restitution* (1978) 9.16, 14.20.
29. (1989) 59 DLR (4th) 161.
30. Ibid., at 195.
31. Ibid., at 197.
32. Ibid., at 168.
33. Ibid., at 169.
34. [1992] 3WLR at 392–3.
35. (1994) 182 CLR 51at 68.
36. Hogg, *Liability of the Crown* (2nd edn, 1989), p. 184.
37. [1977] 2 SCR 576.
38. Hogg, op cit. n 35, p. 184.
39. (1959) 102 CLR 108.
40. In *Hughes & Vale Pty Ltd v. New South Wales* (1954) 93 CLR 1.
41. See (1959) 102 CLR 108, at 115–16, 117 (Dixon CJ), 123–4 (Fullager J), 129 (Kitto J), 130–1 (Taylor J), 132–3, 135 (Menzies J), 146 (Windeyer J).
42. Ibid., at 125.
43. Ibid., at 126.
44. (1910) 11 CLR 258, at 276–7.
45. (1959) 102 CLR 108, at 134–5.
46. Ibid., at 135.
47. Ibid., at 116.
48. Ibid., at 117.
49. See *Commonwealth and the Central Wool Committee v. Colonial Combing, Spinning and Weaving Co Ltd* (1922) 31 CLR 421, at 444, 462–3 (Isaacs J), 474–5 (Higgins J). Dixon appeared as senior counsel in the case.
50. (1959) 102 CLR 108, at 117. Dixon CJ was no doubt guided by that 'certain value' to be set on 'consistency of decision in the British Commonwealth and upon preserving the unity and uniformity of the common law': see Dixon, 'Concerning Judicial Method' in *Jesting Pilate* (1965), p. 152.
51. See *Cam & Sons Pty Ltd v. Ramsay* (1960) 104 CLR 247, at 257 (Dixon CJ). See also Merrals, 'Restitutionary Recovery of Taxes After the Royal Insurance Case', in McInnes (ed.), *Restitution; Developments in Unjust Enrichment* (Law Book Co., 1996), p. 117 at p. 123.

52. (1960) 104 CLR 247.
53. Ibid., at 258.
54. Ibid., at 258. See also Windeyer J, at 272, who made reference to both the Bill of Rights and the Act of Settlement.
55. (1969) 121 CLR 137 at 138–9.
56. Ibid., at 145–6.
57. Ibid., at 142.
58. (1994) 182 CLR 51. See also *Mutual Pools & Staff Pty Ltd v. FCT* (1994) 119 ALR 577; *Commonwealth of Australia v. SCI Operations Pty Ltd* (1998) 152 ALR 624.
59. Ibid., at 87–88.
60. Ibid., at 64.
61. Ibid., at 89. The defence of 'honest claim of right' was first suggested by Brennan J alone as a means of limiting recovery of payments made in error of law in *David Securities Pty Ltd v. Commonwealth Bank of Australia* (1992) 175 CLR 353, at 399, rather than through a notion of 'voluntary payment', which the majority favoured. The defence has, correctly, in my respectful opinion, been recently rejected by the House of Lords in *Kleinwort Benson Ltd v. Lincoln* CC [1998] 3 WLR 1095, 1124 (Lord Goff), 1151 (Lord Hope). The contrived application of the defence in Royal Insurance to permit recovery has been criticised: Merrals, op cit. n 51, 120–1.
62. Ibid., at 89–90.
63. Ibid., at 90 n (96).
64. Ibid., at 92.
65. Ibid., at 67. See McInnes, *Mistaken Payments Return to the High Court: Commissioner of Revenue v. Royal Insurance* (1996) 22 Mon Uni LR 209, 217–18, 219–20. But see now *Kleinwort Benson Ltd v. Lincoln CC* [1998] 3 WLR 1095, where a majority of the House of Lords, Lords Goff, Hoffman and Hope, have adopted a similar analysis of what constitutes a mistaken payment, but in the different context of judicial development, not legislative change.
66. Ibid., at 67.
67. Ibid., at 80.
68. See McInnes, op cit., n 65, 222–5; but contrast Voon, 'Restitution from Government in Australia: Woolwich and its Necessary Boundaries' (1998) 9 PLR 15, 18, who suggests that, if *Woolwich* were accepted in Australia, the judgments in *Royal Insurance* would become redundant. An overpayment would be prima facie recoverable, subject to applicable defences.
69. (1994) 182 CLR 51 at 68.
70. *State Bank of New South Wales v. Commissioner of Taxation* (Cwlth) (1995) 62 FCR 371, at 378 (Wilcox J); *Chippendale Printing Co Pty Ltd v. Commonwealth* (1996) 62 FCR 347, at 366 (Lehane J); *SCI Operations Pty Ltd v. Commonwealth of Australia* (1996) 139 ALR 595 (Sackville J) ('payments made pursuant to the provisions of an invalid statute').
71. See generally Epstein, *Simple Rules for a Complex World* (1994), Chs 6 and 7; Rawls, *A Theory of Justice* (OUP, 1980 reprint), pp. 274–84.
72. See supra, n 30.
73. *Henderson v. Folkstone Waterworks Co Ltd* (1885) 1 TLR 329 (Coleridge CJ England); *Glasgow Corporation v. Lord Advocate* 1959 SC 203, 230–31 (Lord Clyde Scotland); *Woolwich Equitable Building Society v. IRC* [1992] 3 WLR 366, 413–14 (Lord Jauncey).

74. *Sargood Bros v. The Commonwealth* (1910) 11 CLR 258 (Isaacs J); *Werrin v. The Commonwealth* (1938) 59 CLR 150, 163 (Starke J).
75. (1938) 59 CLR 150, 163.
76. *Capital Duplicators Pty Ltd v. Australian Capital Territory* (No 2) (1993) 178 CLR 561, 563.
77. (1997) ALJR 1080; (1997) 146 ALR 355.
78. See the *Franchise Fees Windfall Tax (Collection) Act 1997* (Cwlth), the *Franchise Fees Windfall Tax (Imposition) Act 1997* (Cwlth), and the *Franchise Fees Windfall Tax (Consequential Amendments) Act 1997* (Cwlth).
79. The majority of writers have favoured the adoption of this approach. For Australia: see Mason & Carter, *Restitution Law in Australia* (1995), p. 767; Voon, op cit. n 68, 19. But opposing views have also been expressed: see Wells, 'Restitution from the Crown: Private Rights and Public Interest' (1994) Adel LRev 191, who asserts that a rule against restitution from government subject to defined exceptions is preferable in Australia because of our federal polity. See also Fitzgerald, op cit., n 18.
80. See *Attorney-General v. Wilts United Dairies Ltd* (1921) 37 TLR 884, 886 (Atkin LJ); *Commonwealth v. Colonial Combing, Spinning and Weaving Co Ltd* (1992) 31 CLR 421, 443–4, 463–6 (Isaacs J), 473–4 (Higgins J); Birks, 'Restitution from the Executive: A Tercentenary Footnote to the Bill of Rights' in Finn (ed.), *Essays on Restitution* (1990), p164.
81. *Cam & Sons Pty Ltd v. Ramsay* (1960) 104 CLR 247, 257–8 (Dixon CJ), 272 (Windeyer J); *Woolwich Equitable Building Society v. IRC* (1992) 3 WLR 366, 389 (Lord Goff).
82. Hayek, as part of a general theory of law, has drawn an illuminating distinction between two types of orders, *cosmos* (grown order) and *taxis* (made order). A *cosmos* is an endogenous order resulting from internal processes. Examples of *cosmoi* include language, the market, moral systems, and systems of customary laws. A *taxis* is an exogenous order created for a purpose, hence deliberately designed. The supreme example of this type of order is government. Other examples include the school, the university, the factory, the church. The two types of orders are defined and sustained by different types of rules — *nomos* and *thesis*. *Taxis* or organisation, being directed at particular ends, is sustained by rules called *theseis* — the law of legislation — that are aimed at effecting or facilitating such ends. In contrast, the *cosmos*, being end-independent, is sustained by rules of a fundamentally different nature called *nomoi* — rules of just conduct — making up the law of liberty, that are recognised and declared by the judiciary. Financial legislation is a classic early example of *thesis* enacted for the government of the state by representative bodies. Certain enactments of a parliament, of a corrective or reformatory kind, while taking their force from the statutory instrument at a certain date are end-independent and become part of the *cosmos*. See Hayek, *Law Legislation and Liberty* (1982 revised reprint), vol 1, esp pp. 35–9, 124–7, 88–9; and see the useful summary by Ratnapala, 'The Trident Case and the Evolutionary Theory of FA Hayek', (1993) 13 OJLS 201, 205–18.
83. [1998] 3 WLR 1095, 1122.
84. See cases at n 26 supra.
85. See Cornish, 'Colour of Office: Restitutionary Redress against Public Authority' (1987) 1 J Mal & Comp L 41; Birks, op cit. n 80, p. 164 at p. 203; Law Com CP No. 120, 3.14, 3.54.
86. Rawls, *A Theory of Justice* (OUP, 1980 reprint), p. 236.

87. Beatson, 'Restitution of Taxes, Levies and other Imposts: Defining the Extent of the Woolwich Principle' (1993) 109 LQR 401.
88. Cf. *R. v. Tower Hamlets London Borough Council,Ex Parte Chetnik Developments Ltd* [1988] AC 858.
89. See generally Rawls, op cit., n 86, pp. 240–41.
90. *City of Halifax v. Nova Scotia Scotia Car Works Ld* [1914 AC 992, 998 (PC: Lord Sumner).
91. Ibid., 998; *Matthews v. Chicory Board* (Vic) (1938) 60 CLR 263, 276 (Latham CJ).
92. (1989) 59 DLR (4th) 161, 169.
93. [1949] 1 Ch 409, 411.
94. (1989) 59 DLR (4th) 161, 169.
95. (1959) 102 CLR 108, 116.
96. Ibid., 127.
97. Beatson, op cit., n 87, 415–16; see also Law Commission, op cit. n 7, 6.40–6.45.
98. *Commissioner of State Revenue v. Royal Insurance* (1994) 182 CLR 51, 90 n (96).
99. Burrows, op cit., n 15, pp. 356–7; Beatson, op cit., n 87, 405–6.
100. See Mason & Carter, op cit., n 79, [2029].
101. *Esso Australia Resources Ltd v. Gas & Fuel Corp of Victoria* [1993] 2 VR 99; see also *Air India v. The Commonwealth* [1977] 1 NSWLR 449.
102. See, for example, *David securities Pty Ltd v. Commonwealth Bank of Australia* (1992) 66 ALJR 768, 776, 784, 786; *Kleinwort Benson Ltd v. Lincoln CC* [1998] 3 WLR 1095, 1122, 1139, 1151.
103. (1989) 59 DLR (4th) 161, 169–70.
104. Cf. Law Commission, op cit. n 7, 10.2, and n 1 thereto.
105. Cornish, op cit. n 85, 52–3.
106. See, for example, *Mutual Pools & Staff Pty Ltd v. FCT* (1994) 119 ALR 577 (defence of 'passing on' upheld, where claimant taxpayer had 'passed on' the tax to purchasers and had not refunded it to them); see also *Werrin v. Commonwealth* (1938) 59 CLR 150 (retrospective ad hoc statutory bar upheld); and see the legislation referred to at n 78.
107. See *Commissioner of Road Transport v. Antill Ranger & Co Ltd* (1956) 94 CLR 177; *Barton v. Commissioner for Road Transport* (1957) 97 CLR 633.
108. (1989) 59 DLR (4th) 161, 169 (emphasis added).
109. McCamus (1983)17UBCL Rev 233, 273.
110. Cornish, op cit. n 85, 52.
111. (1989) 59 DLR (4th) 161, 196.
112. (1994) 182 CLR 51, 68. For a similar view, see *Werrin v. Commonwealth* (1938) 59 CLR 150, 163 (Starke J): 'It might be necessary ... where apparently large sums of money were involved, to safeguard revenue that had been paid and collected and protect it in the manner prescribed by s. 12A, and *of that Parliament alone can judge.*' (emphasis added).
113. (1997) 71 ALJR 1080, at 1093 (Brennan CJ, McHugh, Gummow Kirby JJ).
114. [1982] 1 IR 241, adopting the technique of 'novelty stop' as used in the European Court of Justice: *Defrenne v. SABENA Case C-43/75* [1976] ECR 455.
115. See Mason & Carter, op cit. n 79, ch 24; Birks, in McInnes (ed.), op cit. n 51, ch. 3, with commentary by Bryan, ch. 4.
116. (1994) 182 CLR 51, 65.
117. Law Commission, op cit. n 7, 11.10 to 11.22.
118. *Commissioner of State Revenue v. Royal Insurance Australia Ltd* (1994) 182 CLR 51, 87.
119. See McInnes, op. cit., n 65, 228–31.

120. See *Woolwich BS v. IRC* [1991] 3 WLR 790, 836–7 (CA: Ralph Gibson LJ).
121. Ibid., 837.
122. Cornish, op cit. n 85, 52.
123. See, for example, *Gordon Foster v. Langley Corp* (1980) 102 DLR (3d) 780; *Bayview Gardens Pty Ltd v. Musgrave SC* [1989] 1 Qd R 1.
124. A similar question would seem to have been implicitly raised obiter by Menzies J in *Cam & Sons Pty Ltd v. Ramsay* (1960) 104 CLR 247, 271–2.
125. (1989) 59 DLR (4th) 161, 193–4 (La Forest J), 170–1 (Wilson J).
126. (1994) 182 CLR 51, 69–79 (Mason CJ), 90–91 (Brennan J), 101(Dawson J).
127. (1994) 119 ALR 577.
128. See Mason & Carter, op cit. n 79, [2031] [2032].
129. Beatson, op cit., n 87, 418.
130. (1996) 62 FCR 347.
131. (1998) 152 ALR 624.
132. See *Chippendale v. Cmr of Taxation* (1996) 62 FCR 347, 359 (Tamberlin J); see also the text at n 82 and comment therein.

7

Constitutional Convention 1998 and the future of constitutional reform

George Winterton

Introduction

Australia's record of constitutional reform at the national level is often considered poor. In almost a century of increasingly rapid social, economic and technological change, the Australian electors have (so far) approved only eight of the 42 constitutional amendment proposals put to referendum, and none concerned truly fundamental matters. But when compared with the United States, Australia's record appears less dismal. The United States Constitution has been amended only twelve times this century, with only ten amendments having lasting effect since the 18th Amendment (1919) was repealed by the 21st (1933). Australia's record of eight amendments appears comparable to America's ten, although the latter were generally of greater importance than the former.

In comparing the constitutional amendment record in the two countries, account must obviously be taken of their different amendment processes. Alterations to the Commonwealth Constitution must be approved by both the Commonwealth Parliament (by absolute majorities in each House or by either House twice with a three-month interval) and a double-majority of the electors at a referendum (a national majority and a majority of the electors in four States). The Bill must finally be submitted to the Governor-General for the Royal Assent.[1] The methods of amendment specified by the United States Constitution comprise a complex series of alternative procedures reflecting (like its Australian counterpart) the foundational principles of federalism, representative government and popular sovereignty, although direct popular approval is not included. Amendments must be proposed either by two-thirds majorities in each House of Congress or by a Convention called by Congress at the instance of two-thirds of the State legislatures. The former has been the sole method employed; although frequently advocated, no federal Convention has been held since 1787. Proposed amendments must be ratified by either the legislatures or Conventions in three-quarters of the States, the appropriate mode being stipulated by Congress.[2] To date, only one amendment has been ratified by State Conventions: the 21st (1933), which repealed the 18th.

Notwithstanding the similarity in the number of amendments adopted, the experience of the two nations diverges sharply in other respects. First, while 34 proposed amendments were rejected by the ratifiers in Australia (the electors), only six have been rejected in the entire history of the United States, and only three this century.[3] Since an enormous number of amendments have been proposed by members of Congress (and, of course, by others) on a vast range of subjects,[4] the United States Congress clearly acts as a finer sieve than the Commonwealth Parliament. This is, no doubt, largely attributable to the higher threshold for passage (a two-thirds as compared with an absolute majority of the members of each House), but also to the stronger party discipline in Australia. The governing party can effectively ensure that any amendment it proposes will be put to referendum, where it will lose unless it enjoys at least bipartisan support, but neither American party can guarantee the support even of its own members in Congress, let alone a two-thirds majority. Both nations effectively require bipartisan support (at least) for approval of constitutional amendments but, while the United States effectively imposes this requirement for passage in the federal legislature (if not also for ratification by State legislatures), Australia effectively requires bipartisan support only at the ratification stage. It is the relatively high number of proposed amendments which emerge from the Commonwealth Parliament and consequently low proportion of successful referenda (19 per cent) which makes Australia's record of eight amendments appear dismally low when compared with the United States' 20th Century ratification rate of twelve out of fifteen (80 per cent).

Secondly, Commonwealth constitutional reform has been examined by several official Conventions, Commissions and Committees, although relatively few successful amendments have emerged therefrom. The Constitution has been examined by a Royal Commission (1927–29), a Joint Commonwealth Parliamentary Committee (1956–59), two non-popularly elected Conventions (1942 and 1973–85), a Commission assisted by five committees (1985–88), and now a semi-popularly elected Convention (1998). It is striking in contrast that, notwithstanding many calls for a second federal Convention[5] and occasional advocacy for establishing a Constitutional Commission,[6] both of which have been employed extensively in the American States, in more than 200 years the United States has convened neither. It is interesting to speculate why the Commonwealth should have appointed six official constitutional reform bodies this century while the United States has appointed none. Moreover, at the State level the position is almost the converse: American State constitutions have been subjected to frequent and wide-ranging examination and reform, while (except recently in Queensland and Western Australia) the Australian

States have rarely even considered, let alone undertaken, extensive constitutional revision. As an American commentator remarked:

> The national amending process stands in stark contrast to the state experience, where amendments and full-scale revisions are quite common. ... Thus, by 1968, over 4,888 state constitutional amendments had been adopted, with at least one individual state constitution [Louisiana's Charter of 1921] having had over 500 emendations. Moreover, by 1978, more than 145 state constitutions had been adopted, Louisiana alone having had a total of eleven.[7]

This is not the place for a detailed examination of the reasons underlying the contrasting experiences at the national level, noted above, but a few observations may be proffered. First, Americans have probably heeded James Madison's warning regarding the destabilising effect of frequent constitutional change:

> [A]s every appeal to the people would carry an implication of some defect in the government, frequent appeals would in great measure deprive the government of that veneration, which time bestows on every thing, and without which perhaps the wisest and freest governments would not possess the requisite stability.[8]

Nevertheless, American constitutional conservatism must not be overstated. Not only has major constitutional reform been advocated quite frequently — there have been 'about forty serious proposals for major constitutional revisions' since Reconstruction[9] — but the Bill of Rights of 1791 (Amendments 1–10) and the Reconstruction Amendments of 1865–1870 (Amendments 13–15) represented radical constitutional alterations. As Justice Thurgood Marshall noted, '[w]hile the Union survived the civil war, the Constitution did not'.[10]

Secondly, as with other Bills, Congress has naturally employed its committees, with access to expert witnesses, to examine proposed constitutional reforms. Since ratification of proposed constitutional amendments requires the approval of the legislature or a Convention in three-quarters of the States, it might seem judicious for State representatives to participate in assessing such proposals at an early stage. But American thinking has not developed along these lines, perhaps because experience suggests that most proposed amendments passed by Congress will eventually be ratified, and the requirement of approval by a two-thirds majority in the United States Senate is seen as sufficient representation of State interests.

Con Con 1998

The Constitutional Convention held in Canberra on 2–13 February 1998 (dubbed 'Con Con' by the media) comprised 152 delegates, of whom half were popularly elected and half appointed. The latter comprised 40 members of Australian Parliaments (20 from the Commonwealth and 20 from State and Territory Parliaments) and 36 non-parliamentary delegates appointed by the Commonwealth government.[11] The equal combination of elected and appointed delegates originated in a proposal by Alexander Downer when Leader of the Opposition in November 1994.[12] The rationale underlying the Convention's composition was never explained,[13] but the participation of popularly elected delegates and Commonwealth parliamentarians was presumably intended to reflect the two components in the s. 128 procedure. State representation was also appropriate on account of both the s. 128 requirement of approval by the electors in a majority of the States and because the only issue debated — the question of an Australian republic — impacts directly on the States as well as the Commonwealth.

The government explained the participation of 36 non-parliamentary appointees as designed to achieve 'broad representation' by ensuring the participation of 'groups which might not otherwise be properly represented', such as Aborigines and Torres Strait Islanders, and to ensure adequate representation of local government and youth, as well as 'a proper balance between men and women'.[14] Some queried whether the appointed delegates satisfied the stated rationale,[15] but others considered the Convention as a whole 'broadly representative', with 'a representative feel to it'.[16] It was said to be

> a more representative group than Federal Parliament, with more women, more young people and more ethnic and indigenous delegates giving it a more contemporary look.[17]

These observations reflect the inherent ambiguity in the concept of 'representation',[18] which may be a factor underlying the present malaise affecting Australian government. Parliament, the principal organ of representative democracy, reflects, at most, political opinion within the Australian community[19] and even that inadequately in the absence of proportional representation. But political opinion is only one (and perhaps today not even the most important) aspect of a society's multifarious beliefs, interests and concerns as well as personal characteristics such as sex, age, affluence, ethnicity and religion. Hence, as one commentator remarked in respect of the constitution of the Convention, paradoxically 'representation, in the sense of reflection of society may be better achieved through appointment than through some more democratic mode of choice'.[20]

The Convention raised high hopes since it was only the second Convention with a popular component in Australian history, the first being the 80 per cent popularly elected Convention of 1897–98 which essentially drafted the Constitution.[21] Indeed, the 1998 Convention coincided with the final (Melbourne) session of the earlier Convention.[22] That Convention was an essential component in the path to Federation originally mapped out at Corowa in 1893, largely adopted by the Hobart Premiers' Conference in January 1895 and implemented by Colonial legislation: an elected Convention would produce a draft Constitution Bill upon which the Colonial Parliaments would have an opportunity to comment before a final draft was produced, and the Bill would then be submitted to referendum before transmission to Westminster for enactment.[23] The electors proved willing to accept the handiwork of the Convention they had specifically elected for that task.[24]

While employing a Convention to draft the Constitution followed American precedent, Australian federation was achieved more democratically than in the United States, for neither was the Philadelphia Convention of 1787 directly elected nor was the draft Constitution which it produced ever submitted to referendum.[25] As Harrison Moore noted in 1902,

> The federation of Australia was a popular act, an expression of the free will of the people of every part of it, and therein, as in some other respects, it differs in a striking manner from the federation of the United States, of Canada, and of Germany.[26]

John Hirst recently characterised the path to Federation as 'an amazing process ... Quite un-British'.[27]

While the United States' constitutional amendment process — aptly described by James Madison as 'neither wholly federal, nor wholly national'[28] — emulated the process whereby the Constitution was adopted, the Australian framers adopted a more national amendment process which allows proposed amendments to be submitted to the ratifiers (the electors) without first securing broad support. Since the process of adopting the Commonwealth Constitution was modelled broadly on that of the United States, it is hardly surprising that, in securing broad support for the draft Constitution at the proposal stage, it bears less resemblance to the Australian constitutional amendment process than to the American which achieves a far higher rate of successful ratifications.

These conditions suggest that Con Con 1998 was an appropriate mechanism for considering constitutional reform. Indeed the convening of a second popularly elected Convention had long been advocated by constitutional authorities including Sir Robert Garran, Sir Robert Menzies and Professor Darrell Lumb.[29] Former Commonwealth Solicitor-General Sir Robert Garran reasoned as follows:

> Hitherto, an amendment which has reached the stage of being submitted to the

electors has always been initiated by the party in power and has been suspected, usually not without reason, of being intended for use for short-term party purposes. ... In Australia, it was the people who put the seal of assent on the Constitution, and it seems to me that the best chance of getting assents to a systematic plan of amendment is to go back to the people. ... [A] constitutional revision, framed and proposed to Parliament by a convention elected by the people for that purpose, would have a far better chance of acceptance at a subsequent referendum than any amendment framed and introduced by the Government of the day.[30]

Whether future constitutional reform is pursued through Conventions including a popular component will obviously be greatly influenced by assessment of the success of the 1998 Convention. The euphoria displayed in the Convention's final sessions suggested that most delegates — even monarchists, but not supporters of a popularly elected President[31] — considered the Convention a success, although perhaps for different reasons.[32] Indeed, the Convention itself resolved that a similar body, albeit two-thirds popularly elected, should be convened within 3–5 years of the advent of a republic to consider a broad agenda of further constitutional reform.[33] One delegate, the Commonwealth Attorney-General, later acclaimed the Convention 'an outstanding success'[34] while another, Australian Democrats Senator Natasha Stott Despoja, described it as 'pretty incredible ... an emotionally inspiring event'.[35] But, in judging the Convention, what is the criterion of 'success'?

Favourable judgments on the Convention's outcome generally highlight the popular involvement achieved, both through the election of delegates and in following the Convention's proceedings via the electronic media — radio, television, the Internet — and in personal attendance at Old Parliament House, the Convention venue. Newspapers also gave the Convention extensive coverage, including proceedings on and off the Convention floor (press conferences, media interviews, dinners) and the activities of its leading personalities. But, apart from the public education derived therefrom — and some of the media coverage was hardly 'educational' — the lasting benefit of public involvement should be measured by its contribution to a successful referendum outcome; in other words, to adoption of a good republican model. Hence, final judgement on the Convention must await the result of the referendum to be held in late 1999. Meanwhile, any interim assessment must evaluate the Convention's handiwork — its republican model.

The Con Con Model

Evaluation of the Convention's resolutions will obviously vary according to individual preference. The Convention's republican model has six principal components: the nomination, appointment, removal and powers of the President, republicanisation of the States, and amendment of the constitutional Preamble. Since the present writer has discussed most of these aspects elsewhere,[36] a brief overall assessment should suffice here.

It is hardly surprising, but nevertheless reassuring, that the Convention model is most satisfactory on those issues which received greatest consideration: presidential nomination and appointment, the Preamble and republicanising the States. On presidential appointment and republicanising the States, the Convention essentially adopted the 'minimalist' republican position long advocated by the Australian Republican Movement (ARM) and examined in the report of the Republic Advisory Committee in 1993.[37] It favoured, at the national level, a non-partisan, politically neutral President with the same powers and functions as the Governor-General chosen by the people's parliamentary representatives on a bipartisan basis, and wisely left the questions of whether the States should become republican and, if so, on what basis in the hands of the States. Since the President should enjoy broad public support and not be perceived as emerging from some incestuous parliamentary cabal (as was often alleged regarding Ireland's popularly elected presidency before the advent of Mary Robinson), the Convention adopted a broad, community-based mechanism for seeking and evaluating potential presidential candidates for ultimate nomination to Parliament by the Prime Minister and the Leader of the Opposition. The detailed constitution of the Presidential Nomination Committee was appropriately not to be entrenched in the Constitution, but rather left to be governed by Commonwealth legislation capable of adapting to changing community opinion which would evolve in light of experience with the presidency.[38]

Amendment of the Preamble was hotly debated at the Convention. Opinion on the appropriate content and role of a constitutional Preamble varies widely,[39] but the Convention's resolution that the Preamble should, at least, recognise Aboriginal prior occupation of Australia and acknowledge fundamental constitutional principles including popular sovereignty, the rule of law and representative and responsible federal government, social facts such as cultural diversity and core civic values such as respect for the environment was well considered and enjoyed broad support. Its more controversial provision that the Preamble (presumably meaning only additions to the original Preamble) should not be employed in constitutional interpretation[40] reflected the reality of the political balance at the Convention, but is nevertheless justifiable on grounds of constitutional principle.[41]

In other respects, the Convention's outcome was flawed or at least disappointing. The Convention resolved that the powers of the President should be the same as those of the Governor-General. It resolved that the non-reserve powers should be 'spelled out so far as practicable'[42] — which is surely 100 per cent[43] — and the present reserve powers together with the conventions governing them were merely to be incorporated by reference. Although, at earlier stages of the Convention, there appeared to be some prospect of the Republic Advisory Committee's draft partial codification of the reserve powers[44] being adopted, any codification was ultimately abandoned in an attempt to win the government's support. It would be most unfortunate if the Constitution were belatedly to recognise the office of Prime Minister only in the context of presidential appointment and removal, but continue to omit the fundamental requirement of responsible government, namely that the Prime Minister must enjoy the confidence of the House of Representatives.

In its resolution on presidential powers the Convention merely squandered an opportunity for constructive reform of Australian government, but its mechanism for presidential removal constituted a serious lapse of judgement. Under the Convention model, the President is removable by the Prime Minister subject only to the requirement of a general election (but not reinstatement of the President) if the House of Representatives refuses to ratify the removal within 30 days.[45] No ground of removal is specified or procedural safeguard (such as reasonable notice, the right to a hearing) provided.[46] This provision is objectionable on many grounds;[47] essentially, it is both structurally unsound and entirely inappropriate.

It is structurally unsound because presidential removal rests entirely in the hands of the Prime Minister, which would enable a recalcitrant President to thwart removal by a pre-emptive dismissal of the Prime Minister. Moreover, retaining the present mutual dismissibility of the Prime Minister and the Governor-General maintains the risk that the two principal executive officers will play a dangerous game of 'constitutional chicken' (or 'High Noon'), as demonstrated by Sir John Kerr's dismissal of Prime Minister Whitlam without prior warning in November 1975. The Convention mechanism has dashed the hope that Australian government might be improved under a republic by giving the President sufficient security to tenure to encourage openness and trust in dealings between the Prime Minister and the President relating to the exercise of a reserve power.[48]

Moreover, it is surely incompatible with the dignity of the office for the national Head of State to be summarily dismissible by the Prime Minister. No other republican constitution in the world appears to have found it necessary to enable the Head of State to be removed so easily and without specification of any grounds.

It is no coincidence that the two least satisfactory aspects of the Convention's handiwork — its resolution on presidential powers and the mechanism for removing the President — were central features in the dismissal of the Whitlam Government in November 1975. Several commentators have noted the influence of those events on the Convention's deliberations: their 'scars were evident in almost every aspect of Convention discussion';[49] or, more poetically,

> Banquo's ghost in the form of John Kerr, deceased, attended all sessions. At every table and in every corridor he silently influenced most debate.[50]

It is interesting to speculate whether the Convention would have been willing to contemplate a popularly elected President with uncodified reserve powers and greater security of tenure had it been sitting prior to 1975, say in 1970. But that scenario is, of course, fanciful because it is unlikely that Australia would be facing a referendum on the republic in 1999 had the Dismissal not occurred.[51] It is one of the ironies of Australian politics that the 1975 crisis is both catalyst for the republic and one of the principal hurdles in its path. Anger at the Governor-General's dismissal of the Whitlam Government caused many, probably illogically,[52] to consider moving to a republic. Yet the continuing difficulty in specifying how a Head of State should respond to denial of Supply by the Senate is a significant factor preventing codification of the reserve powers, and thus the institution of a popularly elected President, which the public appears strongly to favour.

The Convention's failings are largely attributable to two factors: insufficient attention was devoted to the details of the republican model, and the ARM conceded too much to the Prime Minister and other supporters of the McGarvie model in a futile attempt to secure their support.[53] The Convention must bear some responsibility for this, but much of it was probably an inevitable consequence of the Convention's structure and agenda, which were largely determined in advance by the government.

For several reasons, the Convention was unable to focus attention solely on determining the best republican model to put to referendum. First, much time was occupied with debating the general question of whether Australia should retain the monarchy. Secondly, many monarchists had little interest in contributing to the framing of any republican model. Thirdly, the Prime Minister had undertaken to submit to referendum any republican model enjoying the Convention's 'clear support'.[54] This term was not defined; nor was it made explicit that the earlier requirement for 'consensus' had been abandoned. Once it became clear (on the second day) that the Convention would not favour a directly-elected President, many proponents of direct election opted in favour of the plebiscite which the Prime Minister had promised if the Convention was unable to express a 'clear view'.[55] Hence, the ARM felt obliged to offer concessions to the other 'republican' group, supporters of the McGarvie model. This led to the Prime Ministerial dominance inherent in the Convention model.[56]

Other features of the Convention exacerbated these factors. First, the interval between the election of delegates and the meeting of the Convention, which included the Christmas period, was probably too short to enable delegates to familiarise themselves with the issues and discuss tactics with fellow delegates before the Convention met. Secondly, the Convention's decision to refer to the Resolutions Group (which had been envisaged largely as a drafting committee) any resolution which received the support of 25 per cent of the delegates was an unwise over-reaction to a threatened 'walk-out' by proponents of direct presidential election following the Convention's rejection (on its second day) of full codification of presidential powers, which they interpreted as rejection of their model. This resulted in a deferral of decision on most issues, later resolved with insufficient consideration towards the end of the Convention. Moreover, the Resolutions Group itself, which met in private, appears to have operated unsatisfactorily.[57]

The Future

Comparison of the Australian and American experiences regarding amendment of their federal constitutions and the success of the 1897–98 Australasian Federal Convention demonstrate the advantage of building broad support for constitutional change at the proposal stage. Australian experience indicates that constitutional amendments will not be approved at referendum without at least bipartisan support, and it is politically naive to expect such support for measures which have been promoted solely by the government.

The constitutional amendment process prescribed by s. 128 suggests two appropriate mechanisms for evaluating proposed constitutional reform before a Constitution Alteration Bill is introduced in Parliament. The first is a Convention comprising the four components of the 1998 Convention: popularly elected delegates; Commonwealth, State and Territory parliamentarians; and appointed members of the general public possessing a wide range of personal characteristics and interests, including constitutional expertise. Unlike the first two groups, the third does not reflect a component in the s. 128 mechanism. But the non-elected delegates enhanced the quality of the 1998 Convention's deliberations, in part because many of them were genuinely open to persuasion.[58] Most elected delegates understandably felt obliged to adhere to the platform on which they were elected, so a Convention comprised entirely of popularly elected delegates would find compromise difficult, although that is essential if the necessary broad support is to be garnered.

An alternative[59] mechanism for evaluating proposed constitutional reform is an indicative (non-binding) plebiscite by which the electors chose among two or more alternative proposals. The proposal enjoying most support would then be refined in a Constitution Alteration Bill which undergoes the s. 128 procedure. This was essentially the means by which MMP was introduced in New Zealand in 1996. It has never been employed for constitutional reform in Australia, but Prime Minister John Howard foreshadowed conducting an indicative plebiscite on the republic if the Constitutional Convention proved unable to express a 'clear view'.[60]

The present writer prefers the former mechanism since it is more conducive to reasoned evaluation of proposed constitutional reform.[61] While an indicative plebiscite may be more 'democratic', and possibly offer a greater prospect of success in the ultimate s. 128 referendum, it suffers from the acknowledged defects of such exercises in direct democracy. It is prone to reflect transient community enthusiasms, is costly to conduct (but so is a popularly elected Convention), and enables those with deep pockets to exert a disproportionate influence on the outcome. New Zealand's experience with MMP, with which disillusionment has already set in after only two years, counsels caution regarding indicative plebiscites.

The future of Australian constitutional reform will obviously be greatly influenced by the outcome of the referendum on an Australian republic. If it is carried, the semi (or two-thirds) popularly elected Convention mechanism will receive a great fillip and the government will face strong pressure to honour the 1998 Convention's resolution calling for a two-thirds popularly elected Convention to consider further constitutional reform[62] (on which the government has been notably silent). However, if the referendum fails, constitutional reform in general will undoubtedly be retarded and careful consideration will need to be given to the question of whether to pursue the republic by other means — including perhaps an indicative plebiscite — or to concentrate instead on other issues, such as a Bill of Rights.[63]

But, whatever the outcome of the referendum, periodic constitutional reform is necessary for, as Thomas Jefferson — 'certainly [no] ... advocate for frequent and untried changes in laws and constitutions'[64] — eloquently observed,

> [L]aws and institutions must go hand in hand with the progress of the human mind. As that becomes more developed, more enlightened ... and manners and opinions change with the change of circumstances, institutions must advance also, and keep pace with the times. We might as well require a man to wear still the coat which fitted him when a boy, as civilized society to remain under the regimen of their barbarous ancestors.[65]

Notes

1. Commonwealth Constitution s. 128.
2. United States Constitution art V.
3. For details, see G Anastaplo, *The Constitution of 1787: A Commentary* (Baltimore: Johns Hopkins University Press, 1989), 298–9. (A proposed amendment of 1789 became the 27th Amendment upon ratification in 1992.)
4. For the number and details of proposed amendments since the inception of the United States, see JR Vile, *Encyclopedia of Constitutional Amendments, Proposed Amendments, and Amending Issues, 1789–1995* (Santa Barbara: ABC–CLIO, 1996), 362–80.
5. See JR Vile, *Rewriting the United States Constitution: An Examination of Proposals from Reconstruction to the Present* (New York: Praeger, 1991), 8–10; P Weber and B Perry, *Unfounded Fears: Myths and Realities of a Constitutional Convention* (New York: Greenwood Press and Praeger, 1989).
6. Vile, supra note 4, 77.
7. Vile, supra note 5, 8. For some statistics on American State constitutional amendment, see DS Lutz, 'Toward a Theory of Constitutional Amendment', in S Levinson (ed.), *Responding to Imperfection: The Theory and Practice of Constitutional Amendment* (Princeton: Princeton University Press, 1995), 237, 248–50.
8. JE Cooke (ed.), *The Federalist* (Middletown, Conn: Wesleyan University Press, 1961), 340 (No. 49). For the contrasting views on constitutional revision of James Madison and Thomas Jefferson, see Vile, supra note 5, 3–4.
9. Ibid 10.
10. T Marshall, 'Reflections on the Bicentennial of the United States Constitution' (1987) 101 *Harvard Law Review* 1, 4.
11. For further details, see G Winterton, 'Australia's Constitutional Convention 1998' (1998) 5 *Agenda* 97, 103–4.
12. See L Taylor, 'Downer Pledges Convention to Vote on Republic', *Australian*, 18 November 1994, 2. However, the Convention departed somewhat from Downer's original proposal.
13. For considerations supporting it, see Winterton, supra note 11, 104–5. Convention experience confirmed these observations.
14. Prime Minister John Howard, *Commonwealth Parliamentary Debates*, H of R, 26 March 1997, 3062.
15. See C Saunders, 'Why a Convention?' (1997) 8 *Public Law Review* 213, 215.
16. J M Williams, 'Faith, Hope and Self-Interest: The President in the Future Republic' (1998) 21 *University of New South Wales Law Journal* 897, 898.
17. M Steketee, 'The Politics of the Constitutional Convention' (1998) 21 *University of New South Wales Law Journal* 922, 923. See, likewise, M Handshin, 'Review of the Constitutional Convention' (1998) 6(2) *Rights Now* 10,10 ('[N]o parliament across Australia is, or would ever have been, as broadly representative of the community as this Convention was'); J Bishop, 'The Constitutional Convention' (1998) 25 (3) *Brief* (Law Society of WA) 5, 5 ('If one tried to imagine a truly representative parliament, then the Constitutional Convention was surely as close to it as we have seen in Australia's history to date'); C Thompson, 'The Constitutional Convention' (1998) 25 (3) *Brief* 6, 8 ('Con Con [was] truly representative of Australia in the late 20th century. … Diversity was not only a theme — it was the whole point!').
18. See AH Birch, *Representation* (London: Pall Mall Press, 1971), 15–18 for three common usages of 'representative'.

19. See ibid., 89.
20. Saunders, supra note 15, 214–15.
21. The delegates from New South Wales, Victoria, South Australia and Tasmania were popularly elected, but those from Western Australia were elected by its Parliament and Queensland did not participate.
22. See Saunders, supra note 15, 213–14.
23. J Quick and R R Garran, *The Annotated Constitution of the Australian Commonwealth* (Sydney: Angus & Robertson, 1901), 153–54; J Hirst, 'A Novel Convention: Adelaide 1897' (1998) 1 *The New Federalist* 5, 7–8.
24. Quick and Garran, supra note 23, 154.
25. See Winterton, supra note 11, 98. There were earlier American State precedents for the more democratic Australian path: see ibid. 97–98.
26. W H Moore, *The Constitution of the Commonwealth of Australia* (London: John Murray, 1902), 61, repeated in the 2d edn (Melbourne: Charles F Maxwell, 1910), 64.
27. J Hirst, 'History and the Republic' (1996) 40 (9) *Quadrant* 38, 42.
28. Cooke, supra note 8, 257 (No. 39).
29. RR Garran, *Prosper the Commonwealth* (Sydney: Angus and Robertson, 1958), 209–11; J McMillan, G Evans and H Storey, *Australia's Constitution: Time for Change?* (Sydney: Allen & Unwin, 1983), 357 (quoting Menzies); RD Lumb, 'Methods of Constitutional Revision in the Federal Sphere: An Elected Constitutional Convention?' (1992) 22 *University of Western Australia Law Review* 52; D Lumb, 'Elected Conventions & Constitutional Change' (1993–94) 9 (4) *Policy* 43.
30. Garran, supra note 29, 209–11.
31. See, for example, P O'Brien, 'The Rorting of the Constitutional Convention' (1998) 42 (7–8) *Quadrant* 29.
32. See, for example, H Nathan, 'The Convention from the Inside' (1998) 42 (4) *Quadrant* 21, 25 ('The Convention was a great contribution to Australia'); Bishop, supra note 17, 5 ('[I]t was a remarkable exercise in Australian democracy. ... Whatever the outcome of [the] referendum, the convention itself should be judged a success'); Thompson, supra note 17.
33. 'Final Resolutions of the Constitutional Convention, Canberra, 2–13 February 1998' (1998) 9 *Public Law Review* 55, 58.
34. D Williams, *Realising the Republic: The Government's Perspective* (unpublished paper presented at ANU Seminar Series 'The Republic: What Next?', 6 April 1998), 1. See, likewise, R McGarvie, 'From Rank Outsider to Runner-Up', *Age*, 20 February 1998, A 15 ('an enormous success'); G Williams, 'The People's Convention?' (1998) 23 (1) *Alternative Law Journal* 2, 2 ('a great success').
35. *Commonwealth Parliamentary Debates*, Senate, 2 March 1998, 64.
36. G Winterton, 'The 1998 Convention: A Reprise of 1898?' (1998) 21 *University of New South Wales Law Journal* 856.
37. Republic Advisory Committee, *An Australian Republic: The Options — The Report* (Canberra: AGPS, 1993).
38. See 'Final Resolutions', supra note 33, 56.
39. See G Winterton, 'A New Constitutional Preamble' (1997) 8 *Public Law Review* 186.
40. 'Final Resolutions', supra note 33, 57.
41. See Winterton, supra note 36, 863–4.
42. 'Final Resolutions', supra note 33, 56.

43. See G Winterton, 'A Constitution for an Australian Republic', in G Winterton (ed.), *We, the People: Australian Republican Government* (Sydney: Allen & Unwin, 1994), 1, where they are spelt out.
44. See Republic Advisory Committee, supra note 37, 102–5.
45. 'Final Resolutions', supra note 33, 56.
46. It is possible that the High Court might imply such limitations and thereby subject presidential removal to judicial review: see A Mason, *The Republic and Australian Constitutional Development* (unpublished paper presented at ANU Seminar Series 'The Republic: What Next?', 11 May 1998), 5.
47. See G Winterton, supra note 36, 860–1 for several of them.
48. See G Winterton, *Monarchy to Republic: Australian Republican Government* (Melbourne: Oxford University Press, rev. edn, 1994), 115, 181.
49. S Zifcak, 'Shades of Sir John' (1998) 8 (5) *Eureka Street* 30, 30.
50. Nathan, supra note 32, 22. Moira Rayner has likewise remarked that '[t]he ghost of Sir John Kerr, and what he did on 11 November 1975, haunted the whole Convention': M Rayner, 'A View from the Fringe' (1998) 21 *University of New South Wales Law Journal* 908, 908.
51. See M McKenna, *The Captive Republic: A History of Republicanism in Australia 1788–1996* (Melbourne: Cambridge University Press, 1996), 226 ff; J Hirst, *A Republican Manifesto* (Melbourne: Oxford University Press, 1994), 64–5.
52. Since a republican President armed with the same powers might well have behaved similarly to Sir John Kerr although, perhaps, after warning Mr Whitlam.
53. The following section draws upon Winterton, supra note 36, 865–6.
54. See his remarks: *Report of the Constitutional Convention, Old Parliament House, Canberra, 2–13 February 1998*: Vol 3: *Transcript of Proceedings* (Canberra: AGPS, 1998), 3.
55. Ibid.
56. For a strong critique, see B Galligan, 'The Republican Model' (1998) 42 (4) *Quadrant* 17. For a response, see J Hirst, 'The Republic and Prime Ministerial Power' (letter) (1998) 42 (5) *Quadrant* 5.
57. See Rayner, supra note 50, 912–13. Compare Nathan, supra note 32, 23.
58. See, likewise, Steketee, supra note 17, 923.
59. Theoretically, both mechanisms could be employed, but practically they are alternatives.
60. Supra note 55.
61. Compare Madison's account of the advantages of representative government over democracy: Cooke, supra note 8, 62 (No. 10).
62. Supra note 33.
63. It is, of course, possible to pursue both reforms. Pressure for at least a statutory Bill of Rights is likely to increase once Britain enacts its Human Rights Bill incorporating the European Convention on Human Rights into British domestic law.
64. Letter from Thomas Jefferson to Samuel Kercheval, 12 July 1816, in A Koch and W Peden, *The Life and Selected Writings of Thomas Jefferson* (New York: Modern Library, 1944), 674.
65. Ibid.

Part 2
International Law and Jurisprudence

8 Adjudication theories and hard cases at common law

Alan Fogg

Introduction

In constitutional democracies it is always important to explain and justify the judicial function. Judicial imperialism is sometimes conducted through self-conscious activism and sometimes latent. In all forms it is a negation of the doctrine of separation of powers, and if carried to excess is a threat to the idea of responsible government. Its counterpart, judicial restraint, concedes too much to elected legislatures and unelected bureaucracies. This is why emphasis is often placed on 'balance'.[1]

But a balance requires a fulcrum, and identification of the appropriate fulcrum is elusive and controversial. Darrell Lumb was vitally interested in identifying the fulcrum for superior courts, particularly the Australian High Court. The analytical excellence of his well-known constitutional texts is buttressed by a more expansive critique of judicial decisions in published articles. Merely by way of illustration, Darrell has applied his lawyerly intelligence to critical evaluation of the High Court's expansion of the external affairs power[2] and to the performance of other Australian courts in relation to aboriginal land rights.[3] Darrell was best known as a constitutional lawyer, but earlier in his career also taught and wrote about jurisprudence.[4] In fact, I inherited the jurisprudence teaching from him in 1968. It seems appropriate to offer in his memory an essay that marries legal theory and examples of judicial decision-making.

This is not an ambitious essay. It charts contemporary theories of adjudication and uses two well-known common law cases as laboratories for the testing of the persuasiveness of those theories. Nothing of course can test their validity, which is beyond objective proof. Legal theory is about good arguments, not conclusive answers.

Contemporary theories in adjudication

Natural law theories tend to reside in the United States, where generous entitlements in the Bill of Rights and constitutional amendments have triggered a modern revival of natural law justifications for constitutional adjudication.[5] But constitutions differ, and both reflect and shape the autochthonous values of the society in which they occur. More interesting are theories that accommodate common law, as well as written constitutional law. The dominant modern theory is realism, and its analytical stablemate positivism. Counter-theories include those of Dworkin and Hayek.

Positivism and realism

Realism is the current fashion, and constituted the proximate ethos of the Australian High Court according to its recently retired Chief Justice, Sir Anthony Mason. In 1993 he said: 'In Australia we have moved away from the declaratory theory and the doctrine of legalism to a species of legal realism.'[6] But before summarising what realism is, it is necessary first to deal with its theoretical companion, legal positivism. Positivism is a rule-book analysis of law that anatomises legal systems. Realism is a programmatic theory of judicial function that is parasitic upon the opportunities given by positivism's concentration on rules rather than customs or principles. The connection is clear, and is not invalidated by the current rejection of positivism in the United States, a country where realism had its birth. Recent writings in the United States show a revival of natural law theory that condemns positivism to pariah status.[7] But that development in the see-saw of dominance can be attributed to the contents of the Bill of Rights in that country. In truth, positivism and realism fit neatly together.[8]

The explanatory basis for modern realism as a theory of adjudication is found in Herbert Hart's treatment of hard cases in his influential book *The Concept of Law*.[9] When disputed issues cannot be included in a clear rule laid down by an authoritative institution such as Parliament, then a judge has a strong or semi-legislative discretion to decide the case either way. In a hard case, the judgment is written in language that assumes one or other of the parties has an existing right to win. But this is a fiction. The truth is that the judge has legislated new rights. Hart has elsewhere said that a judge must rely as 'a conscientious legislator on his sense of what is best'.[10]

That view has been subsequently defended by Hart against Dworkin's criticisms.[11] To argue that barristers do not speak of making new law is to confuse rhetoric with reality. The idea that such exercise of judicial power is undemocratic cannot be sustained. Having unelected judges making new law is better than alternative methods such as reference to the legislature. In any event, judges are limited to the specific issues litigated before them. Moreover, delegation to the executive branch regularly occurs, so that limited delegation to the judiciary is no great threat to democracy. Finally, the positivist approach does not amount to retrospective law-making. Creating new law that contradicts the law when the litigated facts occurred is only unjust if it cuts across legitimate expectations. But in hard cases, the law is not clearly established and cannot justify such expectations.

Subject to the primacy of parliamentary legislation, positivism authenticates the role of judges as interstitial legislators. It provides a platform of respectability for realism. There are two versions of realism: the strong version and closet realism.[12] Closet realism can be summarily dealt with. Classical declaratory theory is employed as a facade, because to be too openly realist would shake public confidence in the judiciary. Discretion is the better part of valour when the legislature can attrite the extent of judicial power. Closet realism is weak realism because it is realism in disguise.

Strong realism is the open acknowledgement of what many judges believe they do. Strong realism is a judge-centered approach that emphasises the ambiguity of law and the importance of modernity in judicial functions. At its heart it contains the idea that law is a means to social ends and must be evaluated in terms of its effects. The focus is on empiricism, qualified only by constraints inherent in the court process.[13] The core idea is one of judicial choice of outcome. One of the prime triggers for Caesarism of this kind is the argument that modern society is too complex for governments to handle through legislation alone.[14]

These propositions apply across the spectrum of statutory interpretation, judicial review and common law. This essay concentrates on common law decisions, where the pool is unmuddied by governmental involvement. The convenient focus is Herbert Hart's positivism, since it is Hart who has made a normative evaluation of one of the two decisions chosen for analysis. But Hart's normative arguments are simply the expression of a realism that is licensed by his analytical rule-based positivism.

Dworkin's rights thesis

Ronald Dworkin is doubly a professor, being Professor of Jurisprudence at the University of Oxford and a Professor of Law in New York University Law School. It is thus not surprising that his writings give examples of decisions in both the United Kingdom and the United States. In recent times Dworkin has concentrated on constitutional issues. In particular, he has emphasised the need for moral readings of the US Constitution that exclude a majoritarian or utilitarian premise.[15]

But he has previously written forcefully about the judicial function in extra-constitutional circumstances, including common law. Undergraduate law students will be familiar with Justice Hercules, the superhuman judge hypothesised by Dworkin in order to deal with hard cases. Hercules is the ideal judicial performer modern judges should attempt to emulate.[16] Description of his duties used to be plain. He must construct a political and moral theory that best explains and justifies existing legal materials in constitutions, statutes and cases, and the theory arrived at will be the best guide to the rights he should apply to reach the uniquely correct answer that is discoverable in the hardest of hard cases. He will always decide on principle rather than policy in his pursuit of vindicating the rights people already have. In this way he avoids criticism that he is legislating or that he is unfairly applying law at the time of his decision that was absent when the facts of the case occurred. Dworkin argues his third theory of law avoids the traps of Hart's rule-book approach that gives judges a strong discretion to make new law on policy grounds. Justice Hercules has no real discretion in the sense commonly understood. His decisions run on principled rails to a conclusion that is uniquely right, and the fundamental principle is that people should be treated equally. This means redressing the tilted playing-fields caused by historical inequities and disadvantages.

In *Law's Empire*, the right answer to litigants' entitlements is controlled by two types of test : 'fit' with settled law and 'substance'. Substance contains three components which must be weighed against one another:[17]

- Justice. This means the equal concern and respect an ideal legislator would employ. In common law cases like *McLoughlin v. O'Brien*,[18] this becomes resource egalitarianism.
- Fairness. This entails being supported by majority opinion. Fairness allows Justice Hercules to look at contemporary views about the meaning of a statute, rather than the original intention of the legislature.
- Procedural Due Process. This requires consistency in decision-making. If the community has arranged its affairs on the basis of earlier judicial decisions, it would be wrong to disturb settled expectations even if justice indicates a contrary view.

Dworkin insists that Justice Hercules always finds the law; he never makes or invents it.

Hayek's liberty thesis

Dworkin's theory is superficially a declaratory theory. But those descriptive elements that caused Dworkin to be called Blackstone in modern dress are corrupted by the normative imperative of treating people equally.

Hayek is unselfconscious in his fidelity to classical common law and its processes. It is a declaratory theory that depends on correct judicial articulation of customary rules of just conduct belonging only to non-statutory common law, and which is sharply distinguished from the law of legislation. His objective is to show that liberty is vulnerable if the two types of law are not kept separate, because only rules of just conduct should rightly be enforced against citizens. A rule of just conduct must be:

- abstract, in the sense of being end-independent and applicable to an unknown number of future instances[19]
- negative, in the sense of preventing 'actions towards others' that interfere with a citizen's autonomy and protecting the domain within which he can make feasible plans[20]
- capable of being universalised so that it fits with existing rules of common law[21]
- applied over the long run so that it becomes a settled and tested rule.[22]

There is no imposed will, such as that of parliament in relation to legislation. This is evolved customary law, and rules that are judicially articulated are only part of the corpus of rules that citizens observe, including unwritten rules within a common sense of justice and fair play.[23] Such rules are as much a part of the law as those declared or articulated by judges, and our ignorance of them and our incapacity to verbalise them with precision is immaterial since we can know how to act without thinking about it.[24] They illustrate Hayek's central proposition that it is possible to have order without design; it can be a spontaneous order growing out of a web of culturally inherited rules which have adjusted to each other by processes of time and experience.

The judge's task with respect to common law is restoration of the spontaneous order when it has broken down, not the imposing of an order by resort to result-orientated criteria.[25] He or she will follow customary principles and apply the rule that should have been followed by the parties; such a rule is one which would have been consistent with the spontaneous order.[26] A judge's especial talent is for articulation, even in hard cases. Hayek's theory acknowledges that hard cases like *Donoghue v. Stevenson*[27] alter the nature of articulated common law and extend its scope. But the exercise remains articulation not judicial legislation, since legitimate expectations within a community are capable of being divined by the professional talents of the judge.

This is Hayek's answer to the characteristically perceived difficulty of reconciling declaratory theory with the obvious fact that judge-made law changes. Judging is not an act of will, and positivists and realists are wrong to think that when articulated rules run out the only answer is a strong judicial discretion to change the law by reference to external standards. The sole permissible authentication of the decision in a hard case is genuine social custom in the community,[28] so that the decision will integrate with other rules of just conduct in the spontaneous order. In easy cases where existing rules supply the answer, a judge must identify the facts from the evidence of the parties and then decide on the remedy most appropriate to restore the party injured by the infraction to the position he or she would have occupied apart from the breach.

Sample of hard cases

In 1527 Serjeant Roo, 'who was more eager to show his wit than to be made a Judge', delivered a satire in the royal presence on abuses of the law by Lord Chancellor Wolsey. He was summarily dispatched to prison.[29] The branch of contempt known as 'scandalising the court' seems now to be part of history, which is fortunate for academic commentators because reported hard cases are ideal test-beds for adjudicative theories. The two examples that follow are from common law, since here judges meet squarely with the dilemma of matching existing law with the 'leaping of the gap' involved in landmark decisions. Not only judges but their critics can be subjected to surgical analysis that throws into sharp, comparative focus both legal realism and theories of the counter-revolution.

A dubious case — *Shaw v. Director of Public Prosecutions*[30]

Shaw's case concerns customary criminal law. The House of Lords endorsed a count on an indictment alleging conspiracy to corrupt public morals. Shaw published a directory giving information about services offered by prostitutes, including photographs and a tariff of prices for particular services. The prostitutes paid to be included in the directory which was publicly distributed, and the alleged conspiracy of which Shaw was part was with the advertising prostitutes. He was convicted, with only Lord Reid dissenting, of inducing readers to resort to the advertising prostitutes for the purposes of fornication and of taking part in 'disgusting and immoral acts or exhibitions, with intent thereby to debauch and corrupt the morals as well of youth as of divers other liege subjects of our Lady the Queen and to raise and create in their minds inordinate and lustful desires'. The antique language of the indictment sounds more like Elmer Gantry sermonising in full spate than a criminal charge. It is certainly a colourful way of describing a quotidian transaction with a prostitute.

Shaw's case has been heavily criticised, and the thrust of those criticisms provides a scalpel test for the appropriateness of theories of judicial adjudication. The critics agree that *Shaw* is an example of raw judicial power, but disagree on the basis for attack. Further, *Shaw* starkly represents a judicial dilemma, since there were no binding common law precedents to overrule or distinguish; in terms of common law the issue was in truth completely novel and upholding of the criminal count against Shaw was open on the authorities. That his conduct was morally reprehensible in 1961 was clear, and decent citizens reprobated it. Nonetheless, it is a decision which gave many a sense that injustice was done to Shaw, a feeling that produced the storm of criticism that has surrounded the decision.

Herbert Hart is a noted critic of *Shaw*. The leading British exponent of positivism, Hart attacked *Shaw* as an *ex post facto* decision and called on the shade of Jeremy Bentham to condemn the decision's disregard of the legal value of certainty.[31] Another historical figure was prayed in aid, when he alleged John Stuart Mill would have shuddered at Shaw's case as authorising gross invasions of individual liberty.[32] More generally, Hart disapproved of the enforcement of sexual morality, because this may create a special kind of misery; repression of sexual impulses (and the consequences of that repression) are entirely different from what is involved in 'ordinary crime'.[33] This is a quite extraordinary proposition to apply to Shaw, who was enticed by the profit motive not sexual desire; nor presumably were his unnamed co-conspirators, the advertising prostitutes, sexually damaged by suppression of the publication. Hart seems to be bear-led by his genuine dislike of repression of nonconforming sexual behaviour into a confusion of odd and contradictory arguments.

Can the new declaratory theorists do better? Dworkin has glancingly dealt with *Shaw* as part of a larger argument directed to replacing the rule-book approach to law with his principle-based rights thesis.[34] He points out that the judges in *Shaw* spoke as if they were obliged by existing precedents to reach the conclusions they did, so that they avoided constructing the appropriate overall political theory he fathers on Justice Hercules. Viscount Simonds instead refers to the moral welfare of society, which Dworkin counts as an argument about the character of general welfare which he would allocate to parliament not the bench. The House of Lords should have asked whether the precedents unambiguously required them to recognise conspiracy to corrupt public morals as a crime and, if not, whether a theory that such crime existed was more consistent with Shaw's individual rights than a contradictory theory. 'It would then have been strenuously argued that individuals have a moral right, at least in principle, not to be punished except for committing a crime clearly published in advance, and that in virtue of that right it would be unjust to punish Shaw.'[35] It is clear that Dworkin believes such a right inhered in Shaw, and that it was compatible with British legal and political practice as well as having an instinctive appeal.

Dworkin's approach curiously coincides with Hart's, since both are opposed to *Shaw* on the basis that it constituted retrospective judicial legislation that ignored the defendant's rights. But this is essentially technical not substantive criticism and simply tells us that the House of Lords was careless or mistaken about the way it conducted its judicial business. Clearly, both Dworkin and Hart would have preferred a different outcome in the case, but their analyses are not compelling about whether the decision was substantively wrong. This is where an analysis anchored in Hayek is convincing. Robin O'Hair has marshalled compelling Hayekian arguments to show that *Shaw* is not an authentic articulation of a rule of just conduct in customary criminal law.[36] Lord Tucker did not promote the proposition that it is a common law offence for a single person to corrupt public morals, the advertising prostitutes not having been charged. He relied instead on the idea that corrupting public morals is a type of unlawfulness sufficient to justify a conspiracy indictment but insufficient to justify other official action, whether criminal or civil. The label to be attached to a particular conspiracy was irrelevant for Lord Tucker, who rhetorically asked whether it could be doubted that a conspiracy to corrupt public morals was a conspiracy to effect public mischief.[37]

This approach is cavalier of the procedure for trial on indictment, which is based on the conception of criminal law as a grievance, and converts the law into an engine for the suppression of minorities.[38] There was no 'action towards others' that invaded anyone's domain, whether actually or potentially. The offence was based on a breach of morality from which a grievance was absent, and embraced 'every agreement to do anything which a jury thinks is likely to have that effect'.[39] Moreover, the House of Lords relied on decisions translated from the Star Chamber, a court abolished in 1642 and of offensive reputation, that was established with the authority of the royal prerogative and thus no common law court. It was described by Macauley as a political inquisition that enabled the government of the day to fine, imprison, pillory and mutilate.[40] Such a discredited court cannot plausibly be a source of common law based on public opinion, particularly for an inchoate crime of conspiracy which is open-ended as to future application. The House of Lords is thus likely to have invented the crime rather than identified it as a genuine reflection of custom.[41] Moreover, the court failed to act justly in that it located Shaw's offence in the agreement to combine, which was an accidental element of the impugned conduct.[42] Any outrage to moral susceptibilities lies in the publication of the directory not in the conspiracy to publish which was complete on agreement; the fact that Shaw was not charged with the publication itself was no rationale for identifying a novel crime of conspiracy in order to catch conduct in the criminal net.

A fourth O'Hair criticism stems from Hayek's requirement that articulated common law be based upon a genuine community consensus, otherwise decisions are mistaken articulations. According to the dissenting judgment of Lord Reid, there were 'wide differences of opinion today how far the law ought to punish immoral acts which are not done in the face of the public'.[43] If that be right, then the House of Lords majority transgressed Hayek's theory of common law, since they did not articulate a rule based on community opinion.

A misunderstood case — *Donoghue v. Stevenson*[44]

There can be few cases better known to law students, whether as a staple departure point for negligence in torts or as material for study of judicial technique in introductory courses. The facts of *Donoghue v. Stevenson* are probably better known to lawyers and law students than those of any other case in the tapestry of the common law, and may be shortly stated. The plaintiff brought action to recover damages from an aerated water producer for injuries she suffered from consuming part of the contents of a ginger-beer bottle manufactured by the defendant, and which contained the decomposed remains of a snail. The bottle had been purchased from a retailer by a friend of the plaintiff for consumption by her; it was of dark opaque glass and sealed with a metal cap. The plaintiff claimed it was the defendant's duty to have a system of work and inspection sufficient to prevent snails from intruding into its ginger-beer bottles, and the manufacturer argued that the claim disclosed no cause of action.

Donoghue v. Stevenson was an extremely hard case in 1932, and decided by a bare majority of five judges. There had been no contractual transaction between the parties, who were respectively consumer and manufacturer, and the defendant's argument was that existing law refused recovery of damages for negligence in the absence of a contract. The House of Lords rejected this view, and held that the plaintiff could recover in negligence. Lord Atkin gave the leading judgment for the majority, and offered a principled explanation for a collection of nineteenth century decisions and associated ideas of liability for damage by negligent conduct. They were, he said, applications of a more abstract legal principle that a duty of care is identified when harm to others is foreseeable. Such a principle was not directly expressed in the precedents on which he relied, but he said it was implicit. It was, therefore, right to apply it to manufacturers so far as consumers were concerned unless a principled distinction could be identified justifying a different view.

The conventional modern approach suggests that Lord Atkin tormented the precedents out of recognisable shape in order to reach his conclusion. In particular, a similar principle had been enunciated in *Heaven v. Pender* in 1883,[45] but had failed to gain acceptance by subsequent courts. Lord Atkin attributed that failure in persuasion to a sense of anxiety that a manufacturer would be held liable for a product over which he had lost control once it passed to wholesalers, distributors and retailers. Consequently, he limited manufacturer's liability to goods sold 'in such a form as to show that he intends them to reach the ultimate consumer in the form in which they left him with no reasonable possibility of intermediate examination'.[46]

This amendment, he thought, cured any reasonable reluctance to accept the principle. *Donoghue v. Stevenson* has since been extended and applied to an expanding range of negligent circumstances. The details of those extensions are relevant here as showing the decision is no longer a hard case, and now supplied the dominant justification for identifying negligent conduct. Indeed, so powerful is the gravitational force of the case that it can stop development of other established legal principles in their tracks. *Read v. J. Lyons & Co Ltd*[47] discloses a demarcation dispute between the negligence principle and the strict liability principle contained in *Rylands v. Fletcher*,[48] where the negligence principle prevailed and the defendant succeeded because it was not at fault.

The fascination of *Donoghue v. Stevenson* for realist theories of judicial adjudication lies less in its later triumphs and more in the explanation characteristically given to the process of ratiocination in Lord Atkin's judgment. First-year law students are frequently treated to the alleged insight that, since existing legal materials did not disclose an answer on the facts of the case, Lord Atkin carried out the terms of the Hart thesis. He must have made new law because the manufacturer's liability did not exist before the House of Lords decision. His reputation as a great judge thus rests on his strategic assessment and sense of timing, rather like a good poker player, albeit one with some fairness and humanitarian concern. According to Max Atkinson, first-year law students are then expected to contemplate two antithetical fallacies that have bedevilled theories of judicial behaviour.[49] The first is a natural law sustaining objective moral values, and the second an assumption that judges achieve their decisions by a mechanical process where logical reasoning obliterates any opportunity for them to indulge their personal preference for particular decisional outcomes. It is difficult to find anyone who has seriously advanced the second alternative, but it is a favourite straw man for realists. The only alternative to mechanical extrapolation, say the realists, is to admit the truth that Lord Atkin supplied his own major premise of argument and so invented the law while pretending to vindicate the plaintiff's existing rights.

This rampant cynicism is curable if either of the two modern versions of declaratory theories is applied to Lord Atkin. By the tokens of Hayek's theory, he was justified both in his process of reasoning and in the conclusion he reached. In hard cases it is for the judge to employ his knowledge and skills to focus on the deep structure of the law and the spontaneous order of actions it serves to identify the uniquely right answer. Such self-reflective judicial attitude attempts to reconcile competing purposes,[50] which Lord Atkin did by limiting liability to circumstances where there was no reasonable possibility of intermediate examination. This permits manufacturers with good quality control systems to operate profitably, while at the same time allowing the consumer a remedy against those who are careless. Moreover, the level at which Lord Atkin stated the negligence principle coheres with Hayek's requirement that the law should seek to advance the ends of an unknown individual chosen at random, since the principle proved itself capable of adaptation and application beyond ginger-beer bottles to long-john underpants,[51] to nervous shock claims,[52] and to negligent mis-statements.[53] So persuasive was it that in *Home Office v. Royal Dorset Yacht Co Ltd*[54] three of the judges considered it should apply unless there was some valid reason for not doing so, in effect shifting the burden of proof to those who wish to exclude the principle. This subsequent history goes far to demonstrate that Lord Atkin accurately articulated a rule of just conduct in exercising a judge's dispassionate search for justice.

A similar result is achieved if Dworkin's theory is applied. In both declaratory theories it is wrong for judges to regard precedents as closing off possibilities of extending the common law; both theories also admit the possibilities of mistakes being made by courts, whether in the instant decision or in the precedents being reviewed. The cynical realist view that Lord Atkin manipulated previous decisions to reach the result he wished is thus not a conclusive argument. Does his judgment provide the best explanation of previous decisions? Does it give the most coherent and rational account of tortious liability in those cases against a background of absence of liability for merely being a cause of injury to citizens? These are Dworkinian tests, and scrutiny shows that the earlier decisions identified a duty where there was a special proximity between the parties.[55] Not all judges in *Donoghue v. Stevenson* thought the proximity was one of foreseeable risk, although Lord Macmillan accepted the rightness of Lord Atkin's general approach.[56] But those initial hesitations do not invalidate the use of precedents by Lord Atkin; more persuasively, they indicate that *Donoghue v. Stevenson* was a genuinely hard case where reasonable lawyers could reasonably disagree. For Dworkin and Hayek the plaintiff's right existed before the House of Lords delivered its judgments, so that manufacturers were under a duty of care before 1932 although the courts had not properly appreciated this truth. Realists condemn this as a fiction, or as Lord Reid puts it, a fairy tale. Opposed attitudes of this sort are not capable of conclusive proof either way, but the declaratory approach commends itself as more persuasive than the depressing idea that social goals are being pursued, with the result that judges are sometimes obliged to lie about the way they deal with precedents.

As Atkinson has pointed out, the House of Lords might have come to the same decision thirty years earlier, or even in 1883 if *Heaven v. Pender* had been taken on appeal. It is possible to go back as far as 1869 when the Exchequer Chamber favoured a limited tortious duty for manufacturers in *George v. Skivington*,[57] although the reasoning there was flawed. 'On this view, the fact that we might provide plausible social historical reasons why [the House of Lords] might have been unlikely either to seek or accept such account is not a challenge to this claim about misunderstood rights so much as an explanation of the failure to recognise them.'[58] So a decision which is so often treated as a showcase by realists can surrender more persuasively to nuanced analysis based on modern declaratory theories.

Conclusion

The banner for modern realism is the revolt against formalism. In Australia its main public proponents have been Chief Justice Sir Anthony Mason[59] and Justice Michael Kirby.[60] Sir Owen Dixon's recommendation of a strict and complete legalism as the proper approach to deciding hard cases[61] has been dismissed, even ridiculed. Sir Anthony Mason has characterised the Dixonian approach as resembling an elegantly constructed mansion in which some of the windows have been deliberately left open.[62] It is condemned as elitist and smacking of law as an estoric mystery administered by a priestly caste.[63] The alternative to realism is counted to be sterile logic. In other words, realism (and its stablemate positivism) are a breath of fresh air and judicial honesty.

Puddings are proved by the eating thereof. Both the *Ladies Directory* case and *Donoghue v. Stevenson* surrender better to Hayek's analysis than they do to the cynical pragmatism of modern realism. Dworkin's approach is skewed by his partisan conviction that equality is the basis for common law adjudication. It is, moreover, an approach that offers a revisionist version of formal equality, since treating people with equal respect and concern means reverse discrimination to redress what are perceived as historical disadvantages.

Hayek is the genuine and improved version of Blackstone in modern dress, not Dworkin. Dworkin's claims of right constitute an attempt to quarantine the heterodox from social feedback. It is not going too far to meld Hayek's theory with decisions of the Dixon High Court. That High Court declined to invent new rules to meet ideological claims of social needs.[64] The authenticity of Hayek's analysis with respect to landmark common law decisions goes a considerable distance in support of that view.

Notes

1. The claim about damage to the separation of powers is controversial, but for a crisp assertion of its truth, see Ratnapala, *Welfare State or Constitutional State*?, CIS Policy Monographs 15, 1990. A detailed examination of judicial activism and judicial restraint is found in O'Hair, *The Bankruptcy of Judicial Restraint and Judicial Activism*, PhD thesis, University of Queensland, St Lucia, 1986. A thoughtful article by a modern judge on the 'balance' issue is Davies, 'The Judiciary — Maintaining the Balance' in Finn, ed., *Essays on Law and Government, Vol. 1 – Principles and Values*, Law Book Co., Sydney, 1995 at 267.
2. Lumb, 'The External Affairs Power and Constitutional Reform' (1988) 62 ALJ 679.
3. Lumb, 'Aboriginal Land Rights: Judicial Approaches in Perspective' (1988) 62 ALJ 273.
4. Lumb, 'On a Modern Approach to Jurisprudence' (1960) *Juridicial Review* 143.
5. See, for example, George (ed.), *Natural Law, Liberalism and Morality: Contemporary Essays*, Oxford, Clarendon Pres, 1996.
6. Mason, 'The Role of the Courts at the Turn of the Century' (1993) *Journal of Judicial Administration* 156 at 164.
7. Note 5.
8. Walker, *The Rule of Law: Foundation of Constitutional Democracy*, Melbourne University Press, Melbourne, 1988 at 173.
9. Hart, *The Concept of Law*, Clarendon Press, Oxford, 1961 at 128–32.
10. Hart, *Essays in Jurisprudence and Philosophy,* Clarendon Press, Oxford, 1983 at 7.
11. Hart, *The Concept of Law*, 2nd edn, Clarendon Press, Oxford, 1994. The posthumous postscript contains Hart's rebuttals of Dworkin's attacks on legal positivism, and his criticisms of Dworkin's constructive thesis.
12. See Fogg, 'Dworkin and Hayek: The Declaratory Counter — Revolution' in Ratnapala and Moens (eds), *Jurisprudence of Liberty*, Butterworths, 1996, Essay 10 at 190–200. A similar distinction is made by Dworkin, *Law's Empire*, Fontana, London, 1986 at 152–3.
13. Davies, 'The Judiciary — Maintaining the Balance' in Finn, (ed.), *Essays on Law and Government, Vol 1 — Principles and Values*, Law Book Co., Sydney, 1995 at 267.
14. Note 13 at 272.
15. Dworkin, *Freedom's Law — The Moral Reading of the American Constitution*, Oxford University Press, 1996.
16. Hercules first appeared in *Taking Rights Seriously*, 3rd impression, Duckworth, London, 1981, Chap. 4 (Hard Cases). He recurs in Dworkin's only book that is not a collection of essays, *Law's Empire*, Fontana, London, 1986.
17. For a succinct summary, see Harris, *Legal Philosophies*, 2nd edn, Butterworths, 1997 at 197–205.
18. [1983] 1 AC 410.
19. *Law, Legislation and Liberty*, Routledge & Kegan Paul, London, Vols. 1–3, 1983, Vol. 1 at 19.
20. Note 19, Vol. 2 at 36–7 (negative character); Vol. 1 at 86 (private feasible plans).
21. Note 19, Vol. 2 at 27–9.
22. Note 19, Vol. 2 at 29–30. Hayek is not here dealing with technical validity. A bad decision may be valid, but in a meaningful sense contrary to law. Note 19, Vol. 2 at 50–1.
23. Note 19, Vol. 1 at 74–6. Hart calls these social rules, but excludes them from legality under his rule of recognition.
24. Hayek's view chimes with that of Sir Owen Dixon, who recognised that inarticulate rules

exist, including rules concerning the legal profession. See Woinarski (ed), *Jesting Pilate and Other Papers and Addresses*, Law Book Company, Melbourne, 1965 at 129.

25. Hayek's most systematic account of judicial function is in n 19, Vol. 1 at 94–102, 115–122.
26. For a compatible judicial opinion, see *Robinson v. Mollett* (1875) LR 7 HL 802 per Brett J. at 816–7. O'Hair, n 1 at 231–2.
27. [1932] AC 562.
28. Customary opinion arises from community morals. There can, of course, be morals supporting customary opinion that do not qualify as rules of just conduct because they lack the dimension of 'action towards others' required by Hayek. See O'Hair, n 1, Chap. 5.
29. Lord Campbell, *Lives of the Lord Chancellors*, Vol. 1, 5th edn, 1868 at 405.
30. [1961] 2 All ER 446.
31. Hart, *Law, Liberty and Morality*, Stanford University Press, 1963 at 12. The complaint is odd, since Dworkin accurately identifies Hart's idea of judicial discretion in *The Concept of Law* as exactly producing *ex post facto* law.
32. Hart, n 31.
33. Note 32 at 22.
34. Dworkin, *A Matter of Principle*, Clarendon Press, Oxford, 1986, at 28–9.
35. Note 34 at 22.
36. O'Hair, n 1, Chap. 7.
37. [1961] 2 All ER at 465.
38. Note 36 at 87.
39. *Knuller (Publishing, Printing and Promotions) Ltd v. Director of Public Prosecutions* [1972] 2 All ER 898 per Lord Diplock at 923.
40. Note 36 at 89. The authorities relied on by the House of Lords in *Shaw* are discussed in n 36 at 90–4.
41. This is the second Hayekian criticism.
42. See Hayek's distinction between the relevant and the accidental in n 19, Vol. 1 at 87. This is the third criticism.
43. [1961] 2 All ER 446 at 457.
44. [1932] AC 562.
45. (1883) 11 QBD 503.
46. [1932] AC 562 at 599.
47. [1947] AC 156.
48. (1868) LR 3 HL 330.
49. Atkinson, 'Law Making Judges' (1981) 7(1) *University of Tasmanian LR* 33. The article brilliantly crystallises the advantages of Dworkin's approach over cynical realism. The account of the application of Dworkin's theory in the text reflects this aspect of Atkinson's argument.
50. By the universalisation test of fit with existing rules of the system.
51. *Grant v. Australian Knitting Mills* [1936] AC 85.
52. *Bourhill v. Young* [1943] AC 92.
53. *Hedley Byrne & Co. Ltd. v. Heller & Partners* [1946] AC 465.
54. [1970] AC 1004. Obviously, like *Shaw, Donoghue v. Stevenson* was technically valid as a decision when made. Unlike *Shaw, Donoghue v. Stevenson* triumphantly passes the test of being applied over the long run, which is essentially for a genuine rule of just conduct recognised at common law.
55. Note 49 at 50–4 for these and other arguments.

56. [1932] AC 562 at 619.
57. (1869) LR 5 Exch 1.
58. Note 49 at 52.
59. Mason, 'Future Directions in Australian Law' (1987) 13 *Mon. L.R.* 149.
60. Kirby, *The Judges*, Boyer Lectures, Australian Broadcasting Commission, Sydney, 1983.
61. Note 24 at 152.
62. Note 59 at 155.
63. Note 59 at 159.
64. See, for example, *Rootes v. Shelton* (1967) 116 CLR 383 per Kitto J at 386–7, which emphasised that judges have only riparian rights in the common law.

9

International Trade Law Revisited

Kevin Ryan

Introduction

It is a pleasure to be invited to contribute an article for this memorial volume in honour of Darrell Lumb. We were colleagues at the Law School of the University of Queensland from the time when he was appointed as a lecturer in law in 1959 until I resigned early in 1984. We shared a common interest in constitutional and public international law. We collaborated in writing a textbook on Australian Constitutional Law and in contributing articles to the two editions of International Law in Australia. For many years we had joint responsibility for the courses in constitutional law. More importantly, we were close friends from 1959 until his death in January 1997. His long illness, borne with remarkable cheerfulness, and his death at a relatively early age, were a great loss to all who had come into close contact with him over the years. He was a dedicated legal scholar and a person of wide erudition. It is fitting that his contribution to legal scholarship should be commemorated through the publication of this book.

Darrell's research interest in the field of public international law was concentrated mainly on the law of the sea, and in particular of the coastal jurisdiction. My own interest in that field related mainly to international trade law. In this article I have attempted to give an impression of some major developments which have occurred in the area of international trade law particularly over the past two decades. The treatment is confined to the public law of international trade, as opposed to the law of international trade transactions, and seeks to give an outline of the challenges which have been posed to the post-war aim of creating an integrated multilateral trading system and measures adopted to meet those challenges.

The occasion for these reflections has been my recent participation in international trade law research, after an absence from any substantial involvement in teaching or research in the field for twenty years. At that time, the bases upon which the international trade order had been established were being challenged in several ways. In the course of 1996 I returned after years of work in other fields to a discipline in which old institutions had been basically restructured and new institutions had sprung into existence. Above all, the General Agreement on Tariffs and Trade (GATT) had been massively transformed and given a rebirth under the name of the World Trade Organisation (WTO).

The turning point in the post-war history of the international trading system is to be found, I believe, in the events of the early 1970s. When I wrote a book on international trade law in 1975, I was attempting to give an account of development which had occurred over thirty years since the Second World War. It was already clear by then that the GATT system which had been set up shortly after the war was undergoing severe strain. Two issues had already emerged in the 1960s as serious matters for concern in relation to the functioning of the GATT system. One was the differential treatment accorded to agricultural commodity trade in comparison with trade in manufactured products. The other was the articulation of demands by the developing countries for the adoption of measures which discriminated in their favour despite the non-discriminatory provisions which were basic to the GATT.

In the 1970s the challenge from UNCTAD, which had been established in 1964 as the institution for giving effect to the claims of developing countries, reached a climax in the instruments constituting the New International Economic Order (NIEO) and thereafter rapidly declined. But new issues came to prominence which were handled outside the GATT system which provided a serious threat to its viability as an instrument for the regulation of world trade. Of particular importance were the reliance on non-tariff barriers to trade, the growth in membership of the EEC, its preferential links with other countries and the effect on agricultural trade of its common agricultural policy, the emergence of protectionism within the United States, the trade policies followed by Japan and the newly industrialised economies of East Asia, and the growth of trade in services for which the GATT rules were ill-adapted.

By the mid-1980s it had become evident that if GATT was to survive, it would be necessary to extend it to cover new areas, in particular trade in services and the protection of intellectual property. Agriculture would have to be brought within the GATT system of discipline. The GATT rules would have to be improved particularly by changes to the dispute settlement procedure, and by the adoption of new agreements on subsidies and countervailing measures, on anti-dumping and on safeguards. This became the agenda for the Uruguay Round which culminated in the establishment of the WTO.

It is suggested that the evolution of GATT has passed through three phases. The first covers the period from its establishment in 1947 until the conclusion of the Kennedy Round in 1967. It was a period of high achievement in an expanding world economy. The second phase, which extended until the inauguration of the Uruguay Round in 1986, was one which saw a massive down-turn in the world economy, the widespread adoption of practices which were of dubious consistency with the GATT rules, and a danger of a retreat to protectionism and bilateral or regional rather than global solutions to trade problems. The third phase was the period from the initiation of the Uruguay Round until the establishment of the WTO.

It is of course impossible in this article to give more than a summary outline of these three stages in the life of GATT, but it may be useful to relate some of the major developments in international trade and domestic trading policies to the instrument which was devised fifty years ago to bring legal order into international trading relations.

Phase 1: GATT triumphant

The negotiators who fashioned the GATT rules adopted a concept of an international trading order based on two central ideas. The first was that discrimination as among foreign markets must be eliminated. To achieve this, international trade relations among the contracting parties were to be conducted on the terms of a multilateral most favoured nation commitment. Existing preferences were not required to be dismantled, but they were frozen at existing levels, and no new preferences were to be accorded without a waiver. Where import restrictions were permitted, they were to be administered on a non-discriminatory basis. Where discrimination was permitted for balance of payments reasons, such discriminatory treatment was allowed only temporarily, for the period during which it could be justified on balance of payments grounds. The creation of customs unions and free trade areas was accepted as being consistent with this general obligation of equality of treatment, provided the criteria specified in Article xxiv of the GATT were satisfied.

The second central idea was that the only acceptable form of discrimination in favour of domestic producers was by means of tariff protection. The GATT did not seek to establish a system in which all member countries would be linked through free trade. Trade restrictions in the form of tariff protection could be maintained but machinery would be established which would lead to the mutual reduction of tariff duties, and the extension of the benefits of such reduction to all contracting parties. To this obligation there were exceptions. In particular, there were express exceptions in favour of certain quantitative restrictions, including those adopted pursuant to domestic agricultural support schemes and those imposed under inter-governmental commodity agreements which conformed to criteria approved by GATT members.

These rules were accepted only with a degree of reluctance by several original GATT members. Their willingness to become parties to the GATT was secured only by concessions which had the effect of postponing the strict operation of the GATT system for some years. It was not until the end of the 1950s that the direct controls imposed by the Western European countries on industrial imports from North America were relaxed. Moreover, during the first decade after the war, the trading blocs which had been established by the European powers before the war continued in existence. Britain, for example, exported more to members of the Commonwealth in 1955 than to Western Europe or the United States. But as the 1950s came to a close, two major developments occurred which made possible the full implementation of the GATT system. One was the perception that the most rapidly growing section of trade was that between the developed countries and not that between the developed and the developing countries. There was accordingly no longer the same concern as formerly at building up or preserving sheltered markets in the developing countries. The other was the fact that the Western European countries had reached a stage where they were competitive with the United States and could therefore relax quantitative controls on imports from North America.

Parallel to the emergence of strong economies in Western Europe was their integration in the EEC or EFTA, the building of bridges between these two institutions, and the association with the EEC of many developing countries. The trade groupings which existed at the time when the GATT was negotiated were based mainly on historical links between a metropolitan power and its dominions or colonies. They were superseded or supplemented in the post-war period by new forms of grouping based mainly on regional development and integration schemes. The initial step had been taken with the announcement in May 1950 of the Schuman plan for the establishment of a European Coal and Steel Community which would remove coal and steel production from national control and place it under the control of a community in which the central organ would be endowed with real power over its members. This was implemented through a Treaty signed by France, West Germany, Italy and the Benelux countries. It came into force in August 1955. It was followed by efforts directed to the formation of a European Defence Community and a European Political Community, but their failure led European negotiators from the Six to concentrate on economic integration. Their efforts resulted in the drawing up of the Treaty of Rome instituting the EEC. It came into effect on 1 January 1958. It was quickly followed by the creation by seven other Western European countries of EFTA.

The creation of these regional integration schemes has had an enormous impact on world trading patterns, and on the operation of the most favoured nation principle which is the fundamental rule of the GATT. It was with the trade aspects of these schemes that the GATT was concerned. It must however be appreciated that the objectives sought through the establishment of these integration schemes went beyond those of improving trade. In the case of the EEC, it was always intended to go beyond the establishment of a trading arrangement among the member states in the form of a customs union. A customs union requires the elimination as between member states of restrictions on the movement of goods, and the establishment of a common external tariff. A common market requires in addition the abolition as between member states of obstacles to the free movement of persons, services and capital. The purpose for which the EEC was formed was stated in Article 2 of the Treaty of Rome to be to establish a common market and progressively approximate the economic policies of member states and thereby to promote through the community an harmonious development of economic activities, a continuous and balanced expansion, an increased stability, an accelerated raising of the standard of living, and closer relations between the member states. This looked beyond a common market to an economic union, in which fiscal and monetary policies are harmonised. And beyond that lay the prospect of political union.

Economic arguments put forward for the integration of the economies of the member countries based mainly on the need for larger markets to enjoy economies of scale and the benefits of specialisation, and on the advantages to be derived from intensified competition within the area, were widely questioned at the time and were seen by several European countries as not being sufficient to justify the surrender of national economic sovereignty which participation in the EEC would involve. Their ideal was the establishment of a free trade area embracing the whole of Western Europe, but one limited to manufactured goods because of the particular difficulties associated with securing agreement on trade in agricultural products.

The initial proposal put forward by the United Kingdom in 1956 was to create a European Free Trade Area, within which the proposed customs union of the Six would be constituted. It failed, and in its place there were established an EFTA of the Seven and an EEC of the Six, and bilateral free trade agreements were made between the EEC and individual member states of EFTA. The result was the setting up of a system of industrial free trade throughout Western Europe.

The measures adopted to bring about the economic integration of Europe were taken with close regard to the requirements of the GATT for the creation of customs unions and free trade areas. It is stated in Article XXIV(4) of the GATT that the purpose of a customs union or free trade area should be to facilitate trade between the constituent territories and not to raise barriers to the trade of the contracting parties with such territories. The impact of European economic integration on world trade was both trade creative and trade diversionary. Some countries, and in particular exporters of temperate zone foodstuffs and agricultural products produced in both temperate and tropical zones, were adversely affected by the exclusion from the EEC of products which they had formerly exported to individual member states and by the loss of third markets through subsidised exports from the EEC. Others benefited from increased imports resulting from the growth of income in Western Europe. On balance it was unquestionably trade creative.

There were aspects of the arrangements for European economic integration which were arguably not in accordance with the GATT, such as the exclusion of agricultural trade in EFTA. There were others which seemed to be inconsistent with it, and in particular those provisions in the Treaty of Rome relating to the association of overseas countries and territories. Articles 131 to 136 of the Treaty of Rome sought to promote the economic and social development of those countries and territories and to establish close economic relations between them and the Community. At that time the decolonisation of those territories was still in progress, and critics of the arrangement were not slow to brand it a new form of neocolonialism, as an attempt to continue the privileges accorded to the metropolitan powers by their colonies. This criticism was rejected by the EEC and the associated countries which characterised it as simply a means to provide assistance to the latter to further their development.

In this phase of its existence, GATT activities were centred mainly on the conduct of tariff negotiations and negotiations for accession. In a succession of rounds which culminated with the conclusion of the Kennedy Round in 1967, the industrialised countries made substantial tariff reductions on their dutiable imports and these benefits were extended to all contracting parties through the operation of the most favoured nation clause. There were however two areas in which GATT had only limited success in this period. One was in agricultural trade. Little was done to check the proliferation of protective agricultural policies. Exports were encouraged by export subsidies, and imports were discouraged by quantitative import restrictions. The second was in improving the trading position of the developing countries. The second matter was to provide the major challenge to the GATT system at the beginning of the second phase.

Phase 2: GATT besieged

The challenge from the developing countries

By the early 1960s, the developing countries had become convinced of three matters. These were that it was only by increasing their trade in primary commodities and semi-manufactured goods that they could hope for more rapid economic development; that such increase would not come about unless fundamental changes were made in the rules and practices relating to the conduct of international trade; and that the existing institutions concerned with international trade questions were not prepared to bring about these changes. The objective they pursued was therefore the establishment of a new international trade body which would be the vehicle for effecting reforms in the existing trade system. The measures they sought included the negotiation of commodity agreements to raise and stabilise the price of exports, preferences for manufactured goods of the developing countries in the markets of developed countries, and supplementary financing to compensate the developing countries for losses due to deterioration in the terms of trade.

In June 1964 the United National Conference on Trade and Development (UNCTAD) adopted a set of recommendations relating to international trade relations and trade policies. Many of these recommendations were adopted with the industrialised countries dissenting or abstaining. In effect, they constituted a statement of the changes sought by the developing countries. The Conference also adopted a resolution on the establishment of permanent machinery to continue the work begun at the first UNCTAD.

The issue which above all attracted consideration was the question of preferences for exports of manufactured and semi-manufactured products from the developing countries. It was an issue which split both the industrialised countries and the developing countries. Among the industrialised countries, there were some which had always been resolutely opposed to preferences, and they looked with dismay at the prospect that the GATT prohibition on new preferences would be relaxed. Other industrialised countries which had for a long time granted and received preferential treatment were more sympathetic to the requests of the developing countries. There was general acceptance by the developing countries of the need for preferential arrangements, but there was considerable disagreement among them on the question whether the preferential system to be introduced should be extended to all developing countries in a non-discriminatory way, and as to how the existing preferential systems were to be adjusted to take account of the new system which was to be introduced.

At the Second UNCTAD, held in New Delhi in 1968, a resolution was adopted with the assent of the industrialised market economy countries which recognised unanimous agreement in favour of the early establishment of a mutually acceptable system of generalised non-reciprocal and non-discriminatory preferences which would be beneficial to the developing countries. Three years later GATT approved a ten-year waiver from the most favoured nation obligation to enable members to introduce generalised, non-discriminatory tariff treatment for products originating in developing countries. At the Tokyo Round in 1979 agreement was reached permitting preferential tariff and non-tariff treatment for developing countries as a permanent aspect of the GATT system.

In the 1970s, the proposals by the developing countries for a restructuring of the global economy were formulated in the context of an economic situation which made the demands of the developing countries more pressing and the willingness of the developed countries to meet them more restricted. Inflation and unemployment rose in the industrialised countries to high levels, with consequential protectionist pressures. For many developing countries, the changed economic climate was marked by a serious decline in commodity prices and increased indebtedness as a consequence of this combined with a sharp rise in the price of their oil imports and the decline in aid flows which followed the recession in the developed countries.

The basic instrument which set forth the aspirations of the developing countries for a transformation of the current economic order was a General Assembly resolution: the Declaration on Establishment of a New International Economic Order and the Programme of Action on the Establishment of a New International Economic Order, adopted in May 1974 at a Special Session without a vote but with reservations by the United States, France, the Federal Republic of Germany, Japan and the United Kingdom.

Both in the Declaration and in the Programme of Action which was designed to ensure its application there were explicit references to the need for adoption of the Charter of Economic Rights and Duties of States (CERDS) which was then in the drafting stage. When finally adopted, this set out some fifteen principles which were to govern economic as well as political relations among states, and thirty-four articles on the economic rights and duties of states and on common responsibilities towards the international community.

Throughout the period prior to the adoption of the Charter, there were frequent references by its sponsors to their determination that it would have a juridical character. It was only at the final stage that references in the preamble to the Charter to its effect in codifying and developing rules for the establishment of an NIEO were deleted. Nevertheless, many states, particularly developing countries, maintained that the Charter was an instrument of economic international law. Some went further and argued that the resolutions constituted peremptory norms of general international law (jus cogens) with the consequence that any inconsistent provisions in commercial treaties would be void. This view was rejected by those states which adhered to the traditional position that the United Nations resolutions (apart from resolutions affecting the internal working of the United Nations) have no binding force on members states of the UN. Such resolutions cannot as such be creative or declaratory of legal rights and obligations. They may at most be evidence of a rule which has attained the status of customary law because of a conviction by states that they are obliged to observe that rule, or they may influence the formation of such a conviction.

The most contentious of the principles in the Charter was one which formulated the right of a state to expropriate foreign property. It was asserted that each state has the right

> to nationalise, expropriate or transfer ownership of foreign property, in which case appropriate compensation should be paid by the state adopting such measures, taking into account its relevant laws and regulations and all circumstances that the state considers pertinent. In any case where the question of compensation gives rise to a controversy it shall be settled under the domestic law of the nationalising state and by its tribunals, unless it is freely and mutually agreed by all states concerned that other peaceful means be sought on the basis of the sovereign equality of states and in accordance with the principle of free choice of means.

In 1962 a General Assembly resolution on permanent sovereignty over natural wealth and resources, adopted with the approval of both developed and developing countries, had provided that foreign property could be nationalised on grounds or reasons of public utility, security or the national interest, but appropriate compensation was to be paid in accordance with national and international law. The Charter jettisoned any reference to a duty to pay compensation in accordance with international law. The developed countries which rejected the Charter's formulation on this point insisted that nationalisation or expropriation of foreign property was legitimate only if it was done for a public purpose, and if just compensation in the light of all relevant circumstances was paid; and the determination of those questions must, if necessary, be settled through recourse to internationally agreed dispute settlement procedures.

The matter of rules relating to the protection of investments abroad had been taken up at the Havana Conference of 1948 and included in the draft Charter of the International Trade Organisation, which was intended to incorporate and administer the rules of the GATT. The failure to ratify the Charter had the effect that the issue was not subject to international agreement. Since the further failure to secure agreement on the terms of the CERDS resolution, international protection has been sought predominantly through bilateral or regional agreements. There has however recently been a revival of attempts to achieve consensus on the issue by multilateral agencies, including the OECD, the

World Bank, and the WTO as successor to the GATT. These efforts are currently continuing.

During the first few years after its establishment UNCTAD devoted itself almost wholly to challenging the GATT trading system and to inducing the developed countries to accept changes in that system in the interests of the developing world. But in the 1970s increasing attention was paid to the activities of the dominant agent of world trade and international production — the Transnational Corporation (TNC).

The concern of the developing countries at the activities of TNCs was focused initially on the capacity to impose restrictive conditions on their exports. They were concerned also at the ability of TNCs to determine the conditions on which technology was made available to them. Most developing countries accepted that investment and the transfer of technologies by TNCs were essential to their economic development, but they feared the loss of local control which might come from extensive foreign participation in their economies and in particular from the fact that decisions which deeply affected them might be made by persons or enterprises which were not amenable to their jurisdiction. They were convinced that the task of controlling multinational enterprises must be taken up on a multilateral basis. They sought therefore the collaboration of all states in agreeing upon a set of rules which would apply to TNCs and which would regulate two particular aspects of their activities, namely the transfer of technology and restrictive business practices.

Many developed countries accepted that the elaboration of codes which would define proper standards of conduct for multilateral enterprises was desirable and they agreed that it was useful to secure international agreement on the conditions relating to the transfer of technology and on restrictive trade practices. The matter of transfer of technology was taken up later in the context of the Uruguay Round. The general issue of control of TNCs is currently subsumed mainly in the search for a multilateral investment agreement.

Another matter which was included in the commercial policy provisions of the draft Havana Charter was that of international commodity agreements. This was an area which was of particular importance to the developing countries which relied mainly on exports of primary commodities for their export income and UNCTAD became the main centre for commodity negotiation. Its aim became one of maximisation of export income rather than price stability which was the object of the Havana Charter provisions. Two commodity matters which received particular emphasis in the NIEO documents were the role of producers' associations and the link between prices of commodities and those of manufactured goods. This was a reflection of the particular circumstances which had affected commodity trade in the early 1970s. The specific reason for calling the special session of the General Assembly at which the Declaration and Programme of action were adopted was the deterioration in the economic situation of a large number of developing countries as a result of the sharp increase in the prices of essential imports of food, fertilisers, energy products, capital goods, equipment and services. Advocacy of the establishment of a link between the prices of primary commodities and manufactures was prompted by the view that this would serve to halt the adverse movement in the terms of trade of the developing countries. The support for producers' associations was stimulated by the success of OPEC.

Both these proposals were unacceptable to the industrialised countries. They objected to the proposal to establish fixed price relationships between the exports and imports of developing countries as impractical or difficult of achievement. Their objection to producers' associations was more fundamental. In CERDS it is declared that all states have the right to associate in organisations of primary commodity producers, and that all states have the duty to respect that right by refraining from applying economic and political measure that would limit it. To the major industrialised countries this clause seemed to be an attempt to sanction the establishment of producer cartels. It was precisely to prevent their establishment that in the trading rules adopted after the war, it was stipulated that intergovernmental agreements which involved the regulation of production or quantitative controls of exports of a primary commodity or the regulation of price could be entered into only after a commodity conference had been called in which producing and consuming countries were entitled to be equally represented.

The main thrust of the developing countries in the commodity field was to secure adoption of their proposals for an integrated programme for commodities, designed to stabilise trade in eighteen commodities identified as being of particular interest to them, and to support commodity prices at levels which in real terms were remunerative and just to producers and equitable to consumers. It is enough to say that little progress was made over the ensuing decade in negotiating agreements on the eighteen listed commodities.

The challenge within the industrialised world

By the early 1980s it was clear that the impact of UNCTAD had been limited to the securing of a significant alteration to the no new preferences rule of GATT, and to emphasising the limitations of GATT as a general instrument for regulating international commercial policy. But a much more serious challenge to the GATT system came from policies pursued by the industrialised countries which were of predominant importance in world trade.

Already by the early 1970s it was evident that the commanding position which the United States had enjoyed in determining the rules which were embodied in the GATT and in the operation of the world economy had disappeared. In 1971 it experienced a trade deficit for the first time in this century. There were several reasons for this but emphasis was repeatedly placed on the effect of unfair or discriminatory practices by its trading partners. By the Trade Act of 1974 and amendment thereto the President was authorised to retaliate against foreign countries which imposed unjustifiable or unreasonable restrictions upon United States commerce. It required the President if he determined that action by the United States was appropriate to enforce the rights of the United States under any trade agreement or to respond to any act, policy or practice of a foreign country or instrumentality that was inconsistent with the provisions of, or otherwise denied benefits to the United States under, any trade agreement or was unjustifiable unreasonable or discriminatory and which burdened or restricted United States commerce to take all appropriate and feasible action within his power to obtain the elimination of such act, policy or practice. The Presidential authority might be exercised on a non-discriminatory basis or solely against the foreign country or instrumentality involved. Action taken might include the suspension or withdrawal of trade agreement concessions and the imposition of duties or other import restrictions. Proceedings to initiate Presidential action might be brought by US firms and citizens who alleged that US commercial interests had been harmed by illegal or unfair actions of foreign governments or they might be brought by the government. If an international agreement was involved (as in the case of GATT) the US had recourse to its dispute settlement processes if no acceptable solution was achieved. But even if no violation of an international agreement was alleged sanctions might be invoked on the ground that actions of the foreign government were unreasonable.

The United States sought by these provisions to compel other countries to comply with its views on trade matters including the protection of intellectual property. In so far as the actions of other GATT members were not inconsistent with the GATT, any retaliatory reaction by the United States would probably be in breach of the GATT.

Vigorous action was taken by the United States not only to impose sanctions for unreasonable restrictions on its trade, but also for the granting of unjustifiable exports subsidies or for the dumping of products so as to injure its domestic industries. There were frequent complaints by its trading partners about the processes involved in imposing countervailing or anti dumping duties, and in particular at the time taken in investigations.

In order to provide relief against imports where this could not be justified under GATT Article XIX, the United States relied heavily on so-called voluntary restraints by exporting countries, by which they accepted restraints negotiated in diplomatic proceedings which by-passed the GATT requirements. In addition, the 1974 Act permitted relief to be provided if the International Trade Commission found that imports were a substantial cause of serious injury or threat thereof to an industry. It became unnecessary to establish that imports were the major factor in injury, nor was it necessary to provide any link between increased imports and trade concessions.

While the United States made use of the GATT to resolve disputes, its dissatisfaction with the GATT rules and processes led it to have recourse increasingly to bilateral negotiations outside the GATT system. It was in such bilateral negotiations that its major crises with the EEC and Japan were handled, and the solutions attained were often of dubious consistency with GATT.

By the mid-1980s, the United States had moved from a position where it had been the principal author of the GATT system to one where it was highly critical of many of its basic provisions. It had moved from a position of support for multilateral solutions to one where it relied heavily on bilateral solutions. And it had moved from a position where it actively sought the removal of obstacles to international trade on a global basis to one where it looked favourably upon regional solutions. In 1980 the United States and Canada initiated negotiations on a bilateral free trade agreement. In 1987 the United States-Canada Free Trade Agreement was signed. It came into effect in January 1989. Three years later the United States, Canada and Mexico signed an agreement for a North American Free Trade Area (NAFTA). It came into operation in January 1994. Further extension of the free trade area to include all countries of the Western Hemisphere was advocated in 1990 by President Bush. For the United States recourse to regionalism had been motivated by concern at the developments which had occurred in the European Community which were seen as likely to result in the displacement in Community markets of North American suppliers.

The EEC (now the European Union) has been involved since the 1970s mainly with two matters: enlargement and movement towards a closer union. The process of enlargement began in 1969, and resulted in the admission of Denmark, Ireland and the United Kingdom to membership of the European Communities in 1973. Parallel negotiations were held with the remaining EFTA countries in order to maintain a European free trade area in industrial goods. Subsequent negotiations led to the admission of Greece in 1981, Portugal and Spain in 1985, and Austria, Finland and Sweden in 1994. In 1991 the bilateral free trade agreements between the Community and the EFTA Countries was replaced by the Agreement on the European Economic Area.

The collapse in 1990 of the Eastern European trading system (the Council for Mutual Economic Assistance) has been followed by the negotiation of bilateral association agreements with most of its former members.

In addition to enlarging its membership, the Community entered into association or preferential trade agreements with a number of Mediterranean countries. It also entered into an arrangement (the Lome Convention) with developing countries which included, in addition to the countries mentioned in the Treaty of Rome, twenty-one Commonwealth Countries and six other independent countries not linked with the Commonwealth or the six original EEC members. The result of these measures was that the EEC operated three systems of preferences: one under the Lome Convention in favour of African, Caribbean and Pacific (ACP) states; another under the Mediterranean policy; and the third under the Generalised System of Preferences in favour of all remaining developing countries. The Lome Convention made accession possible to countries with an economic structure and production comparable to those of the ACP states. It was a formula which excluded such countries as those of the Indian Sub-Continent (with which the Communities have commercial cooperation treaties) and those of ASEAN, with which the EEC conducted negotiations through a mixed group of representatives of the Commission and of ASEAN.

The EEC's preferential arrangements were strongly attacked by some GATT members as being inconsistent with the GATT provisions. The attacks came both from the developing countries excluded from the Lomé Convention, in particular the Latin Americans, and from the industrialised members of GATT. The opposition by the latter group resulted in the abandonment by the EEC of reverse preferences in favour of the preference-giving countries. In the case of the former, special account was taken of the interests of Latin American countries in devising the Generalised System of Preferences.

In the early 1970s proposals were made not only for enlargement of the EEC but also for rapid movement towards economic and monetary union. But these aspirations had to be abandoned in the face of the realities dictated by the onset of recession and high inflation and collapse of the Bretton Woods financial system. It was only with the signature of the Single European Act in 1986 that the Community took a decisive step forward in the direction of the creation of a single market. While the EEC had for more than twenty years fulfilled the GATT requirements for the establishment of a customs union, it had lagged behind in the removal of non-tariff barriers to the creation of a single market. In order to secure the harmonisation of national laws which was necessary for a single market, it provided for the use of qualified majority voting for Community regulations and directives.

From a single internal market, progress was quickly made towards an Economic and Monetary Union and a Political Union. The Maastricht Accords, signed in February 1992, established a European Union. It set out a timetable for movement towards economic and monetary union, including adoption of a single currency and establishment of a European Central Bank. It contains commitments to the implementation of a common foreign and security policy. It marks a major step towards European political integration.

The European Community, like the United States, had recourse to voluntary export restraints to limit certain imports from Japan. It had frequent conflicts with the United States on the question of subsidies to agricultural products. This culminated in the adoption by the United States of its Export Enhancement Scheme which was designed to target markets which had benefited from the Community subsidies, but which has created major difficulties for other agricultural exporters.

The most significant development in this period was the emergence of the Eastern Pacific as the most dynamic area in terms of economic growth. Japan came to share with the European Community and the United States a commanding position in world trade. There was an explosive growth in the trading position of the newly industrialised economies of East Asia. And China moved to the position where, as a consequence of transformation of its economic system and its relations with the outside world, it was in the process of becoming a major economic and trading power.

In the case of Japan there was a vast expansion of exports which was made possible by its earlier heavy investment in capital goods. Though this enabled it to move towards liberalisation of imports and investments, it provoked great concern in the United States and the Community at the size of the Japanese trade balance and led to charges of unfair trade practices by Japan. The threat of protectionism in those markets led the Japanese to move towards massive direct investment in manufacturing and service industries and in real estate, particularly in the United States, and thereby created a further cause for friction in their relationship.

South Korea followed a similar path to Japan, and ran into the same problems, particularly with the United States. Its increased exports to the United States were met by demands for the imposition of so-called voluntary export restraints, and by the institution of anti-dumping and countervailing duty investigations in respect to a number of South Korean exports. It was also subjected to insistent demands from the United States for the lowering of its tariff and for the liberalisation of its list of import restrictions and of its foreign investment regime.

Mainland China has moved since 1978 from its previous policy of autarkic development to one where it operates one which it refers to as a 'socialist market economy'. Though stringent controls are still maintained over foreign trade and investment China has recognised the importance of extending its international economic relations and exchanges. It has encouraged direct foreign investment particularly in export and high technology industries and has liberalised imports of capital equipment and consumer durables. In 1987 it made application to resume its membership of GATT. This application is currently under examination.

China's most serious trade disputes have been with the United States. Under the Trade Act of 1974, the United States accorded most favoured nation treatment to China, but this is subject to annual renewal. The renewal has been accompanied by scrutiny of China's human rights record, to China's intense disapproval, and by charges of counterfeiting in violation of intellectual property rights protection.

While the United States and the Community are vital markets for the Eastern Asian countries, there has been a major expansion also within the Eastern Asian region itself. Hong Kong was able to profit from the change in China's trade policy in 1978 by locating industries in China, and by providing shipping and financial services to China, as well as by serving as an entrepot for trade between China and Western countries. Taiwan has been able since 1983 to supply goods through Hong Kong for processing and assembly on Mainland China for export to international markets.

In South-East Asia Singapore has a position which is comparable with that of Hong Kong in East Asia. Since 1976 ASEAN has been reactivated through the creation of an intra-ASEAN preferential tariff scheme, the promotion of joint industrial projects, and the adoption of a common position on international economic matters.

In 1989, as a result of an Australian initiative, there was formed an intergovernmental body, the Asia Pacific Economic Cooperation (APEC). It consisted initially of 12 countries: Australia, Canada, Japan, South Korea, New Zealand, the United States, and the six ASEAN countries. Its membership has been extended to include China, Hong Kong, Taiwan, Mexico, Chile and Papua New Guinea. Its object is to promote among these countries a non-discriminatory trade arrangement. It is not designed to be a free trade area in the sense of Article XXIV of GATT.

The main activity of GATT in this phase was concentrated on the removal or limitation of non-tariff barriers to trade. In the Tokyo Round a number of codes were adopted which in legal theory bound only the contracting parties which ratified them, but which other countries were subject to strong pressure to accept. They comprised a Customs Valuation Code, which set out valuation methods to be used in the valuation of goods for customs purposes; a revised Anti-Dumping Code, which amended an Anti-Dumping Code negotiated in the Kennedy Round; an Import Licensing Code, which was designed to ensure that the issue of import licences and the administration of import restrictions did not operate to restrict imports; an Agreement on Technical Barriers to trade; a Government Procurement Code, designed to ensure national treatment and non-discrimination in purchases by governments for their own use; and a Subsidies and Countervailing Duties Code relating to the interpretation and application of the GATT articles on countervailing duties, on subsidies and on dispute settlement.

The most serious problem for GATT was the decline in the adherence by the major industrialised countries to its rules as providing a legal framework for the conduct of international trade. Solutions were frequently adopted to disputes which by-passed the GATT mechanisms, and were sometimes in conflict with GATT provisions. The most flagrant violations were in respect to the GATT rule in Article XIX which prescribed the conditions on which emergency action might be taken in respect of imports which caused or threatened serious injury to domestic production, and in the adoption of agreements which restricted trade benefits to the parties to agreements in violation of the unconditional most favoured nation clause.

By the mid-1980s a stage had been reached where the multilateral trading system instituted in 1947 had been seriously eroded and was in danger of being largely superseded by bilateral and regional arrangements. The obvious remedy was the institution of another major Round. That was done with the decision taken in 1986 to launch the Uruguay Round.

Phase 3: GATT transformed

From the time when the Uruguay Round was inaugurated in September 1986 until agreement was reached on 15 December 1993 on the texts incorporated in the Final Act, intense negotiations were conducted not only in traditional areas of GATT concern such as tariff and non-tariff barriers to trade, but extending over fields which had never been subject to GATT discipline or which were inadequately dealt within the GATT. They culminated in adoption not only of a number of new agreements but in the establishment of a new institution, the World Trade Organisation, as the 'common institutional framework for the conduct of trade relations among its members in matters related to the agreements and associated legal instruments included in the Annexes to the Agreement'.

There are four Annexes to the Agreement. Annexes 1, 2 and 3, which refer to what are termed the multilateral trade agreements, are integral parts of the agreement, binding on all members. Annex 4 is part of the agreement for the members who have accepted the agreements included in it, but does not create obligations or rights for members that have not accepted them. It consists of four agreements referred to as plurilateral trade agreements drawn up in the Tokyo Round. The task of the WTO is to implement the WTO Agreement and the multilateral trade agreements, and it provides the framework for the implementation of the plurilateral trade agreements. It provides the forum for negotiation among its members concerning the multilateral trade relations in matters dealt with under the agreements in the Annexes and for further negotiations as may be decided by a ministerial conference which is to meet at least once every two years.

Annex 1 is divided into Annex 1A, 1B and 1C. Annex 1A contains agreements on trade in goods. In effect it incorporates the provisions of GATT 1947 as amended prior to the entry into force of the WTO (excluding the protocol of provisional application), the provisions of the legal instruments which had entered into force under GATT, and understandings negotiated during the Uruguay Round on the interpretation of certain articles of GATT. It includes also agreements on trade in goods negotiated during the Uruguay Round. Included in these are the agreement on agriculture, and on subsidies and countervailing measures.

In respect to agriculture, negotiations were conducted mainly by the United States, the European Union, and the Cairns Group of 14 agricultural exporting countries in which a leading role was taken by Australia. These negotiations centred on the three critical matters of market access, domestic support and export subsidies. They resulted in important decisions relating to cuts in agricultural tariffs, the tariffication and reduction of non-tariff measures limiting market access, the decrease of domestic farm supports, and the reduction in the value and quantity of subsidised exports. The Agreement on Agriculture is an important measure for the control of agricultural trade, but it has not made trade in agriculture subject fully to the regime applicable to industrial goods. It is also an area which in the fourth phase which has opened with the adoption of the Final Act will continue to demand attention.

The Agreement on Subsidies and Countervailing Measures advanced the work which had been done in the Tokyo Round negotiations, where it was agreed that the use of export subsidies to increase exports and to limit imports should be more closely circumscribed, and so should recourse to countervailing duties to offset the effects of subsidies. In these negotiations, the prohibition on the use of export subsidies for industrial products were strengthened, and it was extended to subsidies on minerals. Export subsidies were not to be granted on products other than primary products derived from farms, forests or fisheries. In relation to farm, forest and fishery products, the Tokyo Round defined more precisely ways in which export subsidies can give an exporting country more than an equitable share of world export trade, and it provided special procedures for the settlement of disputes about subsidies. The Uruguay Round agreement placed emphasis on the process of resolving disputes about subsidies, distinguishing for this purpose subsidies prohibited under the GATT rules, actionable subsidies which can cause adverse effects to the interest of other members and non-actionable subsidies. There was also a refinement of the work which had been carried out in the Tokyo Round in respect to the imposition of countervailing duties and antidumping duties.

The matter of emergency action was dealt with in an Agreement on Safeguards, in which it was agreed that voluntary export restraints and orderly marketing arrangements would have to be eliminated within four years and their future use was prohibited. Any restrictions imposed by way of quotas were required in principle to be non-discriminatory, but in cases of actual serious injury, selective safeguard action was permitted limited to a period of four years.

Annex 1B contains the General Agreement on Trade in Services. The GATT rules drawn up in 1947 were concerned with the exchange of goods across national boundaries. They did not envisage the growth of international trade in services, which can occur not only across national boundaries but also within national boundaries. That growth has arisen mainly from the development of new technologies, particularly in the telecommunications and information areas, and through the internationalisation of production by multilateral corporations and the consequential need for the supply of services by and to enterprises established in the host countries. The key obligation of parties to the agreement is to provide most favoured nation treatment to all members of the agreement in relation to measures affecting trade in services covered by the agreement, but a member may list exemptions from this obligation which are to be phased out over a period not exceeding ten years. In addition, national treatment is to be provided by a member in respect to services and service suppliers of other members in sectors it has inscribed in its schedule, and subject to any conditions and qualifications set out in the schedule. Successive rounds of negotiations are to be conducted.

In Annex 1 C there is set out the Agreement on Trade Related Aspects of Intellectual Property rights, including Trade in Counterfeit Goods (the TRIPS Agreement). The negotiation of a set of rules designed to protect intellectual property rights was a new venture for the GATT. The United States had taken retaliatory action pursuant to its legislation against what it regarded as unfair practices involving intellectual property rights, and it succeeded in having the matter included in the Uruguay Round Agenda. The Agreement contains a set of general principles designed to protect intellectual property rights, including the principle of national treatment and most favoured nation treatment. It also contains provisions in respect of particular intellectual property rights — patterns, trademarks, geographical indications, copyright, layout designs of integrated circuits, industrial designs — and on the matter of unfair competition.

Annex 2 contains an understanding on Rules and Procedures governing the Settlement of Disputes. There had been a strong tendency to regard dispute resolution as intended to lead to negotiated agreement between the contending parties rather than as designed to resolve a conflict on the basis of applicable rules. The understanding makes it clear that although the processes of conciliation and negotiation should be utilised, the ultimate determination must be made by the application of the relevant rules. It also provides in considerable detail for the procedure by which trade disputes are to be resolved including the establishment of a Dispute Settlement Body, the automatic establishment of panels to hear disputes, and appeals from panel decisions to a standing appellate body on issues of law.

With these measures the GATT has in effect been transformed into the WTO, though it is not a successor agreement to GATT as defined in the Vienna Convention on the Law of Treaties. It has taken important steps towards resolving many of the most critical issues which threatened disruption of an integrated global trading system. The fear that the developing countries might establish a rival institution has been overcome or at least averted by the adaptations made to meet some of their concerns, though it remains to be seen whether these will suffice to ensure to them a growth adequate to their needs. The rival grouping of the centrally planned economies has disappeared, and most of its members — with the great exception of Russia — have been admitted to WTO or are seeking admission. Some of the main points of friction between the industrialised market countries, in such areas as agricultural protectionism and subsidisation, dispute resolution and emergency action through voluntary export restraints, have been addressed in a useful if not final manner. And the range of matters brought within the ambit of the WTO has been extended to make it a more appropriate instrument in the contemporary world. It has opened a fourth phase in the history of GATT. That will no doubt be marked initially by work designed to build upon and extend the results of the Uruguay Round. But beyond this lies what is likely to be the great challenge in the near future: the preservation of a multilateral trading system in a world where regional economic arrangements are being simultaneously developed and where new centres of economic power are emerging.

10

GATT — an impediment to conservation? The Gasoline Case

Peter Gillies

Introduction

A vigorous literature has charted the purported conflict between the GATT/WTO ideal of a free trade in goods among member parties and the pursuit of conservation goals by these same parties. On occasions, it has been suggested, the General Agreement has constituted an impediment to protection of the environment.

The GATT/WTO, of course, provides a multilateral framework for free trade among its membership, subject to certain restrictions, the obvious one being that members are allowed to maintain formal, transparent tariff barriers. GATT has become an issue in the conservation context, because of the determination of certain of its members — principally the United States of America — to employ trade sanctions to further conservation objectives determined unilaterally by themselves.

A technique favoured by the United States has been the employment of embargoes on imports, as a sanction against States which are unable or unwilling to comply with environmental regimes promulgated by it. Such a mechanism can be more readily employed, of course, by a country like the United States with its massive economy and domestic market.

Importation prohibitions implemented by the United States were at the centre of the most celebrated case involving the alleged GATT/conservation conflict, namely, the 1991 challenge brought by Mexico against US trade embargoes designed to protect dolphins from being harmed or killed by tuna fishing in the Eastern Tropical Pacific Ocean — a challenge which resulted in a GATT Panel decision which may for convenience be referred to as the *Tuna I* case.[1]

Tuna I was reprised in the parallel 1994 challenge by the European Economic Community and the Netherlands — a case which may conveniently be termed *Tuna II*.[2]

The disputed trade embargoes were likewise imposed by the United States, in a quest to protect marine mammals, in particular dolphins. In both of these cases the US measures were especially contentious — they were applied to achieve a de facto extraterritorial reach for US conservation law and policy. They illustrate very pointedly how the GATT ideal of the free movement of goods can conflict with conservation objectives.

The third case of particular interest in this context is the most recent one — the 1996 challenge by Brazil and Venezuela against prohibitions on the importation of gasoline authorised by the *US Clean Air Act 1990*. This case will for convenience be termed the *Gasoline* case.[3]

The matter was first referred to a Panel constituted under WTO/GATT; thereafter, its determination was taken on appeal by the United States to the World Trade Organisation Appellate Body. The latter's ruling was its first. Conceptually the *Gasoline* case was a step removed from the *Tuna* cases — the United States was not seeking de facto extraterritorial reach for its conservation policies, but merely seeking to render more effective its internal conservation policies. Nonetheless, the Appellate Body (as had the Panel) found against the United States.

As noted below, the GATT/Panels and the WTO Appellate Body have evinced a protectiveness towards the General Agreement and its objectives. The basic feature of GATT, of course, is that it is predicated on (relatively) free trade among its members, subject to limited and specific exceptions. There is necessarily a heavy onus case upon a member which would, without violating its obligations under WTO/GATT, impose trade sanctions on another member or members.

The General Agreement does not preclude resort to any and all alternative mechanisms for the accomplishment of conservation goals — for example, it is apparent that the members of WTO/GATT (or a subset of them) could, between themselves, conclude other multilateral arrangements for the joint accomplishment of conservation objectives.[4]

Indeed, it is probably the case that the larger ecological issues (such as countering the greenhouse effect) can only be resolved by way of multilateral agreements between States, and could not realistically be resolved by way of individual States imposing trade sanctions on other States, to achieve these more expansive objectives.

Even with the framework of the General Agreement, explicit provision is made for the pursuant of environmental objectives by member States. Article XX operates to save measures which would otherwise be inconsistent with GATT, by reference to a series of alternative tests. Of present relevance are Article XX(b), which excepts measures which are 'necessary to protect human, animal or plant life or health', and Article XX(g), which excepts measures 'relating to the conservation of exhaustible natural resources if such measures are made effective in conjunction with restrictions on domestic production or consumption'. In both cases, however, the measures must not only fall within the terms of each clause, but they must as well fulfil the preamble, or chapeau to Article XX, which requires that the measures are not to be 'applied in a manner which would constitute a means of arbitrary or unjustifiable discrimination between countries where the same conditions prevail, or a disguised restriction on international trade'. (The same qualifier applies to the other Article XX exceptions.) The preamble makes clear that, although member parties may in these defined cases take measures designed to achieve conservation objectives, and although these measures may be prima facie inconsistent with GATT, nonetheless they must not be fundamentally subversive of GATT and its objectives. The preamble undoubtedly vests much discretion in adjudicative panels and the Appellate Body, in disputes of the type canvassed in these cases.

Below, the three leading cases are reviewed. The *Tuna* twins have been adequately discussed in the literature, but the more recent *Gasoline* determination warrants fuller consideration. They are analysed with a view to discerning the extent to which GATT and the obligations imposed by it are inconsistent with conservation goals, the dimensions of any such impediments as may be discerned, and the need, if any, to modify the General Agreement in order to harmonise it with these objectives.

It is to be noted, incidentally, that there have been other earlier GATT disputes airing the environment/trade issue,[5] which have been referred to the Panel.

Tuna I case

Overview

The first *Tuna* case — the Report of the Dispute Settlement Panel appointed to determine whether the US embargo on the importation of Mexican tuna[6] was in breach of the United States' obligations under GATT — is the most often cited instance of a conflict between the GATT and policies directed at environmental conservation. The measures in contention were embargoes on the importation of tuna into the United States in defined circumstances, instituted under the regime provided for by the *United States Marine Mammal Protection Act 1972* (the 'MMPA'). Inter alia, provisions in the Act governed the taking of marine mammals incidental in the course of taking yellowfin tuna in the Eastern Tropical Pacific Ocean ('ETP') and the importation of these tuna and tuna products.[7] In the ETP, dolphins and tuna were observed to associate together, so that fishermen developed a technique (the 'purse-seine' net fishing technique) of encircling dolphins with nets in order to catch the tuna swimming below. Dolphin mortality and serious injury resulted from this technique.

The MMPA authorised but limited the incidental taking of marine mammals by US fishermen in the course of commercial fishing. Pursuant to the regime, one (and only one) permit was granted, covering all domestic tuna fishing in the ETP. This was granted to the American Tuna-boat Association. It limited the killing or injury of dolphins to 250,000 per year (specific ceilings were promulgated in relation to certain types of dolphins within this global ceiling). Specific rules were enacted by way of the MMPA and regulations to govern the use of the purse-seine nets to encircle dolphins, applying to all persons subject to US jurisdiction. The MMPA regime further provided for the mandatory imposition of bans on the importation of commercial fish or fish products from fish caught with commercial fishing technology which resulted from the incidental killing or serious injury of ocean mammals in excess of US standards. It provided for the prohibition of the importation of yellowfin tuna harvested with purse-seine nets in the ETP and products from it unless the secretary of Commerce found that the government of the harvesting country had a program governing the taking of marine animals which was comparable to the US program and the average rate of such taking was comparable to the average rate of taking by US vessels. The burden was imposed on the harvesting country to show that these conditions apply. Further provisions specified more precisely the conditions which had to be met for a positive finding that the harvesting country's regime was comparable to the US regime. Inter alia, the average incidental taking rate (in terms of the dolphins killed each time purse-seine nets were set) for the harvesting country's tuna fleet were not to exceed 1.25 times the average taking rate of the US vessels in the same period. Additional sub-quotas for specified types of tuna applied. This regime was of course unworkable, because the harvesting country's fleet could not know before the end of the period what the relevant US figures for that period were.

The MMPA also provided for the mandatory imposition of bans on all intermediary countries from which yellowfin tuna and tuna products were imported into the United States, unless the intermediary country certified and provided reasonable proof that it had acted to prohibit the importing of such tuna and tuna products from any country from which direct export to the United States had been banned. In effect, these nations were required to apply secondary boycotts, mirroring the primary US boycotts, on pain of having their own tuna exports (or re-exports) banned.[8]

Pursuant to court orders made under the MMPA regime, in 1990–91 the US Government imposed embargoes in certain terms on (1) the importation of yellowfin tuna and products from tuna harvested with purse-seine nets in the ETP from Mexico; and (2) the importation of tuna, etc, harvested in like circumstances by vessels of Mexico, Venezuela and Vanuatu. In 1991 the United States announced the application of an intermediary nation embargo on tuna and tuna product imports from certain countries, pursuant to which such imports would be prohibited unless the importer declared that the tuna did not include yellowfin tuna or tuna products harvested with purse-seines nets in the ETP by Mexican vessels.

The Panel's finding

The US regime in question was a challenging one for GATT. In substance the United States was seeking to impose its environmental policies not only on parties subject to US jurisdiction but on other nations, and to enrol intermediary nations in the enforcement of these policies through its secondary boycott regime. In substance if not in form the United States was seeking an extraterritorial operation for the relevant provisions in the MMPA.

The Panel dealt first with the primary embargoes.[9] These were determined to be in breach of Article XI.I, being (self-evidently) quantitative restrictions on imports of a type prohibited by Article XI. The measures could not be justified under Article III as mere internal regulations enforced at the time of or point of importation.

The embargoes could not be justified under the Article XX(b) or (g) exceptions. Both exceptions are subject to the preamble to Article XX (which in view of the findings on (b) and (g) against the United States, did not fall for consideration). At the outset, the Panel noted that Article XX was to be construed narrowly, with the burden being on the State seeking to invoke it by way of exception, to demonstrate its applicability.[10]

Article XX(b) operates to except the party otherwise in breach of its obligations under GATT, where the disputed measure is necessary to protect human, animal or plant life or health. In the Panel's view, the United States had not shown that its measures were *necessary* in order to accomplish the conservation objectives. The regime enacted by the United States was for practical purposes unworkable, given that the targeted States were unable to know before the end of the relevant accounting period what the US taking rate against which they had to benchmark themselves during this period would end up being. Given this lack of utility, it was by implication difficult to establish that the impeached mechanism and it alone was the only feasible means of accomplishing the objective contended for. The Panel noted that the United States had not explored other reasonable options, such as seeking to regulate the taking rate by multilateral agreements. The issue of extra-territoriality did not arise for consideration given this finding, although the Panel was clearly of the opinion that (b) could not be interpreted as sanctioning such an extended reach for a party's laws. The Panel noted that to accept the United States' broad conception of Article XX(b), so as to permit it to impose unilaterally regulatory regimes in other contracting parties identical to its own, would inevitably greatly weaken parties' rights under GATT.[11]

The United States likewise was not entitled to invoke the Article XX(g) exception. XX(g) excepts measures otherwise in breach, which relate to the conservation of exhaustible natural resources, if made effective in conjunction with restrictions on domestic production or consumption. Inter alia, in the Panel's opinion Article XX(g) was intended to permit contracting parties to take trade measures primarily aimed at rendering effective restrictions on production or consumption within their own jurisdictions — it was not intended to permit a country in effect to justify an extraterritorial (or extra-jurisdictional) reach for its own laws.[12] To approve such an extended application would produce the same problem that it would produce in the case of clause (b), that is, that 'each contracting party could unilaterally determine the conservation policies from which other contracting parties could not deviate without jeopardising their rights under the General Agreement'.[13]

Furthermore, accepting a previous Panel's determination that XX(g) required that the disputed measure be aimed 'primarily' at the conservation policy in issue,[14] the instant embargoes and their underpinning legislation could not be so categorised, given the unworkable nature of the US benchmarks: 'a limitation on trade based on such unpredictable conditions could not be regarded as being primarily aimed at the conservation of dolphins'.[15] The reasoning at this point is somewhat opaque — what is really being highlighted at this point is a requirement that the measures be reasonably or necessarily adapted to accomplishing the conservation objective. Clearly, however, this consideration — of unworkability — would have been relevant to determining whether the United States could satisfy the Article XX chapeau, had this issue arisen (it did not, given the threshold findings in relation to clauses (b) and (g).

The secondary embargo was found to be in conflict with GATT by symmetrical reasoning — it was quantitative restriction under Article XI.4, it was not justified under Article III, nor was it saved by the exceptions in Article XX(b) and (g).[16]

Conclusion

The Panel's conclusion was unsurprising. The determination is clearly justified on technical grounds. At a broader policy level any other result would have been anomalous. The Panel was considerably influenced by the unworkable nature of the US's regime, one which would clearly have failed to fulfil the Article XX chapeau had it fallen for consideration. It would be unusual, were a trade measure in prima facie breach of the GATT, to be excused notwithstanding that it was wholly unreasonable. The other major influence was the Panel's interpretation of the Article XX exceptions as being inapplicable to save trade measures which sought to give an extraterritorial reach to a contracting State's law. To afford them an extraterritorial interpretation would, as the Panel noted, permit a large economy like the United States (with its enormous capacity for importation) to impose its own conservation and other policy regimes upon other member states upon pain of trade sanctions, a process which would self-evidently compromise GATT as a multilateral framework for the (relatively) free trade of goods among contracting parties. The Panel's determination does not preclude resort to other measures (such as multilateral agreements) in order to accomplish conservation objectives with an international dimension, nor of course does it foreclose amendments to GATT in order to provide a stronger underpinning of conservation measures such as by way of amendment of Article XX,[17] although both of the primary reservations expressed by the Panel in this case in relation to the United States' submissions on Article XX and its interpretation and application reflect powerful policy reasons for approaching such a task with circumspection.

The Panel noted that 'the provisions of the General Agreement impose few constraints on a contracting party's implementation of domestic environmental policies'.[18] The extraterritorial issue would not be obviously relevant in a case where a member state seeks to restrict imports as an adjunct to the implementation of conservation policies with a purely domestic reach; but the Panel's stricture on the need for trade measures seeking protection under Article XX to be reasonable and workable applies equally in the intrajurisdictional as well as the extrajurisdictional context.

Mexico did not seek adoption of the Report by the GATT Council, the dispute being overtaken by the North American Free Trade Agreement negotiations.[19]

Tuna II

Overview

The Panel decision in the second *Tuna* case in the 1994 General Agreement on Tariffs and Trade: Dispute Settlement Panel, Report on United States Restrictions on Imports of Tuna,[20] was likewise prompted by the conservation and embargo regime promulgated by the United States *Marine Mammal Protection Act 1972* ('the MMPA'). The European Economic Community and the Netherlands contended that the mandatory primary and intermediary nation embargoes provided for by this regime, prohibiting the importation of yellowfin tuna and tuna products into the United States in defined circumstances, constituted measures that were in conflict with the United States' obligations under GATT.

The MMPA regime has been described in the account of the first *Tuna* case, above. It had been refined to some extent by the time of this second Panel decision. The primary embargo applied to imports of tuna and products from harvesting countries, the vessels of which harvested the tuna by a method (most obviously purse-seine fishing nets) that results in the incidental killing or serious injury of marine mammals in excess of US standards (which were delineated in the MMPA). The harvesting country could escape this prohibition only by proving that it had adopted a regulatory program governing the harvesting of tuna comparable to that of the United States. Inter alia, the country had to establish that its vessels had a rate of incidental taking of marine mammals comparable to that of the United States vessels, that is, a rate no more than 1.25 times that of United States vessels during the same accounting period — which rate could not be known until the end of this period (with the consequence that the United States regime would be unworkable in practice). Ceilings were imposed on the taking of certain types of dolphin, within this global limit.

As an alternative to this proof that it had the prescribed regulatory program paralleling that of the United States, the harvesting country could escape the primary embargo in the first place if it entered into a formal agreement with the United States providing for the country to apply a US-designed regulatory regime designed to minimise the threat to dolphins and other marine animals. Non-compliance would lead to a more comprehensive embargo on imports into the United States, not only of tuna and tuna products but (in defined cases) of fish and fish products amounting to at least 40 per cent of the total of fish and fish imports from that country.

Either way, of course, the United States would be imposing a regulatory regime designed by itself on the affected exporting nations.

Provision was also made for an intermediary nation embargo, pursuant to which the third nation which exported yellowfin tuna or products to the United States, and which imported yellowfin tuna or products that were subject to an embargo on import into the United States, had to certify and provide reasonable proof that it had not imported products subject to the direct prohibition within the preceding six months; otherwise, it would be subject to the secondary embargo on exports of tuna and products to the United States.

The Panel's findings

The prohibitions on imports were of course quantitative restrictions on imports, and were determined to be inconsistent with the United States' obligations under Article XX.I; and they were not protected under Article III as measures relating to the enforcement at the time or point of importation of an internal law, etc. that applied equally to the imported product and the like domestic product. The primary and intermediary nation embargoes were on the same footing in these respects.[21] This reasoning paralleled that applied in *Tuna I*.

The United States sought to except the measures from the consequences of prima facie non-compliance, by reference to Article XX(g) and (b).

The Panel accepted that for the purposes of Article XX(g) dolphins were an exhaustible natural resource. Furthermore, it was accepted that the thing to be conserved could lie outside the territorial jurisdiction of the member seeking to invoke XX(g). A further test, however, had to be fulfilled, namely, the measure had to be one 'relating to the conservation of exhaustible natural resources ...' In the Panel's opinion, a previous Panel had acted correctly in construing 'relating to' as requiring that the impugned measure must be 'primarily aimed' at the conservation of natural resources, in respect both of the purpose of the measure and its effect on conservation.[22] This point was also taken by the Panel in *Tuna I*. This narrow interpretation was endorsed essentially, it would appear, because to do otherwise would provide scope for a contracting party to take measures which would fundamentally challenge the GATT principle of (relatively) unhindered access on the part of members to one another's markets. The Panel noted (echoing the Panel determination in *Tuna I*) that the GATT could no longer serve as a multilateral trading framework as envisaged by GATT were a member to be permitted to invoke Article XX to sanction measures designed to force other contracting parties to change their policies within their jurisdictions including conservation policies.[23] In short, although XX(g) could apply to the conservation of things beyond the territory of the member seeking to invoke it, it was not to be more broadly interpreted to sanction the de facto extraterritorial application of that member's law.

In the present case, the United States measures could not be justified as relating 'primarily' to the stated conservation objective, for the purposes of XX(g). The embargoes could apply to a given batch of tuna or tuna products whether or not the particular tuna had been harvested in a way that harmed or could harm dolphins. Both the primary and secondary embargoes could not per se promote the desired conservation; the primary embargo could only effect this end if it were followed by changes in policy and practices in the exporting country; and the secondary embargo could effect this end only if it were followed by changes in policy or practices, not in the country exporting tuna to the United States, but in third countries from which the exporting country imported tuna.[24] This extraterritorial dimension to United States law and policy was, for the reasons noted, seen to be inimical to the policy objectives of the General Agreement.

The United States also sought to save its measures by resort to Article XX(b), as measures which were necessary to protect, inter alia, animal life or health. Article XX(g) was ex facie more demanding than XX(b), in specifying a 'necessity' test. The Panel accepted that clause (b) could relate to the protection of things beyond the territorial jurisdiction of the party taking the measures in issue,[25] but thereafter its reasoning paralleled that applied to the construction and application of Article XX(g); fundamentally, the Panel would not accept that XX(b) could be interpreted so as to sanction the de facto extension of a member's law and policy to the territories of other member parties. To permit such a broad extraterritorial interpretation of the clause, could lead to a situation in which 'the objectives of the General Agreement would be seriously impaired'.[26]

Clearly, measures of this complexion could not be justified as being 'necessary' for the purposes of Article XX(b). Although the Panel did not spell it out, the unworkable nature of the United States regime would also militate against a conclusion that the disputed measures were 'necessary'.

The preamble to Article XX did not need to be considered, but the tenor of the Panel's reasoning makes it clear that the United States measures would not have fulfilled the requirements set down there.

The intermediary nation embargo could not be excepted under Article XX(d), given the non-compliance of the primary embargo with Article XX:I.

Conclusion

The reasoning, policy premises and outcomes of the *Tuna II* decision parallel those obtained in the *Tuna I* determination. The critical elements of both are the determination of their respective Panels to construe the Article XX exceptions narrowly, out of an apprehension that to permit them to underwrite the extraterritorial extension of a member's law and policy to other member states, on pain of the application of trade sanctions, would unduly disrupt the workings of the General Agreement. As noted, the de facto unworkability of the United States quota regime would in all likelihood have precluded resort to Article XX (a consideration which was pivotal in the *Gasoline* decision below).

Gasoline case

Overview

The dispute centred on complaints by exporters into the United States of gasoline that certain measures instituted by the United States in pursuit of conservation goods discriminated against these exports and as such were inconsistent with GATT.

The quest for cleaner air — the two gasoline programs

The facts are set out at length in the Final Report of the Panel.[27] The United States *Clean Air Act* ('CAA'), which was enacted in original form in 1963, established two gasoline programs to contain or reduce the pollutants generated by gasoline combustion. These programs focused on (a) reformulated gasoline, and (b) conventional gasoline. Both programs were implemented by the Environmental Protection Agency ('EPA'), which adopted the Gasoline Rule for this purpose.

The reformulated gasoline program

The reformulated gasoline program was aimed at improving air quality in, inter alia, specified metropolitan areas exposed to ozone pollution in summer. Reformulated gasoline only (and not conventional gasoline) could be sold in these areas.

The CAA prescribed compositional and performance specifications, which gasoline had to conform to in order that it could be certified as reformulated gasoline. For the period 1 January 1997 to 1 January 1998 these were set by the so-called 'Simple Model'.[28] The specifications applied alike to domestic refiners, blenders and importers, at least formally. The Simple Model applied fixed specifications in respect of certain matters (such as benzene level), and specified that certain other qualities (for example sulphur levels) were not to exceed 1990 baseline levels on an average annual basis.

The conventional gasoline program

So-called conventional gasoline could not (so it has been seen) be sold in the 'non-attainment areas', but it could be sold elsewhere. In essence, the conventional gasoline program (that is, the rules comprehended by it) required that the gasoline sold in these areas generate no higher a level of pollutants than was generated by gasoline sold by domestic refiners, blenders and importers in 1990. The assessment was to be made on an annual average basis. By limiting pollutant emissions to levels no higher than encountered in 1990 gasoline, the program aimed at preventing the 'dumping' of pollutant-generating substances extracted from gasoline in the course of reformulating it for the purpose of the reformulated gasoline program. The 1990 baseline applicable to conventional gasoline comprehended all of its qualities (and not just some of them as under the Simple Model applying to reformulated gasoline). As in the case of the first program, this second program, ex facie, applied alike to domestic refiners, blenders and importers.

The point of contention — establishing the 1990 baselines

The dispute centred on the rules for the establishment of the 1990 baselines, and their implementation. The Gasoline Rule enacted a detailed regime for establishing 1990 baseline requirements for both programs. As noted, the 1990 baseline applies to a wider spectrum of matters in respect of conventional gasoline than it does in relation to reformulated gasoline, but even in the later case it is still important.

The 1990 baselines could be either individual (based on the entity's own stock sold in 1990) or statutory (as determined by the EPA based on the average quality of gasoline sold in the United States in 1990).

Domestic refiners which operated for at least six months in 1990 had to establish an individual baseline using one of several methods.[29] Other domestic refiners (in practice few) would have to use the relevant statutory baseline. Blenders were, subject to one qualification,[30] to be treated identically to domestic refiners.

Importers were in practice in a quite different position. If they were in a position to do so, they could establish an individual baseline by reference to their 1990 imports, but they could only do this by reference to the quality data and volume records of their 1990 gasoline. It was, however, contemplated by the EPA at the outset that few importers would have this data, with the result that the typical importer would have to conform to the statutory baselines.

Discrimination in practice

The Panel's findings of fact were not in dispute during the appeal. According to the Panel, the 1990 baseline regime led, de facto, to a less favourable treatment of the imported product compared with the domestic.[31]

This happened because the importers were in practice, as the EPA contemplated, compelled to use the statutory baselines, while the domestic entities for the most part used individual baselines calculated by reference to the qualities of their own 1990 product. It was 'rare' for an importer to be able to establish one individual baseline.[32] As at August 1995, about 100 United States refiners, representing some 98.5 per cent of the gasoline produced in 1990, had gained EPA approval for the use of individual baselines. Some 97 per cent of them did not (and were not) required to meet the statutory baselines for all parameters.[33] The statutory baselines, then, were in practice rather more demanding than individual baselines. This gave rise to the anomalous situation in which, for instance, 'a batch of imported gasoline which was chemically identical to a batch of domestic gasoline that met its refiner's individual baseline' conceivably might not meet the statutory baseline. If this was the case, the consequence was thus: if an importer sold it, the importer was required over the rest of the annual period in question to sell gasoline which was on the whole cleaner than this non-conforming batch, even as the latter could be sold without complication by a domestic refiner.[34]

The less demanding, self-confirming individual baseline regime afforded the domestics was evidently instituted as an alternative to the more demanding statutory regime, because the United States refiners would have been exposed to physical and financial burdens were they required to comply immediately with a statutory baseline (as were the importers) rather than being given time to phase in the changes eventually to be required. This no doubt helped to ensure that overall supplies to gasoline would not be interrupted. To the extent that the marketing activities of the importers were wound back, the domestic refiners could fill any such gap.[35]

In summary, the Panel concluded that under the Gasoline Rule imported goods would be exposed to a 'highly subjective and variable treatment according to extraneous factors' thereby creating 'great instability and uncertainty in the conditions of competition as between domestic and imported goods'. This, as noted below, was conceived to produce a situation inconsistent with Article III.[36]

The findings — Panel and Appellate Body

The Panel found[37] against the United States on the primary issue — whether the baseline determination regime enacted in the Gasoline Rule was consistent with the 'not less favourable treatment' provision in Article III.4. Prima Facie the United States regime was inconsistent with GATT — the issue then became one of whether it could be justified by resort to the exceptions in Article XX. In the Panel's view, three of these fell for consideration — Articles XX(b) (measure necessary to protect human, animal or plant life or health), XX(d) (necessary to secure compliance with laws or regulations not inconsistent with GATT, etc.), and XX(g) (measure relating to the conservation of exhaustible natural resources, etc.). The Panel found that the United States regime could not be justified by resort to any of these exceptions.

The United States appealed on a narrow (but important) ground — whether the Panel was wrong in finding that, as a matter of law, the facts determined by it did not attract the Article XX(g) exception. The Appellate Body found[38] that the Panel had been wrong in coming to this conclusion; and that the United States regime was within the ambit of XX(g). The consequence was that the Panel was likewise in error in failing to consider whether the regime was within the chapeau (or preamble) to Article XX. The Appellate Body found, however, that the regime was not within the chapeau. For a party to be able to justify a non-conforming measure under Article XX, it had to satisfy not only at least one of the stipulated exceptions but as well the overriding chapeau. Accordingly, the United States regime was determined likewise, on appeal, to be inconsistent with its obligations under GATT. Aspects of the two determinations will be commented upon in turn.

The Panel's findings

Article III.4 — Like products to be treated no less favourably

The Panel's interpretation of III.4 was consistent with prior determinations. Article III.4 is of course integral to GATT, and it is appropriate that it be conceived as setting a high hurdle for contracting parties taking measures impacting on imports from other parties. Article III.4 requires that imports 'be accorded treatment no less favourable than that accorded to like products of national origin in respect of all laws, regulations and requirements affecting their internal sale,' …

The Panel's analysis[39] confirms that a substantive and not a literal approach is to be taken to the interpretation and application of Article III.4.[40] The issue is, does the impugned measure effectively discriminate against imported products? If it does so, then it is prima facie inconsistent with GATT.

In the Panel's view (one not really contested by the United States) the imported and domestically produced gasoline were 'like' products — their places of origin did not alter their sameness, as chemically identical gasoline. The question then became one of whether the import was treated less favourably than the domestic product. The United States submitted that importers were not discriminated against — if an importer could establish an individual baseline it was treated in the same way as a domestic producer, and, conversely, if the importer could not, it was still treated in the same manner as a domestic producer which could not (namely, both had to conform with the relevant statutory baseline). In essence, it was claimed that Article III.4 was satisfied because imports were treated similarly to the product of like-situated domestic producers.[41]

The factual context, it has been noted, established in the Panel's view that the Gasoline Rule did de facto discriminate against imports. It was uncommonly the case that a domestic producer could comply with the statutory baselines, but the vast majority of United States producers could (unsurprisingly) satisfy individual baselines based on their own product qualities in 1990. The practical position was that importers could not — other than in rare cases — establish individual baselines, and that the vast majority of them had to conform to the more demanding statutory baselines, which being based on an averaging system led to great uncertainty in marketing. The discrimination was neatly illustrated by the hypothesis of the batch of gasoline which as produced by a domestic refiner could conform with the refiner's individual baseline, but as imported by an entity without the benefit of an individual baseline could not satisfy the statutory baseline.[42]

The Panel noted further that 'Article III.4 ... deals with the treatment to be accorded like products; its wording does not allow less favourable treatment dependent upon the characteristics of the producer and the nature of the data held by it.'[43]

The acceptance of the non-substantive principle of interpretation urged by the United States would of course, have sanctioned covert discrimination against imports, which would in turn greatly erode the GATT and the primary obligations created by it.

The Panel also disposed of a subsidiary United States submission, namely, that the Gasoline Rule was in conformity with Article III.4, because the statutory baselines were based on the average of the sum of quality profiles of gasoline sold in 1990; that the latter were the basis of all the individual baselines; and that therefore on balance importers were not treated less favourably, even as individual entities among them might be. In the Panel's view this was unsustainable — 'the "no less favourable" treatment requirement of Article III.4 has to be understood as being applicable to each individual case of imported products'.[44]

This process of averaging was little help to individual importers, and at the end of the day imports are (in the usual case) initiated by individual producers and not a collective representing all of the potential importers in all of the relevant contracting States over the averaging period.

The Panel's finding that the baseline rules did not conform to Article III.4 was evidently unexceptionable — it was not raised on appeal.

Article XX(b) — Measure necessary to protect life and health

Article XX(b) creates an exception pursuant to which a measure otherwise inconsistent with GATT may be justified, but it is qualified by the preamble to Article XX, which considerably diminishes its utility for a claimant upon it. Article XX provides, inter alia, that

> Subject to the requirement that such measures are not applied in a manner which

> would constitute a means of arbitrary or unjustifiable discrimination between countries where the same trade conditions prevail, or a disguised restriction on international trade, nothing in this Agreement shall be construed to prevent the adoption or enforcement by any contracting party of measures: ...
> (b) necessary to protect human, animal or plant life or health.

In the opinion of the Panel, the United States could not justify the Gasoline Rule by resort to Article XX(b).[45] In the Panel's view, the United States had to establish three matters — that the policy embodied in the measure fell within the range of policies relevant to the protection of the specified interests; that it was a necessary policy (that is, the interests could not otherwise be protected); and that it was not inconsistent with the preamble to Article XX. The policy was relevant to protecting human life etc., so the first requisite was satisfied — indeed, the complainants did not contend otherwise. In the Panel's view, the second requisite was not satisfied, and because it could not be the policy was not within the ambit of Article XX(b). Accordingly, the Panel did not need to consider whether the policy could (otherwise) pass the threshold hurdle embodied in the Preamble.

In short, the Panel considered that the policy of substantive discrimination against importers comprised in the Gasoline Rule was not 'necessary' to protect human life, etc., even as it was acknowledged that the monitoring and containment of emissions generated by the combustion of gasoline, was necessary to protect human life etc. It is not altogether surprising that the Panel took this view, because a broader, more permissive construction of the exception could effectively sanction overt or covert trade restrictions under the guise of protecting the environment. The key word in Article XX(b) is *necessary*. The Panel's conclusion on the issue is explicable when it is remembered that the assessment of necessity focuses not on the policy sought to be fulfilled in its broadest conception but on the measure adopted to transact this policy. It is the latter which is fundamentally in issue, and in this case the measure was of course the Gasoline Rule. The Panel recalled its interpretation of the term 'necessary' in an earlier case:

> a contracting party cannot justify a measure inconsistent with another GATT provision as 'necessary' in terms of Article XX(d) if an alternative measure which it could reasonably be expected to employ and which is not inconsistent with other GATT provisions is available to it. By the same token, in cases where a measure consistent with other GATT provisions is not reasonably available, a contracting party is bound to use, among the other measures reasonably available to it, that which entails the least degree of inconsistency with other GATT provisions.[46]

In the Panel's opinion, the United States had not fulfilled the onus upon it to prove that there was no other measure (not inconsistent with GATT) reasonably available to it which would fulfil the policy objective, in lieu of the Gasoline Rule in its present discriminatory form. The United States, for example, had not established that the practical difficulties of data gathering, verification and enforcement prevented the institution of an individual 1990 baseline regime for importers; nor had it explained why it could not apply slightly higher overall requirements to domestic and foreign entities alike, with the same overall environmental outcomes, a regime which would more obviously treat importers in a non-discriminatory manner. In brief, the United States had not established that de facto discrimination against the foreign product was the only reasonable way of fulfilling its clear air objectives.

Article XX(d) — Measure necessary to secure compliance with laws or regulations not inconsistent with agreement

The United States sought to justify the Gasoline Rule under Article XX(d), which provided that (subject to the preamble to Article XX), a measure otherwise inconsistent with a provision in GATT was necessary to secure compliance with laws or regulations which were not inconsistent with the Agreement.

As the Panel noted, the United States had to establish several matters: that the measure was one to secure compliance with laws or regulations which were not themselves inconsistent; that the measure was necessary to secure this compliance; and that the measure fulfilled the requirements of the preamble to Article XX.

In the Panel's view, the disputed elements in the Gasoline Rule were not measures to secure compliance with non-inconsistent laws or regulations. Granted that the baseline system was not per se inconsistent with GATT, were the discriminatory baseline establishment rules an enforcement mechanism? If not, they could not be viewed as securing compliance with the overall clean air regime. Conceptually, the baseline establishment rules were but a component in the regime; they were not per se 'an enforcement mechanism. They were simply rules for determining the individual baselines.' As such they were not the type of measure with which Article XX(d) was concerned.[47] Article XX(d) proceeds from the premise that the core elements in a measure relevant to trade between the Contracting Parties in question are GATT-consistent, and its only role is to validate enforcement mechanisms of an ancillary or procedural kind. While the disputed rules were procedural in complexion, they were not concerned with policing.

The Panel did not need, in light of this finding, to determine whether the rules were necessary to secure compliance — logically this could not then be considered. (Based on its reasoning in relation to Article XX(b) above, the answer would have been that they were not necessary.) Likewise, it was unnecessary to determine whether they complied with the introductory clause to Article XX — again the United States would have found this test challenging.

Article XX(g) — Measure relating to the conservation of exhaustible natural resources

Article XX(g) is made subject to the familiar preamble to Article XX. With this qualification, Article XX(g) protects measures otherwise inconsistent with GATT 'relating to the conservation of exhaustible natural resources if such measures are made effective in conjunction with restrictions on domestic production or consumption'. The provision is, on the face of it, a key one in reconciling possible conflicts between GATT and the conservation policies of contracting States.

As noted above, the appeal turned on the construction and application of Article XX(g). The Panel was found on appeal to be in error in deciding that the disputed elements in the Gasoline Rule were not within the scope of Clause (g); but the Appellate Body's determination that they were in any event not in conformity with the overriding preamble to Article XX had the result that the United States' measures were still unprotected by Article XX(g). The Appellate Body's determination is important in its clarification of the scope of Article XX(g). As interpreted, it probably represents as high a hurdle for States claiming its benefit, as was set by the Panel's interpretation; so that the practical outcome will in many individual cases be little different. What the Appellate Body's interpretation does is to attenuate the difficulties represented by Clause (g) for parties claiming the exception, but to confirm that the preamble to Article XX imposes a definite and obvious burden upon such parties. In essence, Article XX(g) cannot be used to subvert the basic policy of GATT. Its limited role is summed up in the cautious language of the report in the Herring and Salmon decision (one quoted in both determinations in the Gasoline decision):

> as the preamble of Article XX indicates, the purpose of including Article XX(g) in the General Agreement was not to widen the scope for measures serving trade policy purposes but merely to ensure that the commitments under the General Agreement do not hinder the pursuit of policies aimed at the conservation of exhaustible natural resources.[48]

Article XX(g) merely clarifies that, if certain conditions are fulfilled, conservation policies can be pursued by member parties, notwithstanding that they do subtract from the free trade objectives of GATT.

The Panel posited four requisites which had to be satisfied by the Party claiming the benefit of the Article XX(g): exception (1) that the disputed measures were within the scope of policies aimed at conserving exhaustible natural resources; (2) that the measures were related to the conservation of these resources; (3) that they were being made effective in conjunction with restrictions on domestic production or consumption; and (4) that they were in conformity with the requirements of the preamble to Article XX.[49]

Requisite 1 was satisfied — clearly the contentious policy was of the broad genus of a conservation policy. The fact that clean air was renewable did not take it outside of the category of an exhaustible natural resource,[50] a conclusion which was not contested in the appeal. Requisites (3) and (4) did not fall for consideration by the Panel. This was because of its finding that the measures were not ones 'relating to' an exhaustible natural resource.

The conclusion that the measures, that is, the baseline determination rules in the Gasoline Rule, did not 'relate to' conservation of an exhaustible natural resource was based upon — so the Appellate Body found — an erroneous construction of Clause (g). Clause (g) (in contrast to Article XX(b) or Article XX(d)) does not adopt a criterion of 'necessity'. Although it did not use the term, or a derivative of it, the Panel implicitly was of the opinion that the clause did import such a requirement, with the result that — as its reasoning in relation to this explicit requirement in Article XX(b) above makes clear — the United States would be unable to fulfil Clause (g). In the Panel's view, Clause (g) required a link between the disputed measure and the conservation measure, and this link was properly characterised in the language of an earlier Report (that in the Herring and Salmon case), that is, the measure 'had to be *primarily aimed* at the conservation of an exhaustible natural resource to be considered as "relating to" conservation within the meaning of Article XX(g)'.[51]

The Panel proceeded further and required (by way of super-addition or interpretation) that there be a 'direct connection' between, specifically, the discriminatory regime founded upon the differential baseline establishment procedures and the conservation of clean air. In the Panel's view there was no such connection, and hence the United States failed to fulfil this third requisite.[52]

The Appellate Body's finding

The Appellate Body considered that the Panel had misconstrued the clear language of Article XX(g) in positing a requirement that a 'necessity' test governed resort to it.[53] The Appellate Body accepted that Article XX(g) and its primary concept of 'relating to' had been properly construed as requiring that the disputed measures be 'primarily related' to the conservation of an exhaustible natural resource; but it did not go further and impose a necessity test. In particular, although the gloss 'primarily related to' was an acceptable one, the term was not a term of the treaty and did not per se function as a 'simple litmus test for inclusion or exclusion from Article XX(g)'.[54] Rather than a requirement that the measure be necessary for the accomplishment of the conservation objective, it was sufficient that it be substantially related to its fulfilment. In this case, the disputed elements in the Gasoline Rule were so related and within Clause (g) because the Gasoline Rule regime was dependent upon procedures for benchmarking air quality. In the Appellate Body's view, 'given that substantial relationship, the baseline establishment rules cannot be regarded as merely incidentally or inadvertently aimed at the conservation of clean air in the United States for the purposes of Article XX(g)'.[55]

In summary, the scrutiny applied to a disputed measure for the purpose of applying Clause (g) is independent of the question of whether it is discriminatory (and violates Article III.4 by instituting 'less favourable treatment'); it is neutral in so far as free trade objectives are concerned and posits the simpler question of whether the contentious measures are substantially related to conservation objectives. (The question of discriminatory treatment, however, is very relevant to the application of the introductory clause in Article XX, the finale hurdle to be cleared by a party seeking to invoke the Article XX(g) exception.)

The United States also fulfilled the requirement that the measures in dispute be 'made effective on conjunction with restrictions on production or consumption'. Once again, the issue of discrimination in trade did not fall for consideration. The ordinary meaning of these words, in context, required no more than that the measures be 'operative', 'in force', or as having 'come into effect'.[56] They did not import a causation test, that is, they did not require that the measures must be demonstrated to be causally effective. On the other hand, their potential effectiveness in accomplishing the stated conservation goal is not irrelevant, because it was clear 'that realistically, if a specific measure cannot in any possible situation have any positive effect on conservation goals, it would very probably be because that measure was not designed as a conservation regulation to begin with'; thus, 'it would not have been "primarily aimed at" conservation of natural resources at all'.[57]

The requisites comprised in Clause (g) having been satisfied, the outstanding issue became one of whether the United States could fulfil the overriding test delineated in the preamble to Article XX(g), that is, that the measures which were within the scope of clause (g) 'are not applied in a manner which would constitute a means of arbitrary or unjustified discrimination between countries where the same conditions prevail, or a disguised restriction on international trade ...'

The Appellate Body's comments provide a valuable exegesis of this chapeau, which is potentially problematic. It clearly is concerned with prohibiting to some degree discrimination in trade; but the invocation of the exceptions provided for in Article XX, of which XX(g) is one, will by definition be unnecessary in situations where the disputed measures have in the first place been found to breach a substantive provision of GATT, most obviously (in this case) the prohibition of 'less favourable treatment' in Article III.4.

The difficulty, then, is to determine when a trade measure which by definition is in breach of a substantive provision in GATT because it involves a proscribed degree of trade discrimination is not so discriminatory as to be outside the scope of protection afforded by Article XX. The test of discrimination posited by the chapeau, that is, is not synonymous with that posited in (say) Article III.4, for otherwise Article XX would be redundant. Logically, the chapeau must permit some degree of discrimination, in order that it (taken with one of the specific exceptions enacted in its subordinate clauses) may function so as to protect a measure which is otherwise in breach of Article III.4 or a like provision.

This the chapeau does by qualifying its proscriptions — it is not any discrimination which falls foul of the chapeau, but only 'arbitrary or unjustifiable' ones. The term 'a disguised restriction on international trade' (which restriction is proscribed) is more troublesome — one superficially logical view would be that (by implication) non-disguised restrictions are all right because they are not proscribed — but this would produce a policy absurdity: why should the transparent restriction be saved but not the covert one, if both are to the same effect?

The Appellate Body resolved this problem of interpretation by analysing the chapeau as creating not a series of mutually exclusive proscriptions so much as a range of overlapping ones — 'arbitrary discrimination', 'unjustifiable discrimination', and 'disguised restriction', which could 'be read side-by-side; they impart meaning to one another'. The same fact situation could attract more than one: so, for example, a disguised restriction could include a disguised discrimination in trade.[58] These phrases were to be interpreted collectively in light of the presumed policy of Article XX, that is, to (1) create certain exceptions pursuant to which measures not conforming to GATT could be justified, but (2) to ensure that resort to these exceptions did not constitute an 'abuse' or 'illegitimate use' of them.[59] When would resort to them not be an abuse or illegitimate use? When resort to the measures, impugned under

GATT but sought to be saved under an Article XX exception, went beyond what was reasonable (or reasonably necessary) to accomplish the otherwise legitimate objective of the claimant (here, the United States and its goal of conserving clean air).

This conception of the role of the chapeau was made clear in the following observations of the Appellate Body:

> The chapeau is animated by the principle that while the exceptions of Article XX may be invoked as a matter of legal right, they should not be so applied so as to frustrate or defeat the legal obligations of the holder of the right under the substantive rules of the *General Agreement.* If those exceptions are not to be abused or misused, in other words, the measures falling within the particular exceptions must be applied reasonably, with regard both to be legal duties of the party claiming the exception and the legal rights of the other parties concerned.[60]

Thus, for example, a trade restriction could not very well be saved under Article XX(g) if the policy motivation for it was to protect domestic industry under the guise of conservation, even if the measure had some conservation value. On the facts, the United States' Gasoline Rule was not of this complexion. Nonetheless, in the view of the Appellate Body, the United States had not acted reasonably in erecting the discriminatory baselines regime. It had not investigated feasible alternatives, such as the application of common baselines to domestic and foreign entities alike, or permitting foreign refiners to apply individual 1990 baselines in lieu of the statutory baselines.[61] The 'resulting discrimination must have been foreseen, and was not merely inadvertent or unavoidable'. As such, the contentious measures constituted 'unjustifiable discrimination' and a 'disguised restriction on international trade', and were not entitled to the protection of Article XX as a whole.[62]

Conclusion

The *Gasoline* determination does not preclude resort to trade measures to aid in implementing a member's conservation policies. Article XX and its exceptions can be invoked to this end. Not unexpectedly, however, the Appellate Body's findings confirm that trade measures employed to this end, which are prima facie in breach of GATT and which are sought to be saved by resort to the Article XX exceptions, must be reasonable if they are to conform with the requirements of the overriding preamble to Article XX. This they will not be if they are prima facie excessive and the responsible member has not investigated feasible alternatives. To hold otherwise would plainly subvert the General Agreement, favouring unilateral over multilateralism.

Conclusion

The *Tuna* cases and the *Gasoline* case shared some common factual elements — for example they all involved the application by the United States of punitive trade measures designed to accomplish conservation objectives formulated by that country. The *Tuna* cases and the *Gasoline* case, however, differed in that in the *Tuna* cases the United States effectively (albeit not formally) sought an extra-territorial role of its law and policy, whereas in the *Gasoline* case it did not, seeking instead merely to effectuate a conservation policy of domestic application. Was the GATT an insuperable barrier to conservation in any of these three cases?

Where *Tuna I* and *Tuna II* are concerned, GATT represented a formidable obstacle to the taking of unilateral and punitive trade measures. Each case reflects the assumption by a contracting party of an extremely ambitious role in applying trade sanctions in order to accomplish an extraterritorial reach for its law, in this case applying it to the vessels of other member States' fishing activities in the Eastern Tropical Pacific Ocean. The application of sanctions against intermediary nations was perhaps even more ambitious. Although the two Tuna decisions do not formally determine that a member's trade measures can never be saved by resort to the Article XX exceptions in a case where to sanction them would be to sanction the de facto extraterritoriality of the member's laws, their reasoning tends towards this end. As the respective Panels noted, to sanction trade measures having this objective would significantly derogate from the fundamental philosophy of the General Agreement, namely, that of a multilateral agreement formed to liberalise trade between members, in which (subject to certain qualifications embodied in GATT) each member has the same formal rights and obligations as any other member, irrespective of their individual market power.

The United States' case was not assisted in *Tuna I* and *II* to the extent that the trade measures pivoted on compliance with a quota regime which was de facto unworkable. This feature of the measures would have made it very difficult to justify them as a bona fide attempt to bring an otherwise non-conforming measure within the protection of one of the Article XX exceptions, least of all the preamble to XX.

The *Gasoline* case was less controversial, in that the United States was not seeking an extraterritorial application for its law and policy. The regime upon which the trade measures pivoted was, however, clearly unreasonable in practice. This problem could readily have been cured by a reformulation of the baselines, so as to harmonise the position of the foreign and domestic refiners and blenders. The *Gasoline* case does not on a fundamental analysis raise a substantive issue of conflict between GATT on the one side and conservation on the other — it was open to the United States to formulate an effective regime which would have been protected under Article XX.

The *Tuna* cases are more problematic — they do go directly to the conflict issues. An obvious, uncontroversial solution to this problem would have been for the parties drawn into the disputes to have entered into multilateral arrangements for the protection of sea mammals.[63]

The only way to resolve an impasse of the type revealed in each of the *Tuna* cases in terms of the General Agreement, and not by arrangements which bypass it, would be to amend the General Agreement to sanction, in particular, conservation-driven trade measures which seek an extraterritorial reach for the policy of the member implementing them.[64] Such an initiative would, no doubt, generate controversy.

This would be to change the character of GATT in a fundamental way. As noted, it would no longer be a multilateral pact promoting liberal trade among its subscribers. Conceivably it would be to presage a new era of protectionism — one not for economic but for other policy objectives, be they environmental, concerned with labour relations, or whatever. Such a policy of social protectionism would be as inimical to the foundation philosophy of GATT as economic protectionism. There is no logical reason why the General Agreement cannot be attenuated — clearly such an amendment is technically if not politically feasible — but it would involve making a choice between relatively free trade and relatively restricted trade. As the *Tuna* cases illustrate, a potentially wide-reaching web of trade barriers could be erected, in quest of a relatively limited conservation objective.

In contrast, as it has been noted, the truly large conservation issues, such as effective methods to eliminate or reduce greenhouse gas emissions, cannot plausibly be dealt with by way of unilateral trade sanctions. Almost by definition, in contexts such as these, effective measures on the required global scale can only be effected by wide-ranging international agreements. There is no reason to suppose that these will, within the compass of their rather more specific subject matter, be in breach of GATT, or that a Panel will determine them to be in breach. As such, the GATT/conservation issue would not be a live one.

Notes

1. GATT: Dispute Settlement Panel Report on 'United States Restrictions on Imports of Tuna', 30 ILM 1594 (1991).
2. GATT: Dispute Settlement Panel Report on 'United States Restrictions on Imports of Tuna', 33 ILM 839 (1994).
3. World Trade Organisation Appellate Body: Report of the Appellate Body in 'United States — Standards for Reformulated and Conventional Gasoline', 35 ILM 603 (1996).

4. It is presumed that such a voluntary arrangement between members would not constitute a GATT-inconsistent measure of which a contracting party which had freely entered into this concurrent arrangement could reasonably complain. Many international treaties committing contracting parties to the accomplishment of environmental goals have been concluded. Discussions of whether a multilateral environmental agreement between parties to GATT would be consistent or not with the General Agreement include: Black D, 'Balancing Trade with the Environment' (1995) 71:3 *International Affairs* 497 at 503; Hunt K, 'International Environmental Agreements in Conflict with GATT — Greening GATT after the Uruguay Agreement' (1996) 30:1 *International Lawyer* 1763 at 187; McLaughlin R, 'UNCLOS and the Demise of the United States' Use of Trade Sanctions to Protect Dolphins, Sea Turtles, Whales and other International Marine Living Resources' (1994) 21:1 *Ecology Law Quarterly* 1 at 78; Palmeter D, 'Environment and Trade: Much Ado about Little?' (1993) 27 *Journal of World Trade* 55 at 60; Petersmann E-U, 'Prevention and Settlement of International Environmental Disputes in GATT' (1993) 27 *International Trade Law and International Environmental Law* 43 at 75; Rege V, 'Gatt Law and Environment-Related Issues Affecting the Trade of Developing Countries' (1994) 23 *Journal of World Trade* 95 at 119; Schlagenhof M, 'Trade Measures Based on Environmental Processes and Production Methods' (1995) 29:6 *Journal of World Trade* 123 at 141ff; Schultz J, 'The GATT/WTO Committee on Trade and the Environment — Towards Environmental Reform' (1995) 89 *American Journal of International Law* 423 at 433; Tietje C, 'Voluntary Eco-Labelling Programmes and Questions of State Responsibility in the WTO/GATT Legal System' (1995) 29:5 *Journal of World Trade Law* 123 at 137.
5. GATT Dispute Settlement Panel Report on 'United States Prohibitions of Imports of Tuna and Tuna Products from Canada' (1982 — BISD 29S/91) (the United States imposed these prohibitions in consequence of Canada's seizure of United States fishing boats alleged to be within Canadian jurisdiction; the Panel determined that the prohibitions were in breach of GATT Article XI.I and that the measures were not saved by Article XX(g), as the restrictions were not 'made effective in conduction with restrictions on domestic production or consumption'); Dispute Settlement Panel Report on 'United States Taxes on Petroleum and Certain Imported Substances' (1987 — BISD 345/136) (environmental issue did not need, in the circumstances, to be canvassed directly); Dispute Settlement Panel Report on 'Canada's Restrictions on Exports of Unprocessed Herring and Salmon' (1988 — BISD 35S/98) (Canadian restrictions on the export of unprocessed herring and salmon, sought to be justified on conservation grounds, determined to be inconsistent with Article XX.1 and not excepted by Articles XI.2(b) or XX(g) — inter alia, the conservation argument was undermined given that the restrictions on the purchase of unprocessed fish did not apply likewise to foreign and domestic purchasers); GATT Dispute Resolution Panel Report on 'Thailand's Restrictions on Importation and Internal Taxes on Cigarettes' (1990 — BISD 37S/200) (Panel dealt, inter alia, with Thai restrictions on the importation of cigarettes, one sought to be justified by resort to Article XX(b); restrictions found to be inconsistent with Article XI.I; and not protected by Article XI.2(c); likewise the measures were not protected by Article XX(b), given that sales of domestically produced cigarettes were not subject to a comparable restriction). A recurring theme in certain of these determinations — one reprised in the determinations to be reviewed below — is that the impugned trade restrictions will not be protected by the environmental exceptions, if there is de jure or de facto discrimination between foreign and domestic traders. These cases are

more fully discussed in Petersmann E-U, n 4 at 55, on whose analyses I have relied in preparing the above summaries.

6. GATT: Dispute Settlement Panel Report on 'United States Restrictions on Imports of Tuna' 30 ILM 1594 (1991). Discussions of the Panel's determination in *Tuna I* include: Black D, 'International Trade v. Environmental Protection: The Case of the United States Embargo on Mexican Tuna' (1992–3) 24 *Law & Policy in International Business* 123; Black D, n 4; Buckley R, 'International Trade, Investment and Environmental Regulation' (1993) 27:5 *Journal of World Trade* 101 at 107ff; Hunt K, n 4 at 173ff; McLaughlin R, n 4 at 9ff; Petersmann E-U, n 4 at 60ff; Schlagenhof M, n 4 at 141; Strom T, 'Another Kick at the Can: Tuna/Dolphin II' (1995) 33 *Canadian Yearbook of International Law* 149 at 152.
7. 30 ILM1594 (1991) at 1599ff.
8. Note 7 at 1600.
9. Note 7 at 1617ff.
10. Note 7 at 1616.
11. Note 7 at 1620.
12. Note 7 at 1621, referring to the Panel Report on 'Canada — Measures Affecting Exports of Unprocessed Herring and Salmon', adopted 22 March 1988, BISD 35S/98, 114, para 4.6.
13. Note 7 at 1621.
14. See the Panel Report on 'Canada — Measures Affecting Exports of Unprocessed Herring and Salmon', adopted 22 March 1988, BISD 35S/98, 114, para 4.6.
15. 30 ILM1594 (1991) at 1621.
16. Note 15 at 1621.
17. Note 15 at 1623.
18. Note 15 at 1622.
19. See McLaughlin R, n 4 at 12–13 surveying responses to the Panel Report by GATT members, and noting that the United States and Mexico entered into bilateral negotiations on the issue. See also the Panel Report on the *Tuna II* dispute — 33 ILM 839 (1994) at 846, 887 surveying the operations of the Inter-American Tropical Tuna Commission's operations and the operation of the Agreement between the United States and certain other American States (including Mexico) in 1992 relating to the reduction of dolphin mortality in the Eastern Tropical Pacific Ocean.
20. 33 ILM 839 (1994). Discussions of *Tuna II* include: Schlagenhof M, n 4 at 141; Strom T, n 6 at 160ff.
21. 33 ILM 839 (1994) at 889.
22. Note 21 at 893, citing Report of the Panel in 'Canada — Measures Affecting the Exports of Unprocessed Herring and Salmon', adopted 22 March 1988, BISD 35S/98, 114, para 4.6.
23. Note 21 at 894.
24. Note 21 at 894.
25. Note 21 at 896.
26. Note 21 at 897.
27. 35 ILM 274 (1996) at 278ff.
28. This was to be succeeded by the 'Complex Model', which was not in issue in the dispute. It was contemplated that new guidelines would be formulated for the year 2000 and beyond.

29. 35 ILM 603 (1996) at 609: for example, pursuant to Method 1 the domestic refiner must use the quality data and volume records of its 1990 gasoline, if available.
30. In establishing an individual baseline, only Method 1 could be used — see n 29; in default of which the statutory baseline applied.
31. 35 ILM 274 (1996) at 294ff.
32. Note 31 at 295.
33. Note 31 at 295.
34. Note 31 at 294.
35. See the Appellate Body Report 35 ILM 603 (1996) at 28, noting that this 'may very well have constituted sound domestic policy from the viewpoint of the EPA and United States refiners. At the same time we are bound to note that, while the United States counted the costs for its domestic refiners of statutory baselines, there is nothing in the record to indicate that it did other than disregard that kind of consideration when it came to foreign refiners.' Similarly n 31 at 279–80.
36. Note 31 at 294.
37. Note 31.
38. 35 ILM 603 (1996).
39. 35 ILM 274 (1996) at 293ff.
40. An approach fortified by resort, pursuant to Article 3.2 of the Understanding on Rules and Procedures, of Treaties Governing the Settlement of Disputes, to the Vienna Convention on the Law of Treaties, Article 31 of which states that 'a treaty shall be interpreted in good faith in accordance with the ordinary meaning to be given to the terms of the treaty in their context and in the light of its object and purpose'. The Panel referred specifically to these Articles in its discussion of the term 'like products' — n 39 at 293–4.
41. Note 39 at 293–4.
42. Note 39 at 294.
43. Note 39 at 294.
44. Note 39 at 285, citing a previous panel determination, i.e. 'United States — Section 337 of the Tariff Act of 1930', BISD 36S/345 para 5.14 (adopted on 7 November 1989).
45. 35 ILM 274 (1996) at 296ff.
46. Note 45 at 296–7, citing 'United States — section 337 of the Tariff Act of 1930', BISD 36S/345, para 5.26 (adopted on 7 November 1989, dealing with parallel Article XX(d).
47. 35 ILM 274 (1996) at 298.
48. 'Canada — Measures Affecting Exports of Unprocessed Herring and Salmon'; BISD 35S/98, para 4.6, adopted 22 March 1988, cited in Panel Report, n 47 at 299.
49. Note 47 at 299.
50. Note 47 at 299.
51. 'Canada — Measures Affecting Exports of Unprocessed Herring and Salmon', BISD 35S/98, para 4.6, adopted on 22 March 1988, and cited in n 47 adding the emphasis.
52. 35 ILM 274 (1996) at 300.
53. 35 ILM 603 (1996) at 620.
54. Note 53 at 620, 625.
55. Note 53 at 623.
56. Note 53 at 624.
57. Note 53 at 626.
58. Note 53 at 629.
59. Note 53 at 629.

60. Note 53 at 626.
61. Note 53 at 629ff.
62. Note 53 at 632–3.
63. Note 19.
64. See the Panel Report in *Tuna I* 30 ILM 1594 (1991) at 1623; and note the comments in Black D, n 4 at 153 (noting that a party seeking to employ a trade measure to enforce conservation goals could, inter alia, seek a waiver from GATT rules; or an amendment of GATT); Rege V, n 4 at 125; Schlagenhof M, n 4 at 151.

11
The Duty of Obeying the Law: the Court of Session, the Kirk and the Disruption of 1843

*Reid Mortensen**

Darrell Lumb

Professor Darrell Lumb's scholarship and profound knowledge of the law are well-attested in this collection of essays. To an unusual extent, he could offer intelligent comment on issues well outside his central interests of constitutional and international law, whether topical or obscure. However, all this would have left but a fleeting impression were it not for his personal touch. His example to fledgling academics like myself was genuinely inspiring. He was notable for his humanity, his humility — despite his knowledge — before the Great Unknown, his interest in others, his civility, and (the quality almost everyone refers to) his decency.

I have little doubt that this sprung from a deep religiosity. Darrell Lumb's character and scholarship lived, moved and had their being in his Catholic faith. It dictated, on a personal level, his essential respect for others and his consistent concern for their welfare, and, even though his faith was no detached mental exercise, his abiding interest in the Catholic natural law tradition. His was a life that exemplified Christian integrity.

It is in this light that I dedicate this essay to the memory of Darrell Lumb. It certainly deals with the problems of a different Christian tradition, and I suspect that he would not have approved the sometimes reckless civil disobedience of the Presbyterian churchmen it involves. However, he would have been interested in the questions of constitutional law and legal history it raises, and he did understand the power of religious feeling that motivated the civil disobedience. This essay also focuses on some practicalities of an issue that Darrell Lumb investigated early in his academic career, the duty of obeying the law.[1] I am deeply sorry that he cannot now give the thoughtful advice on

* I wish to thank Dr John Cairns, Reader in Private Law at the University of Edinburgh, and Professor Francis Lyall of the Faculty of Law at the University of Aberdeen, for helping me with the sources and background research for this article. I am also grateful to Mr Angus Stewart QC, Keeper of the Library of the Faculty of Advocates, Parliament House, Edinburgh, for allowing my access to the Library's excellent holdings of original sources, and to the University of Edinburgh for the use of the Law Library and the New College Library.

this essay that he gave to me on the drafts of others, but I hope that it assists in perpetuating the memory of a man who helped to make the law a more noble calling.

The Disruption

The General Assembly of the Church of Scotland which met in St Andrew's Church, Edinburgh, on 18 May 1843 opened in prayer, as was usual. However, no one expected that this would be a normal Assembly and, indeed, protocol was soon broken. Instead of making up the roll of delegates, the Moderator, Dr David Welsh, read out a Protest. He announced that, at that time, it was impossible for the Church to hold a free Assembly, and recited a litany of ills that had been visited on the Church. The unwelcome visitor had been the Court of Session, Scotland's supreme civil court, and, like the Church, one of the few autochthonous institutions remaining in the country. It had required ministers to be appointed against the wishes of congregations, and had forbidden the preaching of the gospel and the ministration of ordinances in some parishes. It had also cancelled orders made by Church courts, had reconstituted them, and, on occasion, had prohibited them taking disciplinary action against ministers.[2] Dr Welsh then concluded that these built a legal regime 'incompatible with the freedom essential to the right constitution of a church of Christ', and contrary to the principles of the Revolution of 1688 and the Treaty of Union.[3] He and the other leaders of the majority party in the Assembly, Dr Thomas Chalmers and Dr Robert Gordon, then led a file of delegates out of St Andrew's to Canonmills Hall. Lord Cockburn, a judge of the Court of Session and a celebrated diarist, was watching, and counted 123 ministers among them.[4] That was significant enough, but, by the time the new Free Church of Scotland had formalised its separation from the Established Church, numbers had swelled to 469.[5] The schism is known as the Disruption, the last and greatest in the Church of Scotland since the Reformation.

The Disruption made the deepest, permanent impression in Scotland. It prompted decades of rethinking about the relationship between Church and State, which itself led the successor to the original Free Church — and other Presbyterian dissenters — to return to the Established Church in the 1920s.[6] That has made the Disruption the subject of an immense literature: histories, theologies and sociologies. It has also naturally produced its own hagiographies, especially about the remarkable Chalmers.[7] However, legal scholarship on the Disruption is scarce.[8] This is a little surprising, for the Protest of 1843 was no exaggeration. The Church had been in serious collision with the Court of Session on questions of ministry and Church government for the previous six years, and the legal restrictions on the Established Church subsequently expounded by the civil courts were the immediate cause of the exodus of 1843.

Outline

The cases which led to the Disruption are an interesting study in themselves. Taken as a whole, they mark an important point in the development of constitutional law. From 1837 to 1843, in a series of lengthy but passionately argued judgments, the Court of Session endorsed a high approach to the supremacy of Parliament and, as a result, the Court's own statute-based powers. The doctrine does not seem to have been widely accepted in Scottish adjudication until then, and possibly had not even been as clearly stated in the English courts. Secondly, there was a clique of dissenting judges who remained unconvinced by the doctrine of parliamentary supremacy. The dissenting jurisprudence has strong theological currents, and may only be of historical interest.[9] However, in an era which is equally questioning of the doctrine of parliamentary supremacy, it helps to remind how short a pedigree that doctrine has. These cases — the first *Auchterarder*[10] case especially — are therefore among the most important cases the Court of Session ever determined,[11] and, in light of the different theories of sovereignty that competed so intensively for support *within* the Court, provide a rich source of evidence on a critical juncture of constitutional development. Thirdly, it is an important dimension to the controversy that this theory of parliamentary supremacy was applied in cases involving the courts of the Established Church. As such, these courts themselves had constitutional status and political legitimacy in Scotland. So, when the Court of Session and the Church courts came into conflict, obedience to one or the other became a real political dilemma. The *Lethendy*[12] and *Strathbogie*[13] cases show that, whether one chose to obey the Court or the Church, costly personal sacrifices had to be made. The cases which led to the Disruption therefore bring the question of the duty of obeying the law into unusually clear perspective.

In this essay I examine the position judges of the Court of Session took on the doctrine of parliamentary supremacy, and its relationship to any duty the Church had of obeying the law. To this end, it is not really necessary to re-trace in detail all the points on which Court and Church collided in the period.[14] The initial discussion is therefore limited to the legal, religious and social background to the conflict. I then examine the first *Auchterarder* case, which set the theoretical basis for the Court's role in the ensuing controversy. That provides the legal setting for the four cases in which civil disobedience loomed largest: *Lethendy*, the second *Auchterarder* case,[15] *Strathbogie* and *Stewar-*

ton.[16] It then becomes possible to draw some conclusions on the legitimacy of the different decisions the Court made about parliamentary supremacy, and the extent of the Church's duty to obey the law.

Legal, religious and social background

The Reformation in Scotland is officially dated 1560, and soon after Presbyterian government was introduced to the Church.[17] Presbyterianism achieves the regulation of a church through ecclesiastical courts which are both hierarchical and popular. In Scotland, the parish was served by a kirk-session, comprising the minister and lay (or 'ruling') elders. From there, a regional council called a presbytery was constituted by the ministers, at least one ruling elder from each parish, and divines at a university situated within the bounds of the presbytery. The presbyteries sent delegates to a larger regional council called a synod, and, with the royal burghs, to an annual national council, the General Assembly.[18] In practice, the presbyteries and the Assembly exercised the largest jurisdictions. The General Assembly also passed legislation for the internal administration of the Church. It met only once a year (usually in May), and therefore remitted matters that could arise at other times to a Commission of Assembly or, as happened several times through the 1830s and 1840s, to special commissions.[19]

Through the tumults of the seventeenth century and, largely under royal and English pressure, the Presbyterian government of the Church was twice replaced by Episcopacy: government by bishops claiming apostolic succession. The Glorious Revolution nevertheless saw the permanent restoration of Presbyterianism in 1690,[20] and Scottish concerns about the pretensions of the bishops of the Church of England meant that, in the Treaty of Union with England, the Presbyterian government of the Church of Scotland was expressly declared to be unalterable.[21]

However, Scottish Presbyterians were a mixed lot. They ranged from conservatives who merely objected to bishops, to radical anarchists. The former filled much of the Moderate Party, a group which emerged as a disciplined clerical party in the 1750s under the deft leadership of William Robertson, Principal of the University of Edinburgh. Its members numbered other leading scholars of the Enlightenment, Thomas Reid, John Home, Adam Ferguson and Alexander Carlyle included. In the eighteenth century it was closely associated with the universities, a rational philosophical approach to religion, and notions of order, hierarchy and social progress. In the 1790s the Moderate Party also developed a powerful connection with the Government, which in Scotland was effectively the autocratic rule of Pitt's Home Secretary

— Henry Dundas, Viscount Melville. This alliance also marked the beginning of the Moderates' intellectual and moral decline, although, despite representing a minority of ministers in the Church, they managed to retain control of the General Assembly up to 1833.[22]

If the Moderates' rise and fall mirrors that of the Enlightenment, then the Evangelicals offer a similar reflection of Romanticism. Cockburn aptly dubbed them the 'Wild' Party of the Church. Emerging at the beginning of the nineteenth century out of the less disciplined Popular Party, the Evangelicals were the Scottish manifestation of the low church revival. The Evangelical churchman was more likely than his Moderate counterpart to be a conservative Calvinist, or at least biblically centred. He was also probably poorer, and less educated. Yet under the leadership of John Erskine, Sir Henry Moncreiff, Andrew Thomson and Thomas Chalmers the Evangelicals presented an energetic and cohesive alternative to the Moderates. They finally gained a majority in the General Assembly in 1834, and were then in a position to implement a program of mission and Church Extension. Two aspects of this program which soon met legal problems were the new procedures for appointing ministers and the reorganisation of parishes.[23]

The Evangelicals' alliance with the Whigs was not as close as the Moderate–Tory connection, but it was a natural one. Chalmers was by inclination conservative, but had written for *The Edinburgh Review* and was friendly with the young Whig advocates behind it: Francis Jeffrey, John Murray, Henry Cockburn, James Wellwood Moncreiff (Sir Henry's son) and Henry Brougham, all of whom as judges participated in the legal controversies leading to the Disruption.[24] While Jeffrey as Lord Advocate and Cockburn as Solicitor-General in the early Grey Government were trying to extend popular democracy through the Scottish Reform Bill,[25] the Evangelicals were trying to introduce a popular element into the appointment of ministers.

Until 1835, the person who held the right of patronage for a parish (usually the local laird) presented a man to the presbytery responsible for the parish. The presbytery would then 'moderate' the 'call'. This involved an initial decision on whether the presentation was made according to law, and whether the presentee met the formal qualifications for ministry. If the call were sustained, the presbytery would make trials of the presentee's life and doctrine. Finally, if the presentee passed the trial, he would then be received and admitted into the parish. This took place during a service of divine worship, which involved two important acts. Unless the presentee had been translated from another parish ministry, he would first be ordained — set apart for ministry in holy orders by the laying on of hands. Then he was admitted or 'inducted' into his parochial charge, at which point his settlement into the parish was complete. He then became entitled to the stipend, manse and other temporalities of the parish. It was open to the presentee to appeal to the synod (and after that to the Assembly) against any adverse decision made by the presbytery in the process of settlement.[26]

The right of patronage which lay at the beginning of this process originated in the building or endowment of a parish church, and, in the form it took in Scotland at the Reformation, invested the patron with the right and power to present a minister to the church.[27] This naturally tied the allegiance of the parish ministry to the landed interest and to the Crown, which at the Reformation had acquired all rights of patronage previously exercised by ecclesiastical dignitaries. It also made the institution an uneasy companion to a popular form of government like Presbyterianism, and had been abolished when Presbyterian fortunes were highest, in 1649 and 1690.[28] However, in 1712, the Parliament of the United Kingdom restored the right of presentation to the patrons against the votes of the Scottish MPs.[29] The Act of 1712 'restored, settled and confirmed' to thc patron the right to present a qualified person to a vacancy, and obliged the relevant presbytery to receive and admit any such qualified person. The Crown was to exercise any rights of patronage held by Roman Catholics, or by Protestant bishops and archbishops who had held them before the restoration of Presbyterianism in 1690.

This statute assisted the appointment of Moderate ministers throughout the eighteenth century, but was otherwise the main source of religious division in Scotland. It was the primary reason for secession from the Established Church, and therefore the growth of Presbyterian dissent which, by the 1830s, may have represented about 30 per cent of the population.[30] It was also the prime grievance of the Popular Party in the Church. The abolition or qualification of patronage — 'non-intrusion' — was also to become the defining policy of the Evangelical Party. The only real Scottish ministers in the Grey Government — Jeffrey and Cockburn — shared the Evangelical sentiment, but it never had strong support in the Cabinet. Brougham (who had been appointed Lord Chancellor in 1830) came to prefer patronage, although in 1833 he was still sending messages of support to the Evangelicals. In the General Assembly that year, Chalmers moved that congregations be given the power to veto the appointment of a minister presented by a patron, having been warned by Jeffrey that if the Church did not act on patronage the Government would — even without the 'light and encouragement' of the General Assembly. This failed, but succeeded in 1834.[31] In 1835, the Act anent Calls or, as it is better known, the Veto Act also received assents from a large majority of presbyteries, and therefore became a standing law of the Church.[32] In brief, it provided that a presbytery was not to admit as minister any person presented by the patron when a majority of the male heads of families in the parish in full communion with the Church recorded disapprovals of the presentation. There was no need to provide reasons to support a rejection.[33] The Veto Act was drafted by Sir James Wellwood Moncreiff, by then a judge of the Court of Session and a man of noted piety (to the amusement of even his friend Cockburn).[34] However, it was opposed by other eminent lawyers who sat in the General Assembly — including Lord President Charles Hope, Lord Justice-Clerk David Boyle, and the Lord President's son, John Hope, who was Dean of the Faculty of Advocates. It became John Hope's obsession to have the Veto Act declared illegal, and he would continue to argue the cause of patronage vigorously as a member of the General Assembly, an advocate, a judge and a pamphleteer.[35]

Even though the question of patronage came to dominate the Church's collision with the civil courts, a more urgent and practical question for the Church was that of parochial reorganisation. Scotland's population had almost doubled through the period of industrialisation between the 1750s and 1830s, the census in 1831 putting it at about 2.4 million. This was accompanied by enormous shifts in settlement patterns, with a large movement of people into the industrial belt between Edinburgh and Glasgow. In the same period, Lanarkshire's population had increased fourfold.[36]

This created an acute problem for the Established Church. Its pastoral care of a community was, in most cases, exercised by the parish minister. As the parochial organisation of the country dictated how and where the Church's ministry was to be deployed, it also determined how effectively it was ministering to the spiritual needs of the nation. The radical demographic changes of the late eighteenth century witnessed the growth of large villages long distances from the parish church and minister. In Glasgow and Lanarkshire, the population increase in some parishes was so large there was no realistic possibility that the minister could meet the pastoral needs of the community by himself. However, the parochial organisation of Scotland was still largely based on its medieval settlement patterns, and by the 1830s could not even pretend to support of an effective program of mission.[37]

These population changes presented few difficulties for the dissenting churches, as there were no laws dictating where they could build chapels or place ministers. The Established Church alone was limited significantly by the outdated parochial organisation of the country, and faced the additional obstacle of having, at best, a limited power to reorganise it. For, as important as the parish was as an ecclesiastical structure, it also served as the administrative unit of local government. Infrastructure for schools and welfare — as well as the church — was based on the parish *quoad omnia*. The heritors (landowners) of the parish had the responsibility for providing the schoolhouse and for paying the schoolmaster. Together with representatives of the kirk-session, they ensured that monies for poor relief were raised by taxation and collections at the church door, and arranged for them to be distributed to the poor. They were also obliged to make repairs to the church and churchyard walls, and even, if necessary, rebuild the church. The heritors had to build and maintain the minister's manse, pay his stipend and provide other material needs for parish worship, such as the communion elements and church-bells.[38]

That mixture of the parish's spiritual functions with the civil meant that any proposals to redraw parish boundaries involved civil government. Through the seventeenth century, parliamentary commissions were appointed to consider the plantation of new churches, the division of large parishes and the union of small ones.[39] One of the last actions of the Scottish Parliament was to pass this role on to the judges of the Court of Session. In 1707 it made the Lords of Council and Session a permanent Commission of Teinds with power to order new churches to be built and unite or disjoin parishes, as well as the associated power to value teinds and augment ministers' stipends.[40] The legal procedure required to reorganise parishes in the Court of Teinds was, however, time-consuming, and certainly lacked the flexibility the Church needed to respond quickly to rapid population movements. Its most common response was to separate the parish *quoad sacra* from the parish *quoad omnia*. In this manner, some presbyteries approved the building of new 'chapels of ease' in large parishes and, for pastoral purposes only, allotted them a district called a *quoad sacra* parish.

This did not directly affect the civil incidents of the parish *quoad omnia*, and therefore lands in the parish *quoad sacra* remained burdened with the obligation to maintain the church and minister of the original parish.[41] The chapel of ease and its minister were maintained like dissenting chapels, by voluntary contributions.

In 1797 the Church moved to regulate the creation of chapels of ease by presbyteries, requiring the approval of the General Assembly before a chapel and parish *quoad sacra* could be recognised.[42] In 1823 Parliament enabled it to build up to another 40 churches in the Highlands and Islands.[43] Even this was inadequate. It was really not until the Evangelicals took control of the General Assembly in the 1830s that it did deal seriously with the parochial organisation of the Church at its root. Here, it became a central element of Chalmers' Church Extension program.

Chalmers' vision was not merely that the Church of Scotland should provide pastoral care for the country. He intended that it would vigorously 'extend' Christian community throughout the nation, and especially to the working-class poor who were the least accessible to the ministers of the Establishment.

This undoubtedly required a more responsive and intensive parochial organisation, combined with an adequate Government endowment to finance the new churches and ministers.[44] The endowment never came, principally because the Established Church was competing too successfully against the dissenters on whom the Peel Government depended for support. However, the General Assembly did pass legislation designed to enhance the role of the *quoad sacra* parishes. In 1833 it provided that presbyteries could annex parishes *quoad sacra* to any chapels of ease created under the Assembly's Act of 1798 and to parliamentary churches built in the Highlands and Islands. In both cases, the ministers of these chapels and churches were given the full powers and privileges of the regular parochial ministry, and became entitled to sit in the Church courts.[45] Then the Chapel Act of 1835 rescinded the 1798 act and enabled Presbyteries to erect *quoad sacra* parishes, though under the control and review of the General Assembly.[46] The 1839 Assembly passed an Act anent Re-union with Seceders, by which any ministers and congregations of the (dissenting) Associate Synod could be admitted into communion with the Established Church. On doing so, the relevant presbytery could assign a *quoad sacra* parish to the chapel. Its minister would enjoy all the powers and privileges of a parish minister of the Church of Scotland, including the right to sit in the Church courts.[47]

The Church Extension legislation underwrote a radical reorganisation of the Church, and was not without critics. The reliance in parishes *quoad sacra* on voluntary contributions did see a corresponding decline in collections for poor relief which, after all, was a responsibility of the parish *quoad omnia*.[48] Furthermore, the elevation of the status of the ministers attached to *quoad sacra* parishes — most of whom were Evangelicals — further diluted the representation of the ailing Moderates in all Church courts above kirk-session. The cases which brought the Church of Scotland into collision with the Court of Session, from *Auchterarder* on, show that litigants were overwhelmingly preoccupied with the exercise of rights of patronage, but it was the Court's adverse decision on the Act anent Re-union with Seceders in *Stewarton* which ultimately led Welsh, Chalmers and Gordon to disrupt the Church in 1843.

The first *Auchterarder* case

Doubts about the legality of the congregational veto were raised as early as the 1834 General Assembly, but were immediately rested by Lord Moncreiff, Jeffrey and Cockburn. John Hope, nevertheless, waited for an opportunity to test them, and it came in the first *Auchterarder* case. In September 1834 the Earl of Kinnoull, patron of the parish of Auchterarder in Perthshire, executed a presentation in favour of the Reverend Robert Young, with the intention that he be appointed minister of the parish. The presentation was laid before the Presbytery of Auchterarder the next month, and the Presbytery then moved to process — or 'moderate' — the call to Young in accordance with the Veto Act. In December it took 287 dissents to the presentation out of a total of 330 enrolled heads of families in the parish. Finding that a majority of heads of families objected to the presentation, the Presbytery declared that Young could not be settled in the parish. The Synod of Perth and Stirling and the General Assembly upheld that decision, and so the Presbytery rejected Young's presentation.[49]

Lord Kinnoull and Young consulted John Hope, who, in October 1835, raised a summons before the Court of Session. It would have been possible to limit Young's claim to the right to receive the stipend of the parish, but Hope had a larger purpose in mind. He sought the invalidation of the Veto Act, by which the Presbytery's refusal of Young's presentation would become ultra vires, illegal and unwarrantable. It was not until November 1837 that the cause came to the Court of Session, and the matter was thought so important that the hearing took place before the Whole Court. Hope's pleading at the bar alone occupied three days and filled 183 pages of report. Andrew Rutherfurd, the Solicitor-General, led the case for the Presbytery, and was supported by the Procurator of the General Assembly, Robert Bell, and another committed Whig-Evangelical advocate, Alexander Dunlop. They put two basic arguments. First, the matter was ecclesiastical and so, under the constitution, could only be heard in the Church courts. The Court of Session therefore had no jurisdiction to entertain the pursuers' claim. This was nevertheless related to the second, more important point, which was that the Established Church had the legislative power to impose the veto on the effective exercise of rights of patronage. Here, Rutherfurd accepted Hope's argument that, for legal purposes, the Church of Scotland was to be considered a statutory creation. However, in addition to finding its constitutive powers in Acts of Parliament, they could be found in Acts of the General Assembly and a corpus of unwritten law based on custom and immemorial usage. He argued that, as the Established Church had always insisted on the 'call' as an essential part of the procedure for appointing a minister, it was a legitimate exercise of the Church's legislative power to regulate how a call could be made. That meant it was open to the Church to prescribe a role for the congregation in making the call to a minister, as it had done in the Veto Act.[50]

The Presbytery lost in *Auchterarder* by a majority of eight to five.[51] Each of the thirteen judges eventually delivered a separate opinion — a process which took ten days — but they can be grouped according to four different approaches. The first, an unqualified endorsement and application of unlimited parliamentary power, was taken by seven judges. These included the Tory-Moderates: Lord President Charles Hope, Lord Justice-Clerk Boyle, Lord Meadowbank, Lord Mackenzie and Lord Corehouse. The two older Whigs — Lord Gillies and Lord Cuninghame — also adopted this approach.[52] These judges saw sovereignty in the same terms as had John Austin a few years before: it was inherently indivisible and illimitable.[53] These qualities they attributed to Parliament, but the judges held that it was also essential that some court hold comparable unified, plenary powers. This answered Rutherfurd's objection to jurisdiction. As the Lord President held, the Court of Session had jurisdiction in the matter because, in Scotland as elsewhere, 'there must be some supereminent Court or Judicature, to control all other courts or judicatures, and prevent the confusion which might otherwise arise from conflicting jurisdictions'.[54] Similarly, the Court could only recognise as laws those directives that emanated from the legal sovereign, Parliament. Thus, the Church's powers were limited to those found in the statute law. This naturally led to an undisguised erastianism. As the Lord President said:

> For it was an error to hold that the Church of Scotland, as a National Church, was without a temporal Head, which head was Parliament; although, in a proper sense of the word, our Saviour was the Head of the Church of Scotland, as He was also the Head, properly speaking, of every Christian Church.[55]

The Church's powers over the exercise of rights of patronage were therefore limited to those found in the Act of 1712. This restricted a presbytery's powers to an examination of the presentee's qualifications. The General Assembly had no power to repeal an Act of Parliament, but if the Veto Act were allowed to operate its effect would be just that. It would deny the right of patronage its effectiveness and its patrimonial and economic value, and so render the Act of 1712 useless. For that reason the Veto Act was ultra vires the Church, and illegal.

To the modern mind, this might just appear to be a straightforward statement of the supremacy of the Parliament and the statute law, but in 1837 the constitutional law had probably not reached that point. Indeed, in *Minister of Prestonkirk v. Earl of Wemyss*,[56] Charles Hope, when Lord Justice-Clerk, had recognised that the Treaty of Union placed limits on Parliament's legislative powers in Scotland. That decision was made in the Court of Teinds in an application to increase a minister's stipend, so it seems that, at least so far as the Established Church was concerned, he had been prepared to recognise that the Parliament was constitutionally limited.

The only judge of the majority who took a different approach was Lord

Medwyn. He was an Episcopalian dissenter, and his theory of church–state relations was markedly High Anglican.[57] Medwyn's conception of sovereignty was less instrumental. The Veto Act was illegal, not so much because it usurped the authority of Parliament as because it was, in a broad sense, in breach of contract. The Church of Scotland was indeed an independent spiritual institution, deriving its power from no lesser source than that 'which gave Christ to be Head over all things to the Church, which is his body'.[58] However, its powers independent of the civil government were only spiritual. The civil powers it exercised were derived from the contract it made with the State when it sought Establishment. Interestingly, Lord Medwyn did recognise that some matters were so purely ecclesiastical that they were beyond the Court's jurisdiction: but not patronage. The Church was bound to obey the terms of the Act of 1712 'so long as it was connected to the State',[59] and (adopting the conclusions of the majority) held that the Veto Act was incompatible with that connection. Lord Medwyn's opinion is much more sympathetic to the Church than those of the other majority judges. He did not expressly reject unlimited parliamentary supremacy, but his reference to a contract between Church and State recognised enforceable norms which existed independently of Parliament. Medwyn's development of the contract theory in later cases led the other majority judges increasingly to distance themselves from his approach.[60]

Cockburn, who had been elevated to the bench in 1834, dissented. His opinion nevertheless rests on similar legal grounds to that of the majority judges (except Medwyn), and so was the weakest approach in support of the Church. 'The Church, as an establishment, had no power but what the State had conferred upon it.'[61] However, beyond this he was more pragmatic than the majority, holding that, in establishing Presbyterianism, the Scottish Parliament did not create something new, but had built on existing ecclesiastical structures. The statutes which empowered the Church to legislate were therefore cast in the most general terms, and gave it an 'indisputable and indispensable' power to regulate its own internal government.[62] The Veto Act was a measure for the regulation of the call of a minister, and well within the Church's statutory powers. It was therefore legal.

The other dissenting judges rejected the notion of an indivisible and illimitable sovereign, although this is clearer when they speak of the judicial functions of the Court of Session and the Church courts than when they consider the legislative roles of Parliament and the General Assembly. In the judicial sphere at least, sovereignty is pluralised. The Court of Session had a proper and superior jurisdiction in matters civil, and the General Assembly in matters spiritual. These jurisdictions were coordinate — neither court could claim legal precedence over the other. The leader of the minority was undoubtedly Lord Moncreiff, who was recognised by his peers as the ablest judge on the bench, but was also a leading Whig-Evangelical and the sponsor of the Veto Act in the Assembly of 1834.[63] He naturally concluded that the Court of Session had no jurisdiction. Even under the Act of 1712, the Presbytery had power to examine and admit a qualified person as minister, and it could only reach a judgment on his qualifications by reference to the laws of the Church. The matter of qualification and admission was therefore purely an ecclesiastical question, and exclusively within the jurisdiction of the Church courts. However, even if the pursuers could overcome the problem of the Court of Session's jurisdiction, there was still the question of the General Assembly's legal power to pass the Veto Act. Moncreiff had no doubt that the Church of Scotland had some independent status under the constitution:

> And it might well be asked whether [the Established] Church … was not something more than a mere corporation with power to make by-laws, whether it was not an essential and component part of the constitution of the realm, whose independent powers, judicial and legislative, were even more sacred and inviolable, than the powers and jurisdiction of the highest Civil and Criminal Courts of the country. These might be changed or taken away, as they had often been. The others could not be invaded on any vital point, without a direct breach of what was fundamental and essential in the political state of the United Kingdom.[64]

He thought that the Act of 1712 actually recognised the Church's exclusive power over the mode of appointing a minister. It only restored the right of presentation to the patrons, and so continued to respect the Church's exclusive power to prescribe the terms on which the presentee was admitted as minister — including a role for the congregation. Lord Fullerton and Lord Glenlee adopted a similar approach, although Fullerton alone was careful to add that he did not wish to imply that the Established Church was independent of the State, merely that 'according to the policy of the kingdom, a plurality of Supreme Courts was recognised, each independent of the other'.[65] This led to the exclusive ecclesiastical jurisdiction of the Church courts, denying any proper role for the Court of Session in the case. Jeffrey, appointed to the bench in 1834, also concentrated on the idea of coordinate and independent jurisdictions with the Church courts exercising exclusive jurisdiction in matters ecclesiastical, including the appointment of ministers. Unlike the other dissenting judges, he recognised that ministerial appointments might involve civil rights: the right of presentation, and the minister's right to a stipend or some other temporality. In cases which only involved these rights, the civil courts had jurisdiction. In other cases, the Church courts had jurisdiction; perhaps even in all cases where the ecclesiastical and civil rights in dispute were intermixed, but certainly where the 'concluding and most important part' were properly ecclesiastical.[66] *Auchterarder*, however, raised no question of presentation or of the minister's temporal entitlements, and was purely an ecclesiastical case.

When Lord Cuninghame finished delivering his opinion on 5 March 1838, the Court pronounced the interlocutor. The Earl of Kinnoull had legally presented the Reverend Robert Young to the parish church of Auchterarder, and the Presbytery had refused and continued to refuse to take him on trials and rejected him as presentee. The Presbytery had therefore acted illegally, to the hurt and prejudice of the pursuers. In conclusion, the Court remitted the process to Lord Fullerton, the Lord Ordinary, to proceed as he saw just.[67]

Earlier in court, Cockburn had ventured that, as soon as this interlocutor was pronounced, 'the civil and ecclesiastical authorities are in a state of legal collision'.[68] Thus began the conflict. Cockburn thought the judges would be wiser not to take on a quarrel they did not know how to win. Still, they had. He mused:

> No doubt it is our duty to declare the law, and the duty of all to obey it. I cannot doubt that the Church will obey it, both from inclination and necessity.[69]

In truth, he did doubt it. The risk of disobedience to the judgment had been foreshadowed, and so he cautioned the Church to proceed with 'sobriety and candour'. But oddly for one rendering judgment in court, Cockburn also recognised some small utility in the Church's adopting a strategy of disobedience to the law. He hoped that the Church's 'true policy is never to keep itself in opposition to the civil power one moment longer than is indispensable for the maintenance of its authority and usefulness'.[70]

Unsurprisingly, the result in *Auchterarder* was debated at length at the 1838 General Assembly. On 23 May, in an effort directly to contradict the Lord President's opinion on parliamentary supremacy, it resolved that its exclusive jurisdiction in matters spiritual 'follows immediately from God and the Mediator Jesus Christ, and is spiritual, not having a temporal head on earth, but only Christ, the only spiritual King and Governor of his Kirk'.[71] It also promised to 'assert and at all hazards defend' the spiritual independence of the Church, and to enforce submission to the General Assembly's powers by the Church's officials and members where necessary.[72] However, the next day, despite these stirring claims, the Assembly opted for an appeal to the House of Lords.[73] This was taken but, again as Cockburn predicted, was dismissed without real consideration of the issues.[74] The House of Lords decided on the narrow ground that under the Act of 1712 the Church courts could only try the 'qualifications' of the presentee, and by 'qualifications' it meant the man's sufficiency in literature, life and morals. The objection of the congregation to his appointment could not be a qualification.[75] No attempt was made to put the question on the broader footing of the legitimacy of political authority, as had occurred in the Court of Session. However, Lord Brougham, the only Scot to sit on the appeal, did parade his relationship to Principal William Robertson and his Moderate heritage.[76] Furthermore, Sir Frederick Pollock, counsel for the Church in the appeal, foreshadowed more strongly the possibility of the Church's disobedience. Brougham replied:

> ... to menace such lawless conduct on the part of the clergy, of the Christian clergy of a Christian church, the church of Scotland, whose head is Christ himself, is not only indecorous, but it is preposterous, it is monstrous — I will not believe it till I see the fact.[77]

Thinking then that the court's judgment would be 'cheerfully obeyed', he said that, even if it were otherwise, his duty was to state the law.[78] Brougham returned to this topic at the end of his speech, blaming the talk of disobedience on Sir Frederick and the Church's other counsel. Indeed, he thought these suggestions of disobedience would be spurned by the General Assembly itself. Thus Lord Brougham claimed to 'defend the Assembly against the arguments and threats of their advocates'.[79]

Brougham was wrong, but by the time he realised this *Auchterarder* had become only one of many cases in which the Church calculated for civil disobedience.

The disobedience

From *Auchterarder* to the Disruption, the Evangelical and official Church policy was to deny the jurisdiction of the Court of Session in ecclesiastical questions, and to ignore its judgments. Here, the Church's intransigence only hardened over time.[80] True, pragmatically the policy of denying the Court's jurisdiction was occasionally broken by the appearance of churchmen and presbyteries in proceedings brought against them. But no Church court controlled by Evangelicals ever obeyed an order made by the Court or the House of Lords against it in an ecclesiastical question. The four cases which follow show the Church maintaining a remarkably consistent response to the crisis, and also exemplify the different means by which the civil disobedience was expressed.

The Lethendy *case*

The first time a question of civil disobedience came before the Court of Session was in the *Lethendy* case.[81] The Crown, as patron of the united parishes of

Lethendy and Kinloch in Perthshire, presented the Reverend Thomas Clark to be assistant to the incumbent minister, the Reverend Laurence Butter, and to succeed him on his death. However, the Presbytery of Dunkeld rejected Clark in August 1834 on the basis of a congregational veto. The Reverend Butter died in January 1837, at which point John Hope raised a declarator on Clark's behalf in the Court of Session, concluding that the Presbytery was bound to try his qualifications and, if finding him qualified, admit him as minister. In the meantime, the Crown had assumed that Clark's presentation had lapsed on Butter's death and presented the Reverend Andrew Kessen instead. Hope then obtained an interdict from Lord Fullerton to restrain the Presbytery from proceeding with Kessen's presentation. This was served on the moderator of the Presbytery and on Kessen on 22 August 1837, Kessen's call having been approved by the congregation in accordance with the Veto Act earlier that month. However, in accordance with instructions given by both the Synod of Perth and Stirling and the Commission of Assembly, the Presbytery proceeded with Kessen's trials. In June 1838 a second bill of suspension and interdict was obtained from Lord Cuninghame and served on the Presbytery and Kessen. The Assembly was consulted again, and decided that the Presbytery should admit and ordain Kessen as parish minister. This took place on 13 September 1838. In November John Hope presented a petition and complaint for breach of interdict, and in the following February the matter came, once more, before the Whole Court.

This was a low point for the Church, for even Cockburn and Fullerton sided against the Presbytery. The problem of course was that the majority in the Presbytery had openly broken the interdict. So, even if (after trial on the merits) the interdict were recalled, a judicial order with a legitimate procedural purpose had been defied. Robert Bell had argued the case for the Presbytery, and disputed that the Court could punish for disobedience of an order it had no power to make. It was for the petitioner to prove that the interdicts were legal and this, he submitted, had not been attempted.[82] If that argument were accepted, the question came down to the Court's jurisdiction in a question of patronage. That was bound to fail after *Auchterarder*, and a majority certainly held to that effect.[83] However, most also rejected Bell's primary argument that the petitioner had to establish the legal basis of the interdict.[84] Lord Gillies recognised that an interdict could be made incorrectly, but a careful distinction had to be made between the question of the ultimate rights to be determined and that of 'interim possession for the regulation and preservation of the disputed subject'. It was not possible to let the latter question wait until the ultimate rights of the parties were decided. Thus, even if the Court's jurisdiction in the question could be disputed, the interdict requiring maintenance of the status quo until that question could be determined still had to be obeyed.[85] Cockburn disagreed, holding that the interdict could be disobeyed if not founded on a jurisdiction the Court could properly exercise. But he could not deny that, since *Auchterarder*, there was jurisdiction to interdict the Presbytery's proceedings.[86] This brought Cockburn to a more extreme position than he needed to take, for, like Fullerton, he could have decided the possibility of establishing the claim that Clark's trials should proceed was sufficient to sustain the interdict — there being no need at this stage to determine the merits of the claim.[87] The only real dissentients were Moncreiff and Jeffrey, both of whom were concerned that the effect of the interdicts was to order the Presbytery to ordain Clark as minister.

The defence of obedience to superior orders had been submitted on behalf of the Presbytery, as it had been instructed by the Synod and the Commission of Assembly to proceed with the call to Kessen. But, as Lord Justice-Clerk Boyle put it, 'the Commission itself had no right to break the law, and could delegate no right to any of the Church courts to do so'.[88] This did figure, however, in the Court's deliberations on how actually to punish the members of the Presbytery who broke the interdict. They were called to appear at the bar of the Court, but the Whig-Evangelical judges had already opined that the punishment should be light. The ministers, thought Cockburn and Jeffrey, had been motivated by a sense duty, albeit a wrong one.[89] Fullerton thought the breach had not been a wilful contempt of the Court's authority but, given the orders of the Synod and Commission of Assembly, had been motivated by an intention to uphold the authority of the Church courts.[90] Moncreiff thought that, confronted with the conflicting judgments of the Court and the Church, the members of the Presbytery necessarily had to decide which of the two orders had to be obeyed. If they erred in obeying the Church courts, it was an error they felt constrained to make by conscience. This should not only mitigate punishment, it should defend them from punishment altogether.[91] Medwyn also had some sympathy for the dilemma the ministers faced, but did not comment on how this might affect their punishment.[92] Cuninghame agreed that the Court should take the most favourable view possible for the recalcitrant ministers, though he was upset that the same attitude had not been reciprocated in the Church courts, where Clark had been treated with hostility.[93]

The ministers appeared before the bar of the Court on 12 June and apologised, claiming to be deeply impressed by the duty they had to obey the judges, but adding that they were also bound to obey the superior courts of the Church.[94] Cockburn later lampooned the judicial masquerade, admitting that the judges already knew what was going to be said, but that they all pretended to look grim.[95]

Then the judges bargained. The President, the Justice-Clerk, Gillies, Meadowbank, Mackenzie, Medwyn and Murray wanted the ministers gaoled. Moncreiff, Jeffrey, Fullerton, Cockburn and Cuninghame wanted them to pay costs. It was a significant bloc, for the compromise suggested by Boyle, the Justice-Clerk, was a censure and costs, a result much closer to the Whig-Evangelicals' preference than the majority's.[96] On 14 June the Lord President pronounced the solemn censure of the Court. He told the ministers that the Court had been lenient, and if churchmen undertook civil disobedience again in similar circumstances imprisonment would result. This lecture was delivered calmly,[97] but it still shocked churchmen that ministers could be threatened with gaol.[98] The President was at pains to point out that the judges took no personal offence at the Presbytery's disobedience, though that may not have been a necessary comment unless there was some public belief that personal animosities had developed. He claimed that they only wanted to maintain the dignity of the Court. Still, his comment that ministers who in conscience could not submit to the law had no choice but to leave the Established Church was met with applause from the public gallery.[99] The future directions of Court and Church were already set, and disruption was looking like a popular option.

The second **Auchterarder** *case*

Following the disposal of the appeal in *Auchterarder*, the case was remitted to Lord Murray as Ordinary. He declared that the Presbytery was bound to try the Reverend Young's qualifications and, if finding him qualified, receive and admit him as minister. This was read to the Presbytery on 2 July 1839, but, again before acting, a majority voted to refer the question to the Commission of Assembly. This was to meet in August. Lord Kinnoull and Young thought this might be disobeying Lord Murray's declarator, and briefed John Hope in an action for damages and reparation. This time, Hope sought opinions from English lawyers — Dr Joseph Phillimore, a leader at the English ecclesiastical bar, and John Campbell, the Attorney-General and an expatriate Scot, who had led for the pursuers in the first House of Lords appeal.[100] Campbell was confident that damages could be recovered, at least from the ministers who voted to refer the question of Young's trials to the Commission of Assembly. Phillimore was less certain. He had reservations as to whether a court could compel the admission of a man to holy orders.[101] In one sense, this reinforced the Presbytery's central defence, pressed by Alexander Wood (who would succeed Hope as Dean) and James Moncreiff (the judge's son). They argued that Lord Murray had merely indicated the Court's opinion that the Presbytery was bound to take Young on trials. The language used in his declarator did not suggest that any obligation was placed on the Presbytery to do so. In any case (and as Phillimore had thought), the Court could not compel ordination, an essential step to admission to the ministry.[102] The argument was heard by the most senior judges, in the First Division of the Inner House. They were unimpressed. The President, at this point, had come to accept that the Court had no power to compel ordination. However, the statute law allowed it to order that a man be received and admitted.[103] This was really an empty distinction, given the place of ordination in the procedure for admission. Lord Mackenzie refused to make it; he had no doubt that the Court could compel ordination.[104] But putting the question of ordination to one side, the judges agreed that the ministers' disobedience to Lord Murray's declarator made them liable to the pursuers in damages. Even Lord Fullerton thought that Wood and Moncreiff had made too fine a distinction between an order declaring the Court's opinion and one obliging the Presbytery to take Young on trials. For even a declaratory judgment conclusively stated the law as it stood between the pursuers and defenders, and the defenders could not object to that. The Presbytery therefore could not defend against the pursuers' attempts to enforce that legal position, in this case by an action for reparation.[105] As Lord Gillies put it, the declarator bound the Presbytery, and it was obliged to obey it.[106]

So, yet again, *Auchterarder* went to the House of Lords. Unsurprisingly, the Church received few commiserations when the Lords delivered their speeches in August 1842.[107] Brougham sat on the appeal again, but by now had a more realistic appreciation of the Church's motives. Taking the argument that the Presbytery had really only referred the question of Young's trials to the Commission of Assembly for advice, he replied that this was 'an error wearing a more sinister aspect, come of more base parentage, and fruitful of more dangerous offspring'.[108] It was an intentional act of disobedience, and was punished by compensating those who had been injured. Brougham's fear, of course, was that this disobedience would conceive lawlessness, even lawlessness within limited spheres of social life.

> Here, then, would be a complete case of *imperium in imperio*; of bodies existing in the country, and exercising important functions, — functions nearly affecting the rights, civil and patrimonial rights of the subject, — and yet not placed under any control of the law, nor rendering any obedience to those entrusted with the office of administering it.[109]

This, Brougham knew, was what the Evangelicals wanted.[110] Campbell, who, while Attorney-General, had advised that the action for damages could be brought, had been elevated to the peerage in 1839, and now heard the appeal.[111] He naturally agreed that damages could be recovered, but also hinted at the possible solution for the Church.

> *While the Appellants remain members of the Establishment*, they are, in addition to their sacred character, public functionaries appointed and paid by the State, they must perform the duties which the law of the land imposes upon them.[112]

It was only voluntary bodies, like the dissenting churches, which, 'self-founded and self-supported', could govern themselves.[113]

Even with the two judgments of the House of Lords against them, the majority of the Presbytery of Auchterarder never tried Young's qualifications. The disobedience continued until March 1843, when the majority in the Court of Session ordered the minority in the Presbytery who were prepared to proceed with Young's trials to do so.[114] To the Evangelicals, this order was another example of judicial meddling in matters rightly belonging only to the Church, as it reconstituted a Church court. By then it mattered little, because the Disruption took place two months later, and, as the *Strathbogie* case would illustrate at length, the reconstitution of Church courts had by this stage become commonplace.

The Strathbogie *case*

Undoubtedly, the most dramatic collision between the Court and the Church in this period was in the remarkable *Strathbogie* case. This raised circumstances precisely the opposite of *Auchterarder*. The Earl of Fife and Huntly was patron of the parish of Marnoch in Banffshire. His trustees presented the Reverend John Edwards to the parish in June 1837, a presentation sustained by the Presbytery responsible for the parish, Strathbogie. Then the procedures of the Veto Act were initiated. In November it was found that 261 heads of families in the parish objected to Edwards and only one wanted him. *Auchterarder* was decided in the following February, but the Presbytery was directed by both the Synod of Moray and the General Assembly to reject Edwards. It did so, and Lord Fife's trustees, assuming that Edwards' presentation failed, presented Mr David Hendry instead.

However, Edwards had briefed John Hope. From that point, there was much toing and froing between the Presbytery, Synod and Assembly. Hope also raised proceedings on a number of occasions. Finally, on 4 November 1839, the Presbytery resolved, by a majority of seven to four, to comply with *Auchterarder* and sustain the call to Edwards. This immediately provoked a meeting of the Commission of Assembly. On 11 November it overruled the Presbytery's decision to proceed with Edwards' trials, and declared that the majority in the Presbytery had acted against the fundamental principles of the Church. It also suspended the right of the 'Strathbogie seven' to act as ministers of the Church.

The large question in the *Strathbogie* litigation therefore concerned the extent to which the Church could punish ministers who acted in obedience to the law and who, accordingly, objected to the official policy of civil disobedience. The seven initially ignored their suspensions, but sought the help, again through John Hope, of the Court of Session. Interdicts were granted, prohibiting the service of the Commission's sentence of suspension and any other ministers in the Presbytery from preaching in churches and schools in parishes where the seven were incumbent. The Ordinary, Lord Murray, reported that the complainers had only acted lawfully, and should be protected by interdict from any injury threatened to them for doing so.[114] It was largely to comply with these interdicts that the ministers sent by the Commission of Assembly to announce the suspension of the seven did so outside churches and schools in the parishes, and held services outdoors.[115] That led *Strathbogie* to escalate.[116] To exclude any other ministers from their parishes, the seven sought a more comprehensive interdict from Lord Murray. This time he refused, so the seven reclaimed to the First Division. On 14 February 1840 the 'extended interdict' which they wanted was ordered by the Lord President, Lord Gillies and Lord Mackenzie. Lord Fullerton dissented.[117] This interdict was much more serious, as it prohibited all ministers of the Established Church from entering the parishes of the Strathbogie seven and preaching. The Court, therefore, had told the Church that it could not preach the gospel in Scottish parishes — a ban which not only compromised the spiritual independence the Church claimed, but also its very mission as a national territorial establishment. Following a resolution of the Commission of Assembly, the extended interdict was proudly flouted; the most respected ministers rushed to preach in the Strathbogie parishes. Chalmers announced at the next General Assembly that the Church would simply disobey the interdicts and accept the consequences.[118]

Strathbogie, in fact, shows the judges becoming extremely impatient with the Church's disobedience. Incautious remarks were made from the bench, especially by Lord Gillies. He accused the ministers in the Commission of breaking their oaths of allegiance, as disobedience to the Court was disobedience to the sovereign power of the State.[119] And, in a remark calculated to cause the deepest offence to any Evangelical churchman, he claimed:

> The pretensions of the Church of Scotland at present are exactly those of the Papal See a few centuries ago. They not only decline the jurisdiction of the civil courts, but they deny that Parliament can bind them by a law which they choose to say is inconsistent with the law of Christ.[120]

It is easy to get the impression at this point that the judges in the majority were less concerned about reasoning to justify or explain the order they made, as they were to find against the Church. The tone of the judgments had become much more argumentative than deliberative, and the strong suspicion was that the Court was more interested, as Cockburn put it, in 'winging Wild-Churchmen'.[121]

Useless as it was, the extended interdict was made perpetual in July 1840. The Church refused to contest it.[122] *Strathbogie* nevertheless continued. The seven, acting (as the Court of Session held they could) as the Presbytery of Strathbogie, found Edwards qualified. So Edwards, with the consent of the seven, brought an action to have the Presbytery receive and admit him as minister. John Hope represented the seven. This time the Church, by the minority in the Presbytery, appeared, as the question of ordination was at stake. Rutherfurd, now Lord Advocate, Robert Bell and James Moncreiff argued the case.[123] The matter was heard, once more, by the First Division and, once more, it divided — the President, Gillies and Mackenzie holding for the pursuers, and Fullerton dissenting.[124] Lord Gillies and Lord Mackenzie, who was yet to reach the position on ordination he would in *Auchterarder*, still maintained the pretence that an order for reception and admission as a minister was not, regardless of what it implied, an order to ordain.[125] Lord President Hope did accept that the Court had power to order the ordination of a minister,[126] although he would reconsider this.[127] Rutherfurd also argued that Edwards had not undergone trials in any Presbytery recognised by the Church, as the General Assembly had suspended the seven who found him qualified. This brought the Lord President back to the question of civil disobedience. The seven had not been suspended for any lawful reason; to the contrary, they had been suspended because they obeyed the law. The suspensions were ineffective, and so a legally constituted Presbytery had tried Edwards' qualifications. He was entitled to be admitted as minister.[128]

Edwards' ordination took place in January 1841. That brought immediate disciplinary action against the seven, who were deposed from the ministry by the General Assembly later that year. 1841 also saw Charles Hope retire from the Court. David Boyle replaced him as Lord President, and, even more significantly for 'the Church question', John Hope was elevated to the bench as Lord Justice-Clerk.[129]

The new First Division had an early look at the deposition of the Strathbogie seven when they tried to stop the four ministers in the minority from sending commissioners to the General Assembly.[130] Lord Fullerton thought that, as the question touched on the composition of the Assembly, the case was so novel and serious as to be heard by the Whole Court. However, Boyle and Mackenzie outvoted him and granted the interdict.[131]

This interdict was ignored by the Church,[132] but the depositions eventually did come before the Whole Court when the seven brought an action against Dr Robert Gordon, the Moderator of the 1842 Assembly, to have them cancelled.[133] Like the last stages of *Auchterarder* and *Stewarton*, judgment was delivered in the months before the Disruption.

No opinion was given by the Justice-Clerk (who had been counsel in the earlier *Strathbogie* proceedings)[134] or by Jeffrey. The judges otherwise divided on the usual lines: the President, Murray, Meadowbank, Alexander Wood (who replaced Gillies at the end of 1842), Medwyn, Cuninghame and Mackenzie for the pursuers; Cockburn, Moncreiff, Fullerton and James Ivory (appointed in 1840) for the Church. The Church's argument, made by the Lord Advocate, was still that the Court of Session had no jurisdiction. This was a matter of ecclesiastical discipline, and even if it was exercised against the seven for obedience to the law it was exclusively a matter for the Church courts. That point was partly conceded in the joint judgment of Lords Murray, Meadowbank and Wood. The Church courts alone could censure and discipline ministers, but they could only do so in accordance with the law. They held that the proceedings against the Strathbogie seven in the General Assembly had been perverted, as the sole offence they were supposed to have committed was obedience to the orders of a civil court. The result was that the proceedings were beyond the powers of the Church, and the depositions were therefore invalid.[135] The Lord President and Lord Cuninghame delivered similar opinions. Lord Medwyn concurred, but added his unique contractual perspective. In exchange for its established status, the Church had agreed to exercise its powers under particular conditions. It was open to the Court to enforce the performance of these conditions as it could any other contract. Here, the implied condition on which the Church had to conduct its proceedings seems to have been that it not obstruct the lawful proceedings of the civil courts.[136] Then, Medwyn advanced the contractual analysis by outlining what he thought was the only way the Church could respect the law and also honour its conscience:

> If the Church feels itself burdened with this condition, its remedy is not disobedience at its own hands, but a rescission of the contract, and a *restitutio in integrum*, which is always within its power.[137]

The dissent was led by Lord Ivory, who rejected outright the idea that the Court of Session had an indivisible and illimitable jurisdiction.[138] The Church courts were no less independent and sovereign in the province ecclesiastical than the Court of Session was in the civil.[139] Difficult questions of demarcation might arise, but when a collision occurred between the two it was not for one of these tribunals to assume the power to decide which had the right of final judgment. After all, they were equal. The collision could only be resolved by a higher power, presumably Parliament.[140] *Strathbogie* ended in the Court the next day, when it ruled that the man inducted into Marnoch by the four members of the Presbytery who had not been deposed had not been properly admitted as parish minister.[141]

The Stewarton *case*

It was not until 1843 that the Court of Session properly dealt with the Church Extension legislation. The status of *quoad sacra* parishes had arisen indirectly in earlier cases when, sitting as the Court of Teinds, the judges heard applications from ministers for increases to their stipends. Here, the Court had been prepared, in the earliest cases anyway, to recognise that the creation of a *quoad sacra* parish reduced a parish minister's duties and, as a result, tended to counter his argument for a larger stipend.[142] However, by 1839 it was ignoring the impact and, possibly, the legal existence of *quoad sacra* parishes.[143] The question came more directly before the Court of Session when the right of ministers of *quoad sacra* parishes to sit in Presbyteries was challenged. In the First Division, the Tory-Moderate judges did query the validity of the Chapel Act and, alone on this point, Lord Fullerton had unequivocally supported it.[144] However, the Church consistently denied the Court's jurisdiction in these cases by refusing to appear. So, ex parte orders were made against presbyteries on the assumption that the Chapel Act was invalid. But as that same question of validity remained unargued and unsettled until an action inter partes could be determined, the Church continued to act as if the Church Extension legislation were fully effective.

The Church finally appeared in a Church Extension case in *Stewarton*, decided by the Whole Court in January 1843.[145] It was a fatal move, because its chances of success were small. However, it was probably unavoidable. It is possible that the Church had to contest *Stewarton* because it could not, as in other disputes, exercise discipline in its own courts over the suspenders who brought the civil proceedings.[146] William Cuninghame of Lainshaw was patron of the parish of Stewarton in Ayrshire. In November 1839 the Presbytery of Irvine approved the entry of the Stewarton congregation of the Associate Synod into the Church of Scotland. This was in accordance with the Act anent Re-union with Seceders, but against the vote of the parish minister. In January 1840 Cuninghame and heritors of the parish threatened to interdict subsequent proceedings of the Presbytery to allocate a district in the parish to the congregation as a *quoad sacra* parish and to admit its minister, the Reverend James McClelland, to a place in the Presbytery. In March a note of suspension and interdict was raised against the Presbytery. Lord Gillies immediately granted an interim interdict to prevent the division of the parish and McClelland's sitting in the Presbytery until the process of suspension was determined. This was confirmed by Lord Ivory in June, but in the meantime proceedings had continued in the Presbytery, and the Synod of Glasgow and Ayr. In August the Commission of Assembly ordered the Presbytery to continue with the division of the parish, which, despite being served with the interdict, it did on 10 December 1840. The Church appeared to the process of suspension two days later. Cuninghame raised a petition and complaint for the breach of interdict in March 1841. However, this question was absorbed by the more general challenge raised by the process of suspension: that the Presbytery's actions were illegal, a challenge to the Church Extension legislation itself.

Auchterarder and the patronage cases only created a collision between the Church and the Court indirectly. They were incidental to the Church's refusal to recognise the Court's decisions on its direct collision with the patrons. *Stewarton* did raise a direct collision, because the Church Extension legislation assumed that the Church courts had an analogous jurisdiction to that which the judges exercised as the Court of Teinds. Inevitably, the Church's defence failed. Equally inevitably, the Lord Justice-Clerk led the majority. The issue raised the rights of patrons again, as they had a civil right to present a man to the *whole* parish and not to the parish less any *quoad sacra* parochial districts.[147] However, the Act of 1707 gave direct authority to the Court of Teinds to make adequate provision for the creation of new parishes. This was conferred on a civil court, and beyond the statutory powers which alone defined the Church's jurisdiction.[148] As for the power to admit the ministers of *quoad sacra* parishes to seats in presbyteries, he held that the statute law conferred the right to sit in Church courts on parish (*quoad omnia*) ministers. Furthermore, compliance with the statute law generally was a question that the civil courts had power to review, and so the Court of Session had jurisdiction to rule that provision in the Church Extension legislation for *quoad sacra* ministers to sit in Church courts was unlawful.[149] The usual dissents were entered by Lords Ivory, Cockburn and Moncreiff. The latter knew better than the rest that this case — 'the most important cause which I have yet been called upon to consider or to judge of in my time'[150] — spelt the end of the Evangelicals' time in the Established Church. Moncreiff 'trembled' as he contemplated the 'mutilation' of the Church.[151]

Stewarton also shows another dimension of the Church's civil disobedience. Rutherford, Bell, Dunlop and the younger Moncreiff appeared for the Church. Patrick Robertson, Dean of the Faculty of Advocates, appeared for the suspenders.[152] However, it was Alexander Dunlop alone who drafted the answers to Cuninghame's petition and complaint of March 1841. This had alleged that the Presbytery meeting of 10 December 1840 had broken Lord Ivory's interdict. Dunlop pleaded that the Presbytery was bound to obey the directions of the Commission of Assembly, even though an order of the Court of Session demanded otherwise. He continued that the same law and constitution which impelled the ministers to recognise the jurisdiction of the Court of Session in civil matters equally required them to obey the Church courts in spiritual. Then he added a Luther-like flourish:

> They can suffer. But they cannot violate their duty to the constitution, they cannot betray the sacred authority committed to them as office-bearers of the Church, — they cannot sacrifice the eternal welfare of the immortal souls of whom they have the oversight, — they cannot break the vows they have taken to their God.[153]

In the earliest arguments in *Stewarton* in June 1842, Robertson, no stranger himself to rhetorical flourishes,[154] suggested that the majority of the Presbytery were indicating that, whatever the Court decided, they would still obey the orders of the superior Church courts.[155] This stirred some on the bench. The judges generally thought that the pleadings were ambiguous, but the Lord Justice-Clerk, John Hope, noted that, if this pleading were pre-empting disobedience to the Court's orders, it might amount to sedition, and if avowed by the parties at bar would lead to instant imprisomnent.[156] Lord Moncreiff, at the other extreme as usual, thought they were only protesting jurisdiction.[157] Time was therefore given for an explanation. Somewhat embarrassed, Rutherfurd returned to the Court on 1 July admitting that the answers contained 'unguarded expressions'. Having discussed the matter with Dunlop, he indicated that the purpose had been to present an effective denial of the jurisdiction of the Court of Session. It had been Dunlop's intention to strengthen this by ensuring that no plea could be interpreted as accepting that the Court had any right to determine the matter, or as compromising the Church's claim to exclusive jurisdiction.[158] The explanation was a little laboured, but Rutherfurd argued that Lord Campbell had used the same approach when, as Attorney-General, he defended the jurisdiction of the House of Commons against that of the Court of Queen's Bench in *Stockdale v. Hansard.*[159] However, Rutherfurd was happy to do without the offending passages, and they were expunged from the record.[160] This was, in any case, the solution Lord President Boyle had suggested in June.[161]

In this incident the Justice-Clerk was certainly too officious, and was probably just troublemaking. The claim that an ambiguous pleading could amount to sedition was obviously disproportionate, and was not taken too seriously even by the other Tory-Moderates. However, the Justice-Clerk helped to illuminate the twilight between the legally acceptable strategy of denying the jurisdiction of a court and a legally unacceptable act of civil disobedience. The Church's pleading against the jurisdiction of the Court would itself become civil disobedience if it envisaged that the denial of jurisdiction would persist after the Court had held it could determine the case. However, the problem is that, had the Church showed any indication that it would obey the orders of the Court on its determining that it had jurisdiction, it could be taken to have submitted to jurisdiction. In such a case, as the Lord President and Rutherfurd came to agree, it was preferable not to mention how the Church would respond if the protest against jurisdiction did fail. This still needed careful drafting, and it was hardly a time for dispassionate lawyering.

Conclusion

The Court of Session's adjudication on questions of patronage and parochial reorganisation between 1837 and 1843 was, in the true sense of the word, prejudiced. Today, it is tempting but premature to limit this conclusion to the opinions of the Tory-Moderate judges and the others in the majority. The Established Church and, after 1843, the Free Church earned immense popular esteem for the stand taken on the independent jurisdiction of the Church courts, the willingness to engage in civil disobedience for the sake of conscience, and, once the dust settled after the schism, the personal cost the Evangelical churchmen who disrupted paid when they left the comfortable manses, stipends and social prestige of the regular parish ministry. Effectively, the judgment of history is that they were right. The Church settlement of 1921 recognised the independence of the Church of Scotland, and that no statute or law can now limit its liberties, rights and powers in spiritual matters. Indeed, it is not even open to a civil court to declare what matters encompassed by the Church settlement are spiritual.[162] But it is worth remembering that the belle-lettrists on the Court of Session in the 1830s and 1840s — Cockburn and Jeffrey — were in the Whig-Evangelical bloc. Later scholarship has had to rely on Cockburn especially to learn what was happening inside the Court, and that means the controversy is often still seen through his eyes. However, the decisions made by Moncreiff, Jeffrey and, for the most part, Cockburn were as consistent with their known politics and churchmanship as those made by the two Lord Hopes. In many respects, the issues these men had debated in the General Assembly were merely transferred to the Court of Session, but, as the composition of the Court carried more of the legacy of the Dundas ascendancy of the early nineteenth century, the numbers fell differently.

The curial pluralism advocated by Moncreiff, Fullerton, Glenlee, Jeffrey and Ivory had deep roots in the idea of two kingdoms: a doctrine that, in a

Christian nation, Church and State have separate functions but were equal instruments of God's purpose. This was a fundamental theological position to less conservative Presbyterians. These judges elevated it to constitutional status through the Revolution settlement of 1690 and the guarantee of Presbyterianism in the Treaty of Union. Though the parliamentary supremacy of Charles Hope, John Hope, Boyle, Meadowbank, Mackenzie, Corehouse, Gillies, Cuninghame, Murray and Wood had a less distinct theological basis, it correlated neatly with the Enlightenment rationalism that was the common heritage of Moderatism and the emerging school of legal positivism.[163] Throughout, judges on both sides cited Church legislation, the experience of other national churches, confessional documents, ancient church fathers, theologians and churchmen to support their conclusions. In itself, this was orthodox legal reasoning. Scotland in the 1830s and 1840s was not a secular state. In addition, though Scots law developed like English law by a feudal, common law method, the sources of the law recognised by judges in Scotland were much more diverse than was usual in England and the colonies, and included Scottish and continental institutional writers, historical sources, Roman and civilian doctrine, natural law theory and the law of nations.[164] In adjudication on 'the Church question', it was only a matter of course that religious sources would be used.

Still, what is more telling about the majority judgments is that the erastianism they endorsed really represents a hiatus in the Court of Session's approach to jurisdiction in ecclesiastical matters. For, only six years after the Disruption, the Court began again to define an independent sphere of Church jurisdiction in which, according to the constitutional law, it could not intervene. In *Sturrock v. Greig*,[165] it held that a kirk-session could not be sued for damages when it had disciplined a schoolmaster for misconduct, even when the pursuer alleged malice. Even Lord Justice-Clerk John Hope was sounding Evangelical when he held:

> [The Church's] judicatories and its officers are not amenable to the civil courts for alleged wrong. They have been entrusted as a separate government.[166]

Cockburn dissented in *Sturrock*, but sensed the majority was retreating from the broader reading of the Court of Session's powers in the cases from *Auchterarder* to *Stewarton*.[167] There were qualifications to the recognition of the Church's independent jurisdiction in *Sturrock*, such as the Court's continuing power to define the jurisdiction of the Church courts as expressed in statute.[168] However, it was accepted after *Sturrock* that there were questions of law, procedure and discipline inside the jurisdictional bounds of the Church courts that were beyond the supervision of the Court of Session.[169] This certainly did not bring the constitutional law to the point of recognising independent, coordinate jurisdictions as, say, Lord Moncreiff had held in the first *Auchterarder* case,[170] but it would not have allowed the decisions of Lord President Hope in *Strathbogie* and Lord Mackenzie in the second *Auchterarder* case that the Court could compel the ordination of a minister.[171] Thus, in light of the temporary change in the Court's attitude to the Church's jurisdiction between *Minister of Prestonkirk v. Earl of Wemyss*[172] and *Sturrock*, it is possible to see some of the more excessive intrusions of the Court before the Disruption as a reflection of its opposition to the policies of the Evangelical Party. If so, the Court of Session had really become one of the disputants. As a consequence, its decisions lost the credibility they needed if they were to command obedience.[173]

The same prejudices arose in the Court's responses to the Church's civil disobedience. Fullerton and Cockburn, on occasions, demanded enforcement of orders they thought should not have been made. But otherwise, the result the individual judges wanted when dealing with questions of disobedience followed closely from the result they wanted on the questions of ministry and Church government. Here, it is more remarkable how powerless the Court was to deal with the disobedience effectively.

Lethendy is probably the strongest case in which obedience to the Court's order could have been expected. It did not deal directly with the question of the Church's jurisdiction: the order which was ignored was an interim interdict. The case therefore related to the maintenance of the Court's procedural structure, essential to the ordinary conduct of civil litigation, irrespective of the merits of the claim. However, the Court was unable to deal with the breach of interdict properly, because Moncreiff, Jeffrey, Fullerton, Cockburn and Cuninghame were unprepared to punish when, as was inevitable in these cases, the defence of obedience to ecclesiastical superiors was raised. Unable to respond effectively in a case like *Lethendy*, the Court was almost completely paralysed when it had to deal with cases closer to the Evangelicals' concerns about Church independence. It could state, as a matter of law, that Parliament was the legal sovereign, but the doctrine of parliamentary supremacy was a legal fiction while, in practice, the Court could not realise obedience to its interpretation of the statute law.

In fact, it is arguable that, viewed politically, the Church of Scotland had no moral duty to obey the law. Its civil disobedience probably had a legitimate political purpose, it was limited and, to paraphrase Lord Cockburn's remarks in *Auchterarder*,[174] it was only maintained while it was useful. The Evangelicals were no anarchists, they were reformers. They believed that the program of civil disobedience was prophetic criticism of a sovereign that claimed what belonged to God. The goal was therefore to change the heart of civil government in Scotland — not to cut it out. It was a direct challenge to unitarism and its associated concentration of power, and an attempt, characteristically Presbyterian, to have civil government recognise multiple sovereignties, limits to political authority and lateral federalism.[175] And, after all, the independence the Established Church claimed was largely that which dissenters already enjoyed under the common law and the occasional statute.[176] The Church's challenge was also carefully defined and limited to the question of spiritual independence, and the maintenance of its related policies on patronage and parochial reorganisation. The resolutions of the General Assembly and the arguments submitted to the courts on the Church's behalf asserted — with embarrassing frequency — its unqualified submission to the law and the Court of Session's jurisdiction in matters civil, while also making the strongest claims to spiritual independence.

Indeed, the Disruption actually shows that legality prevailed. *Stewarton*, and the Peel Government's unwillingness to initiate legislation that would regularise the Evangelical reforms or support an endowment for the Church Extension program, showed that the civil disobedience was not succeeding, and that the connection with the State was an impediment. Chalmers had raised the possibility of disruption as early as the 1839 General Assembly,[177] but, in the absence of parliamentary intervention, it was also the solution to the Church's concerns recommended by the courts. Lord Medwyn, who was a dissenter himself, had in *Auchterarder* raised dissent as a means of avoiding the restrictions of patronage, and in *Strathbogie* cast schism or disestablishment as a lawful rescission of the contract between Church and State. *Restitutio in integrum* would restore to the Church the liberties it wanted.[178] Lord President Hope and Lord Campbell had also recommended that schism would serve the Evangelicals' ends.[179] Thus, the point at which they finally submitted to the Court of Session's judgments was the Disruption itself. They even evidenced the legality of the event by executing a Deed of Demission, which formalised the separation from the Established Church and the creation of 'the Church of Scotland — Free'.[180] The civil disobedience which followed *Auchterarder* only had real social significance because, in its own administration, preaching and relations with the State, the Church had otherwise demonstrated deep respect for the law and the Court of Session.

Ironically, it seems likely that the civil disobedience of the Church of Scotland did not degenerate into serious lawlessness (as it had in the 1680s) because the constitutional structure of the United Kingdom recognised *imperia in imperio*. In the second *Auchterarder* appeal, Lord Brougham showed real uneasiness about the presence of an *imperium in imperio* in Scotland,[181] but the fact was that the State did allow dissenting churches with high degrees of legal independence to arrange and regulate their own internal affairs. That meant that schism and the opportunity to dissent — both perfectly lawful — helped to stabilise the legal order, and to bring the civil disobedience to an end voluntarily. The bitter conflict between the Church of Scotland and the Court of Session showed how pointless it was to claim sovereignty in matters where it was impractical to enforce it, and the Disruption proves that comparable limits on civil power may even reinforce an orderly society, the law and the duty of obeying it.

Notes

1. Darrell Lumb discussed this obligation from a Catholic scholastic viewpoint in 'The Duty of Obeying the Law' in Tammelo I, Blackshield A & Campbell E (eds), *12 Australian Studies in Legal Philosophy*, Luchterhand, Berlin, 1963 at 195–216.
2. Baillie J (ed.), *Proceedings of the General Assembly of the Free Church of Scotland, with a sketch of the proceedings of the residuary Assembly 1843*, William Whyte & Co, Edinburgh, 1843 at 5.
3. Note 2 at 6–8.
4. Cockburn H, *Journal of Henry Cockburn, being a continuation of the Memorials of His Time 1831–1854*, Edmonston & Douglas, Edinburgh, 1874, II at 21. For another judge's reaction, see Cockburn H, *Life of Lord Jeffrey*, Adam and Charles Black, Edinburgh, 1852, I at 387.
5. Note 2 at 247.
6. Under the terms of the *Church of Scotland Act* 1921 s. 1.
7. The earliest histories are Buchanan R, *The Ten Years' Conflict; being the History of the Disruption of the Church of Scotland*, Blackie, Glasgow, 1849; and Bryce J, *Ten Years of the Church of Scotland from 1833 to 1843 with an Historical Retrospect from 1560*, William Blackwood, Edinburgh, 1850. For a recent collection of essays, see Brown SJ & Fry M (eds), *Scotland in the Age of the Disruption*, Edinburgh University Press, 1993. Theological studies worth consulting include Henderson I, *Power without Glory: a Study in Ecumenical Politics*, Hutchinson, London, 1967; and Donaldson G, *Scottish Church History*, Scottish Academic Press, Edinburgh, 1985. For a sociological study, see MacLaren A, *Religion and Social Class: the Disruption Years in Aberdeen*, Routledge & Kegan Paul, London, 1974. An outstanding modern biography is Brown SJ, *Thomas Chalmers and the Godly Commonwealth in Scotland*, Oxford University Press, 1982. Presbyterian theological libraries often hold *Disruption Worthies: a Memorial of 1843*, John Grieg, Edinburgh, 1876.
8. The following is probably an exhaustive list: Innes AT, *The Law of Creeds in Scotland*, William Blackwood & Sons, Edinburgh, 1902 at 68–96; Lyall F, *Of Presbyters and Kings: Church and State in the Law of Scotland*, Aberdeen University Press, 1980 at 21–53; Taylor TM, 'Church and State in Scotland' [1957] *Jur Rev* 121 at 124–8. I discuss the Disruption in 'Establishment and Toleration: the British Pattern of Secularisation' (1993) 17 *UQLJ* 185 at 195–7.
9. Innes AT, n 8 at 74.
10. *Earl of Kinnoull and Young v. Presbytery of Auchterarder and ors* (1838) 16 S 661.

11. Cockburn H, *Journal* 1, n 4 at 167; Pinkerton JM, 'Cockburn and the Law' in Bell A (ed.), *Lord Cockburn. A Bicentenary Commemoration 1779–1979*, Scottish Academic Press, Edinburgh, 1979 at 111; *Presbytery of Auchterarder and ors v. Earl of Kinnoull and Young* (1839) 6 Cl & F 646 at 723. Lord Moncrieff thought that *Stewarton* was a more critical decision, and in practical terms for the Church it was: *Cuninghame v. Presbytery of Irvine* (1843) 5 D 427: Session Papers (Hope Collection), CCCIII 11, *Opinions of Consulted Judges*, 16 November 1843 at 111.
12. *Clark v. Stirling* (1839) I D 955.
13. *Presbytery of Strathbogie and Cruikshank and ors* (1839) 2 D 258; (1839) 2 D 585; (1840) 2 D 1047, 1380; (1840) 3 D 282; (1842) 4 D 1298; (1843) 5 D 909.
14. For this, see Lyall F, n 8.
15. *Earl of Kinnoull and Young v. Ferguson and ors* (1841) 3 D 778.
16. *Cuninghame v. Presbytery of Irvine* (1843) 5 D 427.
17. Acts of the Parliament of Scotland ('APS') II at 526; III at 541.
18. Acts of the General Assembly of the Church of Scotland ('AGA') 1638–1842, The Edinburgh Printing and Publishing Company, Edinburgh, 1843, 1638 at 32; 1694 V at 236. For special commissions, see *AGA* 1840 XII at 1102; 1841 XV at 1111.
19. Brown CG, *The Social History of Religion in Scotland since 1730*, Methuen, London, 1987 at 28–9.
20. APS IX 133.
21. 6 Anne c 11, art 25.
22. Sher RB, *Church and University in the Scottish Enlightenment*, Edinburgh University Press, 1985; Note 19 at 30; Burleigh JHS, *A Church History of Scotland*, Oxford University Press, London, 1960 at 287–300.
23. MacInnes J, *The Evangelical Movement in the Highlands of Scotland 1688 to 1800*, Aberdeen University Press, 1951 at 79–84; Fawcett A, *The Cambuslang Revival: The Scottish Evangelical Revival of the Eighteenth Century*, Banner of Truth Trust, London, 1971 at 182–209.
24. Cf Brougham HS, *The Life and Times of Henry Lord Brougham*, William Blackwood & Sons, Edinburgh, 1871, I at 243–70; Gray WF, *Some Old Scots Judges: Ancedotes and Impressions*, Constable & Company, London, 1914 at 227–90.
25. Enacted as 2 & 3 Will 4 c 65.
26. See AGA 1711 X at 454; 1732 V at 618; 1748 IV at 695.
27. For the following, see Dalrymple (Viscount Stair) *The Institutions of the Law of Scotland*, ed. by Walker DM, Edinburgh and Glasgow University Presses, 1981, II 8 35; Erskine J, *An Institute of the Law of Scotland*, 8th ed. by Nicolson JB, Butterworths, Edinburgh, 1871, I v 10–11.
28. APS VI part II 205; VII 46, IX 52.
29. 10 Anne c 12.
30. Note 19 at 31.
31. MacIver IF, 'Cockburn and the Church' in Bell A (ed.), n 11 at 90–3; Brougham HS, n 24, III at 76–86.
32. In practice, the Church's *Barrier Act* required (and still requires) the approval of a majority of presbyteries to an act of Assembly before it became a permanent law of the Church; see AGA 1697 IX at 260. But while the *Veto Act* passed through the *Barrier Act* procedure, its supporting regulations did not. These were passed as interim acts every year up to 1842;

AGA 1834 IX at 1037; 1835 IX at 1044; 1836 XI at 1060; 1837 VII at 1069; 1838 XVIII at 1086; 1839 XIII at 1097; 1840 XIII at 1103; 1841 X at 1110; 1842 XVII at 1128.

33. There were Moderates who would have supported a congregational right of veto, if legitimate reasons were given: Omond GWT, *The Lord Advocates of Scotland*, David Douglas, Edinburgh, 1883, II at 23.
34. MacIver IF, n 31 at 75.
35. Burleigh JHS, n 22 at 341; Hope J, *A Letter to the Lord Chancellor on the Claims of the Church of Scotland in regard to its Jurisdiction and on the Proposed Changes to its Polity*, 2nd edn, William Whyte & Co., Edinburgh, 1839.
36. Drummond AL and Bulloch J, *The Age of the Moderates*, Edinburgh, St Andrew Press, 1973 at 184.
37. Note 36.
38. Erskine J, n 27 at I v 24, vii 63, II x 57, II x 63.
39. Black WG and Christie JR, *The Parochial Ecclesiastical Law of Scotland as modified by the Church of Scotland Acts, 1921 and 1925*, 4th edn, William Hodge & Company Ltd, Edinburgh, 1928 at 7.
40. APS XI 10 at 433. 'Teinds' were a tithe, originally one-tenth of the income on land and labour set aside for the maintenance of the Church and clergy: see *Galloway v. Earl of Minto* 1920 SC 354.
41. Erskine J, n 27 at II x 64.
42. AGA 1797 V at 857.
43. 4 Geo 4 c 79, 5 Geo 4 c 90.
44. Brown SJ, n 7 at 249–50.
45. AGA 1833 VI at 1024, IX at 1035. See also AGA 1842 at 1141.
46. AGA 1835 XX at 1053.
47. AGA 1839 VIII at 1094.
48. Note 36 at 184.
49. Note 44 at 227; Grub G, *An Ecclesiastical History of Scotland. From the Introduction of Christianity to the Present Time*, Edmonston & Douglas, Edinburgh, 1861 at 207. The reasons for the parishioners' objections to Young remain unknown.
50. Note 33 at 55–6.
51. *Earl of Kinnoull v. Presbytery of Auchterarder* (1838) 16 S 661; Robertson C, *Report of the Auchterarder Case*, Adam and Charles Black, Edinburgh, 1838; and se Session Papers (Hope Collection), CCLXXXIX.
52. In Cuninghame's case, it was thought that in his time as Solicitor-General in the later Grey and Melbourne Governments he had been influenced by dissenters opposed to the reform of the Established Church: Stephen L and Lee S (eds), *Dictionary of National Biography*, Smith Elder & Co, London, 1908, V at 32; VII at 699–700, 1246 ('DNB'); Note 33 at 96.
53. Austin J, *The Province of Jurisprudence Determined*, Cambridge University Press, Cambridge, 1995 at 189–91.
54. (1838) 16 S 661 at 734.
55. Note 54 at 736.
56. (1808) 28 Fac Dec 92; Morrison's Appendix, Stipend No 6.
57. DNB VII at 407; Note 9 at 74.
58. (1838) 16 S 661 at 759.
59. Note 58 at 760.
60. Note 58.

61. Note 58 at 806.
62. Note 58 at 807.
63. Note 9 at 74; Note 4, *Journal* I at 169; Moncreiff F and Moncreiffe W, *The Moncreiffs and the Moncreiffes; a History of the Family of Moncreiff of that Ilk and its Collateral Branches*, Edinburgh University Press, 1929, I at 165–8; DNB XIII at 615–16.
64. (1838) 16 S. 661 at 791.
65. Note 64 at 771.
66. Note 64 at 801.
67. Note 64 at 811.
68. Note 64 at 809.
69. Note 64 at 809.
70. Note 64 at 809.
71. AGA 1838 XIV at 1085.
72. Note 71.
73. Lyall F, n 8 at 32.
74. Note 4, *Journal* I at 168.
75. *Presbytery of Auchterarder and ors v. Earl of Kinnoull and Young* (1839) 6 Cl & F 646 at 678.
76. Note 75 at 694; see also HS Brougham, *Life and Times*, I at 28–30.
77. Note 75 at 657.
78. Note 75 at 657–8.
79. Note 75 at 720.
80. For the relevant resolutions of the General Assembly, see AGA 1838 XIV at 1085; 1842 XII at 1126; 1842 XIX at II30; 1842 XX at II4I; 1842 XXI at II4I.
81. *Clark v. Stirling* (1839) 1 D 955; Robertson CG, *Report of the Proceedings of the Court of Session in the Lethendy Case*, W Blackwood & Sons, Edinburgh, 1839.
82. The proposition had some support in Lord Thurlow's decision in *Barclay v. Russell* (1789) Dick 729. This argument is set out in the Session Papers (Hope Collection), CCLXXXIX 3, *Minute of Debate* at 11–14.
83. *Clark v. Stirling* (1839) 1 D 955 at 980, 982, 985, 988–9, 990–1.
84. Note 83 at 979, 986.
85. Note 83 at 983.
86. Note 83 at 984–5.
87. Note 83 at 990.
88. Note 83 at 981, 986 and 1017.
89. Note 83 at 986 and 1042.
90. Note 83 at 991.
91. Note 83 at 997–8.
92. Note 83 at 1006.
93. Note 83 at 1017.
94. Note 83 at 1020–1.
95. Note 74 at 233.
96. Note 74 at 233–4. Boyle's 'practical sagacity' became more evident as the controversy deepened, and was even appreciated by Cockburn: *Life of Lord Jeffrey*, n 4, I at 384; see also *Stewarton Case. Report of the Pleadings by Patrick Robertson Esq Dean of the Faculty of advocates and Andrew Rutherfurd Esq Advocate in the Process of Suspension and Interdict, William Cuninghame Esq and Others, Heritors of the Parish of Stewarton against*

the Presbytery of Irvine, June and July 1842. Taken in Short-hand by Simon MacGregor, WD Kennedy, Edinburgh , 1842 at 85.

97. Note 74 at 234.
98. *The Presbyteries of the Church of Scotland threatened with imprisonment in the discharge of their official duty in an address from the Lord President of the Court of Session with an answer to the same in two letters to his Lordship by a minister of the Church of Scotland,* Glasgow, William Collins, 1839 at 5.
99. Note 98 at 8.
100. See Holdsworth W, *A History of English Law*, ed. by Goodhart AL and Hanbury HG, Methuen & Co Ltd, London, 1965, XV at 405–23.
101. Session Papers (Hope Collection), CCLXXXIX; *Case for the Opinion of Dr Phillimore, and Opinion of John Campbell, Attorney-General.*
102. Note 101, *Defences*, 4 March 1840 at 3; *Earl of Kinnoull and Young v. Ferguson and ors* (1841) 3 D 778 at 781–2.
103. Note 101 at 797.
104. Note 101 at 794.
105. Note 101 at 796.
106. Note 101 at 793.
107. *Ferguson and ors v. Earl of Kinnoull and Young* (1842) 9 Cl & F 251.
108. Note 107 at 305.
109. Note 107 at 295.
110. Note 107 at 295.
111. Note 100, XV at 409.
112. *Ferguson and ors v. Earl of Kinnoull and Young* (1842) 9 Cl & F 251at 325 (emphasis added).
113. Note 112.
114. *Earl of Kinnoull and Young v. Ferguson and ors* (1843) 5 D 1010.
115. *Presbytery of Strathbogie and Cruickshank and ors* (1839) 2 D 258.
116. Note 73 at 38.
117. *Presbytery of Strathbogie and Cruickshank and ors* (1840) 2 D 585.
118. Note 73 at 39; Note 44 at 309.
119. (1840) 2 D 585 at 594.
120. Note 119.
121. Note 74, II at 41.
122. *Cruickshank and ors* (1840) 2 D 1047; *Cruickshank and ors* (1840) 2 D 13 80.
123. Note 33 at 59.
124. *Edwards v. Cruickshank and ors (Majority of Presbytery of Strathbogie) and Robertson and ors (Minority of Presbytery of Strathbogie)* (1840) 3 D 282.
125. Note 124 at 295, 298.
126. Note 124 at 307.
127. *Earl of Kinnoull and Young v. Ferguson and ors* (1841) 3 D 778 at 797.
128. *Edwards v. Cruickshank and ors (Majority of Presbytery of Strathbogie) and Robertson and ors (Minority of Presbytery of Strathbogie)* (1840) 3 D 282 at 308.
129. DNB II at 1017; IX at 1206; IX at 1218.
130. *Majority of Presbytery of Strathbogie v. Minority of Presbytery of Strathbogie* (1842) 4 D 1298.
131. Note 130 at 1299–300.

132. Note 74 at 40.
133. *Cruickshank and ors v. Gordon and ors* (1843) 5 D 909.
134. However, it was not Lord Justice-Clerk Hope's policy to abstain completely in proceedings in which he had been counsel and the main protagonist. He did sit on the later *Auchterarder* cases: *Earl of Kinnoull v. Gordon* (1842) 5 D 12; *Earl of Kinnoull and Young v. Ferguson and ors (Members of the Presbytery of Auchterarder)* (1843) 5 D 1010.
135. *Cruickshank v. Gordon* (1843) 5 D 909 at 923–4.
136. Note 135 at 964.
137. Note 135 at 965.
138. Note 135 at 973.
139. Note 135 at 974.
140. Note 135 at 978.
141. *Edwards v. Leith* (1843) 15 Jurist 375.
142. *Brewster v. Marquis of Abercorn and ors (Heritors of the Abbey Parish of Paisley) (1837) 15 s. 991; Gardner v. Heritors of the Parish of Rathven* (1838) 1 D 158.
143. *Gordon v. Heritors of Parish of Monkquhitter* (1839) 1 D 789; *Lord Panmure and ors v. Sharpe and ors* (1839) 1 D 840; *Fleming v. Heritors of Neilston Parish* (183 9) 1 D 1257; *Bell v. Bell* (1840) 3 D 204.
144. *Livingstone* (1841) 3 D 1278; *Wilson v. Presbytery of Stranraer* (1842) 4 D 1294; *Smith v. Presbytery of Abertarff* (1842) 4 D 1476.
145. *Cuninghame and ors v. Presbytery of Irvine* (1843) 5 D 427; Session Papers (Hope Collection), CCXCIV 30.
146. Note 73 at 44.
147. Session Papers (Hope Collection), CCCIII 11, *Opinions of Consulted Judges,* 16 November 1843, at 15.
148. Note 147 at 15–17.
149. Note 147 at 19.
150. Note 147 at 111.
151. Note 147 at 163.
152. Sir Walter Scott called him 'Facetious Peter': n 33 at 84.
153. Session Papers (Hope Collection), CCXCIV 30, *Answers*, 5 May 1841 at 43–4.
154. His handwritten notes on the pleadings refer to the Presbytery meeting of 10 December 1840 as a 'Jesuitical proceeding': *Stewarton Case. Report of the Pleadings by Patrick Robertson Esq Dean of the Faculty of Advocates and Andrew Rutherfurd Esq Advocate in the Process of Suspension and Interdict, William Cuninghame Esq and Others, Heritors of the Parish of Stewarton against the Presbytery of Irvine, June and July 1842. Taken in Short-hand by Simon MacGregor*, WD Kennedy, Edinburgh, 1842 at 21.
155. Note 154 at 11.
156. Note 154 at 86.
157. Note 154 at 87.
158. Note 154 at 89.
159. Note 154 at 90. The Lord Justice-Clerk took issue on this point, denying that these expressions were used in *Stockdale*. Rutherfurd, who had participated fully in the debates on *Stockdale* in the House of Commons, pointed out that the report in Adolphus, on which the Justice-Clerk relied, was not as comprehensive as that in the papers of the House of Commons: see *Stockdale v. Hansard* (1839) 9 A & E 1; note 33 at 76.
160. Note 154 at 94.

161. Note 154 at 85.
162. See *Church of Scotland Act 1921*, Schedule, art 1; *Ballantyne v. Wigtown Presbytery* 1936 SC 625.
163. See Stein P, *Legal Evolution*, Cambridge University Press, 1980 at 69–72.
164. Cf Cairns J, 'Scottish Law, Scottish Lawyers and the Status of the Union' in J Robertson (ed.), *A Union for Empire: Political Thought and the British Union of 1707*, Cambridge University Press, 1995 at 265–6.
165. (1849) 12 D 1220.
166. Note 165 at 1231.
167. Note 165 at 1242.
168. Note 165 at 1231.
169. *Lockhart v. Presbytery of Deer* (1851) 13 D 1296; *Paterson v. Presbytery of Dunbar* (1861) 23 D 720; *Lang v. Presbytery of Irvine* (1864) 2 M 823; *Wight v. Presbytery of Dunkeld* (1870) 8 M 921; see n 73 at 53–9.
170. *Earl of Kinnoull and Young v. Presbytery of Auchterarder and ors* (1838) 16 S. 661 at 791.
171. *Edwards v. Cruickshank and ors (Majority of Presbytery of Strathbogie) and Robertson and ors (Minority of Presbytery of Strathbogie)* (1840) 3 D 282 at 307; *Earl of Kinnoull and Young v. Ferguson and ors* (1841) 3 D 778 at 794.
172. (1808) 28 Fac Dec 92; Morrison's Appendix, Stipend No 6.
173. Cf. n 74, II at 42.
174. *Earl of Kinnoull and Young v. Presbytery of Auchterarder and ors* (1838) 16 S. 661 at 809.
175. Laski HJ, *Studies in the Problem of Sovereignty*, Yale University Press, New Haven, 1917 at 49 and 64–8.
176. Scotland had no comprehensive toleration statute. Formal recognition of lawful dissent first occurred in *Greenshields v. Edinburgh Magistrates* (1710) Coll 427, and a series of statutes to protect and supervise Episcopalians was passed through the eighteenth century: 10 Anne c 7; 19 Geo 2 c 38; 32 Geo 3 c 63.
177. Note 44 at 303–4.
178. *Earl of Kinnoull and Young v. Presbytery of Auchterarder* (1838) 16 s. 661 at 760; *Cruickshank v. Gordon* (1843) 5 D 909 at 965.
179. Note 98 at 8; *Ferguson and ors v. Earl of Kinnoull and Young* (1842) 9 Cl & F 251 at 325.
180. Note 2 at 247.
181. *Ferguson and ors v. Earl of Kinnoull and Young* (1842) 9 Cl & F 251 at 295.

Appendix: Works by Professor R D Lumb

BOOKS

The Constitutions of the Australian States. St Lucia: University of Queensland Press, 1963. 2nd ed. 1965, 2nd rev ed. 1968, 3rd ed. 1972, 4th ed. 1977, 5th ed. 1991.

The Law of the Sea and Australian Off-shore Areas. St Lucia: University of Queensland Press, 1966. 2nd ed. 1978.

The Constitution of the Commonwealth of Australia, Annotated / by R D Lumb and K W Ryan. Sydney: Butterworths, 1974. 2nd ed. 1977, 3rd ed. 1981, 4th ed. 1986. 5th ed. (with GA Moens) 1995.

Australian Constitutionalism. Sydney: Butterworths, 1983.

REFERENCE WORKS

ANZ Commentary on Halsbury's Laws of England, Chapter 32 Constitutional Law / by R D Lumb and C D Gilbert. Sydney: Butterworths, 1976.

LECTURES

The Maritime Boundaries of Queensland and New South Wales. St Lucia: University of Queensland Press, [1964]. (University of Queensland Papers, Faculty of Law, v. 1 No. 4).

New Bearings in the Law of the Sea. St Lucia: University of Queensland Press, 1981. (University of Queensland Inaugural Lectures, No. 56, 29 April 1981).

ARTICLES

Archiv für Rechts- und Sozialphilosophie

"Recent developments in Legal Theory in Australia" (1960) 46 Archiv für Rechts- und Sozialphilosophie 97–114.

Australian Current Law

"Section 90 of the Constitution and Consumption Taxes" [1974] Australian Current Law DT84–DT86.

"Australian Constitutional Convention — Report on Constitutional Conventions" [1980] Australian Current Law AT50–AT52.

"Problems of Characterization of Federal Powers in the High Court" [1982] Australian Current Law AT45–AT49.

Australian Law Journal

"Contractual Relations between Government and Citizen" (1961) 35 Australian Law Journal 45–48.

"Territorial Changes in the States and Territories of the Commonwealth" (1963) 37 Australian Law Journal 172–175.

"The Off-Shore Petroleum Agreement Legislation" (1968) 41 Australian Law Journal 453–461.

"Sovereignty and Jurisdiction over Australian Coastal Waters" (1969) 43 Australian Law Journal 421–438.

"The Law of Wrecks in Australia: *Robinson v The Western Australian Museum*" (1978) 52 Australian Law Journal 198–207.

"The Northern Territory and Statehood" (1978) 52 Australian Law Journal 554-561.

"Uranium Mining: Legislative and Constitutional Aspects" (1979) 53 Australian Law Journal 84–91.

"Section 51, pl. (xxxviii) of the Commonwealth Constitution" (1981) 55 Australian Law Journal 328–332.

"The Judiciary, the Interpretation of the Constitution and the Australian Constitutional Convention" (1983) 57 Australian Law Journal 229–234.

"Aboriginal Land Rights: Judicial Approaches in Perspective" (1988) 64 Australian Law Journal 273–284.

"The External Affairs Power and Constitutional Reform" (1988) 62 Australian Law Journal 679–689.

Australian Marine Science Bulletin

"The Australian Fishing Zone" (1980) 69 Australian Law Journal 4.

Australian Petroleum Exploration Association Journal

"The Continental Shelf" (1968) 8 (1) Australian Petroleum Exploration Association Journal 32–36.

Australian Yearbook of International Law

"The Delimitation of Maritime Boundaries in the Timor Sea" (1976) 7 Australian Yearbook of International Law 72–86.

The Catholic Lawyer

"Natural Law — An Unchanging Standard?" (1960) 6 The Catholic Lawyer 224–233.

Federal Law Review

"Fundamental Law and the Processes of Constitutional Change in Australia" (1978) 9 Federal Law Review 148–184.

"'The Commonwealth of Australia' — Constitutional Implications" (1979) 10 Federal Law Review 287–305.

"Methods of Alteration of State Constitutions in the United States and Australia" (1982) 13 Federal Law Review 1–12.

"The Torres Strait Islands: Some Questions Relating to their Annexation and Status" (1990) 19 Federal Law Review 154–168.

Institute of Public Affairs Review

"Referenda Proposals" (Summer 1984) 37 (4) Institute of Public Affairs Review 196–200.

"Professor Lumb replies to Gareth Evans, 'Referendum Proposals: A Reply to Professor Lumb'" (Spring 1984) 38 (3) Institute of Public Affairs Review 144–145.

International and Comparative Law Quarterly

"Australia and the Law of the Sea: Recent Developments" (1980) 29 International and Comparative Law Quarterly 151–165.

"Native Title to Land in Australia: Recent High Court Decisions" (1993) 42 International and Comparative Law Quarterly 84–100.

Journal of Legal Education

"Natural Law and Legal Positivism" (1959) 11 Journal of Legal Education 503–512.

Juridical Review

"On A Modern Approach to Jurisprudence" [1960] Juridical Review 143–155.

Melbourne University Law Review

"The Scholastic Doctrine of Natural Law" (1959) 2 Melbourne University Law Review 205–221.

"The Continental Shelf" (1968) 6 Melbourne University Law Review 357–369.

Pacific Community

"The Law of the Sea and Australia's Future Maritime Policy" (Spring 1970) No. 6 Pacific Community 64–72.

Philosophical Studies

"Law, Reason, Will" (1960) 10 Philosophical Studies 179–189.

Policy

"Elected Conventions and Constitutional Change" (Summer 1993–94) 9 (4) Policy 43–44.

Queensland Bar News

"Is Australia an 'Occupied' or 'Conquered' Country — How Legal Status of Australia in International Law Affects the Land Rights Question" (December 1984) 11 Queensland Bar News 16, 18–20.

Queensland Lawyer

"Manner and Form in the Australian Constitutional System Post Australia Acts" (1992) 12 Queensland Lawyer 177–183.

"*Mabo* and Aboriginal Title in Queensland" (1993) 14 Queensland Lawyer 15–18.

Tasmanian University Law Review

Review of Julius Stone, Aggression and World Order. (1959) 1 Tasmanian University Law Review 368–370.

University of Queensland Law Journal

"Legal Landmarks, 1957-1958: Personal Property" (1958) 3 University of Queensland Law Journal 310–314.

"Individual Responsibility for Aggressive War: The Crime Against Peace" (1959) 3 University of Queensland Law Journal 333–355.

"The New South Wales Legislative Council Abolition Case" (1961) 4 University of Queensland Law Journal 23–44.

"The Treaty of Rome and the European Economic Community" (1963) 4 University of Queensland Law Journal 297–303.

"Corporate Personality" (1964) 4 University of Queensland Law Journal 418–431.

"The 1973 Law of the Sea Conference: Significant Issues" (1971) 7 University of Queensland Law Journal 256–279.

Review of Jacob A Fagjenbaum and Peter Hanks, Australian Constitutional Law (1972) 7 University of Queensland Law Journal 452–453.

"The Franklin Dam Decision and the External Affairs Power: A Comment" (1984) 13 University of Queensland Law Journal 138–142.

"The Bicentenary of Australian Constitutionalism: The Evolution of Rules of Constitutional Change" (1988) 15 University of Queensland Law Journal 3–32.

"Constitutional Issues Relating to the 'Process of Reconciliation' With Aborigines and Torres Strait Islanders" (1992) 17 University of Queensland Law Journal 111–116.

University of Western Australia Law Review

"Methods of Constitutional Revision in the Federal Sphere: An Elected Constitutional Convention?" (1992) 22 University of Western Australia Law Review 52–71.

Review of H P Lee and George Winterton, eds., Australian Constitutional Perspectives (1993) 23 University of Western Australia Law Review 184–186.

Review of Malcolm Turnbull, The Reluctant Republic. (1994) 24 University of Western Australia Law Review 129–130.

World Review

"Australian Off-shore Jurisdiction" (July 1964) 3 (2) World Review 39–46.

"The Law of the Sea and Australian Off-shore Areas: Recent Developments" (October 1969) 8 (3) World Review 22–23.

"The Border Problem between Papua New Guinea and Australia: Legal Issues" (March 1974) 13 (1) World Review 45–49.

CONTRIBUTIONS TO COLLECTIONS

"The Duty of Obeying the Law" in *Australian Studies in Legal Philosophy* / ed. by Ilmar Tammelo, Anthony Blackshield and Enid Campbell. Berlin: Hermann Luchterhand, 1963. pp. 195–218.

"Alien Property in Australia" in *International Law in Australia* 1st ed. / ed. by D P O'Connell. Sydney: Law Book Company, 1965. pp. 500–534.

"Legality and Legitimacy: The Limits of the Duty of Obedience to the State" in *Studies in the History of the Law of Nations.* / ed. by C H Alexandrowicz. The Hague: Martinus Nijhoff, 1970. pp. 52–82.

"Commentary" [on Reform of the Constitution: The Referendums and Constitutional Convention] in *Labor and the Constitution 1972-1975.* / ed. by Gareth Evans. Melbourne: Heinemann, 1977. pp. 98–101.

"Australian Coastal Jurisdiction" in *International Law in Australia*, 2nd ed. / ed. by K W Ryan. Sydney: Law Book Company, 1984. pp. 370–389.

"Foreword" in *The Decline of the University.* / by Philip De Lacey and Gabriël Moens. Tahmoor, NSW: Law Press, 1990. pp. vii–x.

"The *Mabo* Case: Public Law Aspects" in *Mabo: A Judicial Revolution.* / ed. by M A Stephenson and S Ratnapala. St Lucia: University of Queensland Press, 1993. pp. 1–23.

"Representative Democracy, Federalism and Constitutional Revision" in *Republic or Monarchy? Legal and Constitutional Issues.* / ed. by M A Stephenson and Clive Turner. St Lucia: University of Queensland Press, 1994. pp. 165–182.

"Constitutional Issues and the Native Title Act, 1993 (Cth)" in *Mabo: The Native Title Legislation.* / ed. by M A Stephenson. St Lucia: University of Queensland Press, 1995. pp. 26–35.